From Conciliation to Conquest

From Conciliation
to Conquest

The Sack of Athens and the
Court-Martial of Colonel John B. Turchin

George C. Bradley and Richard L. Dahlen

THE UNIVERSITY OF ALABAMA PRESS

Tuscaloosa

The University of Alabama Press
Tuscaloosa, Alabama 35487-0380
uapress.ua.edu

Hardcover edition published 2006.
Paperback edition published year 2014.
eBook edition published 2009.

Inquiries about reproducing material from this work should be addressed to
the University of Alabama Press.

Typeface: ACaslon

Manufactured in the United States of America
Cover image: Detail from Currier and Ives, *The Battle of Malvern Hill, Va. July 1st 1862:
Charge of the 36th New York Volunteers, at the Battle of Malvern Hill, July 1st 1862, and Capture
of the Colors of the 14th Regt. N.C. Infantry*, Library of Congress
Cover design: Michele Myatt Quinn

∞
The paper on which this book is printed meets the minimum requirements of American
National Standard for Information Science–Permanence of Paper for Printed Library Materials,
ANSI Z39.48-1984.

Paperback ISBN: 978-0-8173-5785-6
eBook ISBN: 978-0-8173-8170-7

A previous edition of this book has been catalogued by the Library of Congress as follows:

Library of Congress Cataloging-in-Publication Data
Bradley, George C., 1947–
From conciliation to conquest : the sack of Athens and the court-martial of Colonel John B.
Turchin / George C. Bradley and Richard L. Dahlen.
p. cm.
Includes bibliographical references and index.
ISBN-13: 978-0-8173-1526-9 (cloth : alk. paper)
ISBN-10: 0-8173-1526-8 (alk. paper)
1. Turchin, John B. (John Basil), 1822–1901. 2. Turchin, John B. (John Basil), 1822–1901—Trials,
litigation, etc. 3. Soldiers—United States—Biography. 4. United States. Army—Officers—Biography.
5. United States. Army. Illinois Infantry Regiment, 19th (1861–1864) 6. Trials (Military offenses)—
United States. 7. Pillage—Alabama—Athens—History—19th century. 8. Athens (Ala.)—History,
Military—19th century. 9. United States—History—Civil War, 1861–1865—Destruction and pillage.
10. Civil-military relations—United States—History—19th century. I. Dahlen, Richard L., d. 2002.
II. Title.
E467.1.T85B73 2006
973.7′3092—dc22 [B]

2006009147

Contents

Illustrations

Acknowledgments

There are many people who deserve credit for helping to create this book, for without the aid and assistance of the countless archivists, research assistants, librarians, and scholars who either broke related ground before we began or who helped us locate, collate, and understand the wealth of material that came before, this work would never have been done. To any and all who thus helped in any way, I give wholehearted, if nameless, thanks.

I could not properly complete this work, however, without giving very special thanks to a few very special people. My wife, Anne, and my son, Christopher, have never had a specific interest in the American Civil War, and yet they did everything a man could hope for to encourage me and my interest in it. For that, and their enduring love, I will be forever grateful.

Nor could I have proceeded without the training and guidance of three very special men. Professors Mason Hammond, Eric Grunn, and Zephaniah Stewart, my tutors at Harvard, taught the highest standards of scholarship, standards that have guided me throughout my life. Thank you all.

Richard L. Dahlen

When I first came to know General Turchin, it was to help a valued friend finish researching and writing a book within the limited time he had left to live. I did not achieve that goal, because Richard Dahlen departed this life in October 2002. However, Dick did me a great favor by asking me to help. After three years, considerable additional research, seven peer reviews, and three rewrites, this book came into being in its present form. The guidance and advice of the University of Alabama Press was essential in developing the story of John Turchin into one with deep underpinnings and significance.

Both Dick and I looked to Dr. Richard Sommers, Randy Hackenburg, and the staff of the United States Army Military History Institute for aid in gathering additional materials essential to the completion of this project. Dr. Sommers's thoughtful insights were invaluable in finalizing the manuscript. Robin DuBlanc proved to be a copy editor extraordinaire. I also owe great thanks to Commander Roger Benton Francisco, USN Ret., Colonel Michael Cross, USMC Ret., Colonel James Aarestad, US Army Ret., and Colonel William Solomon, US Army Ret., for their professional expertise, insights, advice, support and friendship.

This book would never have been completed without the aid and support of many others, including that of the most significant women in my life: my wife, Connie, my daughter, Elizabeth, and my mother, Beverly. Nor would it have been completed without the help of the following great people: Lara Miller, Morgan Bissett-Tessier, Michelle Seagraves, Chelsea Scheidt, Amanda Barton, Emily Mendoza, Erika Wilt, Alyssa Horton, Lindsay Hoover, Amanda Spaseff, Taylor Spaseff, Jenna Cavrich, Elaina White, Amanda Zeiders, Kyla Struncis, Rachel Vollero, Cree Julian, Sam Merkt, Danielle Roher, Zoe Cesarz, Katie Wert, Nicole Joynt, Alex Sikora, Jamie Wilson, Cassaundra Thompson, Rachael Innerst, Amy Sharp, Amanda Weibrecht, Courtney Papinchak, Ariel Butera, Jess Gustin, Tori Moore, Landon Seitz, Katie Lippert, Noelle Harner, Marie D'Angelo, and Mark Culver—Patriots all!

George C. Bradley

From Conciliation to Conquest

Introduction

We, as Americans, have great faith in our form of government, and many of us take considerable pride in the notion that our nation is nearly unique, our people dedicated to lofty principles rather than to high and mighty princes. That pride has at times carried with it a degree of hubris, a conclusion that other people in other places should embrace our ideas and ideals just as readily as do we. Therefore, we believe that when we come into those other places carrying with us this promise of freedom, it is only natural that we should be well received.

Sometimes—for example, in Italy and France during World War II—we have been received just as we had hoped, as liberating heroes, as deliverers from oppression, as the champions of democracy. However, we have not always been so received, no matter how lofty our goals and ambitions. There have been times and places in which we went to liberate or protect or restore the rule of law, and we ended up instead as an army of occupation, facing a large segment of a population that did not want us there. That happened in Vietnam. It appears to have happened again in Iraq. It may have happened for the first time in 1861 and 1862—not overseas, but right here, in Missouri, in Tennessee, in Virginia, and in Alabama.

In times of trouble, when the prospect of war comes over the horizon, Americans, often in great numbers, rally to the cause. Those numbers are never greater than when the country comes under attack. No matter whether the attack falls on a major, if sleeping, naval base and is conducted by a foreign power, or whether it is carried out by troubled countrymen trying to break the bonds of the Union by attacking a small government fort, the lines at the recruiting stations quickly grow long. To ask men, and now women, why they volunteer under such circumstances seems ridiculous. It is the natural and right response for people who care about the longevity of what they believe to be the best form of government on earth, which stands, or so we like to think, as the world's bastion of freedom. Simply put, volunteering is the patriotic thing to do.

However, we can and should ask the question "Why do these people volunteer?" What is it, exactly, that they hope to do after they take up arms? Do they want to restore democracy, order, and the rule of law? Do they want to defeat the powers that threaten our way of life? Or do they want revenge on those who attack us? Whom do these volunteers see as the wrongdoers deserving punishment? Will they focus on the military leaders of the attack and on the heads of the sponsoring regime? Or will they look equally harshly on those wearing the enemy's uniforms, on the people working in the factories supplying the warriors, and on the people at home growing their food and sewing their clothes? It is much easier to lead when the motivations of the people being led are understood.

It is, of course, possible for our government to arrive at answers to these questions, as matters of policy, that differ from those reached by the volunteers who come forward to wage the war. While the volunteers may want revenge, the government may only see a need to restore order. In that case, great care and effort must be taken to ensure that the volunteers are properly trained and indoctrinated, so that the government's policy decisions, and not those of the volunteers, are implemented. We will assume for the sake of future argument here in this volume that an army will fight with more spirit and efficiency when official policy and personal motivations align. Those feelings can be something policy makers and the army can take great advantage of—but only where policy and motivation, as adapted by training, actually do align.

Bring one thousand men together, and the nature of the group you have will depend both on the reason for the gathering and on the men who emerge as the leaders of the group. If they gather in a stadium, cheer the home team, jeer the visitors, and threaten the officials, we call them fans. If they congregate in a public park, angered by events, we call them a mob. If they come together in response to an attack on their country, to rally around the flag, we call them patriots. If they dress in uniforms and stand together on a parade ground, we call them a regiment. The same group can play all of these parts. Civilians can put on uniforms. Soldiers can cheer, and they can riot.

Leadership, or the lack thereof, will be the group's mold. Leaders, good or bad, will set the tone for everyone else. The more tense the atmosphere, the more easily one small act or actor can turn events. A single thrown stone can quickly become hail. In such tense times, the presence or absence of men who can calm and channel the energy of the group will determine whether it becomes a destructive mob or a force of more concentrated, purposeful effort. Also relevant will be the previous experience of the group, especially if it bonds, as do military units.

This book will focus on a group of men, a regiment of volunteers (and to some degree a brigade of four regiments of which that regiment was a part) and the events they experienced in early May 1862. All of them had volunteered to serve in the United States Army. They had done so in direct response to an attack on this country. Within a year, they found themselves in a proverbial tight spot. Arriving in an area where government policy makers assumed they would be received as liberators, instead they found themselves despised as occupiers. What they subsequently did—and why they did it— cannot be fully understood without delving deeply into the man who served as their commander at the time. He set the tone. His actions, or inaction, would do much to determine what sort of group the men he led became.

His anglicized name was John Basil Turchin. He came to America from Russia in 1856, newly married. He had abandoned a promising career in the Imperial Army, in which he had risen to the rank of colonel while still in his mid-thirties. Here, like many immigrants in our own time, he struggled to find a position where he could take advantage of his considerable education and training. Although he soon found work with the United States Coastal Survey in Philadelphia, he became frustrated with the low pay and want of opportunity for advancement and did what thousands of others did: he went west. He tried to establish himself as an architect and engineer on the prairie of Illinois, but finding little business in the small town where he first settled, he took a job with the Illinois Central Railroad in the fastest-growing city in the world—Chicago.

Turchin never expressed any regret for the loss of the prestige he had held while serving the tsar, nor for the loss of income, if he suffered one. (Then, as now, Russian officers were notoriously underpaid.) He and his wife had been drawn to America by the promise of freedom. Better, no doubt, to be free and struggling than to be comfortable and constrained. Feeling the exuberance that accompanied his new unrestricted life in the United States, he had no hesitation in choosing sides when the country went to war with itself in 1861. He stood on, and quickly expressed a willingness to fight for, the side of the Union. However humble his economic circumstances, his military background was well known by people of influence in Chicago, where, as in the rest of the country, men who had actually led military units of more than a company in size were the rarest of commodities. Thus it was that when some of the most powerful men in the city, including the editors of the *Chicago Tribune,* proposed a Chicago-based regiment of volunteers, Turchin's name quickly came to the top of the list of men to lead it.

When he volunteered, Turchin stepped on to a wave that carried along millions of his countrymen. There was, at least at first blush, an important difference between him and most of the others who dropped their civilian lives to preserve the Union that summer. He had been a professional soldier. He had joined the Imperial Army, we can assume, seeking a career, and for nearly twenty years of his life it had been his profession, his livelihood. As a career soldier he had focused on doing those things that bring success to professional military men. First among those was the ability to quickly and efficiently perform the duties assigned to him, to follow orders: in modern parlance, to accomplish his mission. To do otherwise would have ended his ascension in rank and in all probability his career.

Then, as now, another essential element of any officer's duty would have been to care for his men, to keep them sufficiently content to stand and fight, even for a sovereign and a government in which they had no great confidence or investment, except that this was their livelihood, too. His quick, if not meteoric, rise to the higher levels of command in the Imperial Army spoke well of his skill and dedication to both his command and his commanders. Likewise, the men he commanded were by and large in the Imperial Army either as a way to make a living or because their service was required. Although love of country was certainly a factor in motivating the army whenever Mother Russia had been invaded, we can wonder about the depth of commitment any man might muster to a regime of autocrats, when contrasted to a democracy in which a man had a sense of ownership and belonging. Turchin had been in a position where he had the opportunity to quit and look elsewhere. For the more ordinary Russians, such a choice did not exist.

The men Turchin took command of in 1861 were, in contrast, eager volunteers. They had an enthusiastic sense of mission before they donned their uniforms. They came into the ranks with an exuberance Turchin had never seen before, but which, as we shall see, he undoubtedly shared. Many of these volunteers were immature, short on principles and self-discipline, and they had time to spare. What brought them to the war was their enthusiasm for a common cause. They had not joined the army to start military careers. They needed no officers, or anyone else, to help them understand the mission for which they had taken up arms. We will argue here that they volunteered to pick up the gauntlet thrown down at Fort Sumter and to avenge that attack, to preserve the Union, to make war on secessionists, to teach the traitors a lesson, to win and to go home again.

The experience of the Mexican War had given many American professional soldiers, especially those in high command positions at the Civil War's beginning, very clear, if preconceived, notions of what to expect from volunteers when they took to the field. The men who had volunteered for service in Mexico had been enthusiastic about that war, too. They had volunteered to fight, and kill, Mexicans. When the initial war policy of the Lincoln administration became one of conciliation with Southern civilians, many of these Regular Army officers agreed with its premise and substance. They had seen that same policy work in Mexico, where it had been followed by General Scott and the Regular Army. They shuddered, however, at the prospect of using volunteer soldiers to carry it out.

In Mexico, the contrast between the Regular troops of the United States Army, who had treated the Mexican population with great magnanimity, and the volunteers, who had earned for themselves a terrible reputation, had been stark. Seemingly, no one had volunteered for Mexico to befriend the Mexicans. In 1861 there were similar good reasons to think that the men who had volunteered to fight for the Union had not come to the army to befriend the people of the South and cajole them into again being good neighbors and compatriots. There was equally good reason to doubt the ability of the officers of the volunteer regiments to control their men, to restrain a seemingly natural urge, often reinforced by the editorials in the local papers, to commit depredations against the people seen as supporting the other side. If these men were to become more than a mob waiting to riot, someone would have to lead them there, train them to be soldiers who would do what they were told to do, and who would refrain from doing anything else.

One of the Civil War commanders who had shared the career army officer's experience in Mexico was Major General Don Carlos Buell. Thanks in part to the military success of Ulysses S. Grant in western Tennessee, Buell was able to move his forces all the way through central Tennessee and on into northern Alabama by the early spring of 1862. Through seniority, Colonel

John Basil Turchin rode in command of one of Buell's brigades. Because of this deep, early, and unopposed penetration into the heart of the South, Turchin's men would be among the first to test the conciliatory policy as a working tool, as well as the premises that underlay it. Were the Southern people the victims of an oppressive oligarchy? Were they waiting to be freed from it? Would they welcome the return of law and order carried in the wake of the occupying Union troops? Although hopes ran high in the Lincoln administration that this would be the case, overall opinion in the North was deeply divided on these questions. The men on the front line—Turchin's men—would test the validity of the premises upon which the policy rested.

In the study of our Revolutionary War, much serious work has been done analyzing the relative performance of Washington's Continental Army and the various militias called out during the war. Perhaps because Lincoln's formal call-up of the militia was a distinct and limited event in the Civil War, and perhaps because we think of the Civil War militia only in terms of the men who were called out for the first ninety days of the conflict, little, if any, study has been done comparing the performance of the green volunteers of 1861 with the performance of the regiments of Regular troops composing the United States Army. Although we will not pretend to attempt such a massive undertaking here, we will ask questions about the performance and behavior of Turchin's men, and we will discuss how those types of behaviors were hardly unique in the annals of war. We will look particularly at Colonel Turchin and the men under his command, trying to decipher why those men behaved as they did when they did, sometimes looking to other times and places for help in understanding them and the events in which they participated.

We will also explore the contrast between the expectations and behavior of these volunteer soldiers with the training and expectations of career officers such as Don Carlos Buell. Then, as now, career officers preferred disciplined troops because they were considered to be far more effective. As one officer put it, "always in the long run, Discipline has conquered." From an officer's point of view, that is the whole point. As every soldier of World War II learned on opening his *Field Manual,* the "purpose of military training . . . is the assurance of victory in the event of war."[1] However, the contrasting expectations and experiences of the career officers and those of the volunteer soldiers and officers soon led to problems. Because of the circumstances they faced as an army of occupation early in the war, perhaps none came face-to-face with these problems more quickly than did Colonel Turchin and the men he led.

The basic assumptions underlying Lincoln's policy did not anticipate the necessity of occupying hostile territory. Many people expected, or hoped, that the Union army would be greeted as liberators or as restorers of law and order when they arrived in the South. It was hoped that the local civilians might welcome them and thank them for bringing back peace, order, and safety. It was hoped that the Union soldiers could and would cooperate with these friendly citizens. Such situations don't require much planning. Hostile civilians, on the other hand, present a far more difficult challenge. When the newly arrived federal troops encountered many Southern civilians who were cool at best, and others who were openly antagonistic, many issues arose that had not been thought through prior to their entry into the seceded states. These conditions were not addressed by official government policy nor by the general orders issued in compliance with that policy by army commanders like Buell. Could the volunteers be expected to behave like thoroughly trained professional soldiers? Did the men understand and would they support the government's policy? If they failed to behave in accordance with that policy, who would be held accountable? Turchin and his men would be among the first to face these questions.

During the first six months of 1862, the national press and Congress carried on a vigorous debate about war policy. Was the official "conciliatory" policy the right one to accomplish the government's objective of reunifying the country? If not, what should the policy be? As the months passed, the debate gained intensity. While the forces of the government advanced into the Confederacy, the existing policy came to the test, and debate became heated argument. When the storm surrounding the policy reached its climax, Colonel Turchin would find himself in its vortex.

In early May 1862, certain events transpired that served to bring Turchin and the men of his brigade to the center of this argument, one that had begun long before they reached the Tennessee-Alabama state line. The debate spread far beyond them and the little area of Alabama they occupied. It reached from Huntsville, Alabama, to Washington, DC. It filled the halls of Congress and the editorial pages of the national press from Bangor to St. Louis. Here we focus on John B. Turchin and the men under his command, using the events that brought them into the national spotlight to further study the debate that surrounded the nation's war policy. The conclusions reached regarding the events of the 1860s may be very different than those that might be reached today, but the questions about underlying policy presented by the times to those then in charge remain with us. Will we liberate, occupy, conquer, or punish? Why have the people volunteered? What happens when an anticipated liberation becomes an occupation of an area inhabited by a mixture of welcoming and hostile citizens? How should an army of occupation behave? What can we reasonably expect of volunteers in uniform, giving due consideration to their reasons for enlisting, their training, and the level of leadership they have? Knowing what we can or cannot expect of them, is it proper, advantageous, or disadvantageous to deploy them in the troubled territory?

The controversy surrounding John Basil Turchin has been for more than a century only a footnote in the annals of the American Civil War. We hope here to correct that oversight and to give the man once known as "the Russian Thunderbolt" his due. His life and career took fascinating turns. But the crux of that career centered on the events of May 2, 1862. Here we will try to explain, as best we can, why Turchin and his men did as they did that morning and in the days that followed. We will also attempt to place those events in the context of the times, a context that brought Turchin fame rather than the ignominy that might otherwise have resulted. The events giving rise to the controversy moved him to the center of a national debate, the outcome of which had far-reaching consequences for our country, most especially for the part of it that stood in rebellion.

Our goal here is to discuss these men in those times. Similar circumstances have faced other men in other times and places right up to the present. Each time they demand fresh analysis. No matter how high our motives or just our cause, whenever we enter a territory as the champions of democracy, we must accept the fact that there may be some portion of the population that will see us instead as invaders. Each time, we will have to decide anew what to do next.

1
The Policy

It will require the exercise of the full powers of the Federal Government to restrain the fury of the noncombatants.

—Winfield Scott, speaking about
the attack on Fort Sumter

It was, perhaps, somewhat ironic that the clouds, which had pretty much shut out the sun over Washington, DC, on the morning of March 4, 1861, cleared away shortly after noon. Sunlight then fell on the thirty thousand people standing on the great west lawn of the Capitol as president-elect Abraham Lincoln stood and strode forward to address the nation. Just how large a nation he was speaking to was the question that weighed most heavily on a majority of minds. Mr. Lincoln had left his home in Springfield, Illinois, for Washington exactly three weeks before, on February 11. On that very same day, former secretary of war Jefferson Davis also had bid farewell to his family, and to his slaves, at his plantation in Mississippi. He rode off on his own journey, to Montgomery, Alabama, to accept the office of provisional president of a "Confederate States of America," which had been officially formed but three days before. It was clearly the position of those delegates, and of Mr. Davis, that the "United States" was an entity of which they were no longer a part. In Washington, as the great, lanky man they had elected president approached the podium, the vast throng facing the west portico of the Capitol quieted, anxious to hear what Abraham Lincoln had to say about this momentous question. The troops lining the streets, the artillery posted nearby, the riflemen guarding against snipers, all evidenced the tension created by this disparity of views.

Lincoln had begun work on this speech while still in Illinois. No one understood better than he the need for clarity. No one felt with more sensitivity the need for reassurance. No one saw better the need, from the first moment he was in office, for a steady hand at the helm of the government, for an unambiguous statement of policy that would guide, and hopefully heal, the nation during this time of trial. The original themes of the initial draft of his address had survived reviews and revision and incorporated the contributions of men he would work with in the years to come. Abraham Lincoln knew what he was about. He stood before his audience knowing exactly what it was he wanted to say to the people, to all the people, to those who celebrated his election and to those who purported to reject it.[1]

Lincoln approached his inaugural address just as any good lawyer would have. He wrote a legal brief, one that explained the policy he would pursue when he took office, one that set out the legal basis for the course he had chosen. The president came right to the point. After only a few words of greeting to his audience, he said that he saw no need to talk about matters of administration, "about which there is no special anxiety, or excitement." Lincoln's primary concern focused on the fact that many people in the slave states appeared to fear him, so to them he spoke first. "Apprehension seems to exist among the people of the Southern States, that by the accession of a Republican Administration, their property, and their peace, and personal security, are to be endangered. There has never been any reasonable cause for such apprehension. Indeed, the most ample evidence to the contrary has all the while existed."[2]

He quoted his pledge, repeated many times in his campaign stump speeches, that he had "no purpose, directly or indirectly, to interfere with the institution of slavery in the States where it exists. I believe I have no lawful right to do so, and I have no inclination to do so." He quoted the plank from the Republican platform repudiating John Brown's raid as "the gravest of crimes" and assuring each state the right to "order and control its own domestic institutions according to its own judgment exclusively." He told his listeners that he felt bound by these promises made by the party that had nominated him for this office.[3]

What else could he do to reassure these people, many of whom resided in states that already had passed ordinances or resolutions claiming to sever their ties with the United States? "I only press upon the public attention the most conclusive evidence of which the case is susceptible," Mr. Lincoln went on, "that the property, peace and security of no section are to be in anywise endangered by the now incoming administration. I add too that all the protection which, consistently with the Constitution and the laws can be given, will be cheerfully given when lawfully demanded for whatever cause." What more could he say than this? Their property, their peace, their security would not be endangered by him or those who worked for him. What was more, he would "cheerfully" provide them with "all the protection" he constitutionally could. He thus tried to assure his listeners in Dixie that the national government would continue to do that which good government should always do: protect its citizens from those who choose to operate outside the law.[4]

Lincoln now turned his attention to the question of secession, carefully analyzing it according to the common law of contracts. Two parties could make a contract, and those same parties could rescind it, but once made, neither party could unilaterally undo that which bound them both. Therefore, all of these ordinances and resolutions and acts of secession were legally void and of no effect, since the United States had not consented to the severing of the ties that bound the states to the Union. The Union continued to exist, from Maine to California, from the Straits of Mackinac to the Mississippi delta. It was his duty to enforce the laws throughout. He would continue to hold and occupy all of the establishments that belonged to the federal government no matter where located. He would make sure the mails got through. He would continue to collect the duties and imposts on which the government depended for its income. Those things he would do. But, except to hold and occupy that which belonged to the government, he would not invade or use force or make appointments obnoxious to the people of any locale. "So far as possible, the people everywhere shall have the sense of perfect security which is most favorable to calm thought and reflection."[5]

His concluding remarks presented a quiet challenge based in realism and a poetic call to reason. Having done all he could in the form of verbal reassurance, he told those bent on war that "you can have no war, without being yourselves the aggressors." Then came the trusting, soul-stirring prose that captured everyone's attention. "The mystic chords of memory, stretching from every battlefield, and patriot grave, to every living heart and hearthstone, all over this broad land, will yet swell the chorus of the Union, when again touched, as surely they will be, by the better angels of our nature." While those gathered on Capitol Hill offered their polite applause, almost at the same hour the Stars and Bars rose for the first time over the Confederate Capitol. While northern papers generally lauded the president's remarks, the *Charleston Mercury* noted what it saw as Lincoln's "feeble inability to grasp the circumstances of this momentous emergency."[6]

The editor of the *Mercury* had a point, but if Lincoln erred in his judgment of Southerners, he made the same mistake that thousands of others in the North were making at the same time. As was evidenced in his address, Lincoln believed, or at the very least deeply hoped, that the vast majority of the people in the South were tied to the Union with the same strong, "mystic chords of memory" as were he and the people of the North. Given time, reassurance, and evidence of the government's good intentions, the vast majority of the people in the seceded states would happily return to, and support, the national government; or so it was commonly thought by Lincoln and many other men in authority. Subdue the radical few, mostly the powerful slaveholders of the South, treat everyone else lawfully and with an attitude of reconciliation, and peaceful reunion could be easily achieved—or so they hoped. In responding to some supporters from New York who applauded his remarks, Lincoln said, "[T]here will be more rejoicing over one sheep that is lost, and is found, than over the ninety and nine that have not gone astray." That was the basis of the policy the president established on the day he took office. A man of his word, Lincoln and his administration would follow this policy unless and until its premise proved false.[7]

The tension of the times dampened the force of those words. With pressure building at various locations in the South for the surrender of government forts and arsenals, few ears there would have heard anything conciliatory in whatever the president had to say, had they been able to listen. Even Secretary of State William Seward, who had been deeply involved in the preparation of the inaugural address, but who had since been caught up in the whirl of appointments in which the entire cabinet was awash, complained on the first of April that the administration had no policy, either foreign or domestic. Lincoln gave him a brisk referral to the words of the speech. He also reassured Seward of his own steadfastness. "When a general line of policy is adopted," said the president, "I apprehend there is no danger of its being changed without good reason, or continuing to be a subject of unnecessary debate."[8]

The firing on Fort Sumter settled the question of whether there would be war. Low on ammunition, with fire threatening their powder magazine, and out of food, the small Union garrison surrendered on April 14, 1865, after thirty-four hours of bombardment and return fire that had killed no one on either side but that had set everyone, North and South, afire. President Lincoln immediately called for troops to regain control of this piece of federal property and to quell the rebellion. Ominously, rather than hearing calls from the loyal people of the South for those troops to be quickly dispatched, instead, shouts to meet this act of aggression with equal force rose to fever pitch in nearly every state that permitted slavery within its boundaries. Perhaps equally ominously for a leader hoping to calmly reassure the people in the South whose loyalty may have been wavering, the streets of every community in the North filled with men eager to right this wrong, to fight fire with fire.

To many active or former officers of the United States Army who remained faithful to the Union cause, men like George B. McClellan, the policy espoused in the president's inaugural address made perfect sense. This was a war to preserve the Union. It was not, nor should it become, in their view, a war to destroy or alter Southern society or to correct or punish societal wrongs, although even then such ideas had the support of a very vocal minority on Capitol Hill. It was to be fought fairly by men, uniformed and armed, maneuvering on battlefields or to strategically important geographic positions, who would target the uproarious few and leave everyone else alone. Southern civilians were outside the fray. As citizens of the United States, they were entitled to, and would receive, the protection of its laws and government. When Henry Halleck first assumed command in Missouri in the fall of 1861, the first order he received from McClellan was to "impress the inhabitants . . . that we are fighting solely for the integrity of the Union . . . to restore to the nation the blessings of peace and good order."[9] McClellan thus echoed the sentiments of his commander in chief.

Another of the faithful officers was Don Carlos Buell. Orphaned as a young child, Buell was an upstanding, intelligent boy, but one who, perhaps as a result of those early losses, formed few, if any, close attachments to anyone. He was a loner, a man who stood aloof, one who formed opinions internally, too rarely taking into account the feelings or insights of others. He graduated from the United States Military Academy in 1841. While there, he had no known close friends and accumulated an astonishing number of demerits, never fully accepting the disciplinary system, never fully bending to the reality of his situation there. (During his senior year alone, he piled up 193 demerits, the most of anyone in his class, and only 7 short of mandatory dismissal.) The demerits were the first tangible proof of a stubborn streak and a resistance to higher authority that would later mar his tenure in high command. An introvert by nature, when pressed in a crisis he would look to himself for answers, often failing to consider, or ignoring, the demands of his superiors and the challenges presented by his opponents. He never appreciated the value of popularity in a leader and consequently felt himself above politics. When he thought he was right (and that was often), he was intractable. No one, not even the president (especially a president who had no military training or experience), could force him to change course.[10]

But these were faults and traits difficult to discern in the early months of 1861, for in many other, very visible ways, Don Carlos Buell was the epitome of a good soldier. In the Mexican War, Buell had demonstrated tremendous personal bravery in nearly every important battle, right up to the moment a Mexican soldier put a ball through his shoulder at Churubusco, on August 20, 1847. Brevetted all the way up to major, for the next fourteen years he served as an adjutant, at first in his own regiment, the Third Infantry, then from 1848 on in various headquarters, performing very competently, earning two tours in the War Department itself. His diligence earned for him the permanent rank of lieutenant colonel by the time Lincoln assumed the presidency.

That bravery was not limited to his martial exploits. In 1854, although severely burned when the boiler exploded, Buell led the fight to quell the flames aboard a Mississippi River steamboat. He received wide praise for saving not only the ship but also the lives of many others who had been trapped on board. Later that same year yellow fever nearly killed him. He survived and then spent weeks alongside his wife nursing his soldiers, also stricken during the epidemic, back to health. Future corps commander and Gettysburg hero Winfield Scott Hancock put the press on to the steamboat story. For his devotion during the yellow fever outbreak, Buell "won the respect of every officer in the department." He was devoted to his wife, free of any obvious vice, rarely if ever spoke ill of anyone, and was respected as a man whose word was his bond.[11]

Unable to accept the discipline imposed on him at the academy, he yet demonstrated an intense degree of self-discipline and dedication to duty that quickly caught the attention of the officers he worked with. One was a young captain named George B. McClellan, who crossed Buell's path at the end of 1852. McClellan immediately wrote to a friend, reporting that he had met "one of the best men in the Army." In the late summer of 1861, none other than famed West Point professor Denis Hart Mahan reminded McClellan of this acquaintance when he forwarded a list of names of officers who might be, in the professor's opinion, considered for high rank. Despite his disciplinary problems at the academy, Buell had caught Mahan's eye. Originally tapped to head a division in the Army of the Potomac, when Brigadier General William T. Sherman resigned his command of the Department of the Cumberland, Buell received the order to lead the expanded and renamed Department of Ohio.[12]

Buell was one of the few officers chosen for high Union command who happened to own slaves, the result of his marriage in 1851. That fact made him automatically suspect in the eyes of radical Republicans. A devout student of Swiss-born military strategist Henri de Jomini, Buell believed in the science of warfare. Success would come from careful and complete preparation followed by exact execution. "Buell strove for a calculated war, in which every move was contemplated and absolute care was given to logistics, administration, and detail to maneuver for favorable situations for his army, rather than fighting from strategic positions."[13] In addition, he found it difficult to delegate. All official correspondence crossed his desk. Leaves of absence, transfers, and resignations all required his personal approval. Only he could address the public. He banned regimental commanders from his tent, personal interaction with them being outside the chain of command. The incessant delays occasioned by such attention to detail, and his isolation from his subordinates, would create further doubts about the general's devotion to the cause.[14]

Buell wholeheartedly believed that the Civil War was a war of reconstruction, being fought to regain control of a geographic region in which lived a people whose allegiance could easily be regained, if, in fact, it had been lost at all. Therefore, as historian Mark Grimsley points out, he believed he had two missions. The first was to oppose and destroy any recognizable military force raised by the rebels. This he would do according to the teachings of Jomini, with exact planning and overwhelming force. His other task was to protect the rights and property of unarmed civilians, so that they would readily return their allegiance to the United States. Perhaps no other soldier in the Union army was better suited to enforce a conciliatory policy than was Major General Don Carlos Buell.[15]

President Lincoln received his initial chance "to grasp the circumstances of this momentous emergency" (as the editor of the *Mercury* had suggested) just days after the war broke out. The first Union soldiers to die at the hands of the rebels were killed on April 19, 1861, not by rebel soldiers or even militiamen but by rioting civilians, as the men of the Sixth Massachusetts Infantry tried to make their way through crowds of Confederate sympathizers in Baltimore, Maryland. Despite incidents like that, in the opening months of the war the "conciliatory policy" often appeared appropriate. In places like western Virginia, newly arriving Union troops were greeted as godsends, and loud pleas were made for more of them to come to other loyal localities like eastern Tennessee.

For the men joining the fight, trying to discern friend from foe could be dizzying, even when still close to Washington. On July 1, 1861, a company of Pennsylvania militiamen marched from Washington through George-town and on westward along the Maryland bank of the Potomac. They found the reception of the people of Rockville "awful cool," but then passed farms outside town where the owners and their children cheered the volun-teers, waving flags and throwing handkerchiefs.[16] Who was a friend? Who was a foe? Were the Union volunteers to actually treat them all alike? These questions would grow in importance and complexity as the troops penetrated deeper and deeper into the rebellious states.

It was the general view under the then prevailing law of war that civilians who did nothing to support a belligerent stood immune from military action but were entitled to little or nothing from the opposing army.[17] In this war, the civilians living in the South were, in the view of the administration in 1861, countrymen who, in keeping with the president's policy, would be granted "cheerfully" all the protection the laws and Constitution might af-ford. Southern property would be guarded. This in turn meant that slaves might well be kept on Southern plantations by Union troops. Southern rights under the laws and Constitution would be respected and preserved. If the army needed something owned by a Southerner, he would be paid for it. This was far more than civilians in an enemy nation had a right to expect under the rules of warfare, and as questions increasingly arose about the attitudes and loyalty of the civilians living in the slave states, the idea of extending to them benevolent treatment would come under increasing scrutiny.

As Mark Grimsley also points out, Lincoln's policy of "exempting South-ern civilians from the hardships of war made political sense only if their support of the Confederacy was indeed shallow and if they remained passive in the face of the Union armies."[18] Lincoln was above all else a politician. No one would be more sensitive to the continuing political sense of his policies than he. The test of that sense would not occur, however, until the armies of the Union entered the Confederacy and came face-to-face with the people living there. Then two questions would need answers. First, where did the heart of the average Southerner lie? How many sheep had gone astray, and just how far off had they gone? This question, and the varying opinions about the correct answer, would lead to a wide-ranging and extended national debate.

The second question was one never openly discussed by the policy makers, although as we shall see it may have caused increasing anxiety for those who either made the policy or were required to carry it out. Was the volunteer

army about to be sent into the South to quell the rebellion capable of apply-
ing a policy of conciliation? Could this enormous force of volunteers be relied upon to restrain itself, collectively and individually, from exacting a
measure of revenge upon the people of the South? Would they pay fairly and
promptly for any goods they acquired? Would they keep the slaves at home
and at work? Would they assure property owners not only that damage to
farms, homes, and other property would be paid for but, more important, that
it would be prevented? Would they reach out and conduct themselves so as to
reassure the residents of the Confederacy that law and order had indeed returned to their midst? Would they make the average Southerner glad to have
them there? Would they quickly stop the armed rebels opposing them from
committing violent or damaging acts? Answers would begin to develop just
as soon as the Union volunteers left for the front.

2
The Man

Learn to obey before you command.

—Solon of Athens, 638–559 BC

Ivan Vasilevitch Turchininoff was born on January 30, 1822, in the Military Province of the Don Cossacks, between the Black and Caspian seas. His father served as a major in the Imperial Russian Army, giving him a place, albeit on a lower rung, in the Russian table of nobility. This, in turn, gave the son entry into the schools that led to his own commission—not an unusual path for officers' sons, though young Turchininoff did much better at it than most. He had three years of elementary, or "district" school, three more at the gymnasium in the provincial capital of Novocherkassk, a school for children of both the nobility and civil officials. Then, at age fourteen, the boy left for St. Petersburg and the best of the cadet academies.[1]

Even the best military schooling was harsh and by rote. "Our officers are trained just like parrots," a later reformer complained; "prior to commissioning they are kept in a cage and incessantly plagued with: 'Polly, Left turn, March!' and Polly repeats, 'Left turn, March!' 'Polly, Present arms!' and Polly repeats it. When Polly gets to the stage that he remembers all these words, besides learning to be held by one claw, they give him epaulets."[2] Most Russian officers of the period got their epaulets without attending any of the twenty-two cadet academies scattered around the empire. In fact, very few officers serving in the tsar's Regular infantry divisions finished the cadet course.[3] Turchininoff's graduation from the academy in the imperial capital thus gained him advantages, not least his assignment to an elite branch, the horse artillery. In 1841, even here the nineteen-year-old ensign must have found active duty as mindless as the last phase of his classroom education. Russian military doctrine was fundamentally a matter of large-formation drill, leading not to the battlefield but rather to "perfection on the parade ground." All was controlled by "the Regulation (Ustav), which set forth in great detail the various 'battle orders' for the units of infantry, cavalry, and artillery, with complete disregard for the conditions of terrain." Platoon commanders—lieutenants—were obliged during battle to count out an exact number of paces as they advanced to regroup their men in columns for attack.[4]

Over the course of the next eight years, Turchininoff advanced only one grade. As a lieutenant in 1849, he participated in the Russian campaign to help the Austrian Empire suppress the Hungarian Revolution of 1848. In the course of it, he likely gained his first experience dealing with hostile civilians and foraging in enemy territory. Resupply of this sort was not part of official Russian military doctrine. Moving against a Polish insurrection in January 1831, Russian Field Marshal J. K. F. A. Diebitch had tried to feed his army from the countryside, with disastrous results.[5] The commander of the Hungarian campaign in 1849, Prince Ivan Paskevich (who had taken command from Diebitch eighteen years before), learned from Diebitch's example. However, he became so insistent upon amassing vast stockpiles of subsistence along the Hungarian border that his force nearly missed the invasion deadline. Still, Turchininoff may well have become familiar there with foraging as a necessity. (In later writings, he made it very clear that he considered it no vice to make certain that his men never went hungry, no matter where that meant he had to go to get provisions.) Once in Hungary, Paskevich's army met with great difficulty in moving the stores to the troops. As a result, even the men of the artillery were accused of marching at night from village to village stealing oats from peasants. Officers were said to have praised their initiative. That, too, Turchin would do at a later time.[6]

As for the treatment of civilians during that campaign, accounts vary. The Hungarian leader, Louis Kossuth, described the tsar's army as a horde of looters, rapists, and murderers. One modern study, though, has the troops behaving "with exemplary dignity," welcomed by the populace. Perhaps. When the conflict ended "the Russian victors and their Hungarian foes shared a deep mutual respect." The Hungarian commander, Arthur Görgey, chose to capitulate to Paskevich's evidently magnanimous forces.[7] Even if there were such conciliatory feelings, history records, with however much embellishment by the original recorders, that in the capture of the city of Tokaj at the beginning of the campaign, on June 16, after the citizenry fired on the Russian troops from houses, the soldiers "broke into buildings, killed civilians taken 'gun in hand,' and ravaged the whole western part of the city."

A similar rampage was reported in July at the town of Vaæ. Official Russian military code forbade looting and the mistreatment of unarmed civilians. The alleged outrages, which were triggered by civilians acting well outside the rules, and which may be more fairly considered acts of retaliation, were still attributed to uncontrollable Cossacks.[8] Even with Cossacks to be blamed, young officers like Turchininoff learned a larger lesson about the nature of war and the treatment of civilians when some of them decided to play beyond acceptable bounds. He had grown up in the land of the Cossacks. Perhaps he had less of an inclination to look down on the manner in which those untamed horsemen fought.

There are the written, official rules of war. There are also the unwritten laws, the customs. There was no doubt that when the Hungarian civilians took up arms and fired from their homes, they lost their claim to be noncombatants. In so doing, they brought into play one of war's oldest unwritten laws, that of retaliation. Often retaliation was held aloft, bandied about by an army as a deterrent to hostile civilians. But when circumstances presented themselves that brought soldiers into imminent threat of harm from the hands of people who were supposed to be outside the fray, the reaction could be swift and cruel. Because it was retaliatory, the otherwise outrageous behavior became legitimate.[9]

Turchininoff himself seems never to have mentioned being in combat in Hungary. There wasn't much of it to get into. The Hungarians maneuvered to fight their battles against the Austrians, for whom they had a very real hatred. Their campaign ended on August 13, 1849, after just two months. Their army of 200,000 or more lost only 543 men killed in action, another 1,670 wounded, and 11,028 victims of cholera. Whether or not he took part in a battle or in the sacking of a town, it is reasonable to assume that Turchininoff understood the nature of the conflict, and that he knew how the troops behaved and how that behavior was thought of by the officers in command of the expedition.[10] Something about Turchininoff's war service impressed his superiors. His commanding officer recommended him to take the examination for entrance to the Nicholas Academy of the General Staff, Russia's senior military school. There, as he recalled much later, he studied "high tactics, the military history of famous campaigns, topography and geodesy, military statistics, and military administration."[11] He may well have had the chance to compare war as fought in a classroom to his real experience in Hungary.

By matriculating at the academy, Turchininoff entered the progressive wing of the Russian officer corps, at the head of which stood Colonel Dmitrii Miliutin. An academy instructor since 1845, Miliutin brought the life of the mind to his small cadre. His influence was in many respects comparable to that of Denis Hart Mahan, during the same period the intellectual giant of the United States Military Academy at West Point. Miliutin and Mahan shared many of the same broad interests and, curiously, the same aloof personality. Miliutin, though, had been a combat soldier, and ultimately he would carry out major reforms during his twenty-year tenure as the tsar's minister of war from 1861 to 1881. Even before Turchininoff's arrival at the Nicholas Academy, Miliutin had initiated or improved the courses his student would best remember. The most notable, Military Statistics, for which he wrote the text in 1847, provided instruction in "research into a government's strategic plan for military operations in a particular theater of war." In Miliutin's mind, the course was crucial to an officer's training. "Military statistics is like the last page of military history," he wrote. "It is the history of the present, thus providing that essential link between theory and practice."[12]

Turchininoff completed the two-year course in 1852 with, by his own account, the same high honor Miliutin had won in 1836.[13] Turchininoff also acquired at the Nicholas Academy, if he had not already in Hungary, an attitude toward junior officers and soldiers in the ranks that mirrored Miliutin's and guided his own style in America. His ability to gain the warm admiration of the men he commanded in the field was undoubtedly honed during these years. At the same time he developed a scorn for "the strict, narrow, iron-clad martinetism of European states, which would turn sensible men into unreasoning automatons." When he arrived at a station where he did in fact know more about running an army than did many of his superiors, his scorn would breed resentment.[14]

After graduating, Turchininoff gained a post on the staff of the Imperial Guards in St. Petersburg under the progressive Count F. V. Rüdiger. Turchininoff may at first have hoped that reform would recast the "État-major," the general staff, into what he later described as Napoleon's design for it: "to lead the columns, to post the pickets in line of battle, . . . the connecting link between the commander-in-chief and his army; the intelligent conductors of his orders and ideas, and the soul of every movement."[15] This was not, however, the view held by Tsar Nicholas I, who openly distrusted "planners and thinkers." In the 1850s "soldiers who showed intellectual tendencies were called 'scholars' in the pejorative sense of 'eggheads' and were subject to blatant derision." The number of students in Turchininoff's class at the Nicholas

Academy was therefore held to seven, down from twenty-five in the tsar's less crusty days, the 1830s. Graduates were relegated to paperwork, traditional mapmaking, and the organization of the grand parade formations that were the particular and peculiar thrill of Nicholas I. Said Miliutin at the time: "Everything is just great for parades, just terrible for war."[16]

Happily for now Captain Turchininoff, the coming of the Crimean War gave greater scope. In July 1853, as Britain and France hardened their objections to the tsar's adventurism in the Balkans, Vice Admiral Sir Charles Napier, a cautious man, warned Whitehall against the Russian Baltic fleet. With only slightly greater reason, the Russian Ministry of War perceived a threat to the shores of Russia's possessions, Finland and Poland, and to the tsarist capital of St. Petersburg. Colonel Miliutin submitted a memorandum on coastal defense, and the document led to the formation of a special Baltic Committee. Turchininoff played a role—in March 1854—as a topographical surveyor of the Finnish coast (fortified though key positions already were), to identify possible enemy landing spots.[17]

Britain and France declared war on March 28, 1854. Far to the north, Napier's fleet entered the Baltic to scout about and demonstrate against St. Petersburg and its protecting island fortress of Kronstadt. He arrived near Russian waters in May with nine screw and six sailing battleships, joined by eight French, more than a match for the tsar's twenty-five obsolete ships of the line. Accomplishing little by way of combat, the British and French steamed and sailed away in September, even as allied land forces were in transit through the Mediterranean and the Black Sea to invade the Crimea. A second British and French naval expedition arrived in 1855. Both summers, the combined fleet bombarded points on the Finnish coast and landed small parties for trivial engagements. However, the maneuvers were a great strategic success. Coupled with a threat of invasion by the Austrians, the Russians held 200,000 men in the north. A share of them might have tipped the balance around Sebastopol in the Crimea, where 55,000 Russians went into action against 60,000 British and French.[18]

To the Russian army, nonetheless, the defense of the Baltic littoral seemed a clear and splendid victory in an otherwise dismal war. An American visitor, the army's Major Richard Delafield, caught the enthusiasm: "Cronstadt, to the end of the war, set the enemy's fleet at defiance, saving St. Petersburg."[19] Miliutin became a major general in 1854 and in 1855 a member of the tsar's suite. Turchininoff, promoted very quickly through the ranks to colonel at the age of thirty-three, drew a posting at the headquarters of an army corps in southern Poland, which had another fortuitous benefit. Three United States Army officers sent to observe the war appeared in Poland and at St. Petersburg during the summer of 1855. Delafield (superintendent of West Point from 1838 to 1845) was accompanied by Major Alfred Mordecai and Captain George Brinton McClellan. Each wrote detailed, if myopic, reports praising the Imperial Army. "The example of Russia is a lesson every way entitled to our study and imitation," advised Delafield. Published in book form as congressional documents, all three accounts were available to readers interested in military affairs and so could have added luster to the credentials of any Russian immigrant who had a record of service for the tsar.[20]

The visiting American officers, guided by the predispositions of their own Regular service, let themselves be awed by the imperial dress parades and the apparent discipline of troops and cadets. In fact, it was an unsettling time for the Russian army, and a frustrating time for educated officers like Turchininoff, who were being jolted about by the fits and starts of reform. News from the Crimea turned unnerving as early as the battle of Inkerman, in October 1854, when the tsar's commanders had reason to expect victory but were obliged to explain defeat. After the death of Nicholas I on February 18, 1855, and well before the war effectively ended with the abandonment of Sebastopol on September 27, Count Rüdiger's series of memoranda on the condition of the army led Tsar Alexander II to appoint him to head a special Commission for the Improvement of Military Elements. Miliutin was assigned to it in February 1856 and in March produced his own "Thoughts on the Present Shortcomings in the Russian Military System and the Means to Eliminate Them."[21]

This could never become a flood tide of reform. Even when effecting substantial changes as minister of war beginning in 1861, Miliutin himself was no more than an "enlightened statesman of autocracy." Disagreement with the tsar was unthinkable. In 1856 Alexander sought to assure his subjects that "in time of great social turmoil the war ministry would never become embroiled in political machinations." Reformers on the Rüdiger Commission were evenly balanced by mossbacks. The tsar agreed to merit as a basis for promotion only as a distant ideal. Succeeding Paskevich as the new minister of war was, to the chagrin of educated officers, General N. O. Sukhozanet, a man they would just as soon have cashiered for his ignorance.[22]

Isolated in south Poland, but certainly aware of these developments as they circulated through the high command, Turchininoff must have felt the blunting hand of the old order, even as he rapidly climbed through the ranks to colonel, the grade he held when he received the choice assignment of organizing the grand review for the new tsar's coronation. On May 10, 1856, at Krakow, Poland, he married Nadezhda Lvova, the thirty-two-year-old daughter of another army colonel.[23] Most of what is known about her she recorded in a diary while with her husband in the field in 1863 and 1864. Clearly in love, she wrote from camp at Chattanooga, just after the battle of Chickamauga, that she went with him to be where "I know what goes on, I can watch over his needs of every day, and I am there to take care of him in case he should be wounded." Educated in the manner of the Russian upper class, Nadezhda Turchininoff wrote her diary in fine French prose, enjoyed riding horses, and savored fine literature. An aristocratic radical, she believed that the poor of her newly adopted country were "ill-used, fooled, robbed, assassinated by a handful of men fundamentally belonging to the most detestable type that society can produce: the enriched industrialist basely imitating the nobleman."[24]

They married with the apparent understanding that they would make their life together in America, for less than a month after the ceremony they departed for the West. The stated reasons for leaving Russia fit the colonel's background. The *Chicago Tribune*'s account, given on June 24, 1861 (and evidently based on an interview), says that after the Crimean War, "having imbibed Democratic notions, and being thoroughly disgusted thereby with the Russian government," he took a furlough to a spa in Germany for feigned medical reasons. From there, he and his bride kept heading west, until he "made his way to free America." Hope for a better, fairer world lay on the far shore of the Atlantic. On arrival, Ivan and Nadezhda Turchininoff became John and Nadine Turchin.[25]

Turchin brought to America the ability and training that made him the *Chicago Tribune*'s "officer of experience and skill," a man fit for command. Not surprising, though, he also brought an intellectual arrogance and an aptness to be critical of higher commanders. More important, having broken off his career in the Russian army, he retained no stable commitment to the profession of arms. His wife wrote of the officer corps they had known: "A chain of common interests, a solidarity resulting in general security, holds together a multitude that observes itself, studies itself," and perhaps most significantly based on subsequent events, "forgives much to its members."[26] That chain, too, was broken. Having left the profession once, as he said, in part because he was sick of the "tyranny of the army," he would not again assume the correctness of its assumptions or its discipline.[27] He might recognize the professional military community in the United States, but both by his choice and by that of the American Regulars, he would not be a part of it. He was not an officer who would submissively obey orders given by commanders he thought incompetent or one who would ask for forgiveness for doing things in the manner he had come to believe correct.

It would also be obvious from his subsequent writings and behavior that Turchin joined the war effort in 1861 with an enthusiasm akin to that of the volunteers he would lead. He had broken his ties with the Russian officer corps. He developed some degree of disdain for the military leadership he found in America, both professional and volunteer, many of whom were men of much less experience and training than he. It should not be surprising, then, that he developed an even steadier and stronger bond with his men than might have existed for him in Russia. With his American comrades he shared a sense of involvement that no one would have felt on invading Hungary to prop up the emperor. As our story develops and we contrast the professional soldier with the volunteer, we can ask this question: When he signed on to fight in the Civil War, did John Basil Turchin do so as a professional soldier, or did he do so as a volunteer? We can then ponder how this altered his effectiveness as a commander.

By accounts that can have originated only with them, both the colonel and his wife had the good fortune of having a modest amount of family money. A colonel's salary in Russia, even at Turchin's high station, was little better than a third that of his Prussian counterpart. By the book, Russian officers were not allowed to marry without showing independent wealth sufficient to support their wives. Certainly, it would have been difficult to travel abroad without funds.[28] Arriving in New York, the couple first purchased a farm on Long Island, a base from which to learn the language and the customs. Then, in 1857, an economic depression struck. They decamped to Philadelphia, where the thirty-five-year-old Turchin sought to study for American credentials in engineering. There he gained an introduction to the redoubtable Alexander Dallas Bache, Philadelphia native, great-grandson of Benjamin Franklin and superintendent of the United States Coast Survey, a conspicuous employer of well-educated immigrants.[29] Turchin could apply a good coat of whitewash, particularly when recounting times when he was in fact down on his luck, but his 1886 description of important scientific work for Bache in Washington in 1857–58 matches closely what was then happening at the Coast Survey.[30]

Bache had a way of hiring subordinates "on trial," then shedding them.

(Turchin's explanation of leaving the Coast Survey—underfunding of the agency—is belied by the fact that in the late 1850s Bache consistently obtained generous support from Congress.)[31] The search for other work carried him west, in 1858 to Mattoon, Illinois, a rough new railroad stop, where he sought work as an architect. In 1859 he seized the chance to leave the town of but 150 buildings to take work in the thriving city of Chicago, as one of the 3,500 employees of the Illinois Central Railroad. Mrs. Turchin's recollection of their life in their new city: "[I] almost miss the time when John had his temporary job as a draftsman and I worked from dawn to dusk without any help whatever to keep our little household."[32]

In Chicago Turchin become acquainted with some very influential people, including Nathaniel Prentiss Banks, the erstwhile Massachusetts congressman, Speaker of the House, and governor of Massachusetts, who had recently come to Chicago as the Illinois Central's resident director. Banks left after only five months on the job, on May 16, 1861, to accept an appointment as a major general in the Union army.[33] (Never having been in the army or the militia before, Banks, passed over for a cabinet position in favor of Gideon Welles, would begin his army career precariously positioned near the top.) A lesser Illinois Central official, John W. Foster, put Turchin forward as a possible regimental commander. Having failed in the civilian economy— Charles Ray of the *Chicago Tribune* had to guarantee the tailor's bill for his officer's uniform—Turchin must have thought the prospect of serving as the colonel of a new Illinois regiment a veritable redemption of his birthright.[34]

It was not an inopportune thing for an editor of the *Tribune* to guarantee the note of a prospective colonel, especially one who was about to take command of a regiment in which the paper had a great interest. In the form known to readers in June 1861, the *Chicago Tribune* had gotten its start in the spring of 1855. At the suggestion of none other than Horace Greeley of the *New York Tribune,* Joseph Medill had taken very literally Greeley's proverbial advice. Medill had indeed gone west, west to Chicago where he met Charles Ray in the rotunda room of the Tremont House Hotel. Medill had begun as a lawyer in Ohio, but by the time of this meeting he had ten years' experience as a newspaperman. After hard struggles that honed his rather relentless personality, he was already a publisher of the *Cleveland Morning Leader.* Ray's life had been less directed—sailing on a whaler, studying medicine in New York and practicing it in Iowa, writing temperance articles and editing a political journal at Galena, Illinois, then serving as the state senate's secretary in Springfield. The two men enjoyed a wild-game dinner at the Tremont and talked through the night. "A comparison of views led to a determination" to buy the *Chicago Tribune*, a struggling sheet founded in 1847.[35]

Three summers later, the *Tribune* still struggled, nearly undone by the continuing national economic depression that had begun in 1857. Circulation stood at only 4,000. So, on July 1, 1858, Medill and Ray merged their newspaper with another daily of similar size, the *Democrat Press*, published since 1852 by William Bross and John Locke Scripps. "Deacon" Bross, Williams College cum laude 1838, an ardent Presbyterian, an exuberant Chicagoan since 1848 (the year the telegraph reached the town), had begun as a bookseller and editor of the religious *Herald of the Prairies*. His partner, the rather reclusive Scripps, raised in Rushville, Illinois, a former mathematics teacher and a practical economist by inclination, had worked as a Chicago journalist since the time of his partner's arrival.[36]

The combined enterprise worked. Bross and Scripps brought their established reputations as writers to a key group of readers and advertisers—Chicago's rising businessmen. Medill, a typesetter early in his career, kept charge of the printing machinery even while he followed state and national politics with the panache of a modern sportswriter. From Ray's life story the impression emerges that this "intense but hearty man," normally of kindly spirit, was the editor who colored the news columns with human interest—with the stories, for example, about Ellsworth's Zouaves, the drill team that captivated the Northern states during the summer of 1860.[37]

In the hard-driving tradition of Chicago's first mayor and greatest developer, their friend William B. Ogden, all the *Tribune* proprietors were "community makers and community leaders." Any less would have displayed "a lack of community spirit and a lack of business sense."[38] Of necessity, they were boosters. Three of them, all but Ray, claimed to have settled in the city only after close study showed its geographic and economic advantages over every place else on the globe. Ray played his own conspicuous part for business as a trustee of the most important public work, the Chicago Canal.[39] Especially for Bross, the *Tribune's* ambassador to the board of trade, "Chicago became not just a home but a crusade." He would later call its growth "an increase never before equaled by any city in the history of the world." So it must have seemed, for Chicago grew sixfold in just twelve years, from 18,000 residents in 1848 to 109,000 in 1860.[40]

As the cry for abolition of slavery grew to a crescendo in northern Illinois, all four owners of the *Tribune* could honestly claim to have sung their parts in the choir. Medill had become active in antislavery politics in Ohio. Bross was an original Free Soiler. In February 1856 Ray helped write the resolutions at a convention of Illinois newsmen gathered to oppose the expansion of slave territory. Scripps was a fervent, but pragmatic, abolitionist. Like him, the *Tribune*'s editorial page generally held a step back from a stridently radical position, the more effectively to attract readers of moderate antislavery views and those not yet converted. "What shall be done with the slaves?" the *Tribune* asked in a businesslike tone as late as September 5, 1861. "They cannot be exterminated; they cannot be exported; they cannot be forever enslaved." But on occasion the proprietors' personal feelings emerged, as on June 18, 1861, when they denounced any thought of compromise with the Confederate government: "The accursed thing which has alienated the affections of so many thousands from the glorious principles of Republican freedom, is *Slavery*. The conflict will go on until the slave-holding oligarchy is broken down and subjugated, and the Democratic idea is reinstated in the South."

The *Tribune* unabashedly advanced the Republican Party's cause in its editorial columns and also behind the scenes: word-for-word coverage of the Lincoln-Douglas debates in 1858, all to the challenger Lincoln's advantage, gavel-to-gavel coverage of the national convention in 1860, the texts of Lincoln's campaign speeches, the best of them reprinted as pamphlets on the *Tribune*'s presses. During the two years before 1860, when U.S. senator Lyman Trumbull came up for reelection by the state legislature, "we placed some thousands of our papers in the close counties on which the election would turn," Medill later reminded the senator.[41] The *Tribune* came out publicly for Lincoln on February 16, 1860. (Two months earlier, Medill had been in Washington scouting out and promoting his prospects.)[42] As credibly as any Republican operatives, the editors could boast of a role in the Rail-Splitter's narrow victory at the May convention. That summer, Bross stumped throughout Illinois on behalf of his friend, much as he had four years earlier for the first Republican presidential candidate, John C. Frémont. When Trumbull anxiously sought troops to hold "Little Egypt" (southern Illinois, around Cairo) late in April 1861, he wrote to Ray, even a closer friend of the president, or so he must have thought, to urge his intercession.[43]

The *Tribune* prospered. Circulation doubled by 1861, to more than 16,000, allowing the company to pay all obligations overdue from the tight days of 1858. Foreseeing yet greater success, Medill replaced the one-cylinder press (that is to say, a rotary press with a single drum) with a cutting-edge Hoe

four-cylinder, steam-driven printing plant.[44] Public interest in the increasingly gripping news—the excitements over slavery, then secession, then war—
spurred success, but there was more to it. Providing the proverbial well-
written daily paper with broad, general news coverage and features—not
a small feat, yet not uncommon—the *Tribune*'s editors deftly managed to
engage in conversations with their readers, with large, overlapping, non-
antagonistic groups, with politically and economically active people of a wide
region. Midwestern businessmen, abolitionists of all degrees from fervent to
merely interested, Republican politicians and voters, perhaps some opponents, all could find their views reflected or challenged in the *Tribune*.[45] Not
foolishly did Medill boast, "I meet men daily from this and surrounding
States. *They all talk one language.* The *Tribune* is read by a quarter of million of men in the West and it simply indicates as the dial finger, the sentiment of the people. We receive hundreds of letters from Pittsburg [*sic*] to
Leavenworth—from Cairo to Marquette fully endorsing and approving our
views."[46]

As the *Tribune* gathered its power, its editors sought influence at the
White House. The test came in February 1861, before the new administration took office. Lincoln saw it and moved ahead of them. His view of the
press is now often quoted: "No man, whether he be a private citizen or President of the United States, can successfully carry on a controversy with a great
newspaper, and escape destruction, unless he owns a newspaper equally great,
with a circulation in the same neighborhood."[47] The words have an apocry-
phal ring to them, but the sentiment fits. He secretly owned his own newspaper, though not a great one—the Springfield *Illinois Staats-Anzeiger*, purchased in May 1859, with an eye to German-American support in any bid
for the presidency. Immediately upon taking office, Lincoln appointed ten
newspaper editors and publishers as postmasters of major cities, ranging from
Albany to Des Moines to San Francisco (and ten more to tax collectorships
and diplomatic postings).[48] There was nothing novel about this; Andrew
Jackson had favored fifty-five editors with plum government appointments.[49]

For a newspaper owner a postmaster's position was to be coveted, not
merely for the salary, the patronage, and the consequent influence with the
party. Beyond a city's immediate environs, nineteenth-century newspapers
were distributed through the post office and onward by railroads, themselves
dependent on postmasters. Being a postmaster did not necessarily create the
possibility that another publisher's bundles of newspapers might be delayed
or held back, but it was a sure guarantee that one's own paper's fresh packs

would be sped to the readers. In Harrisburg, Pennsylvania, the bundles of the Republican *Telegraph* and the Democratic *Patriot and Union* left the papers' sorting rooms at the same time in the morning, but the *Telegraph* was being read in Pittsburgh that same evening, the *Patriot* not until twenty-four hours later.[50]

Being Chicago's postmaster was of especial importance to the owners of the *Tribune*—its circulation extending, as Medill noted, east to Pennsylvania, west into Kansas—and, what mattered more, to every railroad stop in Illinois. The delay in appointing a postmaster in Chicago turned out to be only that. To handshakes all around at the paper's offices, no doubt, Scripps got the job on March 28. Of greater importance was the role the *Tribune* had in influencing the thought and opinion of those who read it, or who depended upon its owners for patronage and support, men like John Basil Turchin. And although they may not have climbed out to the end of the limb when debating the slave controversy, there was no doubting the fervor of the editors when it came to the manner in which freshly sprouted traitors and rebels should be treated. This was not a question subject to debate. There would be no middle ground, especially when hometown heroes fell in the fray.

For Turchin, new to the country and new to Chicago, the enthusiasm of the editors, who had become his mentors and patrons, would have been contagious. No doubt he had displayed energy of his own that attracted their support. As Turchin's words would later evidence, he was not a timid champion of the freedoms he had come to America looking for. Certainly he would have absorbed much of his understanding of the local cultural norms and societal expectations from his association with men like Foster and Ray. These promoters, who had been so successful in selling Chicago, were no less fervent about promoting the Union war effort. How they called for the war to be fought would matter to the men who left there to fight it. As John Keegan has pointed out, the military usually reflects the society from which it comes. "War," he notes, "is always an expression of the culture" of the society that fights it. If the *Tribune* said to burn the homes of traitors, if it called on the loyal men of America to sink ships, kill rebels, and desolate the very fields those same rebels depended upon to feed themselves and their families, what was there to stop a volunteer from thinking that he should do just that? After the rebels fired on Fort Sumter, the *Tribune* repeatedly made the call to do just those things.[51]

3
The Men

I don't know what effect these men will have on the enemy, but, by God,
they frighten me!

—Lord Wellington

When Hylan Downs and his friends decided to go off to war, they knew
exactly how they wanted to go about it. As he recalled long after the war had
ended, "a member of our company named Sanders and myself had repeatedly
witnessed the drilling of the Ellsworth Zouaves in the old Garrett Block,
corner of Randolph and State, [and] we decided that we must all join the
Nineteenth [Illinois Infantry] because they knew all about soldiering and, of
course, would stand a better show in the future."[1]

Downs was hardly alone in seeking a place with the old Zouaves. John A.
Page was a student at Northwestern University when, on Saturday night,
April 13, 1861, the news broke that the rebels were firing on Fort Sumter.
First attending a student rally where everyone pledged their allegiance to a
flag made of calico (all of the real flags and bunting were already sold out),
he and his friends arose bright and early Monday morning to catch the train
downtown to enlist. The cars were already filled to overflowing with "country boys on the same mission as ourselves" and, as it turned out, they were all
too late. Heading for State Street and the armory of the Zouaves, they found
"the crowd so dense that we could not get near it."[2]

Chicago's Zouave Cadets were the remarkable creation of a driven and
charismatic young man named Elmer E. Ellsworth. In April 1859, just
turned twenty-two, the young man, an impoverished clerk from upstate New
York, decided to seek his fortune in the West. Soon after, by force of personality and imagination, Ellsworth took over and quickly transformed a mori-
bund Chicago militia company into a drill team of national renown.[3] Organizations of the sort had existed around the country for decades—young
men's fraternities, in effect, many of them holding dances and banquets as

often as martial exhibitions. However, as war fever grew during the 1850s, there were never so many such companies, North and South, as in 1859 and 1860.[4]

Ellsworth's own talents "were not those that bring their greatest success in a business career." Nor, perhaps, would they have brought success in the pre-war Regular Army, where innovation and creativity were not the greatest of attributes, for he brought a refreshing verve and many new members to his Chicago club by adopting the extravagant uniforms and the style of drill, "a kind of rapid gymnastics," thought to have been used by victorious French troops in North Africa and the Crimea. Aided by a friend, a French doctor named Charles DeVillers, Ellsworth studied the drill of the French as well as that contained in the books of tactics written by Winfield Scott and William Hardee for the United States Army. From those he worked out his own routines, always seeking to shorten and quicken movements and to improve the physical condition of his men. His volunteers at first drilled three evenings a week, then, as enthusiasm took hold, four hours every night except Sundays, with fast sandwiches for supper. They abstained from alcohol, tobacco, and even from entering pool halls, lest temptation prove too strong. Ellsworth cashiered twelve of the best for imbibing strong drink.[5]

Ellsworth gave purpose to this rigor and boosted the club's elitism and esprit de corps by parading the Zouaves at public events. Their first performance took place on July 4, 1859, in front of Chicago's Tremont House. With their flashy uniforms and crisp movements, they became an instant hit. That September, only five months after Ellsworth had taken over, they entered a competition at the National Agricultural Fair, where the promoters offered a stand of colors for the "championship of militia." They won. Afterward, Ellsworth showed a genius for self-promotion that would be with him to the moment he died. Chided because only one other unit had entered the contest, Ellsworth issued a challenge to all comers. If any militia unit would come to Chicago and best his company, the cadets would pay all the visitors' expenses.[6]

When, despite national advertising of the challenge, no one came, Ellsworth decided to go on the road. First he grabbed the spotlight performing at the Republican National Convention in Chicago in May 1860. Forced to postpone their departure for two weeks because of the death of his brother, in July he took four dozen of his men on a six-week tour of all the major cities in the North, the expenses partly subsidized by Chicago's prominent citizens, with a view to publicizing their booming metropolis.[7] Newspapers in Detroit, Cleveland, Rochester, Albany ("to military eyes, most exciting"), and as far east as Boston and Salem gave them rave reviews.[8]

At West Point on July 26, they drilled before Brevet Lieutenant General Winfield Scott and the commandant of cadets, Lieutenant Colonel William J. Hardee, the authors of the books on close-order drill. The Zouaves wore their billowing red pants, short, open blue jackets, and their "jaunty crimson caps." They all had matching haircuts, moustaches, and goatees. First Ellsworth put them through their own specialized routine, each man bearing a knapsack weighing twenty-five pounds. They did their entire drill at the double-quick, at one point stacking arms and working across suspended horizontal ladders. When Hardee complained of its impracticality, Ellsworth put them through the colonel's official system. When he again complained that some men were cheating by glancing to the side to check their alignments, Ellsworth had his men do it again, again flawlessly, blindfolded. Not wanting to slight General Scott, the Zouaves performed a fourth time, and went through a complete rendition of the general's older system.[9]

A New York City reporter caught something of the Zouaves' own greater-than-West-Point flashiness in City Hall Park, where, in front of 10,000 eager fans, "with uniform speed, and always with an unbroken front, they ran about the field, continually varying their maneuvres [sic], but never verging upon confusion. The vaultings, lunges, thrusts and parryings of the bayonet exercise, were executed with remarkable perfection; the exciting rally upon the center, accompanied with the short Zouave howl, evoked shouts of delight, waving of umbrellas, handkerchiefs, parasols, sticks and hats." The reporter for *Frank Leslie's Illustrated*, which provided full coverage of the New York City appearances, was succinct. "The effect," he wrote, "was electric."[10]

When the cadets returned to Chicago that August, via a triumphal tour of Washington, Cincinnati, St. Louis, and Springfield, the most famous man in America outside of politics stood at their head. Ellsworth's name had become, as the *Philadelphia Inquirer* attested, a household word. More importantly, the building war fever had given rise to thousands of companies of boys marching together in towns stretching from Bangor to Dubuque. Most paraded only in street clothes, and if they were armed at all it was with broomsticks. But didn't they all aspire to be just like Ellsworth?[11] Ellsworth led the best of the best, and the best of the best was the pride of Chicago, all the more so as the war clouds darkened.

It was, perhaps, not coincidental that some of Ellsworth's stops had coincided with Republican campaign rallies. Winning the friendship and admiration of Lincoln himself in the process, in September Ellsworth moved to Springfield, ostensibly to read law at Lincoln & Herndon, but mostly to work on the presidential campaign. He traveled on the president-elect's train to the inauguration, "a sort of pet of Mr. Lincoln," said Henry Villard.[12] Lincoln rewarded him not with a high army post but with a lieutenancy— not yet the time to put twenty-four-year-olds in positions of power but rather, as Lincoln tactfully advised Ellsworth, a time for "justice and courtesy towards the older officers of the army."[13]

He remained in Washington only a month, biding his time, hoping for an appointment to head up a new militia department, when the shells fell on Sumter. Like everyone else, Ellsworth jumped instantly to his feet. In three days he had a plan of action. On April 17, he resigned his commission and caught a train for New York. He went there, he said, to recruit a regiment of firemen, "men who can go into a fight now." In just two days, he had raised enough men to provide a "conspicuous" escort for the men of the fabled Seventh New York Militia, who left that day for Washington. After two additional days, more than 2,300 men, enough for two regiments, had signed his rolls. Ellsworth spent the next week inspecting the hopefuls, whittling down the list of recruits to 1,100, carefully picking only those he thought the most desirable. The people of New York straight off donated over $60,000 to equip Ellsworth's "Fire Zouaves" with custom-designed uniforms, new Sharps rifles, revolvers, and sixteen-inch Bowie knives. The result, thought one commentator, was "a strong, active, and courageous collection of soldiers, men with fine physiques who were acquainted with drills and target shooting, and familiar with hardship and peril."[14]

Back near the shores of Lake Michigan, with the crowd jamming the streets around Ellsworth's old armory, not to mention virtually every other village square in the state, Illinois governor Richard Yates had no problem filling the federal government's call for six regiments of militiamen. Yates, a solid, antislavery Republican, was just as eager to display the Unionism of Illinois as was everyone else. The governor wired Secretary of War Simon Cameron on April 17: "A large number of companies have tendered services. Volunteers are assembling." By April 20, Illinois had accepted the service of sixty-one companies, one more than needed to fill the call from Washington. In Chicago, civic leaders raised $36,000 ("given, not loaned") to equip these men willing to go to war.[15]

Amid this surge of enthusiasm, and besieged by the crowd beating at their doors, veterans of Ellsworth's original Zouave Cadets raised three of those companies. James Hayden gathered eighty-nine men under the name Company A, Chicago Zouaves. John H. Clybourne rallied eighty-three men who took the name Company B, Chicago Zouaves. Frederick Harding, not quite so attached to the Zouave name, took eighty men into Captain Harding's Company, also called the Chicago Light Infantry.[16] To Harding's company a gentleman donated a silk flag bearing the telling legend, "Retaliation—No Mercy to Traitors,"[17] the first real evidence of a sentiment that would be popular both with the press and with a great portion of the public.

For the most part, these militiamen had not drilled with Ellsworth. No doubt some had enlisted in "Wide Awake" groups and had paraded rather sloppily with their friends through the streets as the war neared. Others were simply eager young men caught up in the frenzy of the times.[18] Later careers would show some to be men of fine character and ability. James Henry Haynie, nineteen, joined Harding's company at the first call; he would become, decades later, the dean of the foreign correspondents' corps in Paris. Ira Chase, a sickly twenty-six-year-old sergeant in Clybourne's troop, would become, in the 1890s, governor of Indiana.[19]

These three companies became part of a 908-man Chicago battalion. Another prominent former cadet, Joseph R. Scott, signed on with the staff of the commander of the militia, a banker and militia brigadier general, R. K. Swift, an old (literally as well as figuratively) supporter of Ellsworth's efforts. Typical of so many organizations thrown together at the war's start, this task force entrained for Little Egypt, the area around Cairo at Illinois's southern tip, on April 21, "indifferently armed" (without weaponry, except for the pistols brought from home) and sans uniforms. Notwithstanding, at Cairo some of the Chicagoans had a hand in capturing a steamboat carrying Confederate contraband. Half seriously, they forever resented the government's failure to pay them naval prize shares.[20]

Most of the sixty-one companies originally accepted into state service were organized into six militia regiments to serve for the three months authorized under federal law.[21] The men who had gathered under the Chicago Zouave banners of Hayden, Clybourne, and Harding found themselves on another path. Perhaps the reason really was "the scheming of their officers for promotion," as a downstate Democratic editor scowled.[22] The more likely cause was that sort of aggressiveness that had made the three captains active in the Zouaves in the first place, now reignited by the war's outbreak. They wanted the Zouave flame kept alive in a separate, elite unit, a vaulting, lunging regiment that would build on the teachings of Ellsworth. Still short of recruits, they did, however, have friends in state government, and not just the doddering General Swift, who had repaired to Springfield after being quietly relieved of the command at Cairo. On May 2, the state legislature authorized ten three-year regiments and clearly implied that Chicago—and who else but the Zouave companies?—would be the core for the first such regiment to be sent to the field. Led by Joe Scott, the three companies retraced their steps and camped at the fairgrounds near Springfield, there to await the formation of their little battalion into a full-fledged three-year regiment of volunteers.[23]

For federal service, the president had called for three-year volunteer regiments, but only for forty from the entire country. The secretary of war, "on the other hand[,] was bent on keeping down the numbers," saving the cost of equipping and sustaining troops then thought unnecessary.[24] It took the intervention of Congressman Isaac N. Arnold, prominently a friend of the president and also an ally of the *Tribune*'s publishers, to gain Secretary Cameron's assent to the federal muster of Scott's "regiment," which would be designated Illinois's Nineteenth.[25]

That left a second problem—forming an acceptable unit by hustling up seven hundred or so more men—and hastily, lest the state authorization expire or some other group elbow into the federal slot opened by Arnold. Lincoln's May 3 call had aroused another great, if brief, rush of volunteers. Northern governors, Yates not least of them, began a fervent competition to display their own and their states' valor, boasting to Washington of the regiments they could provide. In fact, in short order the Illinois adjutant general placed more than two hundred companies of additional volunteers on his ledger, enough to fill twenty regiments.[26] For the Chicagoans encamped at Springfield, the problem centered on attracting seven of those companies to go to war with them. Another Chicago drill company, the Highland Guards, stood first in that line. A unit not unlike Ellsworth's Cadets, it dated back to 1855, and as a social club had attracted "the Thistle, Rose and Shamrock," their roster showing names almost entirely from the British Isles. Composed of about fifty men from the city, they enlisted about twenty more in Springfield, and became Company E of the Nineteenth.[27]

The Zouave companies fortuitously came again to public attention when two of them, newly uniformed with a "splendid appearance," returned home on June 7 to march in the funeral procession of the late Senator Stephen A. Douglas, and then remained in camp near the city.[28] The visit may have attracted additional recruits and interest, for another Chicago unit originally raised as an artillery battery came to their encampment. Numerous "out-state" militia companies, mostly from counties that had voted for Lincoln, arrived next. The Cass County Guards from Virginia, Illinois, and the Moline Rifles showed no lack of Unionist ardor. The Anti-Beauregards of Galena, filled with men who had failed to squeeze into the first company their town sent to war with Ulysses S. Grant on April 25, were equally caught up in all the ardor of the hour, as were the Elmira Rifles, who hailed from fertile Republican soil.[29] Lieutenant Alexander Murchison raised the Elmira company's enrollment from forty on June 8 to seventy-five on June 12 simply by posting a few notices and holding recruiting rallies in Stark County churches.

The muster of the regiment was scheduled first for June 14 but, as the *Tribune* lamented, "from the lapse of time and hope deferred, recruits once eager, have turned aside to other pursuits, or have sought active service elsewhere." (The potential recruits jamming the streets in April were still tied by their ninety-day enlistments to the militia regiments.) On Saturday, June 15, the mustering officers arrived at the Zouave encampment but found the companies "not in full rank . . . by reason of furloughs." As would be borne out by subsequent events, company officers were still scrounging the city's streets and wharves for what the Illinois adjutant general's report came to describe charitably as "the floating population." When found and recruited, these men seem mostly to have been taken into Companies C and K, which together had four miscreants drummed out of the service in August and lost another twenty-five to desertion over the following year.[30]

Finally, on June 17, the enlistees underwent their introduction to the tedium of military life—gathered together in ranks, individually running a short distance to demonstrate "motion and gait," then standing in a line as each had his eyes, hands, and arms inspected by a surgeon, Dr. Sims Lee, overseen by the Regular Army's Captain Thomas Gamble Pitcher. That done, they listened to Illinois adjutant general Thomas S. Mather explain the enlistment oath, administered to those who had not already sworn to it in camp Saturday. Captain Pitcher then countersigned the muster roll, accepting the Nineteenth Illinois Volunteer Infantry into the service of the United States.[31]

It was at that moment that the Nineteenth Illinois came face-to-face with its new colonel, the favorite of the *Tribune*, John Basil Turchin. The *Tribune* presented him the next day to its readers, on the front page and with high praise: "We congratulate the Nineteenth in having such a man to lead them.

He is a soldier and a gentleman; and the members of the regiment may be assured that, under his command, they will suffer nothing from the penalties with which ignorance and incompetency [*sic*] are visited." The article was intended as an encouragement to the troops, a comfort to their wives and parents, a satisfaction to the civic supporters of a regiment with "the material for a crack corps."[32] It also gave ample proof of the favorable impression Colonel Turchin had made on the editors of the *Tribune* and presumably upon other people important in the political life of the city. Like so many other men that spring and summer, John Basil Turchin would leave Chicago as a hometown hero seeking his moment of glory, marching at the head of a column of young men with similar expectations.

We cannot now perform any deep, well-documented analysis of the reasons any of these men enlisted. Very few wrote about those motivations. The few who did said what the actions of all the early enlistees demonstrated. They enlisted because Fort Sumter, a symbol of national authority, had been attacked. Although the excitement had been building for years, this had been a tangible and provocative event, just as provocative as the attack on Pearl Harbor to men in other times, that brought them to this point in their lives. But for the boys from the Chicago area, there had been a second, perhaps more personal, event of a like sort that had happened in late May.

On the morning of May 24, 1861, in response to the act of secession of the state of Virginia, new colonel Elmer Ellsworth had been given the honor of leading the first troops to land on the south side of the Potomac in order to retake Alexandria. After moving his Fire Zouaves to the wharves on the Virginia shore of the Potomac and quickly securing the telegraph office, Ellsworth, accompanied only by a corporal, a reporter from the New York *Tribune,* and one or two others, entered the Marshall House Hotel, climbed to the roof, and tore down a large Confederate flag that had been visible for days from the White House. When Ellsworth descended the stairs, the hotel's proprietor, James Jackson, jumped from the shadows and discharged a shotgun through Ellsworth's heart. The most famous man in America became the first officer to fall in defense of the Union.[33]

The news spread with the speed of telegraphy, and it hit hard. The church bells of Washington began to toll. President Lincoln wept. Flags dropped to half-staff. Virtually every newspaper in the country carried the news on the front page. Companies of soldiers donned black armbands. Patriotic envelopes printed with Ellsworth's likeness filled the mails. Poets wrote fresh verse, and choirs sang new songs dedicated to his memory. Perhaps for the only time in history, Elmer became a common name for newborn boys. In Ellsworth's hometown of Mechanicsville, New York, a group of young men playing ball heard the news of his death, immediately quit the game, and enlisted as a group. In New York City, a new regiment, Ellsworth's Avengers, came together in a matter of days. Back in Illinois, the Nineteenth Regiment quickly filled to capacity.[34]

It has been said, "It only takes a year to take a man out of civilian life . . . and really mold him into a very effective soldier," such that the "mission becomes your job. Nothing else but that."[35] These new recruits, like all of the men and boys coming into the Union army that spring, were, at that point in time, little more than a crowd, a group of armed men and boys who had begun dressing alike (if issued uniforms, which were slow in arriving for many). They had a common motivation to assemble. They had been recruited or had volunteered in direct response to the attack on Fort Sumter, and some, particularly those from Chicago, had the added impetus of the killing of Ellsworth to extend their enlistments to three years. In either case, it would have been natural for these boys to believe that they had been asked to come to the war to retaliate for these attacks. Harding's company banner, after all, bore the legend "Retaliation—No Mercy to Traitors."

The unwritten, but widely accepted, law of retaliation had been recognized both in America and in Europe long before the Civil War broke out, and we still see it cited as justification for much of the violence that occurs in the world today. It was then, as Professor James McPherson points out, "an essential component of the masculine code of honor." It gives legitimacy to violent acts done in response to earlier violence perceived by the victims as illegitimate, unfair, or uncalled for. Armies often threaten retaliation, for better or worse, in the hopes that the threat will act as a deterrent. Groups with less training and discipline are more likely to act on impulse and try later to validate their actions by citing prior acts for which their own are "merely" retaliatory.[36]

After the attack on Fort Sumter, Northern newspapers filled their columns with calls for quick, harsh acts of retribution by loyal Union men against the people of the South for what the *Philadelphia Inquirer* called "the greatest of all crimes—the attempted murder of a nation." The fact that a civilian had killed Ellsworth was not lost on the press, nor, we can assume, was it lost on the Northern public at large. The calls for vengeance grew far more shrill after the murder of Ellsworth. In Pittsburgh, the *Gazette* announced, "Virginia will be swept as with the broom of destruction." The

Inquirer quoted the popular dime novelist, Ned Buntline, as saying when he lay a wreath on Ellsworth's casket, "We'll mourn him today boys, and avenge him tomorrow." The editors of the *Chicago Tribune* bluntly suggested just how that should be done. "We shall burn their towns, sink their ships and boats, kill as many of them as we can in battle, and if necessary desolate their fields. This is war." War meant "quick destruction." War meant "a desolated, blackened country." There could be little doubt in the minds of these new recruits about where the folks at home stood.[37]

They all wanted to get even with the "damned Secesh." They said they wanted it burned. Even had they not had this support, we have ample reason, in retrospect, to question the levels of discipline and reserve of these men who answered the nation's call. Perhaps no one had a greater opportunity to cull his recruits and select only the best men for the cause than had Ellsworth himself in raising the Fire Zouave regiment in New York, where he had the chance to review and inspect twice as many men as he needed and sent home all those who failed the initial test. When they departed New York on April 29, observers marveled at Ellsworth's commanding presence, and they proudly announced that the colonel "was unequalled in the matter of managing recruits."[38]

When the Fire Zouaves arrived in Washington, they had the clearly defined task of protecting the nation's capital from imminent threat. Instead, they went off on a two-day bender of "fight, fun and frolic." According to the *Philadelphia Press*, "They have broken into taverns, terrified old ladies, ordered dinners and suppers which they had the impudence to charge to the bankrupt concern, the Southern Confederacy, chased imaginary secessionists through the streets, and performing other irreverent feats." Terrified Washingtonians watched as the Zouaves walked the parapets of the Capitol, knocked down the sentinels assigned there, and hung from the edge of the dome "like monkeys." Ellsworth received direct orders to put an end to their use of local fencing for firewood. If such behavior was displayed by picked men serving under one of the most respected drill instructors in the country while in their nation's capital, what might be expected of more ordinary men serving under less experienced officers in a land perceived by most to be hostile?[39]

The answer to that question, of course, would depend in great part upon the nature and degree of training both men and officers received before they arrived at that post. In turn, the training of the men depended upon the quality of the officers who came to lead them and their own dedication to a standard of professionalism that would over time mold these men into soldiers. If the government, or the army, expected its men in uniform to perform according to a policy that did not allow for a measure of vengeance against Southerners of the sort being called for by the communities they came from, if the government wished to constrain them from acting out according to the unwritten law of retribution, it would be necessary to turn them into real soldiers, ones who would not only do as they were told, ones who would do that which they ought to do even in the absence of orders. Unfortunately, clear senses of duty and honor don't always come naturally.

Of the officers who stood at the front of the Nineteenth Illinois at the time they left for the war, several had little or no discernible military qualifications and would soon prove to have no ability. Governor Yates had seen the Nineteenth Regiment as one that provided places to which he could make his own political appointments of officers, without regard to the political apparatus of the several congressional districts from which they hailed, and so he did. (Turchin was to try for months to get rid of them, with but limited success.)[40]

Officers who had risen from the distinct militia units in the Nineteenth, on the other hand, were mostly able men who had some sense of what they were about—in the Elmira Rifles, for example, Murchison the recruiter and Charles Stuart the elected captain. Lieutenant Knowlton Chandler of the Cass County Guards, age thirty-one, had already been a gold rush miner and innkeeper in California, and at the time he received his commission was a drugstore proprietor and the town police magistrate. Wellington Wood of the Moline Guards, age twenty-one, coauthor of a six-act play, was beginning the study of law, but "his great object, his particular forte, was to ride horses and to command men." In the Highland Guards, Lieutenant David Bremmer, twenty-two, made his real mark long after the war, merging his own baking business with others to form the great National Biscuit Company. Captain Alexander Raffen, born in Scotland, had helped organize the Highlanders, leaving a growing plumbing business to go to war. In 1863, he would become commanding officer of the Nineteenth.[41]

It was the old Zouaves, however, who dominated among the officers of the regiment. Thirty of Ellsworth's Zouave Cadets were in uniform as Union officers by July 13, more of them in the Nineteenth Illinois than in any other unit. Eleven, a third of the regiment's officers, either had been part of the show at West Point the past July or had heard and relished the tale of how, as they believed, their military team had outdone the drill prescribed by the commandant of cadets. Four of the companies came to have one or more officers from Ellsworth's Cadets, beginning with Hayden, captain of Company A. The adjutant, Chauncey Miller, was a Zouave. The governor apparently had a political appointee in mind for the post of major; a petition signed by all of the other officers secured it instead for Fred Harding, who had been the orderly sergeant of Ellsworth's touring company.[42] Joe Scott, Ellsworth's predecessor, then his first lieutenant, although respected as a skilled drill instructor, was only twenty-three, perhaps a little too young to assume command of a regiment, even if he had close ties to the beloved late Elmer Ellsworth. He took instead the position of lieutenant colonel of the Nineteenth. It was the Russian émigré, the man with command experience, who gained the appointment to stand at the head of the Nineteenth. This would be John Basil Turchin's regiment.[43]

As measured against other Civil War regiments, the development of this group of green recruits into a sharp-looking military unit started off with remarkable efficiency and swiftness. Perhaps somewhat surprisingly to those familiar with the military of the twentieth century, Civil War soldiers did not, as a rule, undergo any period of formal basic training. Even for Regular troops, the army did not then provide a standardized recruit training program. The Regular recruits went to receiving stations, like Carlisle Barracks in Pennsylvania or Jefferson Barracks in St. Louis, where they were provided with uniforms and equipment. But a recruit's stay at these posts varied from a few days to a few weeks, depending mostly upon how quickly he was assigned to a Regular unit. As a result, many men arrived for their first assignment who "had no earthly idea of the duties they would be called on to perform, or of the discipline they will be required to undergo." Some cavalry recruits couldn't even sit on their horse at a trot.[44]

Turchin's men had at least a little time to begin training, and from all appearances they made good use of it. The Zouave companies had been in camp since mid-May, first at Springfield and then back in Chicago, where the other companies joined them when they were assigned to the regiment. Thanks to Scott and the others who had learned their trade under Ellsworth, word soon got out about the quickly developing precision of its drill and the esprit de corps growing among the men. According to the regimental historian, both Turchin and Scott from the very beginning "made it clear to every member of the Regiment that ours was to be the very best in the service, if hard work could bring it about." Turchin knew that many of his company officers were ignorant about drill routines. His early training regimen put them in the ranks, where they could learn how to march firsthand. It took him only a week of hard work with company drill and the manual of arms before he attempted a full battalion drill, which he saw as "first rate." By the first of July he was ready to practice battle formations, and he sent the Nineteenth through suburban Chicago in battle line, "skirmishers climbing over fences, loading and firing, dodging around back kitchens and cow stables, jumping over flower-beds and running through verandas, astonishing the natives, particularly the young girls." The mock battle made them headliners in several Chicago newspapers.[45]

Incidents such as those—and, no doubt, its close connections with the *Tribune*—made the Nineteenth a celebrated unit even before it left town. That day came less than four weeks after Turchin took command. With their Russian colonel at the front of the column, the Nineteenth Illinois headed out of camp on Friday evening, July 12, marching down Cottage Grove Avenue to the applause of a cheering crowd. They entrained at the Illinois Central's Lake Shore Depot, off to campaign in Missouri. The Zouaves, said the *Tribune* on the thirteenth, "live again and notably in Companies A and B of the 19th Regiment, that left last evening for the seat of war." In later years, Turchin would comment on the pride and enthusiasm that filled the hearts of his men as they left for the war. "They thought they were ready for the fray, and no doubt they were."[46]

In 1861 the hapless recruit whom the Regular Army shipped off to a fort on the plains without knowing how to ride a horse still arrived at a post where everyone else did. There were plenty of experienced men there who could, and would, show him what he needed to know. Just as important, for the most part he arrived there not because he had volunteered to fight Indians, or because he wanted to avenge attacks on the settlers coming to the West. He was most often, we can assume, there because the army, his employer, sent him there. Unburdened by any preconceived notions about why he was in the army, he needed direction, but not redirection, from his superiors. He lived in a closed community, one with a great capacity to censure his actions if inappropriate and to punish him for them if sufficiently serious. In the old army, few offenses escaped some sort of punishment. The task of molding such a recruit into a soldier who sought solely to please his superiors and perform the duties assigned to him remained relatively simple.[47]

Turchin's volunteers, like nearly all of the volunteers flooding into the armies of the Union at that time, we can assume (from the simple act of enlisting), came for a cause, to right a wrong, to punish the offenders. They were swept up in the *rage militaire,* the patriotic furor, of the time. If they were to be redirected and transformed into dutiful soldiers, it would only happen through the guidance and insistence of their leaders. But here, their leaders, the field and company officers of the regiment, were also recently converted civilians with the same motivations for going to war. Although a number of them were skilled drill instructors, none, save perhaps Turchin himself, had even been a professional military man, and there was a clear recognition, if not a great tradition, in nineteenth-century America honoring the differences between professional soldiers and volunteers. As a major of volunteers in the Mexican War put it, "The American volunteer is a thinking, feeling, and often capricious being. He is not and never intends to be a mere moving and musket-holding machine."[48]

Would precision in drill translate into a finely tuned and well-disciplined fighting unit? The answer would turn on the attitudes taken by the commanding officers, most important by Colonel Turchin himself, and by the experiences of these men during the first months of the war. As Ellsworth's firemen had demonstrated in Washington, early marching proficiency did not in and of itself lead to respectable, let alone honorable, behavior. With somewhere between three and six weeks of drill under their belts, for Turchin's men the second classroom for the study of war, of the style and form of war they would be expected to undertake, would come in Missouri.[49]

4
Advanced Basic

He who makes war his profession cannot be otherwise than vicious. War
makes thieves.

—Machiavelli

A few days before their departure, Turchin met his new commanders. The
first was Stephen A. Hurlbut, who unceremoniously burst into Turchin's tent
to inform the colonel that he was now under Hurlbut's command. Hurlbut
was just one month a soldier and already a brigadier general, his apparent
qualifications for the rank having been that he was a northern Illinois lawyer,
a Republican legislator, and a friend of Lincoln. His abrupt manner, civilian
clothes, and a forty-five-minute conversation combined to convince Turchin
that Hurlbut "did not know his A, B, C's in military matters." The thought
of serving under such a green and inexperienced man, and presumably under
many others like him, left Turchin feeling at first depressed. He rebounded,
however, and soon after concluded that where circumstances called for his
own expertise and experience, he would freely assert himself, even if that
meant resisting or refusing to obey orders.[1]

Turchin next encountered John Pope. Still untested in command, having
served as a mustering officer for the army during the spring months, in the
summer of 1861 Pope had all of the other credentials an American career
officer might want. Pope was Turchin's age, born in Louisville, Kentucky, but
raised in Kaskaskia, Illinois. West Point class of 1842, he had fought gallantly in the Mexican War and had stayed in the service, not behind a desk
but, reflecting his competence as a student, as a topographical engineer, much
of the time as a junior officer on the frontier. His father served as a federal
district judge. His father-in-law in Cincinnati remained a close friend of
Lincoln's newly appointed secretary of the Treasury, Salmon P. Chase. Perhaps not least of all, Pope was also a cousin of the president and had been
another member of Lincoln's escort on the train ride to the inaugural. On

June 14, along with Hurlbut he received his commission as a brigadier general of volunteers—disappointed perhaps, having expected the rank permanently and in the Regular Army.[2]

Pope displayed, a newspaper correspondent in Washington noted, "much of off-hand dignity and authority in his style." However, when Turchin reported to him on July 10 at the Sherman House in downtown Chicago, Pope without a thought put the Russian in an outsider's awkward place. Turchin politely removed his cap, demonstrating his own good manners, quietly expecting the same from Pope, one professional to another. Pope, only partly in uniform, neither removed his hat nor offered his hand, nor did he stand to greet his guest. Instead, he bluntly asked if the Nineteenth was ready to move. Turchin put his cap back on. Their conversation lasted no more than five minutes. What struck Turchin most was Pope's apparent lack of interest in getting to know one of his subordinates. Was Turchin "intelligent or stupid, with military knowledge or without; one to be relied upon in case of an action"? Pope gave no indication that he cared. "He probably saw in me something of a pawn of war chess, and deeming himself to be some sort of king in the approaching game, did not care much to know me." Quickly taking offense, Turchin admitted long after the war had ended that "I did not care much about him either." Pope was the first Regular Army officer with whom Turchin had contact. As with Hurlbut, his opinion of such men started on a low note.[3]

The honest answer to Pope's question should have been no, they weren't ready to move. Turchin's men carried old smoothbore muskets, and they could keep in good order when marching, but in much else they were sorely lacking. "The men were dressed in all sorts of garbs, commencing with the red Zouave breeches and fancy jackets, all worn and ragged, and finishing with Kentucky jean pantaloons and white coats, not in the best of order. As to the headgear, it consisted of caps and hats of all possible shapes, material and condition. Externally the regiment looked at that time a sorry crowd of ragamuffins," Turchin recalled, but with the devotion of a dedicated commander he could also say, "yet it had tremendous material to make soldiers of." Before the issuance of knapsacks, accoutrements, or ammunition, the orders came to head south and west, to Quincy and the banks of the Mississippi. On July 12, the regiment boarded the cars for Quincy and the command of Brigadier Generals Hurlbut and Pope.[4]

Immediately after disembarking at Quincy, Turchin received an order from Hurlbut to cross the river and to set up camp in Missouri. Turchin told the courier that he would cross when his men received their accoutrements and ammunition, which he expected in a day or two. Shortly afterward, the courier returned with a "preemptory order" from Hurlbut to move out. On the same grounds, Turchin again refused. "Now, here was a collision at the start. I was disobeying orders of my superior officer. But what could I do? It was known that Missouri was swarming with rebel sympathizers and guerillas; that the Confederates were raising companies everywhere for their army; that to move across the Mississippi without ammunition would be to risk the chance of attack by troops of armed men and to have a shameful disaster; our guns, without ammunition, were nothing but sticks in our hands, and a dozen daring rebels, well-armed, could slaughter one-half of the battalion." Turchin was right. Although Nathaniel Lyon had very recently cleared central Missouri of organized opposition, only a week before the rebel-aligned State Guard had forced a second Union column to retreat from southwestern Missouri. At a face-to-face meeting, Hurlbut, "noticeably soured," relented, and the arrival of the missing matériel the next day defused the situation. Turchin immediately started crossing and was soon encamped near Palmyra, Missouri, a prominent stop on the Hannibal & St. Jo Railroad.[5]

The situation in Missouri in mid-July 1861, was dire, as Turchin saw it. The governor was a rebel who had appointed another rebel, Sterling Price, to command the state militia, and Confederate recruiting was going on all over the state. It was believed that Gideon Pillow stood at the head of nearly 15,000 rebels gathering near New Madrid in southeastern Missouri, and that Price led a force of close to 10,000 in southwestern Missouri, with other men from Texas and Arkansas about to come over the border. In opposition were about 1,200 men at Cairo, a few troops at Cape Girardeau and Ironton, "several thousand" men at St. Louis, about 6,000 men under Nathaniel Lyon facing Price's buildup, and the few regiments under Pope freshly posted along the railroads in northeastern Missouri.

At the war's beginning, Missourians had no middle ground to hide upon. Supporters of both causes, of the Union or of the revolt, saw those who failed to actively support their side as enemies. Henry Painter, a Presbyterian minister who had supported the candidacy of John Bell for president and who lived by the philosophy "I am for the Union as it was, and the Constitution as it is," found himself counted a traitor by all. He lived in north-central Missouri, where attacks and reprisals happened every day. Marauding bands stalked Union sympathizers, sometimes dragging them off for a summary execution. Small groups of mounted raiders attacked Union patrols, burned bridges, ripped up railroad rail, only to dissolve back into the general population. There were even attempts to hijack steamboats plying the Missouri River. Hundreds of Unionists fled. Those who remained kept circumspect about their allegiance, seeing the beginning of what they thought would be "a war of extermination."[6]

A number of wives, including Nadine Turchin, accompanied the regiment into Missouri. The citizens of Palmyra greeted them cordially, even inviting the officers to take quarters in their homes, but Turchin declined, "making up my mind to never stop at the house of a Southerner, unless it should be vacant and handy to camp." He soon met numbers of Union sympathizers, who came to his tent seeking refuge. Who, he wanted to know, were the most avid secessionists in town? He soon discovered that the majority of invitations "had come from that crowd." Further, his investigation led him to conclude that rebels were gathering at small training camps on farms and plantations all around him, some of them mounted and acting as guerillas.[7]

Turchin devoted himself, as any experienced commander might, to the task of doing all that he could for his men. The initial supply of hard tack was wormy, the bacon rancid, and "the coffee full of gravel and all sorts of beans but the coffee beans." Complaining without effect to Hurlbut, whose answer was "that he could not help it," and after the regimental surgeon told him that the men were getting sick due to the poor rations, Turchin again took the initiative, and

as I thought I was duty bound to take care of the men entrusted to me by the Government, it was my business to find food for them. There was plenty of it in the vicinity. The country around Palmyra being rich and the inhabitants disloyal, I ordered my quartermaster to levy upon all the flour and beef the regiment wanted, and to give proper vouchers for everything taken and let them settle with the Government in any way they pleased. It was none of my business what the Government would do. I reasoned that if for some cause to me unknown the Government could not furnish its soldiers with good rations, it was the duty of the commander to help the Government by finding such rations in the country, and keeping the men in the best trim to do the business for which the same Government enlisted them. It did not take but a few hours before there was plenty of fresh bread and good roast beef in the camp; and if the coffee was not so palatable as it was desirable, the boys had plenty of milk instead from the rebel cows that volunteered to come to the camp and to gracefully surrender their milk to the loyal men.[8]

We do not know where Turchin developed his insights about fighting internecine war, but we do know he had very clear and definite opinions about how this should be done. Perhaps it was taught or debated during his formal military training. Perhaps he gained some firsthand experience when he served as part of the Russian force occupying Poland or invading Hungary. And perhaps, now living in the freedom-loving West, he felt at last free to use an imagination and a level of initiative that had been stifled in Russia, the frustration of which had caused him to leave. We know that he was a man of great initiative, and he saw it as his duty at this time and in this place to show it.

After providing for the welfare of his men, he saw as his next duty the breaking up of rebel activity in his area of operation. As he recalled:

It was a critical and discouraging time in Missouri, and if there ever was a time and place for the display of the greatest energy by our military, it was certainly then and there. I made up my mind to stop rebel recruiting as far as I could reach it by compelling the planters to stop feeding rebel recruits that were organizing and drilling on their plantations, and to refuse them shelter. We had at the time only one solitary horse in the camp, and that was my own saddle horse. We had not a single wagon. . . . I could not chase mounted rebels with infantry alone, so I was bound to have some cavalry.[9]

After being again rebuffed by Hurlbut when he asked for a detachment of mounted men, Turchin decided to grow his own. Finding plenty of mounts nearby, and the local population "inimical," he recruited forty of his men, seized a like number of horses from nearby farms, along with saddles and bridles (all on a temporary basis, for which vouchers were given), and ordered his newly minted horsemen to carry their muskets with bayonets fixed as a substitute for lances and to "scour the country."[10]

For several days I did not see that company, only receiving dispatches from Colby [Turchin's handpicked leader of the band] and a few of the most rabid Secessionists that he arrested and sent under escort. The cavalry was rampaging around striking terror through the country. At the same time I was sending expeditions of infantry in different directions, accompanying some of them myself. Wherever plantations were found, with rooms arranged in the shape of barracks for rebel recruits we would chop all of the bedsteads and cots to splinters, tear blankets and sheets, scatter feathers from pillows and burn mattresses. Then we would take meat out of the smokehouses and flour from closets; sometime we would load corn and oats on wagons, and even would drive away all horses and mules found in those places. Thus in a few days our commissary tent was full of smoked meat, a great pile of corn in the ear was rising by the tent of the Quartermaster, and an improvised corral was rapidly filling with animals.

Private John Vreeland of Company A wrote home to Chicago on July 23 that on one of these raids, at the home of a "Confederate captain," "we confiscated all his personal property."[11]

The result? "When the planter's pockets were so ruthlessly attacked there was a rush to the camp. The delinquent planters were anxious to sign a pledge that they would at once stop feeding and giving shelter to the rebel recruits, and never would do it again in the future" and that if such men appeared, they would be told to leave the area and head south if they wanted to enlist in the rebel cause. The planters also begged for the return of their animals, which Turchin allowed, after warning them that they would be retaken if trouble again arose. Turchin also promised to return the meat and corn after a demonstration of continued cooperation. According to his account, "In 10 days we cleaned the country for 20 miles around Palmyra of all the camps, guerillas and every other rebel organization, and I thought we were doing our duty pretty diligently. Learning what we were doing, the Union men in the neighborhood took courage. There was a company of Home Guards raised on the sly by the Union men of Palmyra," who were keeping a low profile because they had no weapons. Turchin promised to try to secure some and then offered his aid to three other such companies that sprang up near Newark, a town about thirty-five miles away.[12]

Turchin's initiatives, or as he referred to it, the "terror," and the conduct of his men outraged a great many citizens of Missouri. Deputations of prominent men (Turchin considered them all active rebels or at least sympathizers) went variously to Generals Hurlbut and Pope, Illinois governor Yates, and to the Union commander of the department, Major General John C. Frémont, to plead their case. According to Turchin, the Quincy, Missouri *Herald* came out with a flaming article branding the Nineteenth Illinois as "a little horde of barbarians," led by "the worst barbarian ever seen on the free soil of America." The stories quickly reached the Chicago presses, and "a stormy cloud of wrath" gathered over these aspiring heroes. Governor Yates was alarmed. The people of Chicago were, Turchin thought, "scandalized."[13]

Hurlbut wrote to Turchin telling him to "stop such arbitrary proceedings," the arrest of citizens by his roving band of mounted men evidently causing the most distress, but just as he had done so effectively before, Turchin ignored him. A day or two later, Hurlbut appeared in Turchin's tent, but only to tell him that Pope was waiting for him at a nearby railroad depot. When Turchin arrived to face him, General Pope was obviously upset, "pale and excited," and he proceeded to chew Turchin out. "How dare you take private property for the use of your regiment? How dare you to go through the country pilfering, arresting men, taking possession of horses?"

Turchin tried to explain, describing the spoiled rations, what he saw as a duty to destroy rebel camps, his need for mounted men. Pope's response: "You should starve in your tracks before you touch private property."

Turchin stood unmoved. "I think differently," he said. "If the government intrusts [sic] me with 1,000 men, and for some reason cannot furnish them with eatable rations, my duty is to find rations in the enemy's country."

Pope threatened court-martial. "I don't care," Turchin snapped back. Pope, still fuming, assured him that a court-martial was now certain.[14]

The Nineteenth Illinois was, of course, scarcely the only band of offenders pillaging northeastern Missouri. As but one example, Rev. Painter, the unlucky Presbyterian mentioned before, was ultimately arrested, along with five other men, and held as a hostage by other Union troops, to be released only if citizens in the area of Boonville came forward with good information about a pending rebel attack. They did, and the Union soldiers subsequently released the preacher. Pope, commander of the district, could not court-martial them all. He issued an order cautioning his forces "against excesses of every kind, and especially against any depredations upon the person or property of any citizen of Missouri." Although this had been the official government policy, this was the first time any of Turchin's superiors formulated it into an order. By one account, Pope also soon regularized Turchin's solution to the subsistence problem by obtaining a county court order directing citizens of Palmyra to provide rations for Union troops.[15]

Rather than face a court-martial, two days later Turchin received orders to move his men by steamboat from Hannibal to St. Louis. He took a captain of the home guard along to plead his case for arms and ammunition. Early on the morning of their arrival, Turchin presented himself at Frémont's headquarters, seeking to put a claim on a large stand of Springfield rifles, which a militia unit, commanded by future Illinois governor Richard Oglesby and about to be mustered out, would no longer need. There he had a serendipitous meeting with Governor Yates, who also was waiting for a meeting with Frémont. The governor quickly asked, "For God's sake, what were you doing around Palmyra?" Yates was, in fact, at Frémont's office to get to the bottom of it, as well as to complain about the use of Illinois troops for the relatively inglorious duty of guarding railroads. After hearing Turchin's explanation about needing commissary supplies and having a duty to disrupt Confederate recruiting and organizing activities, Yates was completely placated. "Oh, is that all?" he asked, and when assured that it was, he ended the conversation by saying, "Well, it seems to me you are doing the right thing."[16]

Shortly afterward, Turchin was escorted into the sanctum sanctorum of Frémont's headquarters. Immediately struck by the spit and polish (others considered it pomp) of the man, as well as his "lithe and wiry, straight and dignified" appearance, Turchin remained impressed for the rest of his life by this meeting with the Pathfinder. In Frémont, Turchin found common ground, a commander who—like himself, he perhaps thought—combined "generalship with broad statesmanship and intense republicanism." This was, for Turchin, in stark contrast to Pope, who displayed a "narrow martinetism with a decided proclivity to slaveocracy. In condemning me for feeding my men, from necessity, upon rebel flour and beef, and for using a few horses of the Secessionists against the traitors of the country, Gen. Pope either disregarded or was unacquainted at that time with the self-evident truth that 'war must feed war.'"[17]

Frémont, on the other hand, spoke Turchin's language. Having taken command of the Department of the West only a few days before, on July 3, he, too, was just learning the ropes. As subsequent events would demonstrate, he brought to the war the same antislavery passion that had gained him the presidential nomination five years before. He reacted to the turmoil in Missouri, about which he had been ordered to pay particular attention, in much the same way as had his Russian subordinate. In the weeks ahead, he would receive numerous communiqués describing conditions elsewhere in the state much like those around Palmyra, at times with recommendations to take action to foster and bolster the loyal men wishing to form home guard units. He would do what he could to try to build up loyal strength while dealing with large groups of active guerilla and partisan opponents. His order to court-martial any armed man found within Union lines, and to shoot those convicted, could be easily understood in light of the conditions then current. It was an improvement over the summary executions performed by roving bands of thugs then going on. That, and his proclamation of emancipation of slaves used to support the Confederate war effort, would raise hackles in Washington, but no doubt they were heartily supported by Turchin and his volunteers.[18]

At their meeting, Turchin first presented his plea for the Springfields to replace the old smoothbores his men carried. Only after granting Turchin an order for the rifles he sought did Frémont ask about the trouble around Palmyra, saying there had been some serious charges preferred against Turchin and the Nineteenth as a result. Turchin replied, "I told him frankly how I was situated, how I looked upon my duty, what I was doing and what I accomplished during my short stay at Palmyra. He listened attentively, occasionally smiling at my awkward English; and when I was through he simply said: 'That is all right!' and those charges never saw the light afterward." The meeting ended with Frémont issuing one more order, for four hundred stands of arms to equip the home guard. For Turchin, it was a banner day.[19]

The two met only a month before Frémont issued his famous declaration, freeing the slaves and confiscating the property of Missourians actively engaged in rebellion, steps the government would take a year later but that were far too forceful for policy makers to be comfortable with during this opening act of the war. Lincoln quickly countermanded Frémont's proclamation, clearly making the points to his subordinate about who held authority and what official policy was. The experience for Turchin, however, carried with it no such lessons or redirection. Although he had done what his internal sense of duty commanded, essentially he had done as he damn well pleased, clearly knowing that his superiors wanted him to follow other courses. His failure to do things as and when ordered bore no consequences for him or for his men. Turchin, rather than face a court-martial, got lucky, having had the case fall into the lap of the one military commander who would see the sense in what he and his men had done and who failed to see the extreme importance, at this formative stage of the war, of impressing upon his subordinates the necessity of following the chain of command.

As previously noted, Keegan makes the point that "war . . . is always an expression of the culture" in which it is fought. The culture, or the society within which the conflict takes place, imposes restraints on how the war is fought. Wayne Lee, in his book *Crowds and Soldiers,* argues that the combatants respect these restraints out of a need for legitimacy. In the case of the men fighting the Civil War, those supporting the Confederacy needed to demonstrate that theirs was a just cause, and so they insisted that their men fight according to the generally accepted rules. Those fighting for the Union felt a need to do the same. They did, however, have the added knowledge, or belief, that the other side had provoked the fighting. The rebels had shot first. Loyal men thus had a perfect right to shoot back.[20]

In his comparison of the relative discipline and restraint demonstrated by the men who fought the Revolutionary War, Lee strikes a clear contrast between Washington's soldiers, the Continentals, and the various state militias, especially those operating in the Carolinas. Among the factors that Lee finds relevant in accounting for these differences are two that are relevant to the discussion here: first, the inability of the militia to control itself as violence escalated; and second, the operational style of fighting that these differing forces were asked to conduct.[21]

The lack of internal controls Lee ascribes to various factors. Militia companies were highly democratic. Soldiers were free to express their opinions. Orders might well be debated with officers who had themselves been elected from the ranks. General Nathanael Greene said that "with the militia everybody is a general, and the powers of the government are so feeble, that it is with the utmost difficulty you can restrain them from plundering one another." (As he depended upon the militia for much of his fighting force, he would have known.) The absence of discipline, and of leaders who could or would demand it, opened the door to outrageous behavior, dimming the voices that might argue for restraint. Lee notes, too, the motivation of militiamen. They were often recruited directly in response to particular acts of British or Tory aggression. The expectation of a man signing on under such circumstances, when caught up in the *rage militaire,* naturally would have been that he was to retaliate. With officers chosen from a group with similar expectations, voices demanding something other than revenge clearly would have been absent.[22]

The parallels with Turchin's men during their time in Missouri are easily drawn. Although they had demonstrated some increasing skill in drill, nearly all of the officers were as green as the men in learning not only their duties but also how to go about doing them. It would have been natural to expect many of the men to raise questions, first about how to do things, and then to perhaps ask why, or why not, do them. It would have been equally natural to do that which they believed was expected of them or to feel free to do things they would not do in civilian life. Their community and comrades seemed to accept and support such actions, whether it was milking a stray cow, butchering unlucky chickens, taking a few horses, or dragging from his home someone who seemed to be supporting treason. So, too, they were all there for a reason—to retaliate for the attack on their country, to avenge Sumter, to avenge Ellsworth. The papers and their friends called for retaliation and revenge both before and after they stepped forward.[23]

Perhaps just as important in framing the picture a man saw of the war he was asked to fight was the operational style his unit was asked to work with. Washington's Continental Army strove for professionalism. The officer corps, ingrained with senses of honor and duty, worked hard to build a disciplined force of men who could and would stand in line on an open field of battle, giving the British Regulars as good as they received. They maneuvered to gain strategic advantage. They conducted sieges. They loaded, aimed, fired, stepped to the rear, and coolly repeated the cycle while their comrades fell about them. Revolutionary War militiamen, more often than not, were asked to become partisans and loyalty enforcers. They bushwhacked travelers. They went off on raids. They made hell on earth for their Tory neighbors. They instantly and harshly retaliated for any acts of violence done by British soldiers or their supporters, but usually only on the sly, and only where their enemies had left a vacuum of power. Rather than the high-minded response that soldiers make in defense of a nation, acts of retaliation for local acts of violence or disloyalty could quickly become very personal and lethal.[24]

On arriving in Missouri, Turchin's regiment had the task of protecting a railroad. They were not being asked to fight a conventional war. Instead, they found themselves surrounded by partisans and guerillas, in an atmosphere where loyal civilians were living under the impression that they "would have to leave or pitch in and kill as many Secesh as they can before thay [sic] kill [us]."[25] The colonel saw no better way to guard the rail line and take on the partisans than to secure the loyalty of the local people living around him. He saw no ready way to supply his men other than to turn them into raiders. The key lesson in all this was perhaps that this was the Nineteenth Illinois's initial impression of army life. Raiding farms and plantations to secure supplies and drive away traitors (all done mostly in their civilian garb, since uniforms had yet to arrive) was how they were first shown to behave in the field. And while they remained in Missouri, no one acted effectively to change that impression. They could practice and improve their drill all they wanted, but somewhere, somehow, someone would have to make it very clear that other behavior was expected when they went on campaign if, indeed, other behavior was desired.

Turchin himself never gave any impression that he wanted his men to act differently than they had. He organized and mounted his raiders. He supported them with his men on foot. Everything he wrote after the war indicates that he took great pride in the way his men performed in Missouri. In fact, he seemed to nearly get a laugh out of it, as any proud commander might when he sees his men not only performing according to his direction but also enjoying themselves. "I heard incidentally also that there was some foraging going on through hen-roosts and pig-pens in the outskirts of the town after sunset, but as it never alarmed our camp guards I did not pay any attention to the noise; so the regiment was getting on first rate and would not have cared if the Government should have stopped the supply of rations altogether," he wrote for the readers of the *National Tribune* concerning the time his men spent around Palmyra. Commenting on the reaction of his men when they mounted up and began to "scour the country," Turchin told his readers, "It was great fun for the boys to pitch in, and they were so glad to begin the war." No doubt they were, but if they had fun the first time there would be every reason to expect that similar circumstances would again bring about the same behaviors. Professor James McPherson refers to the rhetoric of revenge of this time as something that reveals "the dark underside of the patriotic symbiosis of community and army necessary to sustain the morale of the volunteer soldiers."[26] If this "dark underside" was to be curbed and controlled, someone would have to make certain that it was no longer justifiable or enjoyable for the participants.

It was typical of Turchin that although he talked bravely of his confrontations with his superiors, and although he apparently came out of the situation on top, he also had the good sense to subsequently tone things down. After meeting with Frémont and putting the threat of court-martial to rest, he and his men spent five weeks in maneuvers south of St. Louis. After that, the Nineteenth and its sister regiment, the Twenty-fourth Illinois, were transferred to Brigadier General Ulysses S. Grant's command, who then also served under Frémont. Stationed in western Kentucky, directly across the Ohio from Grant's headquarters at Cairo, they sparred with Confederate cavalry. There is no evidence in the historical record of any material complaints about their behavior while they were there. Then, abruptly, Frémont, to fill a requisition for troops from the War Department, ordered both regiments east to Washington, "with as little delay as possible."[27] Grant received this order on September 15, a Sunday. The Nineteenth and Twenty-fourth entrained before daybreak on Monday. Grant complained, no doubt sincerely, that he had "sent off two of the best regiments under my command."[28]

As the train carrying the Nineteenth rumbled and clacked its way east in the early morning hours of September 17, 1861, forty-six miles east of Vincennes, Indiana, the bridge over Beaver Creek broke under the weight of the locomotive and tender. In the "awful crash of piled-up cars," twenty-four officers and men were killed, most from Company I, the Anti-Beauregards of Galena, riding in the front car that hurtled down the bank. Colonel Turchin jumped up, grabbed an ax, and was one of the first to descend to the wreck, working side by side with his men to free the others trapped by it. Nadine Turchin tore up her undergarments to make bandages and was instantly at the side of the men trapped in the wreck, doing what she could to nurse their wounds and ease their suffering. One hundred and five injured men were taken forward to Cincinnati, where the Twenty-fourth Illinois waited. The disaster created an enduring bond between the soldiers and Nadine Turchin, who accompanied her husband wherever the regiment went. It was but one of the wires in the cable that increasingly bound the men to their colonel, the man who made certain they were always well supplied, the man who never hesitated to show them how much they meant to him.[29]

The accident also provided a talking point for the front-page editorial column of the *Chicago Tribune* of September 19: "The evidence points to a weakening of the timbers of the bridge by some fiend in the interest of Jeff. Davis. . . . This is not a *war*, in any just sense of the term. It is a succession of butcheries on one side, and of prolonged forgiveness by the other." Justified or not, this suspected sabotage became just one more incident in a rapidly growing list that served to strengthen the animosity growing in the hearts and minds of civilians in the North for their counterparts in the South. The editorial also served as proof either that the sins of Turchin's men in Missouri had been quickly forgotten or that they had never been perceived as sins in the first place.

The accident did nothing to dampen the ardor with which the men of the Nineteenth Illinois wished to wage the war they had come to fight. If that ardor was to be limited, controlled, and redirected, that new direction would have to be provided by Turchin's superior officers, men who had a clear understanding of the government's war aims, men who could impose their will on men like Turchin. When the War Department changed its mind and decided to dispatch the Illinois boys to Kentucky, the die was cast as to who those superior officers would be.

5
Leadership

It is absolutely necessary that we shall hold the State of Kentucky; not
only that, but that the majority of the inhabitants shall be warmly in
favor of our cause. . . . It is possible that the conduct of our political affairs in Kentucky is more important than that of our military operations.
—McClellan to Buell, November 7, 1861

At Louisville, Brigadier General William Tecumseh Sherman was about to
succeed to the command of Union forces in central Kentucky when the
Nineteenth and Twenty-fourth Illinois encamped on a defensive line at
Lebanon Junction, thirty-five miles south of the city. However much Turchin and his men may have wanted to strike hard at organized rebel forces,
their commanding general was not, at this point, of a mind for offensive operations. Sherman believed that Louisville was threatened by a Confederate
army of unknown but fearsome size, led first by a native son, Brigadier General Simon Bolivar Buckner, afterward by the formidable General Albert
Sidney Johnston.[1] Sherman took a well-considered, conservative stand, a
holding position just beyond the crest of Muldraugh's Hill, which he intended to hold until he had enough men to do something else. In his depressed state, he told Secretary of War Simon Cameron that he needed
60,000 men for a full defense, 200,000 for an offensive, numbers Cameron
believed "insanely" extravagant.[2] Sherman at this point in the war had a low
opinion of the 18,000 to 20,000 volunteers he did have, chiefly men like
Turchin's, who "with their unbridled will are killing hogs, cattle, . . . and
taking hay and wheat, all calculated to turn the people against us."[3]

Turchin, just as with his other commanders, did not think highly of Sherman either, "that Seminary director," as he described him to Charles Ray.[4]
Their relationship was short-lived, however, for on November 4 Sherman
telegraphed the new general in chief of the Union armies, George McClellan, asking to be relieved. Unlike Sherman, McClellan thought Kentucky an
improbable arena for "real fighting"—"a mere bagatelle," he told his wife.[5]

McClellan immediately replaced Sherman with Major General Don Carlos Buell.[6]

Buell arrived in Kentucky on November 15. In the manner of a thorough professional, he immediately imposed a standard table of organization on the scattered regiments of his freshly augmented and renamed Department and Army of the Ohio. Buell began at the brigade level, and for one of them, eventually designated the Eighth Brigade, he joined the Nineteenth and Twenty-fourth Illinois regiments with the Eighteenth Ohio and the Thirty-seventh Indiana Volunteers.[7] (Buell usually tried to fill his brigades with regiments from different states, the better to thwart the radical Republican governors he feared—rightly, as matters turned out—might wish to interfere with his appointments and operations.)[8] Because of the seniority of his commission, Colonel John B. Turchin rose to brigade command. Certainly Buell found some reassurance in the fact that Turchin's own men were so well drilled and obviously devoted to their commander. We do not know how soon reports reached him describing Turchin's operating procedures in Missouri. The Regular Army was still a small group in 1861, so it would be reasonable to assume that such reports reached Buell's ears sooner rather than later. Subsequent events would demonstrate that Buell had such knowledge.[9]

At the time Buell took command of the department, the enlisted men of the Nineteenth were amusing themselves and the camps around Elizabethtown, Kentucky, editing and publishing an occasional newspaper, the *Zouave Gazette*, to which their colonel submitted articles about close-order drill. To print the publication, they had taken over the abandoned shop of the town's newspaper, whose owner had fled on their approach. Other than that small appropriation of property, we know of no obvious complaints about their behavior while they occupied this pro-secession railroad town. The army's supply system had improved dramatically, and Elizabethtown was on the railway, so men could be well fed without having to seek out provisions on their own. That, however did not end the practice of foraging. One diarist with the Thirty-seventh Indiana noted with reasonable regularity the results of his travels outside camp, often for corn and fodder, at times rather whimsically, once recording that a "cartridge box fell on a goat's head." So far as we know, General Buell never expressed any disapproval of this practice nor about the publication of the *Zouave Gazette*. Nor is there any evidence that he ever sat down with Turchin to talk about the events in Missouri or to make clear the policy that should be adhered to in Kentucky.[10]

If any commander could set a proper, professional tone for the men serving under him, Don Carlos Buell appeared to be such a man. As will be explored more completely in the next chapter, Buell, like many officers of the Regular Army, had a deep distrust of volunteers. But he also had a counterbalancing faith in the value of military training and discipline. His area of command had been enlarged to include the states of Ohio, Michigan, and Indiana, which gave him access to the troops being raised there. Having created his organization chart, Buell used it to drum drill and discipline into the array of recruits now under his command. Turchin himself rigorously carried out Buell's wishes. He began brigade-level drill in midwinter. By the first of February, he had the brigade marching together, loading blank cartridges, firing and moving through the clouds of blue smoke. His men learned not only how they would be expected to maneuver on a battlefield but also how it would look and smell when they got there.[11]

However, even the small, seemingly harmless takeover of the village press illustrated the type of command problem that would challenge Union troops when they entered the South and were not engaged in fighting a rebel army. Lower-level field and line officers would have to make daily decisions about problems or situations involving interaction with the local civilian population. If high-level officers like Buell hoped for a fairly uniform application of policy toward these local civilians, it would happen only through their own vigilance. Directives would have to be clear. Was it proper, or even allowable, for the army to take over a print shop just because the owner was away? Should the army pay rent and reimburse the owner for the printing supplies they used? Did the proprietor's allegiance make any difference? If so, who made the determination, in his absence, about whether the owner was loyal or not?

Once the directives were made clear, the line officers would know what was proper conduct and what was not. Corrective disciplinary actions could then be taken to ensure compliance. However, while Buell's army was based in Kentucky, no orders or directives were issued that covered the subject of dealing with local civilians, be they loyal or not. Decisions were left entirely to the men in the field. Volunteers with the experience of serving in Missouri could thus easily seize a press, or drop a cartridge box on a goat's head, and feel it was completely acceptable. Without corrective actions to rein them in, there also would be a natural tendency for the volunteers to push the envelope, testing their superiors to find out where the line was drawn, if there was one. The men of the Nineteenth simply took over the press and used up the inventory of ink and newsprint they found on hand. No one even thought to ask the question about how the takeover fit with government policy.

Before moving a few miles south on December 12 for a miserable two-month winter encampment at Bacon Creek, Buell assigned Turchin's Eighth Brigade to the Third Division, the new command of Brigadier General Ormsby MacKnight Mitchel. A West Point graduate, class of 1829, from an impoverished background, Mitchel's considerable intelligence had taken him on a career that led from academy cadet to a scientist of national renown. After two years as a mathematics instructor at the Military Academy and a boring year with the Second Artillery in Florida, he quit the army to become a Cincinnati lawyer, a partner of Edward D. Mansfield (later a prominent Ohio journalist and political savant). "Mitchel sat in one corner, reading Quintilian, a Latin author on oratory," until the practice failed, Mansfield recalled years later.[12]

Mitchel then found only spotty employment as a college teacher and civil engineer. He hit his stride in 1843, founding and operating a not-for-profit institution, the Cincinnati Observatory. Nineteenth-century engineers needed to know the night sky in order to measure and survey the earth. Mitchel seems to have had a natural bent for the science and for its adjuncts as well. A popular public speaker and lecturer, he succeeded in importuning public figures to become patrons of his little institution; in finagling support from Professor Bache at the Coast Survey; and in publicizing astronomy, the observatory, and himself with his books, the popular magazine *Siderial Messenger,* and an endless series of strikingly dramatic lectures.[13] Mitchel's tireless efforts made him a prominent figure in the American scientific community, though "his courting of the populace put off serious astronomers, who were touchy, like all American scientists of the time, about the taint of amateurism and superficiality."[14]

When the rebels fired on Fort Sumter, Mitchel was in the thick of a controversy over control of the Dudley Observatory in Albany, New York. He immediately offered his services for the war effort. "I am ready to fight in the ranks or out of the ranks," he called out to a war rally in New York City on April 20, 1861. Wanting to set a dramatic example himself, he exclaimed, "[I]n God's name, give me something to do!"[15] Journeying back to Ohio, he applied his lobbying skills to secure something suitable. Two friends in Washington—Treasury Secretary Chase from Cincinnati and Senator Ira Harris of New York and the Dudley Observatory dispute—obliged him by securing his appointment as a brigadier general of volunteers. The new brigadier turned his oratorical skills to patriotic use at recruiting rallies, but he lobbied equally hard to escape staying behind at Camp Dennison, near Cincinnati, as merely "a drill-master" (albeit one of considerable skill) "of troops to be turned over to the command of other men." In October, after a deal with Secretary Cameron for an independent command marching into east Tennessee fell through, Mitchel submitted his resignation.[16]

Nevertheless, by November 27, resignation forgotten, Ormsby MacKnight Mitchel began serving under the privately amused Don Carlos Buell.[17] By the account of an admiring soldier, Mitchel was "small and slender in stature, not over five feet six inches tall, somewhat brusque and short in his speech."[18] He, like nearly all the others in his situation, also was devoid of training and experience as a commander of a large group of soldiers in the field, a fact that may well have raised itself to Colonel Turchin.

Mitchel and Turchin seem to have accommodated each other well during their first months together. Some of the reason may be found in their mutual acquaintance with science and with Alexander Dallas Bache. Turchin, for his part, must have had a measure of respect for Mitchel's intellectualism, and no doubt also for his aggressive thoughts in military planning. Mitchel sorely needed an approachable subordinate with Turchin's professional knowledge and maturity. His two other brigade commanders, markedly younger men, came with strong credentials but were of another generation. Joshua Woodrow Sill, Ninth Brigade, was of the new generation of West Pointers, class of 1853, a thorough Regular, and a close friend of Philip Sheridan and James B. McPherson.[19] William Haines Lytle, Seventeenth Brigade, known in Cincinnati as "a man of mark," scion of a politically prominent Cincinnati family—radical Democrats, and not contributors to Mitchel's Cincinnati Astronomical Society—had already seen combat, being seriously wounded while leading a failed charge of the Tenth Ohio at Carnifix Ferry in western Virginia on September 10, 1861.

The appointment of apparently competent men to the upper levels of command would not in and of itself solve other command problems that existed lower down the chain in the regiments of the brigade. The Nineteenth Illinois, where Joe Scott stepped up to take Turchin's place, appeared to be well covered, but there were plenty of command problems that had to be ironed out in the other regiments now under Turchin's direction. The German-American Twenty-fourth Illinois spent its two months at Bacon Creek recovering from the errors of earlier commanders. Its ailments began at its inception in May 1861: a group of Chicago's Germans undertook to recruit the men and the company officers, but a prominent out-state Republican, Gustave Koerner, arranged to have imposed upon the unit as its colonel a warhorse from the German Revolution of 1848—Frederick Karl Franz Hecker, lately of southern Illinois. Many veterans of European armies were induced to volunteer but, as with the Nineteenth, the final stage of recruiting had been hard going. Hecker, a martinet, questioned the loyalty of most of his officers—he dismissed several while en route east—and believed, probably with ample justification, that his enlisted men were drunk and deficient. (The regiment's first major, while in Missouri, had once treated the entire regiment to a swim and a cold beer.) Through the fall, the colonel and the company officers squabbled over the command. The factions argued their cases to the German community in Illinois, to Governor Yates, and to the War Department. Mitchel reported on December 16 that the regiment was in "a very demoralized condition." He personally led a search and found many of its soldiers crowding the saloons on the Louisville waterfront, absent without leave.[20]

Hecker at last gave it up, and the worst of the regiment's other feuding officers left with him. Out of the muddle emerged Geza Mihalotzy, a veteran of the losing side in the Hungarian Revolution of 1848, the side against which Turchin had fought. Once a professional officer like Turchin, in America he, too, had struggled to establish himself, in his case as a physician. In January 1861 he organized a militia unit of other eastern European immigrants in Chicago and secured the president-elect's personal permission to call the unit the Lincoln Riflemen.[21] Having led this company to Cairo in April, he brought them into the Twenty-fourth on condition that he become the lieutenant colonel. Mihalotzy took command on December 23 and then began the slow process of reconstructing his control of men who, in Missouri, had been "obliged to adopt the guerilla methods of commandeering subsistence for the regiment."[22]

The Eighteenth Ohio had a similar leadership problem at the top, one that could not be so readily solved. Amiable, well intentioned, devout, Colonel Timothy R. Stanley had been a successful lawyer, banker, and a principal in a stove factory in his hometown of Marietta, Ohio; but he had never been a soldier. Governor William Dennison, who appointed Stanley, tried to assure that at least one field officer in the regiment had some military background and so named as lieutenant colonel Josiah Given, a man with just enough experience in arms to be thoroughly contemptuous of Stanley. With this rift at the top, it took three months to attract enough recruits to fill the ranks. The regiment had not been mustered into the service until November 4 and was thus far behind the Illinois regiments in terms of drill and training.[23]

In the Thirty-seventh Indiana, a serious flaw in leadership of the opposite kind outlasted the encampment at Bacon Creek, even though Mitchel and Turchin took increasingly drastic actions to correct it. When the regiment mustered in at Lawrenceburg in October, Governor Oliver Morton awarded the command to a native Indianan, U.S. Army Captain George W. Hazzard. At first impression, he had the right credentials: fifth in West Point's class of 1847, service in the Fourth Artillery along the Rio Grande in the Mexican War.[24] In fact, Hazzard's career had been spiraling downward. When he and his green recruits first arrived in Kentucky, Sherman placed him in charge of a brigade. Buell's reorganization had knocked him back to the regiment.[25]

There, he may well have resented his reduced authority. His troops unquestionably hated his pointless rigidity. Private Martin Moor noted in his diary on Halloween, "General Inspection by Colonel Hazzard, and the boys tremble in their boots." Another recalled, "The Colonel would not permit any of his men to eat anything but government rations. It was a serious offense to buy cake, pie, fowl or fish from a citizen." Not only did this result in a bland and monotonous diet while camped in a land of plenty, but his men were not blind to the fact that their comrades in the adjoining regimental camps were under no such restrictions. Poor nutrition and the unsanitary conditions caused by being camped in one place too long filled the regimental hospital, and the horrible condition of that place ("worse than the Black Hole of Calcutta," remarked the division surgeon) meant an unusually high attrition rate for the Thirty-seventh at Bacon Creek. Scores of deaths and desertions were recorded there, compared with ten and five in the Nineteenth Illinois: so many, in fact, that the bodies of two men were examined to make certain they hadn't been poisoned.[26]

When Hazzard fined his regimental chaplain for a critical letter published in the *Cincinnati Commercial,* the men of the regiment took up a collection to pay it. Then, one day when the thickly accented Turchin issued an order to the troops that was admittedly hard to understand, Hazzard exploded and "rushed furiously" at Turchin, screaming that there was no such order in the book. "Col. Hazzard," Turchin coolly responded, "you must not address your superior officer in that way; give me your sword." The regimental historian noted that the men "could scarcely keep from cheering." Arrested again later, this time to protect the regimental surgeon (an arrest publicly applauded by the men), Hazzard soon after received orders sending him east, back to the Regulars.[27]

Hazzard's successor was by no means perfect. Hazzard had brought him up on charges—for signing bogus travel vouchers—charges that sounded contrived and went nowhere. Still, Lieutenant Colonel Carter Gazlay, a thirty-three-year-old lawyer from the regiment's hometown, had earned a reputation as a comically hard drinker and had other accusations made about him that would come back to haunt him the following summer. Although his skills in the courtroom would later inspire Turchin's confidence, he showed no sign of any particular military aptitude. Better men would eventually command the Thirty-seventh, but on March 7, 1862, Gazlay took charge. Although the extent of it can be debated, there can be no doubt that the plague of leadership problems retarded the development of this group into a fully fledged military unit already off on its first campaign.[28]

That campaign began on February 10, 1862, when Mitchel's division broke camp and marched south toward Bowling Green, Kentucky. General Buell had seen the rebel concentration there as a threat, perhaps an opportunity, ever since he took command in November. On February 1, exposing for the first time to the commander in chief his own independent streak, Buell had rejected as "impractical at this time" President Lincoln's strong preference that he come to the relief of the Unionists in eastern Tennessee, where a success akin to that seen in western Virginia was hoped for. (Buell's persistence in failing to lend aid to the loyal population of eastern Tennessee would steadily erode his standing in Washington.)[29] Instead, he had informed McClellan of his intention "to move at once against Bowling Green."[30]

Mitchel won the "post of honor," the vanguard, when Brigadier General Alexander McCook, whose Second Division sat poised in the most advanced camp, sensed what would become Buell's natural pace and advised that he could be ready to move in a week's time. Mitchel answered Buell's call with "Tomorrow morning," a response hard to reject. Ordered forward, Mitchel became ecstatic. "I am at last in the position to which my rank entitles me . . . look out my good friends, for moves on the theater of war, that will awake the nation from its long slumber, and send a thrill of joy throughout the land." Filled with men who had once before found it fun to "pitch in," with volunteers who had been "glad to begin the war," Turchin's brigade led the column, with a band marching in front, shouts and songs making clear the joy they felt to be again off to the war. One of his soldiers exulted over Buell's "glorious order" to march.[31] They tramped twenty miles on February 13, and "every ear was open to the sound of the first gun. The conviction that a battle was imminent kept the men steady and prevented straggling." They camped, arose early in a snowfall, marched again in uncomfortable cold, and by Friday afternoon, February 14, they were looking down from a hill across the Barren River at the last remnant of the Confederate forces evacuating Bowling Green.[32]

The Confederate commanders had decided a week before to abandon the city. Some of the rebel troops dawdled in withdrawing, and by February 13 only stragglers remained. They started burning buildings for the sport of it. On Friday morning they destroyed the bridge over the Barren. By afternoon, when Mitchel arrived and directed artillery fire against the town's railroad depot, "fierce-looking Texas Rangers were dashing about in every direction, having sworn as some said, not to leave till they had burnt the city." The first few Union artillery shells sent the Rangers running only slightly faster than most of the townspeople.[33]

The Nineteenth and Twenty-fourth Illinois entered the city first, crossing the river during another night snowfall, fifty men at a time in a flat-bottomed ferry. They found part of the town burnt, notably the depot and storehouses near it, and some other buildings still ablaze, though the damage proved less by dawn's light than the intruders had expected. To them, the principal loss was of commissary stores. "The quantity destroyed by the panic-stricken rebels can scarcely be estimated," one soldier thought. By another account, enough pork, salt beef, and other food items were salvaged, however, to supply the Third Division for a month. Then, too, there were the "fifty or sixty barrels of fine whiskey in one single shed" discovered by another squad of comrades.[34]

Turchin's men quickly evaded the cold by taking up quarters in the many abandoned homes. Looting and vandalism doubtless happened, but not, a witness recalled, in any place where the residents remained at home, thus beginning a pattern that carried through all the armies, of automatically assuming that those who fled before the Union's hosts were disloyal and deserved no respect from the common soldiers who marched with it. Here, in a city where many had fled earlier rebel invaders, that assumption lacked much of the validity it might otherwise have had. No one, however, was known to have inquired as to the loyalty or disloyalty of the people who had vacated the premises. Only Turchin's Eighth Brigade could be blamed for depredations here, for the rest of the division stopped and camped north of the river.[35]

Where better to demonstrate the use and efficacy of the conciliatory policy than here in a community that had been ravaged by the rebels? Where better to establish clear guidelines for the company officers to use when deciding where to quarter their men or dealing with the local citizens? By one account, the occupation of Bowling Green carried an opposite message. Instead,

> the town was nearly given up to the robbery of [Turchin's] soldiers. Every store in the place was broken open and ransacked, and all articles of value abstracted, the grossest insults being bestowed upon all those who offered resistance. Houses were broken into, doors knocked from hinges, windows were smashed to pieces, valuable furniture was split up to kindle fires with, and several houses were literally ruined. . . . Union men, too, who had suffered untold wrongs by the rebels, and who had longed and prayed for deliverance by our armies, were the sufferers.[36]

Where better to strike hard at those who committed or allowed depredations to occur in violation of the spirit of a national policy of conciliation than right here in Bowling Green? When better to establish the rules than at the very outset of the campaign, before bad habits became entrenched? Nothing came of it, not a whisper, not even a friendly hint that such actions might be a bit overboard. The campaign had begun without any departmental orders setting out a policy for the men on how to treat civilians or their property, and no corrective action was taken. Instead, a puffed-up General Mitchel asked Buell to "announce to the country the fall of Bowling Green," which he promptly did. Those headlines were eclipsed almost immediately when newspapers reported Grant's spectacular capture on February 16 of Fort Donelson and with it the decimation or capture of 15,000 Confederate soldiers. For Turchin's men, the loose behavior allowed in Missouri was simply carried forward, its apparent propriety reinforced.[37]

That same day, as Albert Sidney Johnston's rebel troops marched disconsolately southward through Nashville, Mayor Cheatham extracted a promise that there would be no Confederate stand in his city.[38] At almost the same time, Mitchel exhorted Buell to make "a strong and immediate demonstration upon Nashville."[39] On February 22, 1862, with Mitchel's division again marching hard at the head of the column, Buell set off for the capital of Tennessee.[40]

On Monday evening, February 24, the officers and men of Turchin's brigade gazed across the Cumberland River at the recently vacated state capital building. Rebel guerillas had lurked in Missouri, where partisan gangs on both sides had busily carried out summary justice. Entire regiments of men from Kentucky had gone off to fight for the Confederacy. Tennessee, however, had actually seceded from the Union. The state capital building stood vacant. The government officials, faithful to the rebel cause, had run. Despite areas of strong Union feeling in east Tennessee and pockets of patriotism here and there about the countryside, Tennessee officially stood as part of the Confederacy. In Missouri, under Turchin's leadership, the men of the Nineteenth Illinois had gained quick lessons in how to subvert a rebellion, in the realities of partisan warfare, and about how to be self-supporting in a land swarming with both plenty and enemies. Both before that, in Illinois, and afterward in Kentucky, they had learned how to drill and march and do those things that would allow them to fight effectively together on a battlefield.

Their test was about to come. But what sort of test? Would they march on to a battlefield as a part of a great army? If not, they would face a host of questions rarely properly anticipated by those who plan wars. Would they be received by flag-waving civilians celebrating the return of the rule of law under the Constitution of the United States? Or would they be asked to confront the same types of opponents they had faced in Missouri, people in plain clothes whose affiliations were blurred, if visible at all, many of whom operated surreptitiously, who lurked in the dark of shadow and night, who struck terror at individuals, who scattered when challenged, who disappeared into quiet civility until an opportunity to pounce again presented itself? Across the Cumberland, could Turchin's men ever assume on first meeting that any inhabitant could be counted a friend? Past experience tended to indicate no. The locals might be waiting to wreck the train upon which they rode or to shoot them in the back if they turned the wrong way or to ambush lonely sentinels. Their behavior at Bowling Green showed a clear disposition to assume the worst of the inhabitants.

Were they prepared to work with the many other civilians who were caught in the vise of not wanting a war that simply was not going to leave them alone, who wanted nothing more than for all the hotheads to go away and leave things as they had been? Were they prepared to help those people welcome a return of federal authority by being good shepherds of popular opinion? Here these Union volunteers would be on the line testing the popular theory that the rebellion had but scant support among the common people of the South, that Southerners were by and large waiting to be saved and protected from the volatile slave owners who had led them astray. As their experiences and responses in Missouri and Bowling Green proved, this was a theory that had no credibility with Turchin and his men. How would Southern civilians fare if they instead incited these volunteers? If history provided a guide, and Regular Army officers saw in it clear and convincing evidence, that answer was abundantly clear.

6
The Orders

In regard to political matters, bear in mind that we are fighting only
to preserve the integrity of the Union and to uphold the power of the
General Government; as far as military necessity will permit religiously
respect the constitutional rights of all. . . . It should be our constant aim
to make apparent to all that their property, their comfort, and their personal safety will be best preserved by adhering to the cause of the Union.
— George B. McClellan to Don Carlos Buell, November 12, 1861

A day after accepting Nashville's surrender, which the Yankees seized without contest on February 25, 1862, Major General Don Carlos Buell first took
up the question, How should Union troops treat the people of rebel Tennessee? In General Order No. 13a, issued the very next day, he answered with a
straightforward mandate of conciliation. "We are in arms not for the purpose
of invading the rights of our fellow-countrymen anywhere," he wrote, he
thought reassuringly, to the people of Tennessee, "but to maintain the integrity of the Union and protect the Constitution, under which its people have
been prosperous and happy." Accordingly, the order read, "Peaceable citizens
are not to be molested in their persons and property. Any wrongs to either
are to be promptly corrected and the offenders brought to punishment." Lest
there be any doubt of Buell's drift, his adjutant, Colonel James Barnet Fry,
advised division commander Ormsby MacKnight Mitchel on March 1: "The
general desires the protection of our forces to be extended with some liber-
ality, and to reach a class of persons who are not hostile to us although not
warmly our friends."[1]

What did this mean in practical terms? Fry explained with an example.
Should a soldier be shot while on outpost duty, as a Union cavalry officer had
been the night before, Fry advised that the soldiers on picket should be more
cautious and expose themselves less rather than strike back—even with the
relatively bland measures of making arrests or administering loyalty oaths.
Even if such patience and forbearance did not quickly win back the loyalty
of the guerillas firing the shots, it would, it must have been thought, restore
the faith of the rest of the people, and popular support for the rebellion

would ebb and die. If there were Tennesseans waiting for such reassurance, they got it. For the men on picket, for those who had volunteered to fight and kill Southerners, little encouragement could be found in being told to be more careful.[2]

Buell's order followed Lincoln's stated war policy to the letter. There was little doubt, however, that many Americans expected their conquering army to apply a policy of a far different sort. None could recall a war fought along such lines, for American wars usually followed other, harsher rules. In the common memory, or belief, war was hard on everyone. The British had proved it time and again in Scotland and Ireland, from whence many an American family had come. Depredations during the War of Independence had been for decades a subject of every schoolchild's reading. The wars with the Native Americans were ones of no quarter, where communities were torched, where women and children on all sides were often raped, mutilated, murdered, burned, or carried off as captives. Serious historians retold the tales. Many thinking and educated Union men made a call to send Southerners to an equally grim fate, even if they did not join the *Chicago Tribune* and its readers in positively relishing the idea. At Beaufort, South Carolina, in early February 1862, Lieutenant Charles Francis Adams reflected on a looted plantation home: "It isn't a pretty picture, this result of war . . . broken furniture, scraps of books and letters, and all the little tokens of a refined family." But there was nothing for it. "I wandered around and looked out at the view and wondered why this people had brought this upon themselves."[3]

Other thoughtful men, also with good reason, favored conciliation and hoped that soldiers' depredations could be prevented or minimized. The basic philosophy of such a policy was ancient. The prayer to the conquering state "to take mercy on the poor souls for whom this hungry war opens his vasty jaws" echoed over the centuries.[4] More to the point, in 1861 and early 1862, there appeared to be practicality in the hope that friendly persuasion would regain the loyalty of a region believed too vast to be held captive by force and too important to national life to be left a smoldering ruin. In any event, the success of the federal government in securing the border states of Delaware and Maryland and loyal regions like western Virginia and eastern Tennessee appeared to demonstrate the efficacy of a conciliatory policy. If it worked there, the argument grew stronger that it would work at points further south.

At Nashville on February 26, 1862, it fell to General Buell to make a declaration clearly establishing the policy he intended to follow as his men proceeded through Tennessee and into the states where the rebellion had begun. He needed to make a statement that fit with his understanding of national policy and with his view of the proper role of the military as it campaigned in the South. Never mind the reality of the situation he faced or the fears and passions of the people on both sides. General Order 13a was the very appropriate result. The order referred to Buell's belief in the people of the South. He raised the Stars and Stripes over the capitol building in the hopes that "thousands of hearts in every part of the State will swell with joy to see that honored flag reinstated in a position from which it was removed in the excitement and folly of an evil hour; that the voice of her own people will soon proclaim its welcome, and that their manhood and patriotism will protect and perpetuate it."[5]

The men on picket had a different perspective and most probably much different conclusions about who was exhibiting folly in this evil hour. From the beginning of hostilities, many people on both sides of the Mason-Dixon Line had expected the worst from the volunteers joining the opposing armies. Concerned Northerners freely expressed their fears that Southern troops would show no mercy if ever they crossed the Ohio. "Cincinnati and numerous small towns on the river could be utterly destroyed and the country about them laid waste," wrote Wisconsin governor Alexander Randall on May 3, 1861, when asking Lincoln to hold troops in the Midwest; "sacked and burned," was his fear. Confederate Brigadier General P. G. T. Beauregard mirrored the dread, exciting his troops with a message about Union volunteers "confiscating and destroying your property, and committing other acts of violence and outrage too shocking and revolting to be enumerated. . . . they proclaim by their acts, if not by their banners, that their war cry is 'Beauty and booty.'"[6]

Rape and plunder fit easily into this discourse about war. In much the same way, the *Chicago Tribune* urged destruction of Southern towns and watched as its list of subscribers steadily increased. The hyperbole expressed the common expectation. The American nation had been largely made by wars—harsh, partisan frontier wars fought most often by militiamen and untrained volunteers under circumstances in which their families were frequently at risk. King Philip's War, or the Red King's Rebellion, fought to secure New England in the 1670s, remains the bloodiest war ever fought on the North American continent in terms of percentage of people lost. Half of all the towns in New England were attacked. Of the fifty-odd English communities raided, the natives pillaged twenty-five and burned seventeen of them to the ground. When the colonists finally got the upper hand, native settlements fared even worse. The militiamen adopted tactics of torching the palisades and interior buildings of the native settlements. As the people fled, the Pilgrims stood outside the gates discharging their matchlocks and blunderbusses at everyone trying to flee regardless of gender or age. Of the 80,000 people, English and native, who lived in New England at the time, more than one in nine are thought to have died in the conflict.[7]

Such atrocities had marked the way as the frontier moved west. During the French and Indian War and the Revolution, the frontier became a constant scene of depredation, raids, and revenge. The great Iroquois leader Joseph Brandt followed a tactic in the Wyoming Valley of Pennsylvania of driving the white settlers into their blockhouses then burning the nearby homes, fields, and almost everything else he couldn't carry away. His most infamous raid occurred on November 11, 1778, when a party of Tory troops and their Iroquois allies, led by Brandt, fell on the outpost of Fort Alden in the Mohawk Valley. The Iroquois' attention was quickly diverted to the houses at nearby Cherry Valley, on which they descended with a fury. The raiders killed fifteen of the fort's defenders and took forty people captive, leaving the mutilated bodies of thirty-two other noncombatants lying in the ashes of the farms in the valley. The colonists retaliated that autumn by burning the Indian settlements at Oghwaga and Unadilla. On August 26, 1779, General John Sullivan won a decisive victory over a combined British and Indian force at Newtown, near the New York–Pennsylvania border. So many Native Americans died that afternoon that "the sides of the rocks next to the river appeared as though blood had been poured on them by pailfuls." Sullivan continued his push to the west, destroying every native settlement he could find, including the old and well-established communities of Kanadaseagea and Genesee and thirty-nine others, burning grain fields and orchards that had been generations in the making.[8]

The loss of the Revolutionary War by the British opened the land west of the Alleghenies to European settlement, and for another generation almost constant conflict resulted. As soon as settlers pushed across the Ohio River into Ohio and Indiana, the native tribes struck back, burning settlements, ambushing speculators and army convoys alike. Twelve hundred warriors led by Little Turtle of the Miami struck a column of more than two thousand soldiers and militia along the banks of the Wabash in late 1791, killed six hundred of them, wounded four hundred more, and lost fewer than one hundred of their own. The government spent nearly two years planning its response, while the Indians continued to raid the small settlements along the frontier. The army finally encountered Little Turtle and his allies at Fallen Timbers in 1794. General Anthony Wayne followed up his victory there by burning crops and communities as far away as the upper Maumee River in present-day Indiana.[9]

The early decades of the nineteenth century saw more of the same, as Tecumseh's confederacy of tribes tried to stem the flow of white settlement into Indiana and Illinois. Attacks on white settlements in southern Indiana led to the Indian defeat at the battle of Tippecanoe and the burning of the their capital, Prophetstown. An American garrison abandoned Fort Dearborn, only to be massacred trying to reach Detroit. In reprisal, Americans burned to the ground Indian villages across the old Northwest.[10]

A similar sequence occurred in Mississippi and Alabama during the Creek War of 1813—the arrival of white settlers, the attacks by Native Americans, and "brutal repression" by the United States Army. Many of the Creeks fled not west but south to Florida, where they joined the Seminoles. Tensions finally came to a head there in 1835 with the outbreak of the Second Seminole War. The government spent $20,000,000 and the lives of 1,500 soldiers trying to eradicate them. Osceola, the tribe's charismatic leader, successfully battled the army, killed Indian agents, and punished those who aided his enemies. Some of his adherents managed to elude capture and relocation, only to spend miserable decades in abject poverty trying to live in the Florida swamps.[11] One did not need to read James Fennimore Cooper to know that war along the frontier was total war.

Nor was the frontier conflict confined to white settlers and displaced natives. Perhaps nowhere else were the passions of the times better exposed, and along with them the propensity of men on both sides to consider all people on the opposing side as enemies, than on the Kansas plains in the decade before the Civil War began. After the opening of the Kansas Territory in 1854, partisan fighting erupted almost immediately, pitting huge gangs of "Border Ruffians" against equally ardent abolitionists. The Ruffians gutted the city of Lawrence in late May of 1856, burning the business district and many of its homes, killing many unarmed citizens in the process. Three days later, John Brown sought and gained a measure of vengeance, he and his followers hacking to death a small group of slavery's sympathizers along Pottawatomie Creek. These were not the acts of people bent on compromise. Nor were they evidence of people who might see the sense of offering compassion or conciliation to the general population on the other side, or who might see such an offer as a welcome opportunity to sue for peace. These were the acts of enemies, of people who had no desire but to use all available means to attain their own ends.[12]

John Brown reached the apogee of his fame (or the nadir of his infamy, depending upon one's point of view) three years later, when he and a band of followers seized the Harper's Ferry arsenal hoping to instigate a slave rebellion. In that he failed. He succeeded, however, in completing the polarization of the country that had come to the surface in Kansas. In the months following his attack, the people of the South began their own process of retaliation. Postmasters burned "incendiary" Northern newspapers, like the *New York Tribune*. Three dozen Northerners who had relocated to Berea, Kentucky, were ordered by a mob to leave. When they appealed to Governor McGoffin for protection, he offered none, except along the route leading north to the banks of the Ohio River.[13]

In Dallas, Texas, a preacher named Solomon McKinney, a Kentuckian who had used his pulpit in Wisconsin to defend slavery, delivered a sermon in which he decried the sometimes brutal treatment slaves endured. A mob quickly gathered and appointed a committee to whip the preacher and a companion for their pronouncements. Stripped to shirt and pantaloons, McKinney took seventy lashes, his companion eighty.[14] In Columbia, South Carolina, an Irish stonecutter named James Power made the mistake of uttering some antislavery opinions. He was jailed for nine days, after which a gang dragged him through the streets, through a crowd of several thousand laughing and jeering people, among whom stood the speaker of the legislature. They took him three miles out from the city, stripped him naked, gave him thirty-nine lashes, and then tarred, feathered, and retarred the poor man before putting him on a train for Charleston. There he was detained in jail for another week before finally being placed on board a ship bound for New York. Similar incidents of beatings, tarring and feathering, and expulsion happened with great frequency all across the South.[15]

When states started to secede, Senator Ben Wade of Ohio had a simple idea about how to respond. He angrily suggested "making the South a desert." A member of the Ohio legislature urged the appropriation of $1 million to buy rebel scalps. A judge advocated making New Orleans again a swamp, incinerating Montgomery and Columbia, and starving, drowning, burning, and shooting all traitors. As frustration with conciliation grew during the spring of 1862, Governor Andrew Curtin of Pennsylvania added his voice to the clamor. "War means violence," he reminded a crowd in Pittsburgh, "and in time of war man relapses into barbarism. The property, nay, even the life of the enemy, everything he has, we must take and use against him." Senator John Sherman, the general's brother, came to see the war much the same way. "You cannot conduct warfare against savages unless you become half-savage yourself," he said in the early summer of 1862.[16]

Even the renowned pacifist William Lloyd Garrison finally joined the choir. "What have we to rejoice over? Why, I say, the war!" he cried out to his listeners in the spring of 1862. "What! This fratricidal war? What! This civil war? What? this treasonable dismemberment of the Union? Yes, thank God for it all!—for it indicates the waning power of slavery and the irresistible growth of freedom, and that the day of Northern submission is past. It is better that we should be so virtuous that the vicious cannot live with us, than to be so vile that they can endure and relish our company."[17]

Obviously, many people, high and low, saw the coming war as another partisan contest where anything could be expected, whether fair or not. They saw, or perhaps more realistically felt, that the war would be a war between two societies, two peoples. They saw, and advocated, a war that would be a desperate, terribly destructive contest, one that might well be fought to the death by the losing society.

There was, however, a competing philosophy. Those who espoused it envisioned war as a contest between large standing armies. The armies would take to the field much as knights once entered the lists. The forces would face one another and fight until a victor was determined. Everyone else would stand outside the fray, patiently awaiting the result.

The vast majority of the officer corps of the United States Army developed quite apart from the frontier violence and in an atmosphere that in many ways lessened the sectional tensions developing between the Northern and Southern states. By the time the Civil War broke out, three-quarters of the officers of the Regular Army were the products of the United States Military Academy at West Point. The cadets, and the officers they became, developed, especially after the War of 1812, a deep and growing sense of professionalism. That, in turn, encompassed even deeper senses of duty and honor. At the academy the failure to obey a command could lead to immediate dismissal. The regulations required that the cadets "abstain from all vicious, immoral and irregular conduct," the sorts of conduct that would be unbecoming of gentlemen, again under penalty of dismissal. Honor served the academy by providing a means of developing desired behavior. It served the cadets as an end. To be an honorable man among honorable men was both their ultimate goal and reward. If the cadets stood as the stones in the wall, honor was the mortar that bound them together.[18]

They were taught to look upon themselves as men apart, as men set to the highest standards. They were not militiamen on the frontier. They were not British brutes. They were not savages. According to the regulations that governed their lives, should any one of them lose his self control and "beat, or otherwise mistreat any citizen," he was responsible both under the law of the jurisdiction where it happened and to his commandant. Support for a conciliatory policy would come easily and naturally to many who matured in this regulated world.[19]

On August 2, 1861, one of those former cadets, the ascending George B. McClellan (he was not quite yet the army's commanding general), set out for President Lincoln and the cabinet the proposition that by "pursuing a rigidly protective policy as to private property and unarmed persons and a lenient course as to common [rebel] soldiers, we may well hope for the permanent restoration of peaceful Union." McClellan thus marched in lockstep with the policy set forth in the president's inaugural address. In so doing, however, he and his close associates, men like Don Carlos Buell, became owners of that policy. Its validity and broader support for it would be dependent upon their success in bringing the rebellion to an end.[20]

West Point was the beginning of all this, adolescents reciting by rote the rigorous engineering curriculum, marching in columns to their recreation. The "Father of the Military Academy," Sylvanus Thayer, designed the school to foster elitism. In many ways this American institution provided all three stages of Turchin's Russian military education rolled into a single four-year course, although the counterpart of Turchin's concluding Nicholas Academy course in management and strategy was thin—a short series of lectures on strategy from Professor Mahan, an informal club that discussed the campaigns of Napoleon, and an excellent library, well used by the keener cadets. West Point's influence was, however, far more pervasive than that of the school at St. Petersburg.[21]

Strict discipline furthered the cadets' conviction that this was "the best school in the world"—they, therefore, being among the best of the best. No one successfully resisted the code. Dismissal was brutally common. In 1839 a third classman, one year ahead of Buell, wrote a friend at a civilian college, "just to think that three years should reduce a class from 120 to 40." Dismissal claimed those who would not conform, but withdrawals and resignations took the majority who left, those who lacked the perseverance or motivation to endure the Spartan regimen demanded by the academy.[22]

Don Carlos Buell may have stood just thirty-second in his class—near the middle—but he was an apt student of army discipline. Two years out of the academy he stood accused at a court-martial proceeding, charged with striking a private with the flat of his sword. The court gave Buell an "honorable acquittal," not on the ground of self-defense (the man was in custody when Buell beat him) but rather on the strength of Buell's personal plea that he had struck the man "in defense of the service which is bleeding for the arrest of a spirit of insubordination which seems to be sweeping the army."[23]

That affair happened within the insular world of the Regulars at a peacetime garrison post in Missouri. With the coming of the Mexican War, however, Buell and his fellow officers received an altogether broader education in the insubordination and misdeeds apparently inherent in an army of volunteers. With the outbreak of war and the need to geometrically expand the army, President James Knox Polk had started the process by appointing thirteen generals in the new volunteer service. To gain the appointments, political connections proved far more important than military qualifications. In keeping with the practices of the time, governors put forward the names of potential generals and commissioned regimental officers from civilian life, while the president and General Scott kept the Regular units segregated from the volunteer regiments raised for the war.[24] In effect, Polk created a parallel amateur army led by amateur officers, a model that would be used for the expansion of the Union army at the outbreak of the Civil War.

It was in Mexico that the officers of the Regular Army came to know and fear volunteers. "I believe with fifteen thousand regulars we could go to the City of Mexico," concluded Lieutenant George Gordon Meade at Matamoros in July of 1846, "but with thirty thousand volunteers the whole nature and policy of the war will be changed. . . . they (the volunteers) have killed five or six innocent people walking in the streets, for no other object than their own amusement; to-be-sure, they are always drunk, and are in a measure irresponsible for their conduct. They rob and steal the cattle and corn of the poor farmers, and in fact are more like a body of hostile Indians than of civilized whites." Barely three months out of West Point, Lieutenant Ambrose P. Hill described war as it was waged by troops under Indiana politician and new brigadier general of volunteers Joseph Lane. Occupying Huamantla, these soldiers "rushed through the town, breaking open the stores, houses and shops, loading themselves with the most costly articles, rendering themselves brutish by the drinking of aquagardiente. The women screaming and running about the streets, imploring protection, was a sight to melt a heart of stone." "Of course," wrote Lieutenant George McClellan about another outrage, "not the slightest excess was committed by any of the regulars."[25]

There was in fact a huge contrast in Mexico between the behavior of the troops of the Regular Army and the horde of volunteers that came to augment it. The volunteers came to fight "and were in no mood to tolerate offense from anyone, Mexican or American." Reuben Davis, the colonel of the Second Mississippi Rifles, recalled that the troubles began even before his troops left home. Davis saw a dramatic change in his men just as soon as they had been mustered in. It was as if each "felt absolved of any obligation to God or man and, as a consequence, considered himself free to disregard every law of honesty" other than to be loyal to his flag and personally courageous on the battlefield. By the time they reached New Orleans, they had become so uproarious that the city called out its own militia in self-defense.[26]

Some of the Regular officers took quick note of the élan of the volunteers. Meade wrote that the volunteers he met in Monterrey were "sufficiently well-drilled for practical purposes, and are, I believe, brave, and will fight as gallantly as any men." But that very fighting spirit, which was after all what brought them into the service, could just as often be a cause for serious concern. Meade met some Texas volunteers he found outrageous, "for they come here with the sores and recollections of wrong done, which must have been festering in them for ten years, and under the guise of entering the United States service, they cloak a thirst to gratify personal revenge."[27]

The Texans may have had a personal stake in avenging the Alamo, but were Tennesseans equally ardent about avenging the death of Crockett? One of them wrote about his motivation for volunteering: "Politicians may say what they please and decry it as Polk's war, but they only thought then of the fact that we are a portion of the manhood of a great nation going forth to avenge the great wrongs of the past and secure indemnity for the wrongs done us and security for the future." One of the first companies of volunteers Abner Doubleday encountered in Mexico was a group of Tigers from New Orleans, armed to the teeth with Bowie knives and pistols, looking like a bunch of pirates, who ran up to him and demanded, "Now show me your Mexicans!"[28]

It did not help that politicians in many cases led these volunteers to Mexico. Undoubtedly many of them came to lead the regiments and companies they had in tow by whipping up the very sort of patriotic fervor that so shocked and worried the West Point graduates. Controlling their volunteers was almost a foreign thought. In fact, at the beginning of the campaign, "it was a standing joke among the Regulars, that the officers of volunteers found it necessary to enforce every trifling order with a stump speech." Then Lieutenant Doubleday recalled of the volunteers, "many of the officers were politicians and were on such intimate terms with the privates that the latter were utterly regardless of the restraints of discipline. In fact they were more like organized mobs than military forces." One volunteer private shocked Doubleday by poking his head into the tent of Brigadier General David Twiggs, asking the general if he could use his cot to take a nap. It was, perhaps, no small coincidence that Don Carlos Buell then served on Twiggs's staff.[29]

These lessons of Mexico loomed large for an officer corps asked to lead the U.S. Army to victory in the War of the Rebellion. The adoption of a policy carried over from the former war to the latter only seemed to magnify those lessons. Conciliation had been tried before, south of the Rio Grande, with, it was thought, great success. Robert Anderson, the very same man who would be forced to surrender Fort Sumter, observed in 1846,

[I]t seems that Santa Anna can not succeed in exciting the common Mexicans against us—the kind treatment received from us [the Regular Army] contrasts so forcibly with the harsh conduct of the Mexican officers and officials as to operate very much in our favor. Many contend we ought to live on the country and make them feel the horrors of war, and that then they will sue for peace. Perhaps not. It may be that a change of policy on our part would excite the common people so much as to make resistance to the death a cardinal principal [sic] with them; hence would result in an enthusiasm which would render the country unconquerable.[30]

Others had shared the fear that the volunteers would provide the incentive for the Mexican people to rise to repel the invasion. In November 1846 George Meade wrote home, commenting that even though the volunteers were well drilled,

they are . . . without discipline, laying waste the country wherever we go, making us a terror to innocent people, and if there is any spirit or energy in the Mexicans, will finally rouse the people against us. . . . They plunder the poor inhabitants of everything they can lay their hands on, and shoot them if they remonstrate, and if one of their number happens to get into a drunken brawl and is killed, they run over the country, killing all the poor innocent people they find in their way, to avenge, as they say, the murder of their brother.

After the fall of Monterrey, Meade reported that the wealthy families had all fled and would not return out of fear of the volunteers, the locals harboring a well-justified "perfect horror of them."[31]

In Mexico, General Winfield Scott had promulgated and enforced, to the extent he could, a policy of conciliation. He encouraged friendliness toward the Mexican people and a disciplined restraint by his troops, or at least those subject to Regular Army discipline. Scott, an educated, experienced, and thoroughly professional soldier, sincerely believed depredations against civilians would be counterproductive. Like many of his junior officers, he feared the power of an aroused Mexican population. As a veteran of the War of 1812, he may well have looked back to the animosity pointlessly created by American troops (not his own) burning towns on the Niagara frontier where he served. In Mexico he distributed food to the local people within his lines and applied the lash to soldiers who committed crimes against them.[32]

For his junior officers who experienced it, conciliation became a model that fit as well with their experiences in Mexico as it did with their senses of duty and honor. They saw in the policy something that said it was the right thing to do. Accordingly, it became an example of a policy to be used again; and where more appropriately than in a war where the enemy was made up of misguided countrymen? Not least, it fit well with the sense of order of soldiers like Don Carlos Buell.[33]

Officers who had not defected to the Confederacy but who were, nonetheless, in sympathy with the South could take comfort in a policy of conciliation that was by its nature conservative, that respected the South as it existed prior to Lincoln's election, that approved its social structures and accepted slavery as the bottom of what seemed to them a rational hierarchy. Buell, with his Southern family connections and slave-owning in-laws, tilted Southward as much as any officer who kept his federal commission. When he finally left the army in June 1864, he explained himself to the readers of a copperhead newspaper. Secession could be excused, he wrote, because it "was mainly determined by an honest conviction . . . that the control of the

Government had passed into the hands of a sectional party, which would soon trample on the political rights of the South."[34] In addition, Buell and others well and fairly thought it right to be able to say, as Scott had boasted after Mexico, "I carried on war as a Christian, and not as a fiend!"[35]

Thus a dichotomy was born. On the one side stood the professional soldiers and those who agreed with them, promoting a clean, stand-up conflict between armies, in keeping with two centuries of European-style warfare that they had studied as cadets. On the other side stood those who saw war as a harsh and partisan affair, among them the politicians and editors who called for a war of retribution and many of the early volunteers, who had the same quick reaction to the attack on Fort Sumter. For officers who had fought in Mexico, however, a question that must have loomed large in 1861 was this: How were they to enforce a conciliatory policy when they stood at the head of large masses of volunteers rather than among the Regular soldiers upon whom they could count to be restrained and obedient? One answer, of course, was to wait to enter the seceded states until those volunteers were so thoroughly trained and disciplined that they could also be trusted. Both McClellan and Buell would suffer enormous criticism during the closing months of 1861 for the inactivity of their armies. But for them, to invade with an army that would alienate the very people whose loyalty they wished to regain would have been a strategic blunder of epic proportion.

The professional officers who found themselves in high command positions at the outbreak of the rebellion knew the monumental task they faced in converting these gung-ho volunteers into reliable and restrained soldiers. In August 1861, shortly after receiving his first general's star, William Tecumseh Sherman explained the challenge to his wife. "Had I some good regulars," he wrote to her, "I could tie to them. As it is, all the New Brigadiers must manufacture their brigades out of Raw material—Napoleon allowed three years as a *minimum*. Washington one year—here it is expected in nine days." At the time Sherman had great faith in McClellan, noting approvingly that he didn't believe Little Mac would be hurried. The doctrine of restraint would start at the top.[36]

Sherman's lack of confidence in volunteer soldiers, which he, too, had developed during the Mexican War, was confirmed by his experience at the first battle of Bull Run where, after putting up a good fight, the men of his brigade had joined the rout of McDowell's army. "I doubt if volunteers from any quarter could do better," he wrote. "Each private thinks for himself—if he wants to go for water, he asks leave of no one. If he thinks right he takes oats

& corn, and even burns the house of his enemy. As we could not prevent these disorders on the way out [from Washington to Manassas] I always feared the result—for everywhere we found the people against us—no curse could be greater than invasion by a Volunteer Army. No Goths nor vandals ever had less respect for the lives and properties of friends and foes."[37]

Sherman also saw the fault with the manufacturing system he had to produce soldiers from volunteers. He noted that with experienced and trained troops, disciplinary problems could be dealt with by the platoon and company officers, by sergeants, captains, and perhaps on occasion by a colonel. Without this structure of experience in the volunteer units, there was no immediate solution. "Here every woman within five miles who has a peach stolen, or roasting ear carried off comes to me to have a guard stationed to protect her tree, and our soldiers are the most destructive men I have ever known. It may be other volunteers are just as bad," he added, "indeed the complaint is universal." Such conclusions were hardly surprising in light of the observations these officers made in Mexico.[38]

Sherman's correspondence often contains observations that are deeply insightful, even if at this early stage of the war he found himself overwhelmed by the conclusions he reached because of them. He was no less insightful about the people of the South. "I suppose we will have to go into Kentucky & Tennessee to organize an army in the face of the prejudice which you complained so much about in Missouri," he wrote to his wife a few days after he had described his discipline problems. "That prejudice pervades the public mind and it will take years to overcome. In all the Southern States, they have succeeded in impressing the public mind that the North is governed by a mob—(of which unfortunately there is too much truth) and in the South that all is chivalry and Gentility."[39]

Turchin and his men presented a different sort of problem. Here, at least in the Nineteenth Illinois, was a unit that had some depth among the officers. In Turchin, they had a leader who actually had experience commanding a unit of battalion or regimental size. They had many line and company officers experienced in drill. As a result, they progressed much more rapidly than many other units in gaining the appearance of soldiers. They responded quickly to marching orders, did not debate their superiors when doing so, dressed properly, looked sharp on the drill field, and presented a disciplined front while in camp. But were they not led by a man who was at heart, like all the rest of them, a volunteer, a man who had enlisted to fight for a cause, a man who had his own, very independent ideas about how this could best be done? Perhaps Turchin was also fired by the fact that for the first time he led men with whom he shared a cause and a passion. He had been asked to lead a group of men who had volunteered to avenge an attack on a form of government that had become the envy of people everywhere. Was not plunder, in minds such as these, a just and mild end for traitors' property? And in the eyes of his hometown press, was not virtually everyone south of the Ohio River a traitor? They had so seen the people who had fled Bowling Green.

How could generals like Sherman or Buell recognize men such as Turchin's as every bit as dangerous as the "Goths and Vandals" they had seen elsewhere? Certainly, Turchin's men gained a reputation early on that gave clear warning of their proclivities. Sherman confided to his wife in the summer of 1861 that his "only hope now is that a common sense of decency may be infused into this soldiery to respect life and property." That would take time, a fact in all probability recognized by McClellan and Buell as they dragged their feet against the constant push from Washington for quick and decisive action. Changing such deeply ingrained attitudes would take clear direction from the top, and one could not begin too soon to instill in the entire chain of command the importance of following and enforcing the policy. But would time also correct the shortcomings in the system? Could the training process control the motivations that brought the volunteers to and kept them in the fight?[40]

If it were to do so, quick, corrective action would be required when undesired behavior manifested itself. On the western Virginia front in May 1861, George McClellan promised civilians: "All your rights shall be religiously respected." He advised his soldiers, "[Y]ou are in the country of friends." He considered a court-martial for an entire company of three-month militia volunteers who raided the vacant house of a secessionist. He settled for the dismissal of an officer and seven men for the more conventional "small crime of burglary." Having counseled the White House on policy in August, he instructed Buell along the same party line when sending him west in November. "In regard to political matters," the new commanding general wrote in a personal letter, "it should be our constant aim to make it apparent to all that their property, their comfort, and their personal safety will be best preserved by adhering to the cause of the Union."[41]

One would think that a commander contemplating an invasion and knowing the reputation of volunteer soldiers in general would consider taking steps well in advance to drum the necessary sense of restraint into them. So far as we know, Buell did nothing of the sort before his army entered Tennessee, despite having had four months to prepare for that eventuality. General Order 13a was imperative to initiate and uniformly apply the official government policy in Buell's area of operation, but its pronouncement came late in the game, after Missouri, after Bowling Green, after the army had reached Nashville. "The business at hand was not only war, but war of invasion," Buell's chief of staff at the time argued on his behalf years later. "To avoid the active hostility of the inhabitants . . . Buell announced and as far as he could, afforded, protection to peaceable citizens."[42]

For the men serving under Buell, the order and the policy it enunciated could easily have been viewed with suspicion. Many questions had to come quickly to mind. Western Virginia had indeed been reasonably friendly territory for McClellan's men to enter. Many a home had been decorated with the Stars and Stripes. Townspeople had often cheered the arrival of Union troops. Middle Tennessee, on the other hand, rather than welcoming the advancing Union army, had surrendered to it. Dozens of Tennessee regiments had gone into the Confederate service. If a family had a son or a father who had gone off to repel the Yankee invaders, why should those same Yankees protect the farms and manufactories supporting the rebel war effort? Would that protection do anything to bring the rebel warriors back home, back into a love of the federal government?

Might not a Union soldier also ask who his enemies were? Had not he learned in Missouri that rebels wore all sorts of dress and fought in every manner imaginable, from standing in line beside comrades in battle to working stealthily at night loosening railroad rail? If a woman spit in your path or crossed the street to avoid having to exchange pleasantries, what respect should she be given? Even while complaining about the undisciplined excesses of his own men in the summer of 1861, Sherman had noted "[a] good many little incidents, shooting of sentinels & pickets, all the cruel useless attendants of war" that were occurring daily around his camps.[43] The atmosphere only worsened for Buell's men after they descended into middle Tennessee.

Still other forces were afoot in those early months of 1862 that might have provided additional incentive for the issuance of an order such as General Order 13a. Congress had begun an attack on the policy of conciliation. The simple passage of time, which now amounted to ten months, coupled with the failure to end the rebellion through appeals to the better angels of Southern nature, worked on the side of those who had volunteered to wage real war, of those who saw everyone in the South as traitors. The president, his advisors, and many of the generals in charge of the government's armies had taken the opposite view, insisting upon disciplined restraint, thinking that a harsh policy would be not only counterproductive but also discreditable to the nation and a stain upon themselves. Congress, a body more reflective of public opinion, had debated the subject from the first months of the war.

Briefly, during the war's first summer, Congress had seemed to embrace reconciliation. The occasion was the last great effort at compromise made by Representative John Jordan Crittenden of Kentucky, fifty-two years a politician, a disciple of Henry Clay. The Crittenden Resolution announced as national policy "that this war is not prosecuted upon our part in any spirit of oppression, nor for any purpose of conquest or subjugation, nor for the purpose of overwhelming or interfering with the rights or established institutions of those [seceding] States, but to . . . preserve the Union, with all the dignity, equality, and rights of the several states unimpaired." The resolution cleared the House by a wide margin on July 22, 1861. Andrew Johnson of Tennessee introduced a companion bill in the Senate on July 25. A bystander noted in surprise that "almost the entire Republican vote, including such men as Fessenden [of Maine], Hale [New Hampshire], Chandler [Michigan], and Grimes [Iowa], sustained the resolution"—thirty-three aye, five nay.[44] However, during the following autumn the conciliatory atmosphere evaporated. On December 4, the House tabled into oblivion a proposal to reaffirm the Crittenden Resolution by a vote of seventy-six to sixty-five.[45]

The swing in congressional opinion manifested itself almost at the same time in acts to confiscate rebel property and to free slaves. The first of these statutes, touching both emancipation and confiscation, passed by large majorities and became law on August 6, 1861. Introduced in the Senate by Lyman Trumbull, it was largely symbolic: Southern property used in aid of rebellion could be seized, and those slaves pressed into helping the Confederate war effort could not, if they escaped, be sent back by judicial process. Lacking any enforcement mechanism, that act of August 6 led to the formal confiscation of almost nothing and freedom for absolutely no one. It did, however, open the policy debate.[46]

The day after the renewal of Crittenden's resolution failed, on December 5, 1861, Trumbull filed a second confiscation bill. It had a new, harsh thrust: all property, not just the property used to support the revolt, of persons in active rebellion was subject to forfeiture and confiscation. What mattered now was who owned it, not how it was used. Slaves of these rebels were to be set free. The president could devise the enforcement mechanisms.[47] Who were "persons in rebellion"? Old men who provided financial support to the revolt? Women who sewed uniforms? Farmers who provided food for the effort? The statute and the still official policy of conciliation represented polar opposites, with no clearly defined boundary establishing where one ended and the other began. The proposed statute directly contradicted what McClellan and Buell understood as their mission. A month before Buell issued General Order No. 13a, Chairman Trumbull's Judiciary Committee made national headlines by clearing the new confiscation bill for debate by the full Senate. If enacted, the things done by Turchin's men in Missouri would not have been far out of line with the new law.

If this bill were not confusing enough for the leaders of the army, Congress had been hammering away elsewhere at the proposition that the Union army was not to interfere with the South's "rights or established institutions." The issue was the disposition of the escaped slaves who sought refuge in the army's camps—a vexing question, a discrete bellwether of sentiment about conciliation, and a problem that grew as the Union armies moved south. Having begun with Ben Butler's designation of fugitive slaves as contraband of war, the issue again jumped to the forefront on November 20, 1861, when Major General Henry Halleck, at St. Louis commanding the Department of the West, issued his General Order No. 3, referring to "fugitive slaves who are admitted within our lines" and directing that "unauthorized persons of every description" be excluded. The order fast became notorious in abolitionist circles. On December 7, Owen Lovejoy denounced it on the floor of the House. Halleck, with a ready ear, stood down, responding the next day with a message disingenuously pointing out that the order was not political but military, aimed at spies. This was not good enough for Senator Charles Sumner, who on December 18 procured Senate passage of a resolution directing the Committee on Military Affairs to consider "additional legislation that our national armies shall not be engaged in the surrender of fugitive slaves." Halleck, "Old Brains" to fellow West Pointers, sidestepped, instructing a subordinate commander that the order about fugitives of course "does not prevent the exercise of all proper offices of humanity in giving them food and clothing."[48] There the matter stood when Buell fell on Nashville.

By taking on this debate, Congress unwittingly called into question the value of professionalism in the army. Debate over the relative merits of professional, as against amateur, military leadership was nothing new in a nation with a miniscule standing army and a deeply seated belief in the invincibility of volunteer militiamen. More heat could be expected with war, when volunteer colonels came to vastly outnumber their Regular Army counterparts, amateur generals nearly so.[49]

That winter Congress embarked on two other notorious forays against the profession of arms. First, on December 19, it named two radical senators and three like-minded congressmen to the new Committee on the Conduct of the War. "The committee had its birth in the popular demand for a more vigorous prosecution of the war," wrote one of them, Representative George Washington Julian of Indiana, "and less tenderness toward slavery." The members' critiques of military operations seemed generally the antithesis of professional military thought—"simplistic, amateurish, and unrealistic." Their initial investigation into the battle of Ball's Bluff, which was the military blunder that sparked its creation, led famously to the arrest and imprisonment of Brigadier General Charles Pomeroy Stone, West Point class of 1845. "General Stone, the slave catcher, has been broken in his command," reported the *Chicago Tribune* of February 11.[50]

Second, the bastion of professionalism, West Point itself, came under serious attack. The Committee on Military Affairs, quite unlike the upstarts looking into the conduct of the war, served as the army's liaison with the Senate. In December, not surprisingly given the growing magnitude of the war, it advanced a bill, Senate 101, to double the number of cadets at the academy. Opponents boosted instead the idea that the academy should be abolished. "It is aristocratical; it is exclusive; it is a close corporation; and it stands in the way of merit being advanced," suggested Senator Ben Wade of Ohio, "a man of uncommon downrightness" and not incidentally chairman of the rival committee. Backhanded at best was Wisconsin senator Timothy Howe's defense of the academy: "You get martinets in your military school because you send ninnies there."[51] West Point survived, but the bill to expand it failed decisively, twelve to twenty-five. The Committee on the Conduct of the War persisted. Officers in charge of departments, including Don Carlos Buell, would now have to prove in the field the value of their training and policies. The fate of conciliation thus rested in the balance.

With a clear sense that what he ordered was the right thing to do, being both morally correct and in total keeping with the directions of his superiors, through General Order No. 13a Buell put the policy of conciliation on the line in his department. Was he aware of the history of men like Turchin's in Missouri? Had he reflected on the probable behavior of volunteers as his predecessor Sherman had done? Was he informed about the events in Bowling Green? If he was so informed, was he so naïve as to believe that rigorous measures would not be required to keep his men in line? Perhaps he had sufficient faith in General Mitchel, a man of similar training, to believe that he would take the measures necessary to enforce the order within his division. If so, the events at Bowling Green had to be better explained.

Regardless, there was no follow-up, no corrective measures or more specific orders, no real way for lower-level commanders to receive guidance. Buell said "peaceable citizens" were to be protected. Who were they? Anyone who was unarmed? The lower-level commanders were left to make such decisions for themselves. Mitchel, aggressive in his attitude toward the rebellion, made an unlikely candidate to rein in volunteers also eager to fight the rebellious. Buell obviously had faith in Mitchell, well-grounded or not, for he would soon give him the equivalent of an independent command. Had events developed differently and the command remained unified, perhaps Buell could have paid more attention to these matters and achieved a more uniform and desirable result. But he would have been slow to reconsider the policy he set forth in the order. To this disciplined, veteran officer, conciliation and his order enforcing it were revealed truth.

7
The Campaign

If we are not already involved in war, we soon will be. There is no hope for peace, and he is but little better than a mad man who dreams of a long exemption from invasion.

—Jeremiah Clemens, Madison, Alabama, 1861

The men of Turchin's Brigade stepped off in column and marched out of Nashville on Tuesday, March 18, 1862, having rested quietly there for three weeks. With the rest of Mitchel's Third Division, altogether 7,400 strong, they headed south. The Union army had entered the city, as the University of Nashville's chancellor observed, with "[a]ll the air and assumption of a conquering host," no doubt reflecting both the chancellor's and the soldiers' view that the city had indeed been conquered rather than liberated. The advance on the state capital had been unopposed and uneventful. It remained to be seen what kind of war they would be asked to fight as they moved south. Still, the joyless countenance of the local inhabitants did not seem to match the hopes and expectations of the government's policy makers. The Union column reached its first major objective, Murfreesboro, intended to be but a way station, in two more days of very easy marching. Other units served as the occupying force, luckily perhaps, since local sympathies were markedly with the South. Mitchel's division continued its journey deeper and deeper into the Confederacy.[1]

At the same time, General Buell, with the main body of his army, more than 30,000 men, started a slow southwesterly march to join Grant's force, whose recently reassigned subordinate, Brigadier General William T. Sherman, on that March 18, was debarking men on the south bank of the Tennessee's northern reach at Pittsburg Landing, in the neighborhood of a Methodist meeting house known as Shiloh Church. By a March 11 order from Lincoln, Buell's Army of the Ohio had become part of the Department of the Mississippi under Henry Halleck, based at St. Louis.[2] Halleck had immediately busied himself marshaling his armies to confront those being gathered by General Albert Sidney Johnston, thought to be in northern Mississippi somewhere safely south of Pittsburg Landing.

Buell left Mitchel to guard his left flank, to protect against any nuisance from the uncounted rebel forces in east Tennessee under Kirby Smith at Knoxville or from any others that might arrive from the south and east, via Atlanta or Chattanooga, by way of the longest railroad line in the Confederacy, the Memphis & Charleston. The written orders Buell gave Mitchel, dated March 27, contemplated nothing further, simply that Mitchel place his division near Fayetteville, due south from Murfreesboro, northwest of Chattanooga, a day's march north of the Alabama line. No aggressive effort was required, just a good deal of marching in the Tennessee mud. Perhaps the thought that Mitchel would thus command an army of occupation went largely unrecognized, certainly unaddressed. Buell, off to help fight Albert Sidney Johnston's rebel army, would be dealing with traditional military situations. Mitchel, occupying middle Tennessee, would be facing the civilian population of middle Tennessee, discovering whether or not conciliation had a foundation in fact.[3]

Major General George B. McClellan, in his role as general in chief of the army, had established the overall strategic framework for the campaign now assigned to Mitchel six weeks before. The Memphis & Charleston Railroad stood at the heart of McClellan's thinking. The line ran along the Tennessee River Valley, which dipped to the south and ran through Alabama and Mississippi before turning northward again into western Tennessee. Thinking on February 7 to press the advantage gained by the fall of Fort Henry, McClellan had written Halleck that a move on Memphis by both Grant and Buell "will be next in order," increasing the reach of the Mississippi under government control. To support that move, he added, the bridges carrying the Memphis & Charleston over the Tennessee River "at Tuscumbia and Decatur should at all hazards be destroyed at once."[4] Mitchel's men had the inside route to those bridges.

Mitchel's move to them began slowly. "Now we are compelled to halt and rebuild" other bridges on the way to Murfreesboro, wrote a young officer, "before it will be possible for us to move on Alabama." Retreating Confederates and supporting bands of partisans burned the Stones River Bridge and other essential rail spans, initiating a strategy they would use repeatedly to frustrate the advance of Union troops south through Tennessee. General Mitchel could do no more than restlessly order a reconnaissance in force. Between March 25 and 28, Colonel Mihalotzy led a demibrigade through

Shelbyville, Tullahoma, Manchester, and McMinnville, meeting no armed resistance but likewise encountering few welcoming smiles.[5]

As they advanced, the front line became a blur. Union patrols chased rebel "rangers," ran across and arrested Confederate volunteers found on furlough, and released others who were willing to take the oath. They sometimes found Union sentiment present but noticeably subdued. On occasion influential citizens would beg the Union columns to leave behind a platoon or even a regiment to guard them from the reprisals they felt certain would come from their rebel neighbors as soon as the federal troops left. In fact, on March 28, a Union cavalry patrol picked up ten men, taking into custody five who had been rebel soldiers and five others, partisans in plain clothes, who had driven Union families from their homes and threatened to hang any who remained.[6]

Less than two weeks later, Andrews's Raiders reached Marietta, Georgia, and began the episode that became known as the Great Railroad Chase. The Union soldiers involved in the raid had dressed as civilians. When captured by the rebels, they were put on trial as spies. In their defense, their attorney argued that "our being dressed in citizens' clothes was nothing more than what the Confederate Government itself had authorized, and was only what all the guerrillas in the service of the Confederacy did on all occasions when it would be an advantage to them to do so," and he recited the instance of General Morgan "having dressed his men in the uniform of our soldiers and passed them off as being from the Eighth [sic] Pennsylvania Cavalry Regiment, and by that means succeeded in reaching a railroad and destroying it."[7] What was good for the goose was not good for the gander. The rebels still walked a number of the raiders to the gallows.

The fact that the rebels waged a guerilla campaign in central Tennessee made it all the more difficult to differentiate loyal or neutral citizens of the South from rebels and rebel sympathizers or to expect Union soldiers to restrain themselves. Rather than meeting rebel soldiers against whom they could carry on a conventional military campaign, Mitchel's soldiers instead encountered pocket after pocket of partisan fighters, men who would much sooner terrorize their neighbors than face soldiers on a field of battle. As partisans and guerillas, those men fought by other rules, by a code that both allowed and invited reprisal, by regulations that worked to inspire fear and terror.

There could be no doubt that there were many loyal citizens in the area who both needed and deserved protection from the rebels who lay hidden in their midst. In fact, a majority of the voters of Morgan, Lawrence, and

Limestone counties in northern Alabama had opposed secession, tied as they were by trade along the Tennessee River Valley with the North. At Alabama's secession convention in January 1861, that lingering loyalty to the Union had not gone unnoticed. William Lowndes Yancey gave the antisecession delegates fair warning, saying that after secession, any residents who remained opposed to the state's action "will become traitors, rebels against its authority, and will be dealt with as such." Minding one's own business and waiting for the troubles to end would not be an option.[8]

But how could they be protected? Guards left at each deserving house were just as vulnerable to sneak attacks as the tenants. To leave more men would quickly deplete the army of the strength it needed to take and hold the strategically important points on the map or to face organized rebel forces when they appeared. There would be no ready answers to these problems. What there would be were increasing opportunities to want to use the same tactics that the rebel partisans were using. Why not bring a little terror into the hearts of the rebels? Why not scare them into submission, just as Turchin had done in Missouri? Why not let Turchin's volunteers fight the fight they had volunteered for? Why not make the rebels, and all those who supported them, pay?

Further delayed for resupply, only on April 3 did the division as a whole move south. Mitchel had with him Turchin's Eighth, Colonel Joshua Sill's Ninth and Colonel William Lytle's Seventeenth brigades of infantry, three batteries (Peter Simonson's Fifth Indiana Battery, C. O. Loomis's Battery A, First Michigan Light Artillery, and Warren Edgarton's Battery E, First Ohio Light Artillery), and Colonel John Kennett's Fourth Ohio Cavalry. The troops could easily distinguish between the countryside's hostile and friendly inhabitants, although the depth of the mix must have confused them, for they could not know what to expect next. One recorded, "We did not indulge in many regrets at leaving Murfreesboro. . . . Not a farewell was waved at us as we left town."[9]

However, the next day the column reached Shelbyville, settled by New Englanders whom the men found "quite cheering to us in this land of darkness." Nearly every residence displayed the Grand Old Flag. An eighty-year-old Revolutionary War widow stepped forward to greet Colonel Kennett with tears in her eyes. She, a Mrs. Graham, then went to the courthouse and tore down the flag of secession. Her daughter-in-law told of the murder of her husband for his Union sentiments. The correspondent to the *Cincinnati Gazette* told his readers that "cheerful, thoughtful, intelligent-looking faces greeted us at every corner, and beautiful women made us welcome with smiles and tears." Kennett reported, "We have not met such manifestations of delight in any part of Dixie's land." General Mitchel telegraphed for permission to allow normal government, meaning regular local court sessions. Military Governor Andrew Johnson granted it in an instant.[10]

Their stop at Shelbyville represented the crest of the short wave of Union sentiment they discovered as they journeyed toward Alabama. On Tuesday, April 8, Turchin's brigade led the division on the march toward Fayetteville, about twenty-five miles away as the crows flew, separated from Shelbyville by the largely unpopulated hill country of central Tennessee. Perhaps as a gesture of goodwill, General Mitchel sent forward two of his staff officers with a flag of truce to alert residents of Fayetteville of the impending arrival of his troops. Rather than being greeted with welcoming smiles, the flag bearers received threats of personal violence that sent them scampering for refuge in an old hotel, where they hid until the next morning.

Ormsby MacKnight Mitchel had no patience for such insolence. Muscling his way into the town the next day, he fired off a salvo of oral fireworks from his saddle in the town square. "People of Fayetteville," Mitchel thundered, "you are worse than savages. Even they respect a flag of truce. . . . Yesterday, the soldiers whom I sent to your town upon a mission of courtesy and mercy, were shamefully insulted in your streets, and it was you who gave the insult. You are not worthy to look in the faces of honest men. Depart to your homes every one of you, and remain there until I give you permission to come forth."[11] As most homes thus remained occupied, no one noted any depredations of private property, despite the obvious hostility of the locals. Ordering the citizens to their homes was the first example set by Mitchel that Turchin made note of and would later use. Their stay was short. The following day Mitchel resumed the march toward Alabama with Turchin's men again in the lead.

In fact, the movement of Mitchel's division southward through Tennessee resembled the path of an icebreaker. They could break up and push away the obstacles standing in their way, but as soon as they passed the shards drifted back into the path they had cut, and it would all begin to refreeze. Later in April, General Buell ordered some of the regiments left behind in garrison around Nashville, Murfreesboro, and Lebanon to move south and consolidate with others of Mitchel's men. Military Governor Andrew Johnson stood aghast. He quickly telegraphed Washington, hoping Secretary of War Stanton would intervene. "This is substantially surrendering the country to the rebels," Johnson advised. "The effect of removing the troops is visible in the face of every secessionist," he pointedly warned.[12] It seemed that the Union commanders could choose between two equally disagreeable courses of action. They could leave the loyal people of central Tennessee unsupported and open to attack by the partisans and guerillas, or they could leave isolated garrisons of Union volunteers behind that were open to attack from the increasingly strong and active rebel cavalry units operating in the area. To men who had volunteered to grind an ax, neither course provided them with much opportunity to vent their frustration.

Directly south, thirty-five miles away across the Alabama state line, glowed the splendid little city of Huntsville, "the social and intellectual capital of the Tennessee Valley." Founded in 1806 at a large limestone spring, now connected to the river a few miles to the south by a navigable canal, it was home to 3,634 people, 1,980 of them white, not least of those the statesman Clement Comer Clay and his son, Confederate senator Clement Claiborne Clay. It was reported to be "one of the richest cities of its class in the country, and one of the most beautiful in the South."[13]

More than that, Huntsville was the logical point from which to strike at the Memphis & Charleston Railroad, the trans-Confederacy main line. The city lay between junctions with both of the lines that connected the Memphis & Charleston with Nashville. The Nashville & Chattanooga joined the Memphis & Charleston at Stevenson, on the north bank of the Tennessee roughly forty-five miles east of Huntsville. The junction with the Nashville & Decatur occurred where that line crossed a bridge in Decatur—the first bridge that had caught McClellan's strategic attention—only twenty-four miles to the west. From Decatur, the Memphis & Charleston ran along the south bank of the Tennessee River for forty-three miles to Tuscumbia, where it again crossed the river, along the other of McClellan's spans. A Union force holding Huntsville and stretches of rail in both directions could sever communications between the Confederate east and west and would itself be assured of resupply over either of two separate lines from the north. Confused, but generally favorable, reports about the enormous battle at Shiloh gave both Mitchel and Turchin impetus to seize Huntsville. Both would have recognized that a move on one of the two main rail lines supporting the rebel army would be the boldest action the division could take in support of the war to the west.[14]

That Thursday Mitchel sent Turchin and one battery south out of Fayetteville, again in the lead of the division. Just as Buell demonstrated his confidence in Mitchel by giving him an independent command, so, too, did Mitchel express his faith in Turchin. Turchin marched on ahead, while Mitchel followed with Sill's and Lytle's brigades and the rest of the cannon. Soon after crossing the state line, Turchin's column strode over the enormous plantation of Leroy Pope Walker, the Confederacy's first secretary of war, more recently a brigadier who had found garrison duty at Montgomery so insulting that he had resigned his commission. His mansion house stood deserted, already emptied of its furnishings. His slaves remained. They danced, they sang, they laughed. One wore a leg shackle that a Union cavalryman gladly removed. Although the mansion was spared, some of the men set an outbuilding ablaze. As they continued the march, the correspondent for the *Cincinnati Gazette* felt his confusion growing. He found pockets of "strong Union feeling . . . mingled with many false notions concerning State sovereignty and the duty of submission thereto." The only consistently friendly faces he could count on were black. After twenty-five miles on "a common country by-path, in awful condition," nighttime found the advance of the column within ten miles of Huntsville.[15]

After four hours of rest, Turchin's brigade, now accompanied by Kennett's cavalry, moved on and struck the town just after daybreak. The only Confederate troops on hand happened to be a detachment of 170 recruits and their officers bound for the Ninth Louisiana, pausing en route to Virginia, "taken in tents and disarmed before they half comprehended their condition." The great prize lay in the railroad yards—seventeen locomotives, perhaps 150 passenger and freight cars—and, of course, control of hundreds of miles of strategically important rail.[16]

"To swoop down on a large city, take charge of it and require the citizens to act as you dictate to them, gives one a good idea of the prerogatives of war," the Thirty-seventh Indiana's historian wrote of the troops' entry into Huntsville. Mitchel, when he arrived later in the day, personally directed the troops as they secured the town. Taking no chances on the political alignment of the residents, the general himself stood sentinel at the street corners, watching as his men spread out in squads to search private homes for firearms. Order 13a or not, no secret cache of rifles or muskets would go undiscovered in Huntsville under General Mitchel's watch. Legal niceties like search warrants had become an early casualty of the conflict. Again, Turchin would later follow Mitchel's example.[17]

In this theater, Union generals had not yet awakened to the value of using their roughest, most unruly regiments as military police, turning one set of malefactors against another, neutralizing both. A posse of Irish wharf rats enlisted from Cincinnati's slums, the Tenth Ohio, would later provide William S. Rosecrans and George H. Thomas with exemplary service as their provost guard. These men had already shown promise, attempting at Nashville to brain another regiment's major with a stove and threatening while collectively drunk at Fayetteville to mutiny rather than march farther south. A night in camp with the Tenth Ohio, as bandsman Dan Finn described it, could provide great amusement if you could stay windward of the fray. "Johnny Montague got his fighting propensities aroused and gave Kroll a left-hander over his right peeper which was returned by Kroll who gave Johnny a sou-western clout on the smeller. At this stage of affairs Charles Colean stepped into the arena and made himself a peacemaker. By grabbing with his herculean grasp ahold of the belligerents and held them at bay until quiet was restored." Although the Tenth was at hand in Huntsville by Friday afternoon, General Mitchel instead made his provost guard from the farmers in Gazlay's Thirty-seventh Indiana.[18]

At Huntsville no great need arose to restrain the troops. The restlessness of most still found a channel into forward motion. The day of the occupation, units went east and west along the railroad to protect the new position. That day and the next, April 12, Mitchel began to exploit Huntsville's strategic value. He personally went eastward with Sill and a large part of the Ninth Brigade past Stevenson to destroy the railroad bridge at Widden's Creek, five miles short of Bridgeport. That move blocked any possible Confederate rail movements from eastern Tennessee or northern Georgia.[19]

Turchin went west by train on April 12 with the Nineteenth and Twenty-fourth Illinois and orders to burn the bridge at Decatur. He found it already burning at the far end, on the south bank, set afire by precipitously retreating Confederates. One witness said of the rebel retreat that he had seen fast races before, "but never anything equal to that!" Turchin's troops crossed the bridge, put out the fire, and instinctively continued marching toward Tuscumbia. On that side of Huntsville, too, the enemy could not react. With Albert Johnston dead, General P. G. T. Beauregard and the divisions battered on the Shiloh battlefield were encamped near Corinth, their attention focused on the armies of Grant and Buell threatening to grind southward, which they soon did. Turchin's force, now including parts of three regiments but only six hundred strong, easily occupied Tuscumbia on Wednesday, April 16.[20]

Evidence that they now strode in a hostile land stood everywhere in plain view. "At Huntsville we saw the first whipping post to which negroes were tied," and at Tuscumbia the first bloodhounds, looking ready to "eat a niggah up in a minute, shore."[21] Acts of random, stealthy, in-the-back violence made the case even more plain. At Tuscumbia on April 19, bushwhackers caught up with Private James A. Davis of the Nineteenth Illinois. Davis, the first man the regiment lost in enemy territory, fell the victim of partisans, not of enemy soldiers, while he stood his tour on picket that night, killed by stealth and in the dark. Two days later Company E drove off a band of Southern sympathizers attacking a squad on guard at a railroad bridge near town. Retaliation came swiftly. "They [the soldiers] acted very badly while in town," wrote a citizen, "breaking open cellars, etc. taking what they pleased."[22] The complaints went no further, either by citizens attempting to gain official redress or by commanders stepping in to enforce government policy. The pattern of behavior learned early on had resurfaced and again went unchecked.

Two weeks later General Mitchel detailed the reactions that came about due to his seizure of Huntsville and the railroad. The people were bitter. "Armed citizens fire into the trains, cut the telegraph wires, attack the guards at bridges, cut off and destroy my couriers, while guerilla bands of cavalry attack wherever there is the slightest chance of success." Mitchel went on in this wire to Stanton to say that he had arrested some of the citizens and was certain he could convict them in court using the testimony of blacks. But could he do that, convict white men based on the testimony of their slaves? Could he send the more notorious to be held in Northern prisons? Could he offer government protection to the African Americans brave enough to offer the testimony? Such unresolved policy questions only further muddied the quagmire into which Mitchel and his men had entered.[23]

The small size of Turchin's force at Tuscumbia made it vulnerable to counterattack. From the armies advancing on Corinth, another seventy miles to the west, 100,000 rations arrived by riverboat but no reinforcing troops.[24] Turchin's officers resorted to a ruse to pump up their apparent strength, entering a dozen regiments' numbers behind their names in hotel registers. The Confederate command, preoccupied to the west at the real "seat of war in the Mississippi Department," did much the same sort of thing. A Methodist parson and a Sunday school teacher were dispatched toward Tuscumbia on a pair of nags, their mission to spread the gospel that a well-armed force was "embarked on a campaign to clean out North Alabama of Yankees." Albeit a rumor, it was one taken seriously.[25]

Whether from lack of reinforcement or preferring to interpret equivocal instructions safely, Turchin quit Tuscumbia on Thursday morning, April 24, and began a tedious march back to Decatur, hampered by enemy cavalry, losing four men as prisoners (forty, the *Mobile Advertiser* implausibly reported). As soon as they recrossed the bridge, his men fired all of the twelve wooden spans, turning the bridge into a luminous pyre. They completed their mission on April 26, when a similar blaze brought down the bridge at Decatur. Turchin led his men back into Huntsville the following day.[26]

Once Turchin returned, Mitchel set out with Sill's and Lytle's brigades on another expedition to the east, past Stevenson, to capture Bridgeport and its long span across the Tennessee. Mitchel made himself no less than a "Protean commander," thought a *New York Herald* correspondent, "as he appears at one and the same time at different places, 100 miles apart, burning and building, contracting and expanding, retreating and attacking." Issue was joined Tuesday evening, April 29, when the Third and Thirty-third Ohio regiments marched over a hill above Bridgeport, accompanied by two guns from Loomis's artillery. Though entrenched, the Confederates at the town's edge again chose to demonstrate their prowess as sprinters. "[W]e had before us a foot race and not a battle," recalled the Third Ohio's Colonel John Beatty. The enemy commander, Brigadier General Danville Leadbetter, proved "a regular blue-grass trotter for speed." According to the *New York Herald*'s lengthy and excited account, "A stampede began, and was not finished until the river was placed between themselves and our infantry."[27]

The Bridgeport affair was Mitchel's first direct command of men in combat. An observer wrote that the astronomer moved his forces "with great rapidity and skill, but he showed a nervous temper, which gave the impression that in a great battle he would become too much excited for a commanding officer." By another analysis, the incident merely "made a great deal of noise by telegraph."[28] Turchin's brigade had no part in it. Resting quietly at Huntsville, three of the regiments watched as the fourth, Stanley's Eighteenth Ohio, moved out that April 29, headed, with all its camp equipage, twenty miles west by northwest to garrison the small but picturesque town of Athens, Alabama. Mitchel claimed that a deputation of worthy citizens had invited his men to come, and he promised that the locals would "raise the flag the moment our troops enter."[29]

Union strategy at the time would have led Mitchel to send troops to Athens whatever the residents thought about it. It was an important stop along a rail line supporting the advanced Union position. It would be garrisoned. Athens had grown in a location that placed it near the Elk River and Limestone Creek bridges of the Nashville & Decatur, with Decatur itself and the junction with the Memphis & Charlestown only a few miles to the south. North along the rails lay Pulaski, sparsely garrisoned, then Columbia, Franklin, and finally Nashville. Although an understandable command decision in a country where there was no large, organized rebel force, the garrisons were often unwelcome guests of people openly hostile to the intrusion of the federal government. Small and isolated, the garrisons provided easy targets that would help build the notoriety of some of the Confederacy's most famous horsemen. As one commentator noted, the garrisons "better served the mission of population control than as a deterrent to rebel incursions."[30]

The seat of Limestone County, Athens had but 887 inhabitants in 1860, 338 of them slaves. No whipping post or slave-hunting hounds were reported, but cotton plantations, some of them places of obvious wealth, surrounded the community. Visiting later in the summer of 1862, reporter Henry Villard perhaps unfairly found Athens shabby, "an even more unclassical place than Florence."[31] Citizens could claim a slender attachment to the Union and would boast with a degree of truth, when it served them, of living in the last place in Alabama to remove the Stars and Stripes from atop the courthouse cupola. On a Saturday night in January 1861, local workingmen had held an antisecession parade, ending it in the courthouse square by burning in effigy Alabama's proslavery orator, William Lowndes Yancey. This was not an unnatural protest. Northern Alabama had factories—cotton mills nearer Huntsville, for example, one running 3,000 spindles. White mechanics could calculate how black chattel slavery affected the local wage scale. Athens also had tolerated an antisecession newspaper, unique in the state, the *Union Banner*, but only until February 1861, when editor A. B. Hendren concluded, "I cannot of course expect to survive the mighty powers brought against me." That same month, a citizen reported, the flag came down from the courthouse, after "a good deal of animosity" and "sober second thought," to be "buried in oblivion." In fact, it was stored in a drawer in the home of the town's mayor, Press Tanner.[32]

A likely purveyor of Athens's pro-Union reputation was the town's most prominent pro-Union native, Judge George W. Lane. He sat on the circuit bench for Limestone County from 1835 through the 1840s, "an erect and imposing presence," then exchanged his robes for a private law practice in Huntsville and a pleasant life at an imposing and well-known estate, Oaks Place. In April 1861 the Lincoln administration had appointed him the

United States District Judge for the Northern District of Alabama, in effect the senior federal official in the area, and paid him from Washington, albeit not without difficulty, a munificent salary of $2,780.55 per annum. Lane kept his Athens connections, hoping to hold his court sessions there, but thus far he had not done so.[33]

The only other conspicuous Unionist resident still walking the streets in Athens, so far as it appears, was sixty-year-old "Captain" D. H. Bingham. Born in Vermont, a relative newcomer, he had moved to Athens from Huntsville in 1858. His neighbors seem to have regarded him as a "monomaniac" to be protected from his own eccentricity. He had a talent for offending his neighbors.[34]

Some prominent Limestone County political figures entirely opted out of the secession controversy. The even-tempered George Smith Houston, for one, was "opposed to the whole Southern movement" but left Congress in 1861 upon Alabama's secession, stayed home, then refused to take a federal oath of allegiance when the time came. It would probably be fair to say, moreover, that for many others at Athens in May 1862—as at Farmington, Connecticut, when Tryon's Loyalist raiders swashed through in April 1777 and as at other towns in other times—the bulk of the citizenry were "apathetic, apolitical men, who simply did not want to become perilously involved in a civil war." Athens's postmaster, Richard C. Davis, kept Southern stamps in his drawer along with Northern currency but, he said, always called himself "a Union man." He, like many of his fellows, was doing his best to keep his neck off the block—off of everyone's block.[35] Actively and unabashedly Confederate, however, were those citizens of Athens who had committed to take a side. Limestone County contributed the officers and men for two companies in the Ninth Alabama Infantry, two more in the Twenty-sixth, other soldiers to the Thirty-fifth and Fifty-fourth, and troopers to Alabama's Ninth and Eleventh cavalry regiments.[36]

As Mitchel's division began taking its hold on northern Alabama, Captain Thomas Hubbard Hobbs's company of the Ninth Alabama stood in defense of Richmond. Hobbs, by the evidence of his own lifetime diary, was an engaging and intelligent thirty-six-year-old whose view of the universe was comfortably centered at Athens. He had grown up in its small-town society, had graduated from the University of Virginia's law school, preferred local planting and railroad development to law practice, and had represented Athens's interests in the legislature from 1855 to 1861. A bitter argument between Hobbs and Houston, his former mentor, came incongruously close to fisticuffs, shutting down a secession debate in their hometown in March 1861. (But the slender young Hobbs and the burly old Houston soon "agreed to go on with friendly relations.") Before marching east, doubting not at all the Confederate cause, Hobbs publicly denounced Judge Lane as worse than a foreigner, "an appointee of Lincoln, with a Black Republican commission in his pocket."[37]

On the Confederate home front at Athens, a self-described "speculator," Thomas Jefferson Cox, acted as the local state tax agent. He collected both taxes and voluntary donations to the Confederate cause. Plantation owner Dr. James F. Sowell contributed from his evidently substantial means toward clothing and cloth for soldiers from Limestone. His son William served with the Thirty-fifth Alabama. George Peck had tailored a coat for Thomas Hobbs's twenty first birthday in 1847; now he was cutting and making uniforms for Hobbs's soldiers. "On the whole I think the sympathies of the people here are with the Confederate Government," J. W. S. Donnell would later testify.[38]

Donnell had his own slant on the subject, having sent that government $500 in advance of his taxes. But evidence suggests he was right, and that the presence of Mitchel's forces across north Alabama did nothing to elicit or free suppressed pro-Union feeling. When a federal cavalry detachment visited Athens on Saturday and Sunday, April 26 and 27, twenty-nine-year-old spinster Mary Fielding wrote in her diary: "Five of them came to Sunday School this morning & there were several at Church. They had the impudence to join in the singing with us, tho' they look sheepish & mean. I couldn't help thinking all during the sermon, 'how I do wish that Capt. [John Hunt] Morgan's or some other boys of ours would come galloping into town! How I would like to see you all scamper.'" Notably, when the Eighteenth Ohio arrived to garrison the town, the Stars and Stripes that had been removed a year earlier from the courthouse cupola remained in the mayor's drawer.[39]

In quieter times, Colonel Timothy R. Stanley would have been a fine choice to put in charge of this little county seat. He had prospered in another small town, Marietta, Ohio, as a furnace manufacturer and lawyer, and had succeeded well enough in local politics to reach the state senate in 1860 and to raise his own regiment in 1861. A peaceable fellow, entirely devoid of military knowledge, he had but one earlier experience in a challenging spot—at Bowling Green in February, when he had been left behind as provost marshal of the thoroughly subjugated city. At age fifty-one he had the advantage of maturity, if not that of more direct experience.[40]

Arriving with his regiment on Tuesday evening, April 29, Stanley took up lodgings on the courthouse square at the home of the young mayor, William Presley Tanner, known about town as Press, one of a family of merchants. Not all of the regiment stayed in town. Company E moved out to guard the railroad bridge over Limestone Creek to the south. Company I went north to Pulaski. Half of another company rode guard on the trains. The remainder of the regiment, three hundred men by Stanley's rough count, tented together at the local fairgrounds racetrack, four blocks north of the square. The next day most of these troops left on a scout south to Brown's Ferry under Lieutenant Colonel Josiah Givens. Confederates had been reported north of the Tennessee between Huntsville and Decatur. Finding none, Givens's expedition returned before nightfall.[41]

The behavior of the men of the Eighteenth Ohio in town was, as Mayor Tanner later declared, "Unexceptionable! The citizens were congratulating themselves on having such a quiet and orderly set." The soldiers, for their part, had no complaints about the citizens.[42] Their stay in Athens as April ended remained quiet and uneventful. All of that changed at 7:00 in the morning of Thursday, May 1. The men heard pistol shots from west of the town. Stanley had pickets out in that direction, down the Florence Road. Rather than call them in, he sent a company to reinforce them. It became lost, or at least out of touch. Stanley sent another. It, too, disappeared. Soon after, the sound of musketry rolled toward the square, followed in twenty or thirty minutes by the banging of cannon and incoming artillery shells.[43]

Stanley, under fire for the first time, became "excited"—better put, panic-stricken. Down to half strength due to the scattering of his companies, facing unseen enemies equipped with artillery, he could think of no better action than placing his remaining men in formation in the square.[44] He had always hated to give orders. Now the other flaws in the Eighteenth Ohio's command structure began to take their toll. The colonel had never enjoyed his officers' confidence, at least not since training at Camp Denison in Ohio months earlier, when he had obliged them to share tuition fees for a veteran brought from another unit to do his own job, instructing them in regimental drill. He especially lacked the confidence of his lieutenant colonel, Givens, who was far more of a military man than himself, as he readily admitted. Stanley had made a militarily unthinkable (but in the early days of the Civil

War hardly unique) arrangement with Givens, ceding to him the duty of command in combat.[45]

Standing in the courthouse square, faced for the first time with the imminent arrival of armed enemy troops, neither Stanley nor Givens could decide what to do. Time slipped away, then scouts sent out earlier on horseback returned to report, and with no motive to underestimate, that the Eighteenth faced three to four hundred cavalrymen, two artillery pieces, and three battalions of infantry (more precisely, they had seen "three flags"). Before any enemy force came into sight, Givens ordered retreat, and Stanley ordered the wagons packed with all equipage but the tents. Givens's order was obeyed. Stanley's was not. There was no time to divert wagons or men to the racetrack, just north, for the equipment. The regiment moved south at the quickstep, empty wagons clattering close behind.[46]

Townspeople openly loitered about, watching as the soldiers fled. By all accounts, women derisively waved kerchiefs and no doubt pointedly jeered the backs of Stanley's men. As to the rumors of gunfire from the houses, which played a great role in justifying subsequent events, the best evidence is Stanley's own testimony. On horseback, he had the opportunity to observe. Later he had every reason to exaggerate the peril. He reported nothing but hearing a "great shouting" to his rear after his men were well out of town. Givens's account and those of several enlisted men also gave no indication that the civilians actually threatened the Union troops with firearms. But such would be the reports.[47]

Marching at first by the road paralleling the railroad line, the column's advance met an oncoming train carrying, of all people, Major General Ormsby MacKnight Mitchel, en route to Athens. He had stopped, literally on the tracks, when the engineer heard the sound of gunfire ahead. The general's orderlies found Stanley, passed on an order to stand and fight—by then Lieutenant Colonel Givens's choice also—but soon relayed a contradicting order: to retreat until the regiment met reinforcements. Mitchel's train chugged away in reverse, the general safely on board.[48] The Eighteenth trudged along southeasterly, away from the tracks. Under the afternoon sun, the men could see smoke rising from the direction of the bridge over Limestone Creek. Part of missing Company G somehow found the column. Remnants of Company E, left to guard the bridge, arrived to report a cavalry attack that had burned the bridge and with it a Union supply train from Nashville.[49]

At Athens, moments after the Eighteenth left, Confederate troopers entered, perhaps as many as two hundred of them, some in civilian clothes, together with a section of mountain howitzers, two small cannon each drawn on a two-horse carriage. They rode as the First Louisiana Cavalry under the command of Colonel John S. Scott. The regiment had been active in middle Tennessee since February, chiefly in burning bridges, and appears to have been the group that dogged Turchin's withdrawal from Tuscumbia a few days earlier. As it happened, the First Louisiana was a paper tiger. Its junior officers were as disgruntled with their aggressive leader as the Eighteenth Ohio's were with the passive Stanley.[50] However, on this Thursday all was joy around the Confederate horsemen. "The streets were lined with exultant ladies and shouting men," no doubt the noise heard by the fleeing Stanley. The ladies gathered in a body and presented Scott with a Confederate flag, which they had kept hidden. It is hard to believe that some of this sentiment was not displayed before the Eighteenth Ohio completed its withdrawal from town.[51]

The rebel commander soon dispatched Captain Fenelow Cannon and the thirty men in his Company G on a brief foray to burn the Limestone Creek Bridge, over which Mitchel must just have passed. They did so, though not without a half-hour firefight. The gap in the rails led to the wrecking and burning of a southbound supply train and the capture of a thousand bags of coffee. Scott sent out other detachments, and with one of them went two new volunteers from Athens, George Mason and James B. Hollingsworth, who left at home a wife struggling with a late-term pregnancy. The pair returned later with a prisoner, a soldier from the Eighteenth, whom Mason had winged with a rifle shot. Before the whole troop left town that afternoon and evening, the colonel ordered that the Ohio infantry's camp at the racetrack be cleared of everything that could be used and the rest torched. Some of the abandoned knapsacks, at a citizen's suggestion, were distributed to local blacks. Others fell into the hands of white children. Scott issued an order to the town fathers that his men be provided with a meal. It was happily provided, gratis.[52]

Back in Huntsville, Mitchel took prompt steps to counter the incursion. Turchin received a terse written order to take five hundred men by rail to reinforce Stanley. To tighten a noose that was obviously too loose, he ordered John Beatty's Third Ohio back to Stevenson from its camp east of Bridgeport. Curran Pope's Fifteenth Kentucky was put to a forced march down from Fayetteville.[53] As the afternoon wore on, Turchin obtained Mitchel's leave to lead the expedition himself and to expand it to a comfortable form, in effect, to the three battalions he had been trained to take into combat as a

Russian colonel. He called on eight companies from the Twenty-fourth Illinois and 250 men each from the Nineteenth Illinois and the Thirty-seventh Indiana. Enough men would remain to tend to the regiments' gear, which in the rush could not be brought along, and to leave a provost guard in Huntsville. Mitchel added Edgarton's battery, a section from Loomis's battery, and five companies of Colonel John Kennett's Fourth Ohio Cavalry. Turchin's official orders, as Mitchel told him, were "to march on Athens, to attack the enemy there, and take and hold the town at all hazards."[54]

Mitchel evidently spent the entire afternoon at his impromptu command post, the Huntsville train station, an imposing new brick structure, two and a half stories tall, itself a center of attention in Huntsville. The commanding general was already notoriously angry about earlier guerilla attacks in the region. Embarking soldiers gathered into an audience. Nothing was more natural to Mitchel than flights of oratory, and in the heat of the moment he shouted out an order to "leave not a grease spot" at Athens. Apparently liking the sound of the phrase, he repeated it. Drive the Confederates into the river, he told the troops on a westbound train, annihilate them. Hearing a report that two soldiers from the Eighteenth had been killed, he announced to all present, "I will build a monument to these two men on the site of Athens. I have dealt gently long enough with those people. I will try another course now." Captain Knowlton Chandler of the Nineteenth Illinois came to the conclusion that Mitchel "intended that we should clear things out generally." The captain would have no qualms about seeing to it.[55]

Kennett's troopers and Edgarton's artillerymen headed west on the dirt road to Athens, followed by Mihalotzy's Twenty-fourth Illinois. Turchin, accompanying the Nineteenth Illinois under Scott and the Thirty-seventh Indiana under Lieutenant Colonel Ward, went by train to Madison Station, halfway to Decatur, thence to march northwest. At points en route each part of the force encountered men from Stanley's regiment. Turchin encountered the bulk of it near Madison Station, belying a cavalry scout's early report that "most of the 18th" had been taken prisoner.[56]

The stories these bedraggled volunteers had to tell were at least as lurid as Mitchel's speechifying. By many reports, the Athens townsfolk had jeered the retreating regiment. Some told of men yelling, "God damned sons of bitches." One claimed less tamely that "the women had spit on their guns." A further account had it that at Limestone Creek rebel gunfire kept two wounded soldiers from escaping the wrecked train, and that they had burned to death in the locomotive cab. The force of the tale was not diminished by the improbability that a Union eyewitness would have stayed to watch. If there was a time to recall how a soldier had felt when he had volunteered, this was the time. Vengeance could be swift. They were in the South. Captain Edgarton concluded then and there that the troops believed "Athens was to be sacked and burned on our arrival there."[57]

During the evening and early morning hours, Turchin's two columns arrived in the vicinity of Athens. The colonel stopped them a few miles short of the courthouse. There they waited for dawn, no doubt mingling to talk about Southern treachery, undoubtedly spreading and inflating the reports about the insults and injuries that had been inflicted by the people of Athens on the men of the Eighteenth Ohio the day before. Thoughts of revenge would easily have grown in many of the young men's minds as they waited for the order to fall in. They had the echoes of the old editorials from the *Tribune* to think about, the call to "burn the homes" all too plainly recalled in General Mitchel's refrain to remove every last grease spot, every trace of rebellion, no matter how minor, from the little town of Athens. Turchin gave his men but a brief respite, time enough to churn the thoughts and rumors and exaggerations, during what would have been in any event a sleepless night. They would be marching into Athens nervous and excited about the events that had called them there. Frazzled, tired, and with minds unaccommodating to reason or patience, the men of the Eighth Brigade would find it much easier to remember how they dealt with the rebels in Missouri than to recall the specifics of any order of conciliation when the sun rose on Athens, Alabama, in the early morning hours of May 2, 1862.

8
Outrage

The sacking of Athens was the most shameful affair of the war. Soldiers of Turchin's Brigade were then and there guilty of outrages unfit to be named.

—*Cincinnati Commercial,* July 17, 1862

[A]n impartial observer . . . will express his surprise, not that so much mischief was done, but so little; and that, under the circumstances, the entire town was not plundered and destroyed. . . . Now as to the outrages themselves, I unhesitatingly pronounce that they have been greatly exaggerated.

—*Cincinnati Gazette,* dispatch datelined Huntsville, July 23, 1862

Turchin's aide, Lieutenant William B. Curtis, galloped back to report that the Confederate soldiers were gone from Athens. Curtis had gone forward around 3:00 a.m., accompanying Kennett's advance—two hundred troopers and one artillery piece from Edgarton's battery. Turchin had ordered Kennett to strike hard and fast: "[I]f the town held only a cavalry force he was to attack it right-off." No need for that. Now, while Turchin's infantrymen finished their early breakfast, Kennett went in pursuit of Scott's Confederates down the Florence Road west toward the ferry across the Elk River.[1]

Turchin advanced the remaining four miles to Athens in column, Lieutenant Colonel Scott and the Nineteenth Illinois in the vanguard, just as Turchin's seniority dictated. Turchin sent Curtis to direct Mihalotzy and Edgarton to stop before entering the town proper and to stack arms on the grounds of J. W. S. Donnell's mansion, Edgarton's artillery to unlimber there and on an empty lot adjoining, the guns aimed to cover the south and west, the enemy's presumed location. Standard army doctrine called for a large reserve to be held in the rear, and Mihalotzy's men provided it. Donnell's home and front lawn sat on one of the area's two elevated points, a prominent place for a prominent residence in times of peace. War made it a proper site for artillery, and men and horses immediately began trampling the grounds under foot.[2]

Leaving Curtis to finish placing the reserve, Turchin pressed forward to the courthouse square, five blocks to the north and two blocks west across the railroad tracks, a space the size of a block, the small two-story courthouse in its center. He found that at the square's southwest corner the slope down to the town creek created a salient around the second elevated point for artillery. From it, Chandler's two pieces could be aimed west and south toward the Florence and Brown's Ferry roads. There stood Mayor Tanner's store and residence. The mayor watched as "the soldiers were breaking down the board fence in front of my yard, and the artillery men with the long knives they had commenced cutting down my peach trees . . . [and] broke down another fence on the other side exposing my whole garden." Turchin himself placed the guns. In his view, "if some damage was done to the fence of Mr. Tanner it was a military necessity." Such an action certainly fell within the definition of proper military conduct.[3]

Turchin immediately sent a divided company of his Nineteenth Illinois forward as pickets on the roads west and south and ordered the rest of the regiment to stack arms in the street on the south side of the square directly behind the artillery. The Eighteenth Ohio, the next regiment to arrive, also stacked arms before being posted in the courthouse yard. The time was perhaps 8:00 a.m. The residents of Athens began to gather and gawk. Turchin, nervously trotting about on his horse, and some of his officers ordered them to their homes, among them the snickering Bill McEnary as well as Robert Mendrum and Thomas Cox. They all appeared to resent being warned off, no matter how proper such a directive may have been if a counterattack was anticipated.[4]

Next, and also widely begrudged by the residents, came the searching of homes and stores for weapons, standard operating procedure since Huntsville if not before, no doubt accelerated at Athens by thoughts about the town's farewell to the Eighteenth Ohio and the rumors of citizens firing at the backs of the hapless Union troops. Turchin's men scattered for this duty almost immediately after stacking their arms. When Cox went home as ordered, he found that two soldiers already "had been there, and got my shotgun, and a valuable map." The brash young fellow ran the soldiers down and, oddly enough, recovered his weapon. Two other volunteers barged into the home of a thirty-eight-year-old widow, Mildred Ann Clayton, "demanding arms and I told them there were none there. One said I was a 'God damn liar.' . . . Called me a 'Goddam Bitch.'" After being threatened with a revolver, she proved the offending soldiers correct and surrendered a couple of guns hidden in the house. To that point, the behavior of the volunteers was still within legitimate bounds, even if a bit uncouth. Firearms and maps had genuine military value. However, the men then proceeded to ransack her home, perhaps justified in their minds by her initial deception, no doubt angered by the lies they had first been told. They made a mess, soiled the carpets, but took nothing other than the guns.[5]

The men of the Eighteenth Ohio had their own further reason to enter homes. Even had common sense not suggested to them that the citizenry had filched their abandoned knapsacks and gear, local slaves reported as much. So, too, did the patriotic whites, who had approached the Unionist Bingham very early in the day and "told me they had blankets and clothing belonging to Col. Stanley's [regiment], and asked me what they had better do with them. I told them to carry them to the railroad depot and inform Col. Stanley or his men on their arrival in town where they were." Thus tipped off that the locals had picked up some of their belongings, the men of Ohio began a search that rapidly degenerated into pillage, finding their missing property and more. Houses near the square were "broken open generally and goods carried away by the troops," recalled the Eighteenth's bass drummer, Joseph Arnold. "A large number of the knapsacks of my men were recovered," recalled his colonel.[6]

The stores on and near the square had opened for business before Turchin's men marched into town, a few of them at least, and now, unwillingly perhaps, they stayed open. The pretext for legitimate searches, the search for firearms, soon became superfluous. At Peck & McAllister's general store, young George Peck was in his room "upstairs looking on at the plundering . . . between 9 and 12 o'clock a.m. I saw and heard a teamster on horseback draw the attention of a crowd of soldiers to the store I was in, and they rushed over and burst in the door and stripped the store of its contents. . . . I rescued the books from the safe and went up to my room, a soldier was putting on a pair of my shoes and an officer of the 18th Ohio, they called him captain, was helping a private put on some of my clothes. I afterward saw him, he came around and told me I had better nail up my store." Locks were no protection. At Madison Thompson's establishment, Thompson later found, "the back door was broken open. . . . The front door had been unlocked from the inside. Nearly all my stock of dry goods and groceries was gone, worth about three thousand dollars."[7]

From Thompson's and other stores, increasing numbers of soldiers were seen emerging with dry goods and shoes, carrying the merchandise mostly to the Eighteenth Ohio's post in the courthouse yard. With a bit of hyperbole the Thirty-seventh Indiana's historian recalled, "The sidewalks of the town were almost covered with dry goods." Not to say that the soldiers neglected to go for an obvious prize, the store safes. At Peck & McAllister's, Peck remembered, "The iron safe was broken open in my presence with about a half dozen sledge hammers and axes. Three different parties worked at it. . . . A Lieutenant waited on this until he got bored." The safecrackers took $240 in Confederate currency and, worth even less, $4,000 in promissory notes. At Peterson Tanner & Sons, a store owned by the mayor's older brother, the strongbox yielded $2,000 in funds held as deposits (Athens had no bank) and as much as $25,000 in notes. Evidently realizing it would be pointless to try to collect from the signers, the troops later returned most of the notes.[8]

The soldiers next found a target to attack even less sensibly and with almost unaccountable wantonness—books. The behavior fits, though, a curious pattern and practice of men set loose among enemy civilians. Witness the affair of the Four Towns Book Club in Doagh, County Antrim, sacked by an English yeoman regiment, June 1798: "The books were trampled underfoot or torn asunder, . . . the globes broken to atoms. . . . A soldier, unable to destroy in an instant a volume of 'Gibbons' decline and fall of the Roman empire', proceeded to kick it down the stairs leading from the club room to the street." Witness the affair when Sherman's march reached the Georgia state library in the capital at Milledgeville in November 1864: a Union soldier rode his horse through piles of books thrown out on the wet ground (but an Illinois college graduate, First Lieutenant Alfred Trego, thought to rescue a classical dictionary and a volume of Macauley's essays for his own use). Witness William Gilmore Simms's 10,000-volume library, burned at his Woodlands estate in South Carolina by stragglers from the same army in February 1865. Pages bearing the novelist's bookplate were found in the gutters of Columbia days later.[9]

So it was at Athens that morning. Breaking into Richard Davis's post office, residence, and store, Union soldiers took $1,000 in cash and removed all the bedclothes except the featherbed. They also trampled and tore as much of his inventory of two hundred Bibles as they did not care to steal. At the library belonging to the scholarly physician J. F. Sowell, soldiers stole some of his books, destroyed others, and scattered the remaining volumes on the floor. The senior member of the local bar, William Richardson, had his library ransacked. One soldier went about town trying in vain to peddle one of his treatises.[10]

All this profitless bibliophobia was a handy sort of revenge against Southern aristocracy and learning, expressed rather less thoughtfully than Lieutenant Adams's sentiments in the ruined library at Beaufort. Passing Simms's library a few days before it was ransacked and set afire, Oliver Otis Howard's thoroughly literate and usually humane artillery chief, Colonel Thomas W. Osborne, reflected, "I think it will be saved. I should have no objection to seeing it burned. His influence has been very great in carrying on the war."[11] Perhaps also, though, the tearing and burning and waste of hostile civilians' books was a way of reaffirming that by rebellion, by attempting to opt out of the great American experiment with democracy, the rebels had made an inexcusable threat to the very being and meaning of the United States, which even the most coarse, common soldier would punish accordingly.

Turchin himself was in the square when the pillaging began, riding about on horseback, giving orders, sitting on the front steps on the courthouse's north side, awaiting reports, at least until Lieutenant Curtis arrived from positioning the reserve. Turchin then gave Stanley permission to use squads led by commissioned officers to search homes for knapsacks—by this time a retroactive authority. After that he left with Curtis to inspect Stanley's former regimental camp at the fairgrounds and to survey other possible campsites and posts for the brigade, tasks that took as long as an hour.[12]

By the time they returned to the square, no one could have failed to notice the goings-on. This was, after all, a town of but seven hundred souls. The sight of men carrying their plunder, their shouts of discovery and encouragement, no doubt accompanied by the clang of safecrackers hard at work in Peck & McAllister's store, would have been impossible to miss, even for officers whose thoughts may have been fully occupied preparing for the possibility of a counterattack. "The noise of knocking open some of the doors was very great," Thomas Cox added, but Lieutenant Chandler thought that "it was the movement of the things about the street that drew more attention [than] the noise." The movement conspicuously included volunteers appearing "with citizens' clothing, caps, hats, &c. such as would naturally come from stores."[13] According to a Thirty-seventh Indiana soldier's anonymous account, at Athens that morning one man from the Nineteenth Illinois obviously took the cake. He "had dressed himself in a fine pair of cloth pants, a vest and boots, and a striped pigeon-tailed coat far too big for him at the shoulders, but too short, the tails of the coat coming only to his waist. He also wore a silk stove pipe hat, around which he had wrapped one end of a richly-colored ribbon . . . streaming out behind him as he swaggered, or staggered, up the street singing, 'The girl I left behind me.'"[14]

Turchin ostensibly paid no attention to this sideshow. He cannot but have seen some of it, and Stanley was later quoted as remarking after the fact "that it would not have been so bad if they had taken only what they needed, or words to that effect." Certainly the troops thought they had their commander's sanction. "Colonel Turchin allowed us to take our revenge, which we were not slow in doing, although it was not his orders, still he winked at our proceedings." Much was later made of the idea that Turchin, a European soldier, had sanctioned a supposed European custom of allowing his troops the freedom to loot the town because it had, if only the day before, resisted conquest.[15] Turchin never acknowledged any such an intention. No witness to any such order by him at Athens ever stepped forward. No one, however, could avoid the obvious inference that he "winked at" the proceedings that morning to give his men a chance to vent their anger and excitement. That alone, in many professional soldiers' eyes, would be sufficient to condemn the colonel.

Turchin had, however, other, more pressing matters to tend to. Shortly after his arrival back at the square, he received two messages in quick succession from Kennett: first, "the woods were swarming with cavalry"; second, the enemy had dug in near the Elk River and an assault by the Ohio cavalry had failed, taking casualties. Kennett wanted reinforcements. Turchin sent a detachment of the Eighteenth Ohio. One hundred and fifty men under Lieutenant Colonel Givens trundled off in the regiment's wagons. He ordered Lieutenant Chandler to go along with one of his guns. That crisis addressed, Turchin appointed Stanley the town's provost marshal, made a provost guard of the Eighteenth Ohio's men who were staying behind, and issued orders to clear the streets and keep the troops in place. It was now about noon. Pressing business finished, Turchin and Curtis went for dinner to the town's hotel, J. B. Davidson's, on the east side of the square toward the railroad station.[16]

Turchin's decision to send the Eighteenth Ohio to the aid of the cavalry was deliberate. "I knew the officers and men were anxious to cast off the suspicion cast upon them of having shown the white feather when they were driven out of town by the enemy."[17] This deployment left untouched his three stronger regiments, and it cleared many of Stanley's vengeful troops and some of the misbehaving artillerymen from the square. However, that same decision left Stanley understaffed to post an effective provost guard, and the men of the Eighteenth Ohio had the least motivation of any present to preserve order and keep the peace.

As the afternoon wore on, marauding soldiers roamed to more and more homes around town. Four and a half blocks from the square, at the residence of the two widows Malone, a visitor the next day found everything "torn to pieces. I found preserve jars about, open—the house smeared with their contents, the dining room especially and the carpets. . . . I noticed a fine large trunk smashed in." Soldiers of the Thirty-seventh Indiana and Twenty-fourth Illinois made their way to the center of town to join in the excitement. To the list of stores plundered there, D. H. Bingham would add Samuel Tanner's shoe shop, John Tunentine's store, John Danforth's, and (likely sources of demon alcohol) Dr. Malone's drugstore and Allen's drugstore, "the floor covered over with medicine bottles and all the contents of the store . . . to the depth of about two feet."[18]

Stanley was all but powerless. "Stanley called up his regiment and told them to stop it," one of his soldiers observed. "The pillaging went on by the rest of the troops and by this time he could not stop it." Turchin ordered Stanley to send patrols about the town. He sent only three, "using nearly every available man I had left during the remainder of that day."[19] The sentinels posted at Bingham's home stayed only "two minutes" before they were called away for the Elk River expedition. Stanley kept trying to furnish guards "when requested," and two were posted in front of Mason's store, two more at Hope's drugstore, and both establishments went unharmed. Madison Thompson's store fared less well, but when bothered by a party of men "drinking and threatening in the yard of my house" Thompson succeeded in having them arrested by Lieutenant Quentin of the Nineteenth Illinois. Thomas Cox solved his own domestic security problem by meeting Captain William Edmiston of the Eighteenth Ohio in the square and bringing him home to dinner. Later Cox would testify that "while there he drove soldiers out of my house."[20]

Turchin himself, after a postdinner rest at Davidson's, embarked sometime between 1:00 and 2:00 on military duties, making a reconnaissance of the roads and fields outside the town. "His invariable custom was as soon as he got into camp to reconnoiter the whole country in the vicinity," as the Nineteenth's adjutant, Lieutenant Chauncey Miller, had noted. He thus missed the afternoon rampages, perhaps thinking that, if Stanley could be entrusted with Bowling Green and if men of the Thirty-seventh Indiana were adequate to keep the peace at Huntsville, then the brigade could handle Athens while he attended to his own military duties.[21]

There was ample and obvious military need for reconnaissance. Turchin knew that Kennett, his Ohio cavalrymen, and now some Ohio infantrymen were in a firefight with Scott's Louisianans to the west, the outcome unknown. In fact, that fight continued as Turchin scouted Athens's more immediate environs. With Kennett's first charge repulsed, the Confederates had bought time to draw back to the ferry across the Elk. When the reinforced Kennett advanced again, half the rebels were across the stream, carrying with them a good deal of the Eighteenth Ohio's stolen camp equipage. Kennett's second charge was met "by our boys with a yell and a perfect sheet of bullets and buckshot," as the *Charleston Mercury* told the story. Then the Union artillery went into action, according to the *Cleveland Plain Dealer*, and with three shells sank a flatboat nearing the farther shore, forcing another boat just leaving the eastern shore back with twenty-three surrendering Confederates. Unbeknownst to Turchin, the bulk of Scott's rebels turned to cross the Tennessee six miles to the south, which they did at their leisure.[22]

Turchin also had reason to think other rebel cavalry units and bushwhacker gangs were operating in the general vicinity. In fact, that Thursday and Friday at Pulaski, Tennessee, a day's ride up the railroad, Confederate cavalry under the fabled "aristocratic knight of the Bluegrass," Colonel John Hunt Morgan, scored a great coup. With 1,500 cavalrymen, by one greatly exaggerated Union estimate (more likely about 400), using another of his clever ruses, Morgan had rounded up, detachment by detachment, altogether 15 union officers and 368 enlisted men, including Lieutenant Edward M. Mitchel, General Mitchel's son, along with Captain John F. Jumper of the Eighteenth Ohio's Company F and at least four members of its Company I.[23]

In the evening Turchin and Kennett arrived back at Davidson's Hotel, Kennett bringing with him twelve men wounded during the day's fighting. Caring for them required the requisitioning of bedrooms, beds, and bedclothes, further disrupting the daily lives and routines of Athens's residents. The detachment of the Eighteenth Ohio sent to Kennett's aid spent the night in the field. Turchin set about repositioning the bivouac sites of the other regiments in town.[24] That change must have ended the pillaging for Friday, if exhaustion and satiety had not already done so, but it led to new problems in the days to come.

It would be too easy to say that Turchin's troops omitted to burn Athens because they needed its buildings for shelter. True enough, they had brought no tents and little camp gear on the hurried march from Huntsville. And notwithstanding the distant harsh words from the *Chicago Tribune* and the recent angry exhortations by General Mitchel, no home or other structure was destroyed, not on May 2, not during the three weeks the Eighth Brigade remained in town. The extent to which Turchin's men vented their frustration was in fact remarkably limited. They took—stole—numerous personal items for which they had no need. They made a mess of a number of stores and homes. But they never seized civilians who might reasonably have been suspected of being rebel sympathizers. They burned no buildings, took no prisoners, although they did wait outside the home of James B. Hollingsworth's ailing wife, hoping the new rebel volunteer would return to her side. Athens was not made a grease spot.

Events might as easily have gone more harshly. On April 13, while proceeding toward Tuscumbia, Turchin's own soldiers had "burnt a house most splendidly furnished that belonged to a man who burnt one of the bridges."[25] As will be discussed in more detail later, also on May 2 civilian bushwhackers had stopped the train carrying the Third Ohio while it rushed to reinforce Huntsville, firing into the cars and wounding two soldiers. "We proposed to hold the citizens responsible for these cowardly assaults," decided the commanding officer, and "to make them more uncomfortable than they should be in hell." At a nearby hamlet, Paint Rock, "in a few minutes a dense column of smoke, rolling up high into the air, from the buildings which he had ordered to be fired, announced to the people of the surrounding country what they might expect if they persisted in this dastardly warfare." The village burned "to ashes." Such acts of direct reprisal had justification. The taunts of the citizens of Athens did not rise to that level.[26]

At Athens, as the town settled into darkness, the worst new incidents were merely the irritants to be expected from troops forced to quarter themselves either without shelter or in civilian lodgings. Turchin and his aide found rooms arranged for them at Davidson's Hotel. The commander's mounted escort had not yet arrived from Huntsville. Other troops were at hand to freeload, and in less than a week, the bill at the hotel ran to $140, even though Curtis was contributing provisions from commissary stores. Turchin, who preferred the comfort of his own tent, to which he soon moved, later claimed ignorance of the amount due the innkeeper. Likely he was naïve about the costs incurred. Free board and lodging were the perquisites of a traveling senior officer in the Russian army.[27]

His disposition of troops for that and the next few nights rounded their formation in a shallow bulge toward the enemy threat from west and south. The Thirty-seventh Indiana took position on the right, at the fairgrounds north of the courthouse square, without shelter. Happily, rain was scant for the next two weeks. Until a brigade officer noticed, the men amused themselves running requisitioned mounts on the racetrack. At the center of town, the Eighteenth Ohio stood post near the courthouse and its yard. Some companies in the Nineteenth Illinois were quartered in vacant houses around the square. Two others, an advance post, went forward to the Coleman residence grounds on a low hill overlooking the Brown's Ferry Road.[28]

Edgarton's battery and Mihalotzy's Twenty-fourth Illinois remained stationed on the left, to the east at the substantial residences of J. Haywood Jones and J. W. S. Donnell. There, off to the side, the greatest problems arose. Some artillerymen took lodging under their own gun carriages, some in slave huts, but Edgarton and his officers took over part of Jones's house, "a first-class residence," then only slightly used since the mansion was not yet finished. The occupation was amicable at the start. Jones provided Edgarton with dinner the first evening, and Edgarton helped Jones lock all his valuables in an upstairs room. The relationship soured, however, when the room came unlocked and silver went missing, to the embarrassment of Mihalotzy, who also quartered himself and some of his men in the Jones parlor. With a search of the men, Mihalotzy recovered some of the silver.[29]

The rest of the regiment camped half a block away on the Donnell estate, a "magnificent" property that included detached offices, slave quarters, stables, and a ten-pin bowling alley. An unblushing complainer, Donnell thought "the worst inconvenience we had for several days, besides the annoyance of the soldiers around the negro huts and kitchen, was their taking the oil cloth covers to my buggies to protect them from the rain and the cushions of the buggies to sleep in." He also lost some children's clothes and a box of silver stored, foolishly as it turned out, in a servant's house taken over by the regimental band.[30]

Lesser citizens suffered more amid random misconduct that continued through Sunday, May 4, and beyond. Food was the soldiers' target of choice—ridiculous quantities of it—eight barrels of molasses, for example, taken from John Malone's house by a squad of drunks. Mayor Tanner's boardinghouse behind his general store faced a stream of men demanding free meals. Donnell found his poultry missing and his cows milked. Army provisions arrived early and regularly from Huntsville, but an officer there remarked, "Our boys find Alabama ham better than hard crackers." Writing from Athens on May 15, a soldier told readers of the *Cincinnati Commercial:* "Whatever fresh meat appears upon the table, the eater philosophically resolves that if his cook has violated the scriptural injunction, 'Thou shalt not steal,' he will not magnify the offence by violating another, but will 'eat what is set before him, *asking no questions.*'"[31]

Colonel Carter Gazlay, Adjutant Chauncey Miller, the rest of the brigade's troops, and all of its baggage train arrived the evening of May 6. Nadine Turchin arrived, too, but not to stay in the hotel. The couple moved immediately to the colonel's headquarters tent, pitched on Donnell's grounds— "nearly in the midst of my lawn about sixty yards from, and in view of my premises." As he had resolved while in Missouri, Turchin continued to refrain from sleeping in a Southerner's house.[32]

Thereafter the harshest impositions on the townsfolk affected slaves and horses. In both cases, Turchin acted under explicit orders. On Saturday morning, May 3, he received a note from Mitchel ordering him to "[i]nduce the negroes to bring you information [from along the river west toward Florence], and to have it conveyed from plantation to plantation, by promising them protection within our lines for any real valuable service." Only one man was actually deployed on this project—"Mrs. Vasser's boy Joe." "He was sent at one time to Pulaski, twice to Brown's Ferry, several times to Lucas Ferry, and several times to ferries on Elk River, and once to Florence, but he did not get there." He learned nothing. The "grapevine telegraph" proved a total failure. Joe, however, won his freedom; he left with Turchin's troops at the end of their stay.[33]

Union employment of slaves, with an aim to allowing them to earn their freedom, was hardly conciliatory. Impressments of horses might not have been as hot a political issue, but it rubbed local citizens nearly as hard. With Kennett's cavalry gone, Turchin received the orders on Monday, May 5. His raiders could ride again. "You are authorized to press horses, and to mount your best riders among the infantry as scouts." He grasped the order enthusiastically. He called on each regiment to produce twenty-five riders (in the event, the Thirty-seventh Indiana had not so many), and from town and plantation as far as fourteen miles away they gathered 104 horses. (Owners would later claim 200 to 300.) Vouchers were given when requested. Through Bingham's good offices, some needy owners were able to retrieve their animals. Training infantry on horseback led to more complaints. The new cavalrymen knocked down the fence at Robert Davis's farm, "letting the cattle on it for 3 weeks." Robert Mendrum saw another field trampled, ruining "a crop of corn that was 3 or 4 inches high."[34]

Farmers may have chafed at the loss of horses and the spring planting. Certainly, no resident could have been amused to see Nadine Turchin cavorting through the fields on a riding pony "borrowed" from an Athens lady, a sight remarked on as far away as Huntsville.[35] But at bottom the Union command had a sound claim to military necessity. Men of all ranks in the brigade must have shared a bit of the dread Private John Vreeland felt when he wrote home May 17: "For the last ten days we have had a force of 4 or 5000 of the enemies cavalry hovering around us, but as yet have had no Collision." The numbers were elevated, but the threat was real. On May 8, the First Kentucky Cavalry and 120 Texas Rangers, all under Kentucky's Colonel Tom Woodward, fell on Company E of the Thirty-seventh Indiana, guarding a railroad trestle at Elkins, just a few miles from Athens. They killed five Union soldiers (whose bodies arrived back in Athens draped on a handcar) and captured a large number of others.[36] Ten days later a detachment of the Third Ohio sent north of Athens to Winchester, Tennessee, "passed through a region most thickly infested with the most daring raids of guerrillas, and at Winchester had an encounter with some of [Brigadier General John] Adams's regular [rebel] cavalry, who, after making a rash charge into the town while we occupied it and losing a few men, retreated eastward to the mountains."[37]

For all this excitement, while penned up in and around Athens the rougher members of the Eighth Brigade still continued with their petty crimes. William McEnary had nailed shut his harness shop windows on May 2, but a few days later found several men inside, "taking away tack and buckles, pieces of webbing, tools, parts of harness mounting. They had them in a sack and when I entered the door ran to the back door and tried to get out"—the scene the same as at a million other botched burglaries. Bingham himself lost a gold watch, a revolver, some of his wife's jewelry, none recovered, even after the knapsacks of the Twenty-fourth Illinois were searched. In response to thievery and other crimes, Provost Marshal Stanley "had a great many men in jail at Athens, and I sent a great many men to jail at Huntsville, and they were mostly returned, some with the same guard I sent with them."[38]

Law enforcement could never be simple in these circumstances. When bass drummer Joseph Arnold of the Eighteenth Ohio, posted to guard the home of one Little (or one Butler, depending on the account), found a silver platter (or pitcher) in "an old ice house," he reported it to Stanley (or so he claimed) and turned it over on written orders (lost) to a purported member of Turchin's escort. Again depending on the account, the object appears to have become confused with a cheap piece of silver plate "purchased" by the Nineteenth Illinois's drum major but placed in the brigade quartermaster's custody. Citizens complained and officers noticed, but as the war moved on, the booty, whatever it may have been, vanished.[39]

Despite all of the fierce rhetoric that preceded the entry of Turchin and his men into Athens, only one serious crime against the person was reported, and it was treated with all the diligence it would have gotten in a peacetime garrison. On Saturday, May 3, a small squad from the Thirty-seventh Indiana, foraging seven miles southeast of town, came upon the home of the widow Charlotte Haines. There, in the plantation's kitchen, one of the Indianans ordered a young servant girl named Mammy to put down the infant in her arms and proceeded to rape her while Mrs. Haines watched. Coming to Athens a few days later to complain about the outrage, the mistress identified one Private Ayer Bowers as the rapist. Turchin, over Gazlay's objection, immediately ordered the man's arrest and placement in the stockade of the Nineteenth Illinois. Gazlay argued that the accused should be held in his own regiment's friendlier embrace, and in any event that he should not be prosecuted solely on a slave's testimony about consent. If, after all, slave testimony wasn't sufficient to try traitors, how could it be used against government soldiers? At that place and time that was a legitimate, if thorny, legal point. Adjutant Miller questioned the girl, inquired after "white witnesses," and remanded Bowers to the provost marshal at Huntsville. Two weeks later Bowers presented himself at Gazlay's headquarters tent in Fayetteville, "said he had been turned out of Huntsville jail and ordered to join his regt."[40]

Turchin's brigade stayed in and around Athens until May 26 and then headed back to Fayetteville, Tennessee, thence to spend the first fortnight in June on another of Mitchel's projects, General James Negley's roundabout and inadequate assault on the Confederate position at Chattanooga. The soldiers left behind a town whose citizens had been robbed, insulted, inconvenienced and, to a degree, terrorized. If any people in the South had just cause to resent the presence of the avenging angels of the United States, certainly the people of Athens now did. In what had been undoubtedly hostile surroundings, the soldiers could have, and did, exercise physical power in uncouth ways, much like some of them had done before in Missouri. But when compared with the behavior that the rhetoric of the times had called for, had they not acted with great restraint? There had been no wholesale destruction of buildings, public or private. The courthouse still stood. Its records were intact. The homes of Athens may have been made a mess, but they still provided comfortable shelter for the residents who remained in town. Only one assault had been reported, and when challenged the wayward Union soldiers had usually scattered and run rather than confront or harm their accusers, which they could have easily done.

These events were not the scene that might have been expected of Turchin's volunteers when they entered Athens the morning of May 2. They had spent five weeks marching about exposed in hostile territory. They had discovered a civilian population more often than not openly bitter about their presence—people who sneered at them by daylight and who stalked them in the dark of night. Sent to Athens with General Mitchel's express orders and exhortations to make the place a wasteland, they had indeed taken a measure of revenge. After the tension of a night's march, spiced by tales of rebel outrages, and then entering the town to find no armed enemy, they must have experienced enough nervous excitement to offset their exhaustion. Whether their brigade commander expressly agreed to allow them to "have a little fun," or whether discipline had simply collapsed, much more damage than the ransacking of stores could have occurred. Whether extreme or not, restrained or not, understandable or not, one thing was certain. The events of those early days in May in no way conformed to the sorts of actions envisioned by General Buell in his General Order 13a or to the overall conciliatory policy of the Lincoln administration.

The wonder was, as reporters noted later, that more damage was not done, that the town had not become a scene of unspeakable outrage. The soldiers—most of them—had moderated their behavior to live for a time among people who in many ways proved to be very like the neighbors they knew at home in the North. The men did little permanent damage. Fields were trampled, but there was no scorched earth. No townspeople died. None were injured or maimed save the slave girl, whose assault had been promptly addressed. Homes and fields did not suffer the torch. No townspeople complained about a shortage of provisions or the threat of starvation. No one saw in the Athens of May 1862 any evidence of "the introduction of grave new acts such as the poisoning of wells, maiming of livestock, widespread desecrations."[41]

When the Eighth Brigade quietly marched out of town and turned Athens over to the successor garrison, a single regiment, the Twenty-first Ohio, the evil or merit in what the brigade had done stood to a great degree in the eye of the beholder. To those who thought the hearts and minds of the residents of the Confederacy could easily be reattached to the Union, the events at Athens were heinous and self-defeating. To those who thought that Southerners should get a taste of retribution for bringing on the conflict, the disruptions at Athens appeared not only just but perhaps too mild. For the Southerners who saw the people of the North as an uncouth mob, they had their proof of the fact, as did the army officers who feared the undisciplined nature of volunteers. For the volunteers who had been frustrated by months of camp living, they had finally gotten to act out some of the fantasies that had brought them to the enlistment offices.

Into this otherwise innocuous bed of uncertainty one gentleman laid the spark of scandal. Other towns silently suffered subjugation by Union troops during the late spring and early summer of 1862. Occupied Murfreesboro, Winchester, Fayetteville (known to the soldiers as "one of the meanest secession holes in Tennessee") cannot have been pleasant places for the inhabitants. When the army reclaimed Pulaski from John Hunt Morgan, also on May 2, a "reign of terror prevailed for three days" at least the equal in description of that at Athens at the same time, yet events at Pulaski were little noticed then and have barely escaped oblivion since.[42]

Athens, however, had its native son, United States District Judge George W. Lane. Even as the town was being plundered, Lane began trying to serve two masters. On May 3, the *Mobile Evening News* took snide notice of a rumor that he might be appointed military governor of Alabama. "He will have to . . . have a powerful and trusty bodyguard to watch over the safety of his regal person." Lane must have winced sharply again a few days later when prominent Huntsville citizens—the elderly former governor, Clement Comer Clay, for example—were grilled in public about the low crimes of bushwhacking and bridge burning before an "Examining Board of Commissioners," composed of a supercilious Union major and two captains.[43] But Lane was at heart a Unionist, and besides he wanted the adornment and pay due his federal position.

He tried to resolve the conflict by serving both sides as a self-appointed mediator of the troubles at Athens. On May 7 he jumped onto reasonably tenable ground, appearing before Turchin with a citizens' delegation to protest against an oath of allegiance Mitchel had printed and sent up from Huntsville on, of all dates, May 2. Much of the oath was offensive if not legally objectionable ("we will not only duly abstain from any act of hostility, but will do our utmost to persuade other citizens to do the same, . . . we will give information of intended attacks to the Federal Officers").[44] By complaining about this sort of thing, Lane did not compromise his Union position, nor did he diminish his local stature.

Whatever Turchin said or did at the meeting about this matter—the loyalty oath issue appears to have been deferred for a full month—Lane and his citizens' committee were emboldened to go further, to turn to a more concrete subject, the outrages committed by Turchin's soldiers. They had no need to ask Mitchel or Turchin for formal orders forbidding depredations: Mitchel had already issued such paperwork on May 3, 5, and 7, contradicting his own oratorical rants on May 1, and on each occasion Turchin had promptly followed suit. Instead, after meeting with Mitchel in Athens, they sought money damages, drawing up a detailed bill of particulars. Under the judge's guidance, the delegates listed the injuries suffered by no fewer than forty-five residents. Collectively, they claimed $54,689.80 as restitution for the damages done by the visiting Yankees.[45]

Lane did not sign this petition—he had no claim of his own—but he cleverly moved it forward. At his estate near Huntsville on Saturday evening, May 17, he hosted a "strawberry supper" for General Mitchel, officers of his staff and command, and local luminaries, including Limestone County's notable George Smith Houston. Mitchel took center stage, talking about how he would have "knocked the Confederates to pieces" already, given free rein. "The evening was a very pleasant one," recorded a military guest.[46]

The social affair failed to secure approval for the Athens claims. The general was pleased to partake of a fancy country feast, even more to have an audience for his boasts. He had been deeply disturbed by details of thefts. He went so far as to order that enlisted men's baggage be searched. But he believed he had no authority whatever to pay civilian claims with federal funds. Nor, evidently, did he want to try. "I sincerely hope," he answered the claimants, "that no remarks of mine could have led you to imagine that the Government of the United States would pay individuals for robberies suffered at the hands of individuals, actions not only without orders, but contrary to the most positive and repeated orders."[47]

And yet Mitchel left Lane with the door ajar by asking the citizens for "a finished report" with which he could "convict before a court-martial those guilty of robbery and pillage." The wantonness in the Eighth Brigade's behavior, as the experienced trial judge must have conceived, could fairly be shown alongside the resulting costs, a complementary picture inviting compensation. The project was in preparation before Turchin and the brigade left town.

The assignment found ample support from the new garrison commander, Lieutenant Colonel Jesse S. Norton. Norton served as living proof that if placed in the right hands, volunteer soldiers could both garrison a town and act in a conciliatory manner toward the inhabitants. Norton had already built a sturdy reputation during the relatively short time his regiment, the Twenty-first Ohio, had been in the South. So pleased were the citizens of Huntsville with the conduct of his men, and with him as their provost marshal, that hundreds of them signed a petition to keep him in that office. Norton had every intention of carrying out the provisions of General Order 13a to their fullest extent. He kept his men off the streets and made certain they did nothing to interfere with any of the business of the community, including the return of runaway slaves. He moved from Huntsville to Athens. Reportedly fostering an abiding hatred of Mitchel, Norton quartered at an estate outside town and "bent his attention to forming the acquaintance of the planters, and the prominent men of the country," as his Twenty-first Ohio's disapproving historian remembered. The local citizens, however, heartily approved. "He certainly has his Regt. under better control than the others, who have been here; you rarely see any of them in the streets," one local recorded. Norton earned even more respect when he stepped forward to help Judge Lane pursue their claims.[48] No matter how well supported or by whom, the cause and complaints of the citizens of Athens never would have placed their little community near the center of a debate over national policy, however ably prepared and pressed by Judge Lane. For that to happen, Colonel John Basil Turchin himself would have to be thrust into greater prominence.

9
The Nomination

The time of the Senate has been chiefly occupied of late in Executive Session on the perennial shower of new Brigadiers. . . . The rank of Brigadier has almost ceased to be a mark of distinction, and if we go on at the present rate, we shall soon have enough officers of that grade to take Richmond without the aid of any privates.
—*Chicago Tribune,* May 2, 1862

Illinois governor Richard Yates visited the nation's capital from June 14 through June 21, 1862, accompanied by John Wood, his state's quartermaster general. Staying at the National Hotel, they spent time with their senators, Lyman Trumbull and Orville Hickman Browning, and gained an audience with the secretary of war, Edwin Stanton. The main objective of their trip was routine but important. They came in search of money, federal money, to reimburse the state for funds spent recruiting troops. Then, too, Governor Yates had another pet enthusiasm: putting stars on the shoulders of senior military officers from Illinois. As it happened, western Virginia's Francis Harrison Pierpont was also in Washington on Friday, June 20. Pierpont served as the Unionist governor of West Virginia, a state recently proclaimed by its citizens but not yet admitted by Congress. Pierpont's mission paralleled that of Governor Yates.[1]

Yates, the Republican governor of the fastest-growing state in the West, had real clout, even with Secretary Stanton. Pierpont, no less influential as a loyalist governor of at least a portion of a seceded state, had earlier gotten the irascible secretary overridden on military matters. Thus, there was little surprise that day when the honorable secretary of war dictated, signed, and forwarded to the president a document, which the president forthwith sent to the Senate, containing the nominations of Joseph Andrew Jackson Lightburn of western Virginia and John Basil Turchin of Illinois to be brigadier generals of United States Volunteers.[2]

There is no reason to think that Stanton forwarded these names in order to make a point about the government's war policy. Pierpont had been obliged to shield his citizens from depredations by Union troops as well as from rebel-sympathizing bushwhackers. Lightburn, for his part, had been a diligent regimental commander in his home territory, where it had been far easier to raise troops loyal to the government than it had been for rebels to organize.[3] The abolitionist secretary was the bloodiest-minded member of the cabinet, accepting his post only "if no other pledge than to throttle treason shall be exacted." A lawyer with no military experience, he held to views of war quite as lurid as anything in the textbooks of his boyhood.[4] Turchin's nomination resembled Lightburn's in that he was the best his sponsors had to offer at the moment. Strategic policy considerations regarding such appointments, if they were to arise at all, would only come later, if and when the nominations required action.

No one could have expected on June 20, 1862, that the Turchin and Lightburn nominations would come to anything. Weeks earlier, orators in the Senate chamber had tried to call attention to the fact that serving brigadiers were already overabundant, and a move had been started to limit the number of promotions. Typically, the upper house then proceeded to approve a further raft of them. As a result, few places now appeared open. (Lightburn, in fact, did not receive his star until March 1863.)[5] In the summer of 1862, his and Turchin's nominations were a matched pair of political accommodations, forwarded to the bottom of a deep and thickening pile.

In the American army before the Civil War, as one thorough study has it, "promotion was an all engrossing preoccupation among the increasingly career-minded officers." Political influence in Washington carried no slight weight, particularly when an officer sought to make the great leap up from colonel to brigadier.[6] The war provided a bonanza of opportunity for aspiring officers, whether veteran Regulars or new volunteers. It was no less a bonanza for politicians, men who, when advancing the right constituents, might accumulate political chits and enhance their own and their faction's prestige by the number and quality of their military protégés. Even the president, holding the power to nominate, found himself with a valuable fund of influence among officers' political sponsors.

Through 1861 and on into the summer of 1862, governors, senators, and congressmen all carried on an unabashed campaign of political patronage, not necessarily disadvantageous or discrediting to the military service. The act of June 25, 1861, calling for half a million federal volunteers more fuzzily allowed the president, with the Senate's advice and consent, to appoint "such number of major-generals and of brigadier-generals as may in his judgment be required for their organization." Lincoln's political savvy led him at once to send word to each state's congressional delegation soliciting names. When the War Department issued the resulting list of new brigadiers on August 3 to a swarm of colonels waiting outside the adjutant general's office in Washington, one of them, crusty Samuel P. Heintzelman, West Point class of 1826, hearing his own and some of his comrades' names, incredulously exclaimed, "By —— ——, it's all a lie! Every mother's son of you will be cashiered." In fact, most of the list was respectable. The Ohio caucus yielded stars for William Tecumseh Sherman, West Point 1840, and Alexander McDowell McCook, class of 1856, though also for Robert Cumming Schenck, a former Whig congressman, avid Lincoln supporter and, much later in life, renowned authority on draw poker.[7]

The political machinery more often than not continued to promote men with actual military experience, mainly because of the influence of Senator Henry Wilson of Massachusetts, chairman of the Committee on Military Affairs and the Militia. Every nomination had to cross his desk. A firm friend of the Regular Army and prone to heed its recommendations, Wilson could advance a particular nomination or delay it, but he could not of his own power kill it. Thus, in early March 1862, a request from Major General Henry Halleck led to a motion to confirm made by Wilson himself that propelled Regular Colonel Edward R. S. Canby to a brigadier's slot in only nine days.[8] On the other hand, Chairman Wilson, an ardent teetotaler, could as easily throw barricades across the route. When career officer William Farrar Smith's name came up in December 1861, he appeared well qualified. However, Wilson suspected Smith of being a tippler. The chairman's position was clear: "I have recommended no man who is guilty of intemperance; and I do not intend to do it." Nor did he, thus stalling Smith's confirmation for more than seven months.[9]

Other powerful senators could sometimes organize an end run. When Wilson's committee failed or refused to report on the nomination of Erastus B. Tyler, an Ohio fur trader of indifferent military ability but a popular figure in his part of the state, Ohio's senator Benjamin Wade forced the committee to disgorge it, and his wealthy constituent was confirmed the very same day, May 14, 1862. Similarly, Attorney General Edward Bates quickly pushed through the nomination of volunteer colonel James Henry Van Alen, whose main claim for patronage arose from the fact that he had been sufficiently wealthy to personally equip the New York cavalry regiment he stood in front of. Bates went directly to the president to intercede on Van Alen's behalf.

Word immediately went from the White House to Capitol Hill to get it done.[10]

Politicians who sought advancement for men from their states usually had no reason to discount military education and experience, it being always best in any political horse race to back a likely winner. Combined with Wilson's predilections, this wisdom usually tilted the balance of brigadier's openings to real soldiers. At the end of December 1861 Wilson could boast, responding to the outcry against West Point, that of the 110 brigadiers confirmed to that time, 75 were either academy graduates or veterans of American combat service, and half the rest had attended state or foreign military schools. On May 7, 1862, after several spates of further promotions had pushed the total to 167 serving brigadiers, Wilson still could tell the *New York Times* with some understatement nearly the same thing—"a majority are trained military men from the army."[11]

Promotion was an accomplishment sometimes hard-won. Marsena Patrick of upstate New York was a logical candidate for general officer: West Point class of 1835, fifteen years of active service, including the Seminole and Mexican wars. At the Civil War's outbreak, he left a college presidency to become a brigadier and inspector general in New York's state militia. In March 1862, in Washington and renewing his Regular Army acquaintances, he got himself detailed to McClellan's staff as New York's liaison officer. He then sought a federal commission with the acquiescence of Governor Edwin Morgan and the clear and active support of Senator Ira Harris, another Republican and a noted purveyor of military patronage for upstate constituents. Patrick's diary for the month rather pettishly records the moves in their campaign. On March 10 Harris warned of a fight, as "New York has had more than her share of Generals." The next day Patrick was advised to visit Senator Wilson. "I did so & was disgusted with him." On March 13 pressure from McClellan's staff finally started Patrick's ball rolling. During the evening on March 17, Wilson personally advised Patrick of his confirmation.[12]

In the atmosphere prevailing in Washington, Governor Yates's advancement of Turchin did not stand out in the flurry of activity, no more than Pierpont's of Lightburn or that of Maine's governor, Isaac Washburn, Jr., when in April he had proposed the name of John Curtis Caldwell, the schoolmaster-colonel of the Eleventh Maine. With much the same political right as senators and cabinet members, governors did that.[13] Yates had been doing his best for Illinois officers for a long time. In June 1861 he made a pest of himself with Lincoln by urging a brigadier's position in the Regular Army—a permanent, not merely a wartime, rank—for John Pope. That July Yates suggested to the president that the lack of a major general from Illinois meant that the state "has no identity, no distinctive recognition." On April 9, 1862, when Pope stood as a major general of volunteers, Yates pleaded for his elevation to that rank in the Regulars "as a token of gratitude to Illinois." Lincoln responded immediately that such promotions "are not as plenty as blackberries." Yates nonetheless earned a nominee's undying fealty, and presumably also that of the nominee's admirers. "No Illinois soldier who did his duty in the war," wrote Pope in his *Military Memoirs*, "will ever cease to remember Governor Richard Yates, and to honor his memory."[14]

When in Washington on June 20 (and just as Pope was about to assume command of the newly created Union army of Virginia), Yates had additional reason to try to amplify the Republican recognition of Illinois by securing an appointment for another able brigadier. At that moment the state was embroiled in an electoral campaign over a new constitution that, if adopted, would redistrict in the Democrats' favor. Republicans were concerned and aroused—none more than Medill and his colleagues at the *Tribune*.[15]

In hunting for party prestige through conspicuous military promotions, Yates had a record of success. Pope was in the ascendant. He had successfully commanded the left wing of Halleck's advance on Corinth in May, and on June 26 he would be appointed to command all Union troops in the East except those on the Peninsula. Illinois now had two other major generals of volunteers, Ulysses S. Grant and John A. McClernand, giving it more than any other state. Of the brigadiers thus far confirmed, Illinois had garnered only twelve by Henry Wilson's count, eleven by Yates's (career officer John M. Schofield, attributed to Illinois by Wilson, had far closer ties to Missouri). This was hardly a just number when compared with the thirty-seven from New York, twenty from Pennsylvania, and twenty-two from Ohio.[16]

Those eleven had benefited most from the political interests of Yates, the Illinois Republican Party, and the president. Three had solid party credentials. John M. Palmer was now proving himself a solid soldier, as were Stephen A. Hurlbut (despite the naïveté shown in Missouri) and Benjamin M. Prentiss, both proposed by the Illinois congressional caucus, much as the Ohio caucus had put forward Sherman, McCook, and Schenck.[17] One, John A. Logan, was a noted Democrat, but a "War Democrat," and his successive promotions fit Lincoln's policy of co-opting suitable men from the opposition.[18] Eleazer Paine, a personal friend of Lincoln, became a colonel at Yates's behest at the start of the war. He proved to be "an old fogey [and] a martinet, and was constantly electioneering"—enough, evidently, to make him a brigadier by fall. Napoleon Bonaparte Buford, who had served with Pope at Island No. 10, had solid political connections and also benefited from Pope's rising tide.[19]

Four others had been promoted for their gallantry, or at least their fortunate presence, at the reduction of Fort Donelson. Three of them were Republican politicians: Leonard F. Ross, John Cook, and future governor Richard Oglesby. None would again attract military attention (though Oglesby was promoted to major general by Lincoln after being wounded in October 1862). The fourth, John McArthur, was, like "Black Jack" Logan, an officer with conspicuous military ability who had the added panache of having captained a militia group, the Chicago Highland Guards, not unlike Ellsworth's Zouaves.[20] What had Stanton and the Senate done for Illinois lately? Nothing more than seeing through the nomination of Julius White of the Thirty-seventh Illinois, who had been confirmed on June 9. Briefly the collector of customs at Chicago, but with political ties only in Wisconsin and without military experience, White carried little promise of luster for Yates's delegation of Illinois Republicans. Once nominated, his appointment had taken six weeks.[21]

Yates clearly wanted more. Turchin's original appointment, to command the Nineteenth Illinois, denoted connections to the *Tribune* and so to Chicago's elite, connections that the only Chicago brigadiers, McArthur and White, did not have. In fact, Ray and Medill had recommended Turchin's promotion in November 1861 in letters to Illinois adjutant general Alvin Fuller. At that point Turchin had little to recommend him in Washington, only the Nineteenth's controversial service in Missouri and his own prior rank in the Russian army. Not insignificantly, Turchin himself was not so much interested in promotion as he was in the improbable goal of increasing his regiment to sixteen companies, the size unit he would have led for the tsar. Nothing had come of his sponsors' recommendations.[22]

By June 20, however, Turchin and the Nineteenth had gained martial fame in the Illinois press for their intrepid service marching from Huntsville to Tuscumbia. Events at Athens had yet to be mentioned either in the *Tribune* or elsewhere. A dispatch by the paper's Nashville correspondent, published on April 14, gave Turchin all the credit for instigating the march on northern Alabama (and prematurely gave him the title "general," presumably because he commanded a brigade). An item from Decatur published on May 2 had him holding Tuscumbia and Florence. "The 19th Illinois is in the advance as ever."

The most direct evidence of what motivated Yates to recommend Turchin in particular is a letter supporting the nomination, manifestly written at someone's request, sent on June 23 to Illinois senator Lyman Trumbull by Grant Goodrich, as prominent an endorser as could have been found. Goodrich stood as an elder statesman among Chicago Republicans and was a good friend of the *Tribune*'s publishers. Judge Goodrich recounted Turchin's Russian military background, praised his regiment ("many of the first young men of the city"), and argued, "Those who were present say the successes of Mitchel have been more due to his [Turchin's] skill than to that of any one else."[23] The keys—Chicago, Huntsville, and the favor of Chicagoans who mattered—all appeared to be in place.

News of the events at Athens had begun to surface. On May 29 the *Cincinnati Commercial* published an article (which the *New York Times* reprinted) datelined May 15 that began: "One of the most disgraceful outrages ever perpetrated during the war was the indiscriminate and general sacking of this city, by certain forces in Col. Turchin's Brigade." Written by a soldier of the Thirty-seventh Indiana (and naturally absolving that regiment of any complicity), the piece provided exciting detail—cracking safes, stealing silver plate, the impoverishment of a widow and her "four little children." At this moment in time, both the *Commercial* and the *Times* inclined to a conciliatory view of the war. Lincoln's secretaries, John Nicolay and John Hay, regularly read both newspapers, and their office was directly across the hall from Stanton's. Still, if by chance they brought this news to Stanton, he likely would have brushed it off. The secretary of war was not entirely indifferent to misconduct by troops. On May 22 he granted Mitchel's melodramatic request for authority to inflict the death penalty upon straggling soldiers found guilty of "robbery, rapes, arsons and plundering." Gratuitously, but evenhandedly, he added the authority to exact the same penalty upon Southerners "guilty of irregular or guerrilla warfare." His attitude toward the rebels, as the *Washington Star* famously paraphrased it, was "Let them swing."[24] During May and June Stanton had already signed and sent on to the Senate the names of thirty-three nominees for brigadier general. He did the same for Lightburn, about whom there was not a whiff of outrage, and for Turchin.

Never during the Civil War did the Senate routinely rubber-stamp a nomination. At the moment Turchin's name went forward, an overabundance of existing brigadiers and a glut of nominations awaiting Senate action dimmed his prospects, all the more because the Senate seemed bent on trying to limit the number of further promotions it approved. If an excess of brigadiers had not already been noted, it had been forcefully put on the agenda in the upper chamber on March 28 by Senator James Wilson Grimes, Iowa Republican, possessed of a "keen, incisive, and disputatious turn of mind" and a sharp eye for unwanted government extravagance. Pointing out with some exaggeration that the army already had 172 volunteer brigadiers (in fact, about 135 confirmations, another 40 nominations pending), Grimes moved to express as the Senate's opinion that such promotions should be limited to men who showed "superior competency" or "gallantry in action." The motion failed, though Senator Wilson of the Military Affairs Committee himself agreed in principle that "we have had quite enough general officers nominated."[25]

A month later Senator Grimes got another chance to object. On Monday, April 28 the Senate confirmed eighteen brigadier generals and sent to Wilson's committee fourteen more nominations. (Perhaps as evidence of the Senate's growing inclination to restrain itself, only seven of those particular nominees would eventually be approved.) On Friday, May 2, in response, the Iowan introduced a bill, S 297, to amend the year-old open-ended act of July 25, 1861, and limit to two hundred the number of brigadiers in the volunteer service. Grimes personally saw no need for more than one hundred, but he left the final number to the Military Affairs Committee.[26]

Chairman Wilson welcomed the bill, welcomed it so much that he supported it publicly by providing the *New York Times* with a list, later printed in full in the *Congressional Globe,* showing the army's generals, state by state: 167 of them brigadiers already confirmed, with a disproportionate number from New York State. On May 7 Wilson rose in the Senate chamber to suggest that a mere 150 would have been adequate. Grimes responded with his rationale for an even 200: the army could have 160 brigades, and "I then allowed a certain percentage for casualties, for sickness, for the command of divisions, for the temporary command of corps d'armée, and I concluded that forty brigadiers were enough to cover that entire amount." By May 8 Senate Bill 297 passed without dissent, though not without a nearly successful motion by New Hampshire's John Hale (twitting Grimes, his antagonist on the Naval Affairs Committee) to adopt a lower number, 180.[27]

The significant support for Hale's proposed amendment (sixteen of thirty-five voting senators favored it) might seem on the surface to have shown real resolve for limits on promotions. If so, that resolve melted in the coming weeks. Perhaps McClellan's peninsular campaign, where action reached its opening crescendo at Fair Oaks, gave thoughts of new nominations of competent and gallant men, allowing the Senate to show its appreciation of combat experience. From the lush crop of fourteen brigadiers confirmed between May 7 and June 20, three were then serving on the Peninsula: Charles Griffin, captain in the Fifth Artillery; Albion Parris Howe, captain in the Fourth Artillery; and George W. Taylor, colonel of the Third New Jersey Infantry. Two other officers received nominations during this period for their service before Richmond: the controversial John Cochrane of New York (a New York Democrat already rejected once by the Senate on a voice vote) and Colonel Joshua Howell of the Eighty-fifth Pennsylvania.[28] The Senate confirmed five more officers that season after combat service elsewhere. Stephen Burbridge of the Twenty-sixth Kentucky and James Tuttle of the Second Iowa had both fought bravely at Shiloh. Able cavalry leader Washington Elliott had been recommended for his work under Pope before Corinth. Service in the Shenandoah Valley garnered stars for Erastus B. Tyler of the Seventh Ohio, with both his political connections and a gallant charge by his men at Kernstown, and George H. Gordon, a graduate of West Point and Harvard Law School who had raised and personally trained the Second Massachusetts.[29]

Turchin's achievement of tearing up the Memphis & Charleston, however much touted by Governor Yates, still left his confirmation subject to the real dynamics of promotion in the early summer of 1862: politics as usual, even for the combat veterans. James Grimes, ironically, was no less a practitioner than any other senator. New brigadier Tuttle, for example, himself an Iowa political figure, may have owed his star as much to the "recommendation of the Senators from Iowa," recorded by the Senate clerk, as to his service in the field. Grimes probably championed Pope's cavalryman, Washington Elliott, a career officer from Pennsylvania, as much because he served as colonel of the Second Iowa as for any service in Mississippi.[30] Among others promoted between May 7 and June 20, Henry Hayes Lockwood, a sometime Naval Academy professor commanding Maryland's coastal defenses, had Henry Wilson's favor and a border state background. Peter Joseph Osterhaus of the Twelfth Missouri, born in Prussia, may have been an able officer and "a pleasant, genial fellow, brave and quick," but more to the point Republicans saw the support he had among his fellow German-Americans in St. Louis.

(Nearly all of Lincoln's 17,028 Missouri votes in November 1860 came from that bloc.) Green Clay Smith was enough of a politician in his own right to be elected to Congress from another border state, his native Kentucky, in the fall of 1862.[31]

Grimes's bill to limit the number of generals failed to become law. The *New York Tribune*'s astute young Washington bureau chief, Adams Sherman Hill, wryly said in a dispatch on June 24 that it was "ignored by the House, which thought that the Senate should have moral courage enough within itself to decide each case on its merits, and in view of all the circumstances." Perhaps to throw back on the nominator the blame for the surfeit of nominations, the Senate in executive session on June 9 unanimously passed a resolution directing the secretary of war to advise "how many brigadier-generals are supposed to be necessary" and "the basis on which the necessary number is calculated."[32]

Stanton finished his report two days before he signed the nominations of Turchin and Lightburn. As it happened, the flow of nominations abated somewhat after June 20. Only one reached the Senate between then and July 3, the administration being not so much chastened about its nominating practices as it was preoccupied with the mounting conflict on the outskirts of Richmond. In the same short period the Military Affairs Committee routinely reported nine nominations to the floor. A lone confirmation resulted.[33] Still, the Senate felt that it faced an unmanageable backlog in Wilson's committee and at the clerk's desk. By one analysis bruited about at the time, more than fifty nominations stood against a supposed rational need for no more than eleven further confirmations. (A limit on July 3 of two hundred would have left seventeen places to be filled, but the numbers seemed to be growing beyond the ability of reporters and clerks to keep count.)[34]

The one confirmation voted between June 20 and July 3 shows the intensity of the pressure behind individual nominees. Military Governor Andrew Johnson sorely wanted a brigadier's position for Whig Unionist William Bowen Campbell, venerable Tennessee politician and veteran of the Seminole and Mexican wars. Assistant Secretary of War Thomas Scott thought Campbell politically a "reliable man" and would have given him Johnson's job. Even the rebels regarded Campbell highly. On June 15 Johnson wrote Henry Wilson about the nomination. "It is right and will do much good at this time. Please let it go right through." It did. Campbell was nominated June 16 and confirmed on June 21.[35]

Campbell did not especially want to be a general. Lesser candidates very much did and applied their own pressure, heightening the backroom competition. On May 22 Senator John Sherman placed in nomination the name of Colonel Crafts J. Wright, West Point class of 1828, an Ohio lawyer and sometime editor. Wright could plead his own case. "I was part of the army arriving before Fort Henry. I was *in* the entire battle of Fort Donelson. . . . We were in the battle of Shiloh and fought under [your brother] Brig Gen W. T. Sherman [who had been confirmed as major general May 2] during *all* the two days fight, and there, at his request held our line by the bayonet and force of appearance. . . . Whilst *many* have been promoted to rank as Brig Gen for *one* appearance in battle I have not for several." Another aspirant, Colonel James S. Jackson of the Third Kentucky Cavalry, had been a congressman, knew the ropes, and knew letters might not be enough. He journeyed from his duty station in northern Mississippi to visit the capital for "official transactions," mostly interviews with reporters, probably also with senators, trumpeting his own abilities.[36]

As if all that competition were not enough, Turchin had other notable competition from Illinois. Colonel Edward Needles Kirk, a downstate lawyer, had gained no small measure of fame when wounded at Shiloh leading a brigade in Buell's Army of the Ohio. Unlike Buell, and more than a bit like Turchin, it was later reported of Kirk that "this officer can never be reproached with lack of activity or daring." Kirk's nomination went to the Senate on June 16, two days after Yates arrived in Washington.[37]

Turchin, as a recent Russian immigrant, could not claim any great constituency, as many German- or Irish-born leaders could. His military experience had been gained largely at the farther edge of distant Europe. Just as his name was about to be put forward, an embarrassing scandal made this a potential source of doubt, if not a distinct black mark. J. Napoleon Zerman, a sometime staff officer under John Charles Frémont, had been proposed for a brigadier's star by the abolitionist Major General David Hunter. The dashing European's star appeared secure after his confirmation on May 5 on the motion of Ira Harris of New York, the state where he claimed citizenship. Then, just two days later, on May 7, the *New York Times* reported the word from European diplomats in Washington. The new general was "an exiled Austrian," known as a "defected adventurer and imposter" at the Spanish court, and "a convicted swindler and forger, who has served in the galleys and pined in the jails of Europe so often that such facts ceased to be novelties worth mentioning." Worse in some circles, he was said to have once been willing to accept a post as a mere master's mate in the navy. Despite the confirmation, the administration magically withdrew Zerman's nomination on June 18, only two days before they submitted Turchin's.[38]

What was more, as an experienced officer and departmental commander, Major General Don Carlos Buell had his own thoughts about which of his subordinates deserved promotion, about who would best lead and guide the components of his army. In the mind of this impeccable professional, Turchin would soon appear to be a miscreant nearly as foul as Zerman had proven to be. Buell would then need to make a point, a point about discipline in his army, about who was in command of his department, about the policy they would use while occupying middle Tennessee and northern Alabama, about how war would be conducted by the men under his command. He would act, for once, decisively.

10
The Indictment

If, as I hear, the promotion of Colonel Turchin is contemplated, I feel it is my duty to inform you that he is entirely unfit for it. I placed him in command of a brigade, and I now find it necessary to remove him from it in consequence of his utter failure to enforce discipline and render it efficient.

—Major General Don Carlos Buell to Secretary of War Edwin McMasters Stanton, June 29, 1862

Don Carlos Buell spent the middle two weeks of June 1862 marching his men from the area of Corinth, Mississippi, eastward toward Chattanooga. As had been the case with virtually every prolonged movement of his army, the advance had the pace of molasses running along a 3 percent grade. Henry Halleck had ordered Buell to move out on June 9. On June 25 the headquarters of the Army of the Ohio had gotten only so far as Tuscumbia. Buell had the additional job of repairing the Memphis & Charleston main line as he went along. That work provided another excuse, if not quite a valid reason, for the snail's pace of the advance. (On June 20 Buell let Ormsby Mitchel know that it was going to take his troops a week to repair a bridge over a creek.) The extra work served as an irritant, but reliable rail lines would be essential if the army was to avoid raiding Southern farms for food and fodder. Buell suggested switching his base of supply to the north and McMinnville, but the idea fell on deaf ears. So the Army of the Ohio continued inching its way to the east.[1]

With the mail on the evening of June 25 came, as always, current newspapers. The enlisted men and junior officers of Turchin's command and many of their midwestern comrades probably favored the *Chicago Tribune*. However, the usual mailbag also included recent editions of the *Louisville Journal*, the creation of the renowned conservative editor George Dennison Prentice. A New Englander who first came to Kentucky to write an admiring biography of Henry Clay, Prentice let his paper's columns reflect the debate raging in his own mind, pitting slavery's supposed virtues against the evils of secession. The resulting clash, which so clearly reflected the dynamic of the crisis for Kentuckians, who took great pride in their traditional role as compromisers, made his an important voice in the ensuing commentary about General Mitchel and Colonel Turchin. In this favored paper the senior officers would have noticed a short news item in the edition for June 23: "Col. Turchin, of the 19th Illinois, and Col. Briggs, of Mass., have been nominated Brigadier-Generals."[2]

This notice alone would have grated on Don Carlos Buell. As long ago as April 11, he had recommended seven of his colonels for promotion to brigadier, and John Basil Turchin had not been on that list. What was more, thus far only one of Buell's men had been confirmed.[3] Buell, like McClellan before him, faced a predicament. Washington politicians had usurped the management of his command. Rather than encouraging him to use his experience and expertise to make decisions crucial to the structure of his command, the War Department and the president, with the collusion of the Senate, were naming his subordinates. Were they competent? Were their commands disciplined and efficient? Had they been effective in implementing official orders and policies? The lack of action on Buell's candidates and the putting forth of others in their stead indicated only too clearly that Buell's opinion on these subjects was not of overriding concern.

General Buell and his entourage reached Athens on Friday evening, June 27, making camp just outside of the town. Buell's chief of staff, James Barnet Fry, busied himself in Athens, arranging the transfer of ammunition and meeting with Colonel Jesse Norton of the Twenty-first Ohio, always a citizen's advocate. Complaints about the treatment of the local residents by Turchin's men surfaced almost instantly.[4]

Those complaints took no time at all to reach Buell himself, and they struck a raw nerve. He quickly assured the people of Athens that the men under his direct command would give them nothing to fear. He stopped the supply trains well out of town to keep the men orderly and, notably, issued an express order to his subordinates to allow "no depredations." During the train ride to Huntsville all the next afternoon, through the welcoming reception, the provost marshal's brass-band concert, and the tour of Mitchel's headquarters south of the city, Buell took ample time to consider his course of action. He started at the top. On Sunday, June 29, he wrote directly to Secretary of War Edwin Stanton voicing his adamant objection to Turchin's nomination. That same day a nameless aide-de-camp wrote to Brigadier General Mitchel. "General Buell desires to know whether any formal reports have been made to you of unauthorized or improper conduct on the part of

Colonel Turchin and the troops of his command at Athens, Ala., or else-where. If so you will please forward them, with such remarks as you deem proper."[5]

Mitchel responded the next day, saying that no formal report had been prepared, adding the ill-considered remark that the pillaging at Athens "is a matter of general notoriety." He also said that he had asked a committee of local citizens to examine outstanding claims for damages, and that they apparently totaled more than $50,000. He finished by saying that he had ordered a search of the brigade's knapsacks that had found no plundered goods, and that Colonel Turchin had declared "that he did his utmost to prevent his troops from pillaging and from every irregularity." Mitchel added his own rather obvious conclusion: "It is certain he [Turchin] has been unsuccessful." Subsequently asked for the citizen's report of damage, Mitchel quickly forwarded it to headquarters. Ever a meticulous officer and student of military law, Colonel Fry personally reviewed copies of the citizens' claims. When a report arrived of additional trouble caused by a couple of Turchin's men near Fayetteville, Tennessee, Fry immediately directed staff officers to investigate those as well.[6]

One complication likely to impede a court-martial abruptly departed. Buell seemed to value Ormsby Mitchel's opinion, but to the latter's increasing level of frustration, his advice rarely seemed to have any effect. For three days in late June, Buell conferred with Mitchel at Huntsville. Mitchel did most of the talking, while, in his opinion, Buell was his "usual uncommunicative self." Mitchel had a great enthusiasm for the war. He came to hunt rebels. Serving under "one of the most hesitating and slow men he ever met" had drawn the popular astronomer to the end of his rope. After three days of unsuccessful attempts to convince Buell to press the advance on Chattanooga with speed and dispatch, Major General Mitchel gave it up. He stormed out of the tent, demanding a three-week leave of absence. On July 2 Secretary Stanton called him to Washington, "to repair to this city without an hour's delay," where his services could be put to better use. Mitchel jumped aboard the next available train.[7]

In Washington, Mitchel was for a short time without a command. Many of his men in Huntsville were sorry to see him go; some wished to leave with him, such was the contrast with Buell.[8] Buell promptly appointed as Third Division commander Brigadier General Lovell H. Rousseau, a lawyer, a former member of the legislatures of both Indiana and Kentucky, and a Mexican War veteran. The Kentucky riflemen he recruited to the Union cause in 1861 esteemed him as a military commander, particularly after his gallant conduct at Shiloh. His own frustration with the policy of conciliation had become clear just a few weeks prior to his elevation to division command. At a banquet in Louisville on June 16 he had this to say: "We have taken none of [the rebels'] property; we have excluded their slaves from our lines, when needed we have placed guards of our soldiers around their houses to protect them, and yet they persist in calling us abolitionists and Negro-thieves." From a military point of view, Buell made a sound choice. At Perryville and again at Stone's River, Rousseau would demonstrate his competence as well as his devotion to the cause of quelling the rebellion.[9]

With Mitchel entirely out of the picture, on Saturday, July 5, the inquiry yielded up formal charges and specifications. Special Order 93 on that date appointed seven officers and a judge advocate to sit as the court and ordered it to convene Monday morning in Athens itself. On the same date, in response to the charges, Colonel Turchin sent a wire listing his accomplishments and tendering his resignation, to be "accepted immediately."[10]

The outrages committed by Turchin's men did not stand alone. Other well-publicized, and probably more serious, atrocious acts had been perpetrated during June across the western counties of Tennessee and Kentucky. The wild-eyed horsemen of the Seventh Kansas Cavalry, led by Colonel Charles Jennison, known in his home territory before the war for "banditry, brutality, and cold-blooded murder" in serving abolitionism (hence, "Jennison's Jayhawkers"), had been led through perdition for the past seven months by Lieutenant Colonel D. R. Anthony. Over the winter the unit had already embarrassed Halleck west of the Mississippi. Now east of the river, the Jayhawkers sometimes stooped to outright highway robbery. They were much more an affront to military good order and discipline than anything charged against Turchin's brigade. Their conduct had met with indifference, if not express approval, from their brigade commander, another Kansan, Brigadier General Robert Byington Mitchell. The matter had finally fallen into Halleck's lap.[11]

Halleck, in that affair, ordered the arrests first of the more conspicuous enlisted wrongdoers, had them brought from the field "in irons" on July 3, then ordered the arrest of Colonel Anthony on July 6. Writing to Stanton the next day, he despaired of the regiment's conduct. "Since the Kansas troops entered this Dept. their march has been marked by robbery, theft, pillages and outrages upon the peaceful inhabitants, making enemies of our cause wherever they went." Nothing, it seemed, could be done about it, mostly because of Congress. The Jayhawkers had the ears of the Kansas senators, James H. Lane and Samuel Clarke Pomeroy. "I have brought these troops to this place [his headquarters at Corinth] and shall do my best to reduce them to proper discipline, but am very doubtful of success so long as bad officers, supported, as they allege by political influence at Washington, encourage them in violating law, regulation and orders." Court-martial charges had already been drawn against Anthony, but for trivial offenses. They were shelved. Halleck, or one of his clever staff officers, devised a more expedient remedy, a plan to force the lieutenant colonel's resignation by putting him in an uncomfortably subordinate position, making him want to resign and thereby ending the problems, political as well as disciplinary. Halleck adopted the plan, and it worked.[12]

By accepting Turchin's proffered resignation, Buell had the opportunity to avoid a trial and a public display of the incident, allowing it to go quietly away. He did not. He ignored Turchin's offer. The court-martial of Colonel Turchin would proceed as ordered, and his offending subordinates would be dealt with in short order afterward. Why the difference in approach? Halleck and Buell were two very different people. Henry Halleck was at first appearance an unmilitary major general, "inclined to fatness, with a double chin, bald forehead," who "could not ride a horse out of a walk." No less firmly advocating the Regular Army's prerogatives and professionalism, he had learned how to deal cannily with the civilian world and its politicians. Posted to California during the gold rush year of 1849, five years later Halleck resigned his commission, learned the law, became an expert in mining rights, and pursued a career as a jurisprudential engineer for San Francisco's thriving entrepreneurs and politicians. To succeed in such an atmosphere, he had to become a keen observer of human nature as well as a skilled negotiator. He had a good sense of when to go all in and when to fold.[13]

Don Carlos Buell had a very different frame of reference. He wore a brigadier's plain front uniform. He displayed a soldier's rigid demeanor. His approach to a problem always came straight from an army manual. He remained very much the young man who would strike with the flat of his sword rather than tolerate disobedience. For the entire period between the wars, while Halleck cut mining deals, Buell wrote orders, serving exclusively in the peacetime adjutant's well-ordered world. "His Alma Mater was not West Point, but that more pitiless school, the adjutant general's office," wrote William F. G. Shanks, the only newsman sympathetic to him. "[C]onstant service in that department of the army made him too systematic—smothered the fire in his heart, the impulsiveness in his nature,"[14] and evidently the creative in his thinking. Confronted with the ruckus created by Colonel Turchin's men, Buell would never see the need for a more clever solution in the context of a broader world. If possible political and popular ramifications of the decision ever crossed his mind, he would have seen them as completely subordinate to the need he had to restore and maintain discipline in his area of operation. Orders were orders. Now, more urgently than ever, Buell had signals to send: to the troops in the field and to their regimental officers, that punishment would surely be inflicted for any failure to heed General Order 13a. The government had never issued any orders to him informing him of a policy change. He certainly would have believed that his neck was on the line should he not follow the orders he had received the previous November.

He had no time to lose. The Union volunteers coming to fight the war now lived, in ever-increasing numbers, in the South. After the victories at Shiloh and Huntsville, and even more after the forced Confederate evacuation of Corinth on May 30, the men in blue found themselves in the towns and plantations of western Tennessee and northern Alabama and Mississippi, where seemingly no one welcomed their arrival. Nothing about the experience led them to want to return fugitive slaves to their owners nor, by extension, to respect the property rights of the Southern gentry.[15]

Turchin's Eighth Brigade shared in that experience, observing the whipping post at Huntsville and the slave-hunting hounds at Tuscumbia. What effect did such sights have on them? We have no direct evidence, but the reaction of the men of the Fifteenth Wisconsin Infantry, a unit recruited almost entirely from Norwegian immigrant farmers, not a bunch notorious for riotous misbehavior, may give us a hint. From their leader, Colonel Hans Christian Heg, upstanding chief among his state's Norse settlers, comes the detail. Encamped at a plantation near the Mississippi River, Heg wrote his wife as early as March 23, "I have protected [the owner's] property so far, and not allowed the soldiers to destroy any thing, but if I can be assured he is a rebel—I can assure you I will not give him much protection to his Negro property." Heg's attitude steadily hardened. On May 9 citizens complained to Military Governor Johnson that the Norwegians, now encamped at Island No. 10, "have daily and nightly been allowed to prowl around the country persuading and in many instances forcing off our slaves, especially the women and children, secreting them in camp and upon the Island and sending off upon transports large numbers." By July 2, writing home from a headquarters he had commandeered at Humboldt in the center of west

Tennessee—the local hotel's "fine large parlor with a piano in it"—Heg wrote, "[T]here are a good many of the troops here that are behaving very badly, stealing and robbing the Houses nights. I have arrested a few."[16]

Buell knew of the increasing indiscipline in the ranks and among free-thinking volunteer senior officers such as Heg. One of Buell's adjutants at Nashville reported on June 20 that the march led by Brigadier General James Negley—a militia volunteer, not a professional soldier—against Chattanooga had, earlier that month, left "one scene of pillage and robbery" in the middle Tennessee mountains. If the overall news failed to grab Buell's attention, the statement that "officers have aided and encouraged and benefited" from the pillage certainly must have. The complaints reached all the way to the top. "General Negley laughed at and did not attempt to prevent the outrages." The author of the confidential report, Oliver D. Greene, then delivered the news conciliatory men most feared. Because of the outrages, "hundreds of Union men in East Tennessee have been transformed into secessionists." Nor was Negley the only miscreant. Greene went on: "I am reliably assured that [by] all reports, official or otherwise notwithstanding, the troops in Negley's and Mitchel's commands, with few exception, have become bands of robbers and thieves." How many of these outrages had been acts of reprisal or retribution? It did not matter. It did matter that Colonel Turchin, a trusted brigade commander in Buell's command, had been part of it.[17]

On the other hand, strident dissatisfaction with the conciliatory policy burst forth from an unexpected quarter on Independence Day. During a celebration at Major General George Thomas's divisional headquarters in Tuscumbia, new brigadier general Robert McCook, a member of a famous fighting family of generals, got his fill of fellow officers' "effusions" about "southern brothers," and perhaps also his fill of Southern liquor. Springing to his feet, young McCook announced: "If they will not submit reasonably, they must be exterminated. My men and I are ready to do just *that*, even if it means the South is to be laid waste."[18] Buell had reissued General Order 13a on June 15 in a composite order for the governance of the Army of the Ohio. Obviously, those orders had not stemmed increasingly angry sentiments such as McCook's.

Nor would orders alter the nature of the war these men were being asked to fight. Even Oliver Greene had not been blind to this other side of the conflict. In the same dispatch in which he complained about the behavior of Mitchel's and Negley's men, he reported that the male citizens who had de-clared for the Union as Negley marched through had been either chased out or murdered once Negley's troops left. Governor Johnson complained at the same time to both Halleck and Stanton. "The rebel cavalry are committing the most atrocious outrages upon the people, and there are no means to protect them." When he asked for two regiments of cavalry with which to provide that protection, Stanton told the governor that although he, the governor, was authorized to raise them, the government had no troops to send. Johnson was free to grow his own. Buell himself faced the daily inconvenience of railroad rail being loosened or removed and of telegraph wire being cut. Dispatches sat unsent sometimes for days at a time.[19]

In Washington, all that spring Congress had steadily chipped away at the policy of conciliation. On March 10 the Senate had approved a new article of war prohibiting officers in the field from returning fugitive slaves to their owners. The House followed suit, and Lincoln signed the bill into law on March 13.[20] The prospect of slaves, female slaves, hiding in army tents especially irritated General Buell. On March 11 he had written to General Mitchel to complain of a specific instance. The new article of war did not, paradoxically, directly effect any change in the prior contrary Fugitive Slave Act, and the army's bureaucracy was not quick to publish the new law in general orders, blunting its effectiveness. By one account, as late as June 15 Mitchel got into a brouhaha with junior officers of the Nineteenth and Twenty-fourth Illinois regiments by insisting that they follow General Order 79, coincidentally dated March 11, by rousting slaves, mostly female, out of camp, not the sort of situation envisioned by Congress when the law passed. But the new law was at least on the books.[21]

As a portent of harsher measures to come, "proof positive that a new order had begun in Washington," on April 3 Senate Republicans found constitutional objections insubstantial, asserted their branch's plenary right to govern the District of Columbia, and voted to a man to emancipate the 3,000 slaves domiciled there. The bill, S 108, thus passed 28 to 14. They headed in the same direction on May 6, keeping the confiscation bill very much alive, and with it the threat to emancipate slaves held by actively rebellious Southerners, by sending the measure to a friendly conference committee. Congressional support for conciliation still existed, but its trial period had neared its end.[22]

While all this took place, all eyes, including those of the Army of the Ohio, started to focus on Richmond. In mid-June, Colonel Manning Force noted the demoralized expressions on the faces of the people of Corinth, Mississippi, and the almost polite deference they demonstrated when coming in to deal with Union officers. He also noted in his diary that "every person who has been near Corinth, or any other place in communication with America, is assaulted for news from Richmond."[23] On June 26 the Army of the Potomac could see the church spires of the Confederate capital. They could listen to the peal of the bells. Then, at 3:00 that afternoon A. P. Hill's division struck the lone Union corps on the north side of the Chickahominy River near Mechanicsville, Virginia. The Seven Days' battles began. All Northern hearts looked for news of McClellan's great victory. With that victory would come the need to occupy the entire South.[24]

For Buell, formal charges and specifications against Turchin would tell the troop commanders in the Army of the Ohio that good order would prevail. They, along with their men, would be punished for the depredations they committed or allowed, for letting their men prowl about and steal and even worse, for alienating people on the brink of being restored as citizens of the United States. It would provide a not-so-subtle basis for his junior commanders to stop making Fourth of July speeches threatening Southern brethren with extermination. Formal charges against Colonel Turchin, based on a knowing disobedience of General Order 13a, had to be filed to restore order in the command, an order that had been too much ignored. A more active campaign could have easily prevented much of the mischief among the men, and it would have served equally well to relieve the frustration of Buell's subordinates like McCook and Mitchel, not to mention the increasing frustration with the progress of the war evidenced at the Capitol. For Buell, that was water over the dam. He had to take a stand. There was, at this point and time, no other priority. How else could he contemplate leading volunteers into the South?

As he readied the charges against his Russian colonel, Don Carlos Buell had no way of knowing just how swiftly, and decisively, events were about to turn against him. He would never have predicted McClellan's defeat before Richmond. He had no idea about, or apparent concern for, the tremendous level of frustration with him, with McClellan, and with the policy of conciliation that was about to be unleashed from the halls of Congress to the streets of Chicago. The advance of the court-martial proceedings never missed a step. Buell's staff prepared the indictment. His West Point–trained inspector general signed it. Captain Swaine, who arrived in Athens just as court was to begin session, probably saw the charges for the first time when he read them aloud in open court.[25]

The indictment presented a comprehensive complaint, its disciplinary and political ends being plainly displayed. The charges as drawn would yield

Buell precisely the verdicts he would want to review, approve, and include in a general order to be read by every officer in his army. A skeptic, however, could read the charges as overblown, inflammatory, and stretched beyond the facts that Captain Swaine or any lawyer could in good faith expect to prove in court. They thus demonstrated both the pressure Buell now felt he was coming under and his frustration over the repeated violations of General Order 13a. To any reader, the indictment contained a message about the wrongs that came with deviation from the conciliatory policy.

The first of the three charges accused Turchin of neglect of duty. Recitations of twenty or so instances in which Turchin supposedly had, to his own knowledge (even if that knowledge was merely ascribed to him because of the acquiescence of his officers), allowed soldiers to plunder and pillage the citizens of Athens "without taking adequate steps to restrain them" supported the claim. The instances began with sexual impropriety and religious desecration: the attempt of "an indecent outrage" on the servant girl and the destruction of "a lot of fine Bibles and testaments, which were torn, defaced, and kicked about the floor" in a shop. Most of the rest of the specifications charged depredations at nine homes and ten stores. The charge emphasized the magnitude of the monetary losses suffered by the people of Athens as documented by Judge Lane. The rape served as the ultimate example of Turchin's failure to have his men properly under control. The charge had shock value and demonstrated how bad things could get if volunteers ran amuck. Another accused "[a] part of this Brigade . . . quartered in the Negro huts for weeks," of "debauching the females and roaming with the males over the surrounding country to plunder and pillage." Other accusations ranged from the laughably specific ("spoiling . . . the beds by sleeping in them with their boots on") to the implausible and unanswerably vague.

Under the second and third charges, conviction would serve specific objectives that mattered to Buell. Each contained few specifications, but they both flowed from the conduct detailed in the many specific acts already enumerated under the first charge. The charge that Turchin had conducted himself in a manner unbecoming an officer and a gentleman mattered to the general because under Article 83 conviction meant automatic dismissal from the service and the end of Turchin's military career. It would serve as unanswerable proof to everyone from Stanton to the Zouaves as to Turchin's lack of fitness. The only specification added here concerned a failure to pay the bill at Davidson's Hotel—a low sort of crime, defrauding an innkeeper. The third charge, failing to obey orders, mattered because it recited in the first of three specifications Buell's General Order 13a. Convicting Turchin on this charge would send the clearest possible message to the officers of the Army of the Ohio. They would make certain that their men did not despoil the property or offend the sensibilities of the Southerners in their midst, or they would pay the price of disgrace by dismissal. The final specification in the indictment alleged disobedience of the army's hoary General Order 4, barring officers' wives from camp and field. Turchin was undeniably guilty, but so, too, had been other general officers, including Ormsby MacKnight Mitchel, who had very openly brought his wife and daughters south to enjoy Huntsville's charms. Obviously, in General Buell's view, it was time to put the army back in the full military mold from top to bottom.[26]

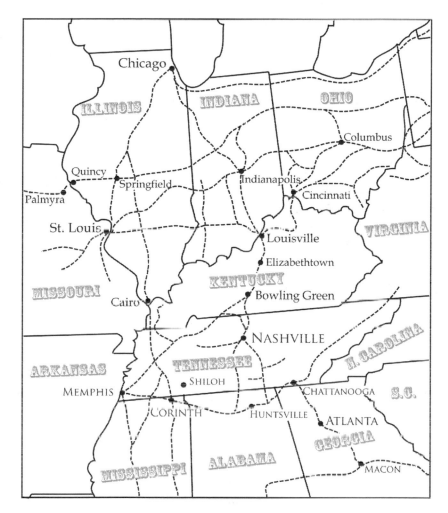

Figure 1. Turchin's area of operations, 1861–62.

Figure 2. Colonel Elmer E. Ellsworth became a national celebrity at the age of twenty-three parading with his drill team, the United States Zoauve Cadets. His death at the hands of a hotelkeeper at the start of the war was a cause for national mourning—and of widespread calls for revenge. Photo courtesy of the U.S. Army Military History Institute.

Figure 3. Don Carlos Buell was forty-three when he took command of the Department of the Ohio. Although he was a hero at Shiloh, his failure to move on eastern Tennessee (both before and after the battle) and his con-ciliatory politics would ultimately cost him his command. Photo courtesy of the Library of Congress.

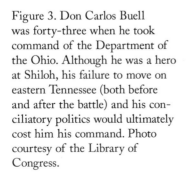

Figure 4. Ormsby MacKnight Mitchel left the military and made his fame as a scientist before the war. Ardent in his desire to defeat the rebellion, he was frustrated with the leadership of Don Carlos Buell. His faith in Turchin's training and ability led him to give his brigade commander numerous independent missions before the events at Athens. Photo courtesy of the U.S. Army Military History Institute.

Figure 5. Illinois governor Richard Yates wielded considerable influence in Washington as the Republican governor of the president's home state. His request resulted in the nomination of Turchin to the rank of brigadier general. He later served in the United States Senate. Photo courtesy of the Library of Congress.

Figure 6. Senator Henry Wilson of Massachusetts, chairman of the Committee on Military Affairs, had every general's nomination cross his desk. He opposed Turchin's promotion. He went on to serve as vice president of the United States in the second Grant administration. Photo courtesy of the Library of Congress.

Figure 7. Thirty-year-old Brigadier General James A. Garfield presided over the Turchin court-martial. He went on to serve on the board that heard the Fitz-John Porter controversy, as William Rosecrans's chief of staff, and as the twentieth president of the United States. Photo courtesy of the Library of Congress.

Figure 8. James Barnet Fry served as McDowell's chief of staff before performing the same role for Buell. He probably wrote the indictment under which Turchin was tried. He was named provost marshal general of the army in March 1863, where he performed with distinction through the end of the war. Photo courtesy of the U.S. Army Military History Institute.

Figure 9. John Beatty began his distinguished military career with the Third Ohio. He received his brigadier's star in November 1862. He later served three terms in Congress, ran for governor of Ohio, and published numerous books, including his diary. Photo courtesy of the U.S. Army Military History Institute.

Figure 10. Senator William Pitt Fessenden of Maine served as the floor leader for Turchin's nomination. He went on to serve as Lincoln's Secretary of the Treasury and as chairman of the Joint Committee on Reconstruction. Two of his sons became Union generals. Lithograph courtesy of the Dahlen Collection.

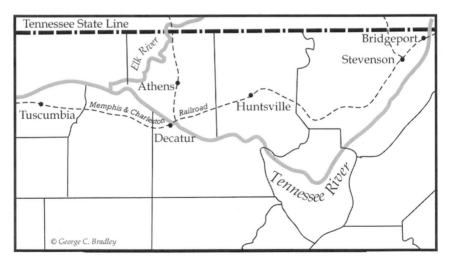

Figure 11. Northern Alabama, spring of 1862.

Figure 12. Brigadier General John Basil Turchin proudly
displaying the brigadier's stars he was awarded in the summer
of 1862. Photo courtesy of the Chicago Historical Society.

11
The Court-Martial

Our court . . . is now in full blast.
—Colonel John Beatty to his diary, July 10, 1862

Major General Don Carlos Buell could not have doubted that in James Abram Garfield he had the right young brigadier to preside over a trial on these accusations. Garfield, a proven combat leader, had spoken earlier in the spring publicly affirming his support of conciliation. His keen intellect and sharp political skills had gained for him a brigadier's nomination from high in the government. Garfield had entered military service only in August 1861. An ordained minister, before that he had been a state senator and head of small Hiram College in northeastern Ohio. Although militarily untrained, he was not a typical volunteer. He already possessed the personal attributes that would carry him to Congress and beyond: "hunger for knowledge, unflagging industry, and ambition for distinction." He gained his volunteer colonel's commission by raising his own regiment from his legislative constituents.[1]

Garfield appeared before Buell with that regiment, the Forty-second Ohio, at Louisville, Kentucky, on December 17, 1861. A novice but senior colonel, and with a leader's natural charisma, Garfield took command of a brigade composed of three fledgling Ohio regiments and a Kentucky cavalry troop. Buell quickly sent him off to repel an invasion of eastern Kentucky from Virginia led by the Kentucky lawyer Humphrey Marshall, West Point class of 1832. On January 10, 1862, at the battle of Middle Creek, Garfield's force prevailed, sustaining in a day's fight twenty-one casualties to twenty-four for the rebels. Driving Marshall from the commonwealth, Garfield garnered his first success as a field commander and enhanced the growing esteem felt for him by Don Carlos Buell.[2]

It did not hurt that Garfield's initial campaign had been a standard military mission, his men joining battle with a similarly equipped and formally organized foe. He and his men did not begin the war as partisans. Thus, after driving Marshall away, it was easier for him at that earlier stage of the war to announce to the citizens in the captured Big Sandy Valley: "[T]o those who have taken no part in this war—even to those who hold sentiments averse to the Union, but yet give no aid or comfort to its enemies—I offer the full protection of the Government, both in their persons and property. . . . The Army of the Union makes no war of plunder, but comes to bring back the prosperity of peace." Quite clearly, Garfield was not a volunteer in the sense that Turchin and his men were volunteers. He took great care to enforce the government's official policy and, demonstrating his own political skills, he was quick to send Buell's chief of staff, Colonel Fry, a copy of the proclamation, letting his commander know that he was doing the job expected of him.[3]

Such attentiveness to the sensibilities of those around him had made Garfield a political success when he sat in the legislature in Columbus, where he befriended the rising Jacob Dolson Cox, supported Governor Dennison's move on a federal Senate seat (though evidently not enough to offend the victor, John Sherman), and acted as a protégé of Salmon P. Chase. Success on the battlefield for such a man bore quick benefits. Garfield's promotion to brigadier, obtained with Chase's aid, carried the same date as his victory over the hapless Humphrey Marshall.[4]

Garfield continued to lead a brigade in the Army of the Ohio, arriving on the field at Shiloh near the end of the battle. From then on, there had been no combat glory to be found. There were opportunities, though, to observe and gain a measure of respect for Buell. "Few officers in the service possess a greater reticence, terse logic, and severe habits of military discipline," Garfield noted when recalling his commander. In June Garfield gained a little experience in courts-martial, presiding over the trial of Second Lieutenant Sasser Sullivan of the Fifty-eighth Indiana for charges that were ultimately dismissed.[5]

Camping across the South that spring, the good soldier Garfield held to his own underlying habits of mind, inculcated before he graduated from Williams College in 1856. Stern Puritanism governed all his thought. He adhered to the abolitionism that he had suddenly chosen to advocate at school in 1855. From Tuscumbia, in June, he wrote to his wife that he could "chill your blood with the recital of horrors that have resulted to slaves from their expectation of deliverance." At the same time, Garfield privately had no confidence of finding any real Union sentiment in the South. Without it, conciliation was senseless, and thus began his doubts about the underlying policies governing the conduct of the war.[6]

Garfield did not outwardly waver in his obedience to Buell and to the thinking ingrained in the established military order. Over years in public life, his sincerity would be questioned on various points, but not now.[7] By one astute view, at this time in his life he accepted "every implication connected with the business of war and the status of being an officer, and wasted no further thought on the matter." On June 25 he wrote to a close friend and mentor, his words chosen carefully as always, arguing "it better, in this country, occupied by our troops, to be a rebel than a Union man," given the protection afforded slave owners. Garfield liked to take the long view: "There will spring up out of this war a score of new questions and new dangers . . . of even more vital importance than the ending of the war." In due time, in the proper place, Garfield would want a hand in forging the answers: "I do not hesitate to tell you I believe I could do some service in Congress in that work, and I should prefer that than continue in the army."[8] In the army Garfield would conform to the army's policies, as any subordinate officer of quality should, but a time would come, he foresaw, when he would have a hand in charting the course himself. Until then, as an ambitious man, Garfield was well aware of the advantages of pleasing one's superiors.

As Turchin's court-martial began, Garfield had not yet come to color events at Athens in any light cast by abolitionism or, for that matter, conciliation. As he wrote his wife the night before testimony began, the town simply "had been given up to pillage and in the presence of the Russian . . . was sacked according to the Muscovite custom."[9] He was apparently under the impression that Turchin had done, or had allowed things to be done, in keeping with his past experience. Deeper issues would appear with the evidence, ones that could easily be missed by jurors thinking they knew the real story already. If there was any question about Garfield as presiding officer, it was whether he could separate his personal and military thinking. Thus far, he gave every indication that he could.

No such question at all need have been asked about the next two most senior members of the court, both of them well versed in the discipline and customs of the Regular Army. Jacob Ammen, born in Virginia but raised in Ohio, West Point class of 1831, had worked for twenty-four years as a mathematics teacher at small colleges in the South and Midwest. Coming into the Civil War as a fifty-five-year-old captain of a volunteer company, he had led the Twenty-fourth Ohio at Shiloh and Corinth.[10]

Ammen was "a stern, unbending disciplinarian," unthinking, by every account ever written about him, seized by the old soldier's mental outlook, and with old, influential friends throughout the newly expanded service. One was General Charles F. Smith, who had stayed on active duty and had just served as Grant's model before Shiloh. In April 1861 Ammen, then working as a civil engineer in a small town in southern Ohio, became colonel of the Twenty-fourth Ohio. He expressly doubted whether all decent men in the Confederate army had been forced into service, "as they claim," and suspected more were rebels than might be conciliated. But he would do nothing to disappoint Buell, whom he greatly admired, whose behavior at Shiloh he would defend for the rest of his life—and who, by putting him on the April 11 list of colonels recommended for promotion, was giving him an honor every academy graduate appreciated. He would fully recognize the disciplinary problems Buell sought to address by bringing Turchin to trial.[11]

Curran Pope, a product of the academy's class of 1835, had served as a long-term county court clerk for Jefferson County, Kentucky, sitting in Louisville before the outbreak of the war, at which time Pope had raised his own regiment, the Fifteenth Kentucky Infantry. A wealthy and prominent border state Unionist, true to the thinking of editor George Dennison Prentice and others of his political set in Louisville, Colonel Pope had no doubts whatever about the efficacy of the conciliation policy. In April he wrote to political acquaintance Andrew Johnson that, save for battlefield reverses, "mild yet firm measures in the course of two or three months will bring the people back to their allegiance."[12] Two decades as a court clerk had, moreover, given him the practical experience of dealing often but not too closely with the rough and routine criminal sorts.[13] Just as he knew a Kentucky gentlemen, Pope knew a wharf rat, knew what a crowd of them might perpetrate, and no doubt had irreversible opinions about what a dishonorable, or simply inattentive, commander of such a crowd should expect when punishment was meted out.

Another Louisville colonel on the court, Marcellus Mundy, age thirty-two, had been pursuing his considerable ambition as he commanded the Twenty-third Kentucky Infantry in garrison in Tennessee towns, where he showed the insecurity peculiar to a Kentucky native who had practiced law in Philadelphia only to return home to participate in the war. In speeches to citizens and letters to Andrew Johnson he adhered to the military governor's position that Tennessee's Southern sympathizers should pledge allegiance or be sent into exile. But Mundy's position was just nominally harsh. He sought the citizens' affection and, trained to act for his client as the occasion seemed to demand, he got that affection, at least on the surface. Residents of the town of Lebanon came to praise "Col. Mundy's manner of getting along with our people" and, so far as Mundy could tell, "by selective exiles" a "healthy tone" was later established among the pillaged people of Pulaski. (That town also had been torn up on May 2.) Buell and Fry could count on Mundy. When other Union troops committed further outrages, he was one who reported it posthaste.[14]

Colonel Thomas D. Sedgewick had earned a brigadier's star in combat, but earning it and receiving it were two very different things. He had signed up from Louisville as colonel of the Second Kentucky Infantry in July 1861 and fought ably across western Virginia through the fall. His gallantry at Shiloh, where he was knocked down by a spent ball, earned praise for his "marked ability" from prominent Kentucky general William "Bull" Nelson and led to brigade command in the advance on Corinth. But at 4:00 a.m. on May 30, just as the Confederates were effecting their evacuation, Sedgewick was succeeded in command by a green-behind-the-ears brigadier, Mahlon Manson of Indiana, a point that did not escape Sedgewick's hometown paper. Sedgewick might be expected to be a bit sensitive about the promotion of men less battle-tested than he and, as a border state colonel, sentient to the rights of Southern civilians.[15]

Thus far, the court-martial board was made up of three border state colonels, who could be expected to be sensitive to the charges of mistreatment of civilians, and by a fourth colonel well-versed in the disciplinary needs and expectations of the army. To the mix was then added Colonel James G. Jones of the Forty-second Indiana. Jones, who left the management of his regiment to his lieutenant colonel and major, had time that could be put to better use.[16] Moreover, he had served as a state attorney general until 1856, when he was chosen as a Millard Fillmore elector on the Know-Nothing or "American" ticket. With that antiforeigner campaign having taken place the very year Turchin and his bride arrived in America, little sympathy could be expected in this quarter for the defendant. Perhaps the regiment's major, James M. Shanklin, provided a glimpse of Colonel Jones's conciliatory attitude when he described an incident on the march from Nashville to Murfreesboro in March 1862:

Coming along the road we met a man on horseback, who inquired if we had seen his two runaway niggers. . . . espying the Negroes he made them come out, and drove them at a full run up the hill, urging his horse fairly on them, and cursing and hooting after them, striking them as they went. Will you believe it? We all stood there and saw him do it without lifting a finger. It was a brutal affair, yet there we stood, each waiting for the other to interfere. No one but Colonel Jones really had the right to stop him. He seemed to have forgotten his Republicanism, and the man was allowed to drive and ride down the panting Negroes right past us.[17]

Colonel John Beatty, the thirty-five-year-old colonel of the Third Ohio Infantry, became the junior officer on the court, a Yankee banker from Sandusky, in the old Western Reserve of northern Ohio. He was of another mold than the more senior members of the court. Beatty was conspicuously a Republican (and on principle, not in pursuit of office), a supporter of the aggressive Free Soil New Hampshire senator John P. Hale for president in 1852, of John C. Frémont in 1856, and a Lincoln elector in 1860. On May 2, 1862, while Turchin's men ransacked Athens, about forty miles to the east, near Paint Rock, Southern bushwhackers fired into a train carrying Beatty's men. The fusillade wounded six Union soldiers. Beatty had stopped the train and with an armed guard had called upon the people of Paint Rock. He made himself clear. The bushwhacking and sabotage would stop. "Hereafter, every time the telegraph wire was cut we would burn a house; every time a train was fired upon we would hang a man; and we would continue to do this until every house was burned and every man hanged between Decatur and Bridgeport."[18]

Beatty put on an immediate demonstration of his sincerity. In retaliation for the cutting of the telegraph wire and the wounding of his men, then and there he set fire to the little hamlet and carried off three civilians to the military jail at Huntsville. A party returned three days later and arrested twenty-six more men suspected of burning bridges. Beatty noted in his diary, "The burning of the town has created a sensation, and is spoken of approvingly by the officers and enthusiastically by the men. It is the inauguration of the true policy, and the only one that will preserve us from constant annoyance."[19] Moreover, Beatty was a great admirer of the recently departed Ormsby MacKnight Mitchel, whose honesty, aggressiveness, and indifference "as to whether this traitor's cotton was safe, or that traitor's Negroes ran away" he looked up to.[20]

Beatty kept a journal, now a minor classic in Civil War literature, in which he recorded with exceptional honesty all he perceived as he sought to apply "good sense" to his duties. Beatty was not the perfect juror in any jurisprudentially ideal sense. He had too much of his own views on policy, and he was not hesitant in following them. He was, however, a proven soldier entirely satisfactory to his superiors, one who would not be swayed by another's rank or position. In addition, he had earlier served on courts-martial and had gained experience with troop misbehavior as provost marshal of Huntsville. Finally, he, too, was available, his regiment in garrison, and he recovering from a bout with jaundice.[21] Nonetheless, the cut of Beatty's cloth did not match that of the rest of the court.

To complete the court, they needed only the judge advocate, Captain Peter T. Swaine. When he left West Point in 1852, a brevet second lieutenant, a modest twenty-fourth in his class, Swaine had taken with him no training in military law. The academy's curriculum included no practical instruction in the subject until two years later. Swaine did offer the cause of military justice at Athens his own devotion to the army as a career (likely encouraged by a wife whose military forebears went back to the Revolution), practical experience from several years in frontier garrisons, and whatever help he could find in the Articles of War and in treatises, the most accessible of them the elementary legal chapters in Colonel H. L. Scott's *Military Dictionary.*[22]

Decisions on hard points of law—on procedure and evidence especially—were left not to the judge advocate but to the court as a whole, guided not by any specific code, apart from the Articles, but by the members' perception of "the general usage of the military service, or what may not unfitly be called the customary military law." United States Supreme Court Justice Joseph Story had pointed them there in a fundamental case, *Martin v. Mott,* in 1827, where his opinion granted nearly carte blanche to military tribunals to decide their own procedures.[23]

In northern Alabama in 1862, Judge Story's decision had wide-ranging effect. Colonel Turchin or his counsel remained free to make a wide variety of legal arguments based on any rough cut they could make of experience and logic. Brigadier General Garfield, the presiding officer, was left to puzzle from the first day of trial over "a good many intricate questions of law constantly coming up." Captain Swaine had to try to give the case direction and keep the trial moving by calling witnesses in some sort of logical sequence, conducting prosecutorial direct and cross-examination. Then, each evening, he had to do his ministerial duty of assembling the mandatory transcript of the testimony.[24]

General Buell might have been well advised to wait patiently for the verdict that must have seemed certain from this carefully assembled court on the indictment so carefully drafted. With his campaign against Chattanooga up in the air because of Stanton's call for troops to aid McClellan (since suspended), and with a mind to soothe the souls of the people of northern Alabama who had been the object of the outrages perpetrated by Turchin's men, he instead stepped into the limelight. He cut to a further point in the exercise, that of assuring the most substantial citizens of northern Alabama that conciliation was the official policy, one that he planned not only to pursue but also to enforce. By trying and punishing Turchin, he would vindicate the honor of those harmed. Though for months he had been confirmed as a major general, Buell had never worn the rank's splendid uniform. On the evening of Monday, July 7, hot as it was, but with the charges and specifications drafted and the court's members appointed, he donned his new coat, adorned with its "double-starred rectangles" and "rows of three buttons," to pay a visit to the most substantial loyal citizen in the area, Judge George W. Lane.[25]

The judge advocate, Captain Peter Swaine, had tried courts-martial before, presumably a fair number of them. In fact, he was delayed in convening this one, delayed at headquarters in Huntsville by another court.[26] When he arrived in Athens, though, he thought to get off to a fast start. He had in his repertoire the lawyer's standard ploy of beginning with a very respectable victim. Athens's postmaster, Richard C. Davis, admirably filled the role. He took the witness stand on Thursday, July 10, 1862.

First, however, Swaine and the court had to respond to a formal written motion (likely prepared by Carter Gazlay, though he had not yet made his formal appearance as defense counsel) asking that each witness "be required to state under oath whether he or she is for the United States or Confederate States, and that each witness be required to take the oath of allegiance." This was the chief, if not the only, "intricate question of law" posed to Garfield that first day, and it arose from sound legal thinking. For long ages English and American courts had barred as "incompetent" testimony by witnesses who had been adjudged convicted of certain offenses—notably treason, perjury, bribing or "seducing away" witnesses, false accusation—on the theory that the conviction evinced a "total disregard to the obligation of an oath."

The rule stood firm in Macomb's *Practice,* which flatly postulated that testimony by such a witness "is regarded by the law as of too doubtful a character to be admitted in a Court of Justice."[27]

The rule was weakening. Colonel Mundy, once a Philadelphia lawyer, may well have known that it had been abolished altogether in Pennsylvania in 1859. The rule had been done away with by statute in Alabama in 1852, "leaving the [prior] conviction as matter directed only to the credit of the witness." Court clerk Curran Pope would have known, however, that it still stood, tenuously, as good law in Kentucky and so, had he been inclined, might have lent his support to this defendant's position. By Macomb's, or Kentucky's, or any other formulation still standing as late as 1862, the rule required the party invoking it to bring forward authenticated proof of the challenged witness's prior conviction for treason or perjury or whatever.[28] Turchin did not have that proof for any Athens resident. The court members, "having maturely deliberated upon the matter[,] decided not to entertain the proposition." The court did give the defendant full benefit of the thought behind the rule, "reserving to him the right to ask the witness any proper questions" going to bias and credibility.[29]

Questions about allegiance would, of course, be allowed during the trial, and the responses would have their effect, however minor, on court members. Far more dramatic, however, would be the treatment such witnesses received in the press. The very proposition that a court, military or otherwise, could allow a patriotic volunteer to be tried based on the testimony of people who declined to take an oath of allegiance would appear inherently misguided to many people in the North. This was the sort of thing from which headlines were born.

Postmaster Davis had time to tell the court, when finally allowed to testify shortly before adjournment at 5:30 p.m., that on May 2 Union troops had broken into his office and had generally vandalized the personal property they found there. Most notably, they had spoiled some two hundred Bibles and testaments and purloined $300 in cash, half of it silver, belonging to the American Bible Society and the local Masonic lodge.[30] With Davis, as with most of the witnesses, Swaine had three straightforward points to make in his direct examination. First, men of the Eighth Brigade had engaged in wanton, purposeless, and expensive destruction of civilian property that fell well outside any claim of military necessity, or even that of justifiable retaliation. Probably forced to it by starting the court-martial on the run, Swaine did this first by eliciting the witnesses' long narrative, then by seeking rote responses to a short set of questions, asking the same of nearly all, rather than by more convincingly using questions eliciting specific answers. Of Davis he asked, perhaps a bit energetically: "Narrate what you know in regard to the conduct of the troops of Col. J. B. Turchin's command when they entered the town of Athens, Ala. Mention times, places and circumstances!"[31] He received in response lengthy testimony about destroyed Bibles and missing Masonic money. (One never knew who might be an initiate of that widespread fraternity.) If any members of the board had received their third degrees, the witness provided the prosecutor with a dandy response.

Second, the charges as framed obliged Swaine to show that the soldiers' conduct had seriously offended the sorts of citizens who ought instead to have been brought back to the Union fold. Proof on this point was always implicit, and who better to give it than a friendly postmaster confessedly "acting for the Confederate States at that time"—but who had, he said, "always called myself a Union man."[32]

Third, as a matter of effective advocacy if not of strict law, Swaine must have known he had to prove that Turchin himself either ordered or at least clearly condoned wanton misconduct and pointless destruction, preferably with a bit of personal spite toward the hapless civilians. Here Swaine struggled. With Davis Swaine merely danced around the subject: "Was the accused Col. J. B. Turchin aware of what you have said was going on?" He got nowhere: "I do not know whether he knew it or not." As the case progressed, the prosecutor became more direct, perhaps more desperate. Of William McEnary, the second day's third witness, the brash young harness maker whom Turchin himself had chased out of the courthouse square as the regiments were stacking arms, he asked, "Did you hear Col. Turchin give any order or permission to the Soldiers on that day? If so, report it!" No luck. "No," replied McEnary, "none but the order to arrest me."[33]

Swaine must have realized about his first point, damages, that the pile of proofs that originated with Judge Lane smacked too much of claims for money, even if the postmaster's losses did include the vandalizing of the wardrobes in his living quarters as well as stealing cash from his till. Swaine must also have realized that more was on trial here than an officer for disobeying orders. The conciliatory policy that underlay the order was being challenged. To both defend it and prosecute the defendant, evidence was needed that would demonstrate the atmosphere created by poorly disciplined troops. Swaine turned to his first such witness during the second day of trial, the widow Mildred Ann Clayton. Her story was one of being terrorized. Soldiers had come to search her home. On May 2, after being threatened at gunpoint, Mrs. Clayton had surrendered the few guns she kept in her house.

Marauding volunteers, probably artillerymen, had visited her again the next day, sometimes in groups as large as ten or fifteen. The men of one group laid their eyes on Mrs. Clayton's servant girl and "threatened an indecent outrage" on her. The threat scared Mrs. Clayton enough to send the girl away to a safer place, although she testified she never reported the incident to an officer.[34]

However, in the narrative testimony by the widow Charlotte Haines, albeit from a farmstead seven miles outside Athens, Swaine had even better goods, and a witness who typified the bind that many civilians in northern Alabama and elsewhere found themselves in after the outbreak of the war. Union troops had visited Mrs. Haines on several occasions, always scrounging food, beginning shortly after the Eighteenth Ohio first came to Athens. At times two or three men would come by, at others closer to a dozen. Before May 1 "they were generally peaceable and behaved very well and did not molest me in any way. The soldiers usually asked me for milk and offered to pay for it, but I would not charge them for a little milk. I was a lone woman, having no children but a son in the Southern Army and I always told these persons so, who said they were sorry my son was fighting against the government and I told them I was sorry also. He was a married man and I had tried to persuade him to remain at home."[35]

The congenial atmosphere disappeared after the events in Athens on May 1 and 2. On Saturday, May 3, three sullen soldiers walked into her farmyard, saying they wanted some ham. Mrs. Haines said she had none to spare and was told by one of the men that he guessed they would have some anyway. They left with three hams and a vague promise of payment. Soon word got out about the contents of her smokehouse, more parties arrived, and they quickly took all she had, which included 1,500 pounds of bacon. The troops left the door to the smokehouse open, and the pigs and livestock quickly made the place filthy.

The following day the trio who had first taken the hams returned, this time carrying their rifles and with things on their minds other than food. Mrs. Haines saw them coming. "My negroes, whose huts are all in a row were in their quarters as is usual on Sundays. These 3 soldiers came up to them and at once commenced indecent familiarities with them, calling the women 'Sissy' and throwing their arms around them, running their hands into their bosoms. I was setting in the door of my house with a book in my hand pretending to read, but watching the men all the time." This went on for nearly an hour.[36]

Their attention then turned to Mrs. Haines and her home. On the pretext of searching for weapons, they forced their way into the house. She told them "I was a lone woman and had none. I never had fired a gun and did not know how." The attention of the men diverted to the sideboard and the other furniture. They tossed open drawers looking for medicine and money. While one kept watch at the front door, the other two headed upstairs. In fear, but not wanting them to break down doors, Mrs. Haines went up, too, unlocking rooms, trying to placate the intruders. Finding nothing but stored lumber, the men ordered one of her servants to hitch up a carriage to take them back to camp; and then their attention turned back to the women they had fondled in the slave quarters.[37]

Mrs. Haines continued her narrative.

All had left the place except one woman and her daughter, the latter about 14 years of age. One of the men asked her how old she was. She answered, "I don't know how old I is." He then said to her, "put down that child," (meaning a baby she was nursing in her lap) "I want to use you." Her mother came to me in great distress saying they were going to ruin her daughter. The daughter cried for her mother. The man said "God damn your mammy, we will have her next!" I was so much frightened I did not know what to do. The mother begged me to save her daughter, and I ran out to the yard, and there before me a horrid outrage was committed on her person by the man, and afterward the outrage was repeated by one of the others, but not by the third man. These men acted more like brute creation than human beings, and had no regard for me or anyone. The mother I locked up in a closet but let her out to escape them and she ran away into the thicket. They tried to hunt her up, thought she had gone into the cellar, but could not find her. I was so much alarmed that although I wanted to protect my property I was afraid to stay and got a neighbor to send me across the Tennessee River. When I returned about ten or twelve days afterwards I found my property almost a complete wreck. All my outhouses, such as hen houses, dairy, etc. were broken open. The door of the hen house had been chopped down with an ax. My house had been entered and all the sugar, coffee, and provisions I had were gone.

The Union army had not only cleaned her out of food, they had taken the little bit of money she had secreted in her sewing box and had even walked off with her photograph albums and pictures, some of which were the only keepsakes she had of a departed daughter-in-law.[38] Here was a witness who served as a perfect example of the type of person who deserved the full protection of the law and government and who had instead fallen victim in the most intimidating manner to the very men who should have provided it.

As testimony unfolded on the third, fourth, and fifth days—Saturday, Monday, and Tuesday—the prosecution brought forward its most articulate witnesses. Thomas Jefferson Cox covered very well the ruckus in the square, the gutted stores, and the defendant's presence nearby, but he could not say anything about any affirmative order directing misbehavior. Members of the court, with their own questions, tried to bring out some bit of proof implicating Turchin directly. All of them failed, but by asking the questions they clearly hinted that they thought such proof was technically necessary for a guilty finding. And toward the end of each witness's testimony came the sort of question Turchin himself asked Cox: "Were you or not at any time agent for the State of Alabama, connected with the rebellion. If so, when, and for what purpose." To that there was always a clear and predictable answer: "I decline to answer the question as it may criminate myself." The court felt the obligation to respect the constitutional claim. Neither the press nor the public would.[39]

The testimony by prominent and well-to-do citizens—Mayor Press Tanner, John Haywood Jones, and notably J. W. S. Donnell—did its intended job, presenting a convincing picture for the court's members that injury had been done worthy of the notice of the military's criminal law, if the thoughts recorded by the banker on the panel are any indication. Surely it was hard for John Beatty not to sympathize with Tanner for the burden placed on him at his little store and kitchen. "One day 47 [soldiers] took dinner, 18 took supper that same day and 18 took breakfast the next morning." Some descriptions of damage in fellow citizens' stores were compelling: "I next went to Allen's drug store," testified Donnell, "found it open, a great many soldiers in it, it had been plundered and rifled, and great destruction had been done in there, I found the floor covered over with medicine bottles and all the contents of the store, and the soldiers were then tearing down the contents of the shelves, and throwing down on the floor everything they did not want." The court heard enough, in fact, that "after mature deliberation" it granted a defense motion to exclude the testimony of another Donnell, Jonathan, about something the soldiers of the Eighth Brigade were alleged to have done somewhere else in Limestone County as early as April 19.[40] Although not pertinent to the case itself, such information would weigh in heavily with General Buell.

John Beatty busied himself totaling up the damages. Disregarding court rulings on the admissibility of evidence, he started his own tally. He correctly recorded in his diary that one witness (the wealthy, voluble J. W. S. Donnell) "swears that Turchin's brigade robbed him of twelve hundred dollars' worth of silver plate." Beatty added in the next line, moreover, information that must have been extrajudicial and gained around the evening mess table from other officers or during recesses in conversations with friendly townsfolk: "Turchin's brigade has stolen a hundred thousand dollars' worth of watches, plate, and jewelry in Northern Alabama." So far during the trial, Swaine had offered proof of thievery miniscule by comparison: another $1,000 in silver plate, fifty chickens here, "some turkeys" there, John Jones's $275 in fowling pieces, and yet other piece of plate, allegedly melted.[41]

It mattered not to Beatty how high the total might run. On July 14, after only three days of testimony, he reached some conclusions about the significance of the evidence quite different from those Buell—or for that matter, Turchin—wanted. "Turchin has gone to one extreme," Beatty was already sure, "for we cannot justify the gutting of private houses," of which in fact no evidence had yet been presented,

> and the robbery of peaceable citizens, for the benefit of individual officers or soldiers; but there is another extreme, more amiable and pleasant to look upon, but not less fatal to the cause. Buell is likely to go to that. He is inaugurating the dancing-master policy: "By your leave, my dear sir, we will have a fight; that is, if you are sufficiently fortified; no hurry; take your own time." To the bushwhacker: "Am sorry that you gentlemen fire at our trains from behind tree trunks, logs, and ditches." "Had you not better cease this sort of warfare? Now do, my good fellows, stop, I beg of you." . . . "in the meantime we propose to protect your property and guard your Negroes." Turchin's policy is bad enough; it may indeed be the policy of the devil; but Buell's policy is that of the amiable idiot.[42]

Beatty thus seemed disposed not to excuse men in uniform for a straightforward crime of theft, and presumably he would convict any culpable thieves, but without especially much enthusiasm. To him, the weakness of official national policy had become clear.

On the next point important to Buell, the desire to show that the crime had the further effect of alienating the likes of Tanner, Jones, and Donnell, Swaine's case looked to Beatty as though it were based on a policy grown moronic. When Donnell's testimony ran gratuitously past countable losses and into the bruises to his sensibilities, injured as he claimed they were by petty vandalism, Beatty's enthusiasm for it must have collapsed quicker than a camp chair. "I rush to mention," Donnell told the court July 14, "one act of annoyance more grievous than the rest. [A] wagoner of Captain Schardy Company E 24th Ill[inois] drove against a large self acting gate . . . which he knew he could not do so without breaking the gate down. It was an expensive structure. . . . In fact I repeat it was contemptible compared with the annoyance caused me and my family, but I should say it was about six thousand dollars."[43]

The gate may well have been Donnell's most visible prewar expression of conspicuous consumption, sited as it was on his grounds on the hill entering Athens. Beatty, who had not blushed when ordering the burning of human habitations at Paint Rock, did not bother to note this $6,000 item in his diary. Years later, though, he had occasion to think about Donnell's airs and his own response to them. In a historical novel he wrote in the 1900s, after establishing a reputation as a writer and speaker on the Civil War, he included a carefully written lecture to an aristocratic secessionist, a character in his fiction who could have been his best recollection of James West Smith Donnell: "War, Mr. Brenar, . . . is not a holiday pastime; . . . those engaged in it are not expected to adjust the scales of justice to a hair, and to award to each one his exact due. . . . you, and such as you, are far more responsible for the present condition of affairs than the rank and file of the Confederate army; by your wealth and influence you have arrayed whole communities against this flag, and there is no good reason why you should be exempt from the evils which you have precipitated on the country."[44] That was the sentiment of a Union volunteer.

On the third point in the proof—Turchin's direct involvement in the depredations—Swaine ought to have found his best evidence in the testimony of Union officers and men. He called the witnesses. The desired testimony proved hard to elicit. The strongest of them took the stand late Tuesday morning. First Lieutenant Robert G. Chandler of Loomis's Battery implicated the defendant in the outrages but, as his testimony began, only after the fact, not directly proving any order sanctioning misconduct before it occurred. Chandler recalled hearing a conversation the afternoon of May 2 in which Turchin "remarked, about the affairs then going on, that he did not care so long as they did not take what they did not need, or words to that effect."[45]

Albeit void of any substance as to any prior order, if true, Chandler's story clearly indicated that Turchin was well aware of what had been going on and that he condoned it. It was the most damning evidence Swaine would adduce from any witness, and perhaps it gained emphasis when the court adjourned for lunch.[46] The witness's credibility came into question, however, when the court reconvened at 4:00 that afternoon. Lieutenant Chandler failed to reappear and was found asleep in his quarters. After an hour's wait a brigade adjutant sent to arrest and retrieve the groggy witness "returned and informed the Court that Lieutenant Robert G. Chandler was too drunk to be arrested." Next morning Chandler managed to extricate himself from the resulting finding of contempt (by admitting that during the break he had had dinner, he said, with a bottle of wine, then took morphine to promote his postprandial nap, and did not awake until 7:00 p.m.). How much credit should be given to testimony given by a man under such obvious stress? Seemingly little or none—the weight of Chandler's testimony had evaporated. The young artillerist had had his fill of the proceedings. Fortified by his drug-induced sleep, he returned only to recant. When asking for proof of Turchin's "permission to pillage the stores or dwellings," an inquiring member of the court elicited no more than a flat denial that there had been any. As for the store goods he noticed in his own soldiers' hands, Chandler testified, "They said they bought them and I took no further steps in the matter."[47]

From then through July 17, the prosecution's evidence was cumulative. Witnesses told story after story about messing around in stores and houses, enticing slaves to leave their masters, impressing horses and, incomprehensibly to one reading the transcript, a disappeared piece of silver plate soldiers found in an icehouse. Nothing damned Turchin directly. Still, at the end of that Thursday afternoon Swaine rested the government's case.[48]

Sitting down that evening in the "best of accommodations," a room in Dr. Benjamin Maclin's spacious home two blocks north of the courthouse, mingling relief with sarcasm, General Garfield summarized for his wife the prosecution's efforts. If the case as he set it out did not command an acquittal, still it fell far short of compelling enthusiasm on any point needed for a resounding vote to convict.

The horrible character of the outrages which have been committed here are in striking contrast with the character of the officer (Colonel

Turchin) who is charged with the responsibilities of allowing their perpetration. . . . For ten days he has sat patiently while citizen after citizen (rebels all) have rehearsed and we have recorded the outrages of the men under his command. Though by a fiction of the military law, the prosecution has been striving to fix upon him the responsibility for robbery of citizens and rapes of female slaves, yet during all that time he has borne himself so much like a noble-souled man that he has quite won my heart.[49]

It would be unthinkable in a modern court proceeding for the defendant and the jury to interact. Yet in the hours after the court adjourned for the day, Garfield entered into friendly conversation with Turchin, learning of his training and position in Russia, his attraction to the United States, of his efforts "to show the rebels their treachery to the Union was a terrible crime." Garfield wrote to his wife detailing the conversations, concluding by saying, "I have tried to give you the substance of a man who will probably be dishonorably dismissed from the Army in a few days, but who nonetheless has won my heart and whom I will always be glad to call a friend." Bad acts had been committed, to be sure, but the complaining victims were "rebels all," and the defendant was not personally a man with whom the presiding officer, the church-college headmaster, could find moral fault. Garfield himself, it seemed, would be reluctant to convict a patriot based on the testimony of people who would rather plead the Fifth Amendment than take an oath of allegiance.[50]

The end of the prosecution's case meant, as the military-court manuals sensibly provided, a day or two of respite for the defendant to prepare his case, a break here stretched only over the weekend. Garfield and Beatty were both ill, Garfield seriously. The others undoubtedly experienced the dulling effects of the boring strain of slow, repetitive testimony in a summer-hot room. Other courts-martial based on the same events had been set down on their docket—those of Stanley, Edgarton, Mihalotzy—and the evidence was not likely to have become more interesting in the retelling.[51]

However much the court members wanted to hear the end of the case and be done with the matter, the court could not prudently continue sitting at Athens. One week before his promotion to brigadier, at daybreak on Sunday, July 13, Confederate colonel Nathan Bedford Forrest "burst upon the town of Murfreesboro' like a thunderbolt from a clear sky," capturing a garrison of 1,400 men of the Ninth Michigan Infantry, Third Minnesota Infantry,

Fourth Kentucky Cavalry, Seventh Pennsylvania Cavalry, and at least two sections of artillery. Losing the position cut the Nashville to Stevenson rail line. Among the prisoners were Brigadier General Thomas T. Crittenden and Colonel W. W. Duffield, the pair of whom had arrived on post only two days earlier and, it was now thought (somewhat predictably), had not properly placed their forces. Duffield had been on Buell's April 11 list of colonels worthy of promotion. His nomination quickly and quietly disappeared. Turchin's court hurriedly moved its sittings to the better-protected position at Huntsville.[52]

Forrest's brilliant raid entirely blocked the flow of supplies south to Stevenson, thence to Huntsville. Within two days, officers' messes at the latter post went on half rations. Regiments were drawn closer together to coordinate mutual defense.[53] It was, on reflection, an imprudent time for a brigadier and six colonels to be sitting in a courthouse in little Athens without so much as a corporal's guard. The convening authority duly rescheduled the court-martial to resume proceedings at 8:00 a.m., Monday, July 21, at the Madison County courthouse on the hill overlooking the Huntsville train station. Garfield and Beatty traveled there Saturday afternoon.

One unexpected result of moving the trial to Huntsville, to Buell's Army of the Ohio headquarters, was that suddenly, for the first time, members of the press corps discovered that Colonel Turchin was on trial. Happenstance had to this point conspired to keep all details of the story of Turchin's court-martial out of the newspapers. One voracious news-gathering organization might have caught on to the item early and as a matter of course, but the *New York Tribune*'s chief correspondent in the West, Albert D. Richardson, in a message dated June 6, threw cold water on a proposal by the paper's careful managing editor, Sidney Howard Gay, to hire a reporter to go to Huntsville.[54]

Another aggressive paper that missed the story, Richard Smith's *Cincinnati Gazette*—supporter of the radical Senator Benjamin Wade, opposed to Buell, in favor of aggressive war—had a man in the area early in May. But that man was W. C. Furay, personally no fan of Buell, either, charitably to be described at any time during the war as an overly imaginative news writer, who was just then experiencing one of his runs of covering the wrong location. Furay, who got along well with John Beatty, had been on the march with the Third Ohio on May 1 near Stevenson, where he kept quiet about the happenings at Paint Rock, just as Turchin's regiments began their adventures at Athens, miles away.[55] There was no telling where he was on July 10 and for the next week, but his paper's usually more somnolent rival, the *Cincinnati Commercial*, clearly without a man anywhere in Alabama, mentioned in an editorial about Ormsby MacKnight Mitchel the incidental fact that Turchin "was at last accounts being tried by courts martial," but in Huntsville, not Athens—a tip that a reporter with Furay's grit would have turned into a full-blown story.[56]

A nameless reporter wanting to cover the story had approached Judge Advocate Peter Swaine earlier in the past week asking to sit in. Sensitive to the implications of such a request, Swaine wrote to Colonel Fry on Tuesday, July 15, asking whether it would be "proper to allow a reporter to take down points in the testimony for publication?" Wiser in reporters' ways and the army's response to them, Fry had a pat response: "Reporters are not even allowed in the camps."[57] Finally, with the dateline of Athens, Friday, July 18, the *Cincinnati Gazette*—presumably Furay—transmitted the first detailed story of the case that had been brought against Colonel John Basil Turchin, but still only summarizing the three charges with specifications, describing the court as being "in full tide of business." Other developments in Washington, DC, were about to turn this little-noted trial into a celebrated incident.

12
The Switch

If we are ever to put down the rebellion we cannot afford to refuse any
of the means recognized by the usage of civilized warfare. The slave
must be armed and sent against his master—our armies must find
subsistence as far as possible at the expense of the enemy . . . [Those]
who would do for the best interests of their country without regard to
slavery must be put at the head of our columns. . . . The people are ripe
for extreme measures.

—R. R. Enos, of Springfield, Illinois, to
Senator Lyman Trumbull, July 14, 1862

The conflict that had simmered since the war began, pitting Lincoln's policy
of conciliation against the likes of the widespread and popular demand, echoed in the *Chicago Tribune*, that the South be rendered "a desolated, blackened country" had come to its boiling point. Now, in July 1862, the point of
decision arrived. The army, its ranks being depleted by casualties, disease, and
the discharge of many men who should never have been accepted in the first
place, needed a fresh influx of new volunteers. McClellan's resounding and
unexpected defeat shocked the country, calling into question all the premises
upon which the war was being fought. As significant as it was, that defeat was
but part of the ever-increasing evidence that the people of the South had no
desire to be liberated, that instead they had a deeply seeded desire to go their
own way. Lincoln needed to quickly and clearly establish a war policy that
would inspire confidence all across the Union, a new policy by which he
could carry on the war to a successful conclusion.[1]

Responding rather too late to the predictable result of Secretary of War
Stanton's suspension of recruiting in April—a shortage of soldiers in July—
Lincoln had on July 1 issued a call for 300,000 new volunteers. He would
settle for half that number, he told New York governor Edwin Morgan, "if I
could have them now." They were not forthcoming. Peter Watson, Stanton's
dour and cautious assistant secretary, confidentially passed word to the *New
York Tribune*'s Adams Sherman Hill on June 22 and again on July 14: "As to
enlistments, he says they are very slow—slower in the West than in the

East." In fact, during July the state of Illinois managed to raise and muster only two regiments. The problem became obvious to the interested general public. "Recruiting is dull," wrote the New York Union League's George Templeton Strong in mid-July, reflecting on a massive rally calculated to liven it up in his city of New York.[2]

Nothing figured more drastically in the inability to recruit than McClellan's defeat at the gates of Richmond. The euphoria of 1861 had long since evaporated into the reality of war as men endured it. In the spring of 1862 there had been a universal hope that a few swift victories would quickly end the war. Even a pragmatist like Ulysses Grant thought so as he took Forts Henry and Donelson.[3] However, rather than melting away after their defeats, the rebels had staged their massive counterattack at Shiloh. When the rebel army at Richmond succeeded in driving McClellan's host back down the James Peninsula, all prospect of an early victory vanished. Then, as the rebel armies launched offensives that drove the Union armies out of Virginia and most of Tennessee, the possibility of victory at any foreseeable time dimmed as well.[4] It was time for the Union to regroup, to harness new weaponry, to adopt new policies that would attract the recruits needed to win the war.

Many observers linked the recruiting problem perceived in the early days of the summer of 1862 to the presence of the conciliatory policy. "Freemen are reluctant to join the army, expose their lives and destroy their health merely to enforce Order No. 3 [Halleck's regulation turning fugitive blacks out of the army's camps] & guard rebel property," argued the *Chicago Tribune*'s Medill to his senator, Lyman Trumbull. At a recruiting rally in Bangor, Maine, Vice President Hannibal Hamlin felt obliged to promise new recruits, "[W]e want to send forth no Federal bayonets to protect rebel property. We don't fight the rebels to save their property."[5]

No one, it seemed, was quicker to realize the need for a clear statement of national war policy after McClellan's defeat than was McClellan himself. On the evening of July 7, 1862, at his field headquarters, McClellan handed Lincoln a carefully drafted essay, now known as the Harrison's Landing Letter, making a well-reasoned, albeit last-ditch, argument for the continuation of the "professional" war making he had been trying to carry out. Little Mac argued as strongly as he ever had for a war in which "all private property and unarmed persons should be strictly protected." The prospect of emancipation concerned the general. "Military power," he wrote, "should not be allowed to interfere with the relations of servitude," but he argued more broadly against any behavior by Union soldiers that fit the mold a very substantial part of the population, not least many present volunteers and potential recruits, had for a long time thought the appropriate way to suppress an insurrection. He wrote as the professional soldier he had been trained to be that "pillage and waste should be treated as high crimes; all unnecessary trespass sternly prohibited; and offensive demeanor by the military towards citizens sternly rebuked."[6] McClellan also wrote as a general in charge of an army fighting for the most part a conventional war against a very competent and conventional foe.

Lincoln politely took the document, quietly read it, thanked the author, but said nothing more in reply.[7] One military historian has commented about the letter, "[I]n the normal course only successful generals could impose policy."[8] McClellan had failed, and everyone in the country who supported the war shared in the disappointment. As William Pitt Fessenden observed the day before, "We have had a terrible fright during the past week, and have hardly recovered from it yet. At one time it was feared that the Army of the Potomac would be obliged to surrender."[9]

Lincoln's silent response to what was obviously a heartfelt plea demonstrated not only his reserve and self-control but also his own understanding of just how quickly and dramatically things had changed. His actions in the days and weeks ahead would demonstrate without question how far he had fallen away from the policy McClellan still argued for. In a letter written at the end of the following summer, Lincoln would most clearly enunciate the lessons the rebellion had taught him during his first year in office. Then he would write, "Is there—has there ever been—any question that by the law of war, property, both of enemies and friends, may be taken when needed? And is it not needed whenever taking it, helps us, or hurts the enemy? Armies the world over, destroy enemies' property when they can not use it. . . . Civilized belligerents do all in their power to help themselves, or hurt the enemy, except a few things regarded as barbarous or cruel." The only exceptions he noted were the massacre of the vanquished or of noncombatants. In the summer of 1862, he had decided that he had to do all in his power to aid the Union cause. Conciliation fell by the rail.[10]

McClellan, however, carried remarkable credibility as he pled for a continuation of a conciliatory policy. Lincoln actually feared repercussions within the army if McClellan's views went unheeded, expressly on the issue of emancipation, implicitly on the broader issue of conciliation. The president said at the beginning of July that to any step toward emancipation "there were two objections: 1. That half the army would lay down its arms, if emancipation were declared; 2. . . . three more states would rise, Ky, Md, Mo."[11] Senator Charles Sumner, who reported the president's thoughts, had no reason to magnify the problem, though it was an old fear.

The politician Lincoln would not have missed, however, the other long, loud, and broadly based calls heard everywhere to begin wreaking havoc in the South. At this point, with an outcry against conciliation rising everywhere, from the halls of Congress to the columns of the nation's most influential presses, Lincoln would gain an obvious advantage by rolling up everything the South perceived as detrimental, calling it all "harsh war," and properly harsh, and thereby moving in accord with the mass of public opinion while smoothing over some specific objections to the freeing of slaves. Confiscation in general had broad appeal, constantly pumped up by such newspapers as the *Chicago Tribune*. There was political sense in stressing confiscation as the administration's program. While it remained true that many Regular Army officers—McClellan's constituency—could rise in protest over a policy that included either confiscation or emancipation, the president would have known that for many a volunteer, the end of conciliation would mark the sort of call to arms they had been waiting for. Lincoln had much to weigh as the time for decision approached.

McClellan had received broad support from the administration, and he had failed. Don Carlos Buell, now having been in command of his department for nine months, had trended dangerously close to insubordination. During the past winter he had begun to acquire a reputation for recalcitrance, most notably in his failure to follow either broad hints or orders to move on eastern Tennessee, a pet project of the president's.[12] Now ordered to advance on Chattanooga, and doing so at a pace that wandered between agonizingly slow and unwilling, Buell drew a direct rebuke from Halleck, still commanding at Corinth, that amounted to a curt, insulting, and ultimately correct lesson on elementary strategy: "The President telegraphs that your progress is not satisfactory and that you should move more rapidly. The long time taken by you to reach Chattanooga will enable the enemy to anticipate you by concentrating a large force to meet you."[13]

As Buell sat languidly in Huntsville during the second week of July, moreover, word had begun to arrive in Washington of his effort to rid the army of Colonel John B. Turchin. The pendency of the trial must have become known at the White House not later than Saturday, July 12, perhaps a day or two earlier. With the news of it came the prospect of using the appointing power to raise Turchin as an example for the policy wanted by the government, a neat reversal of Buell's use of the same circumstance. The colonel had already been nominated for brigadier, obscurely but handily enough. It remained only to bring his name before the Senate. This, however, would be no small task, for there were perhaps fifty other nominations pending. In order of nomination, the Russian's name stood far closer to the bottom than the top of the stack, and none of the others was on trial. On that July 12, on Senator Lyman Trumbull's motion, an executive session ordered that "a list of general officers not acted upon is to be printed in confidence for the use of the Senate."[14] That list has been lost, but evidently it was superseded immediately when Henry Wilson's Committee on Military Affairs took up the subject that same day and "selected twenty-nine [nominees] to report to that body, notwithstanding that there are only eighteen additional officers of that rank required by law," or so reported the *New York Herald* the following Monday. Wilson's list undoubtedly included Turchin's name. Any later inclusion of him in the group being considered would have led to undue notice, remark, and probable objection.

Intimations must have been already abroad in Washington that Turchin's very recent record—to wit, his men's activities at Athens and Buell's response in the Athens courthouse—might well make his appointment controversial. Prentice's *Louisville Journal* had broadly thundered on July 10, "Gen. Mitchel and a portion of his command have perpetrated in North Alabama deeds of cruelty and guilt the bare narration of which makes the heart sick. The particulars in the case will be laid before the authorities in Washington in the course of a few days." Offhandedly, the *Cincinnati Commercial* commented on July 11, "Col. Turchin . . . was at last accounts being tried by court martial at Huntsville." Both papers circulated widely in the capital. The sponsors of Turchin's competitors would not have kept this interesting news under wraps. Nor would those who wished to promote and protect the good order and honor of the United States Army.

In fact, the news reached even so obtuse a legislator as Pennsylvania's Edgar Cowan. On Friday, July 11, standing on the Senate floor, he made light of it. "I pay no attention to these rumors of any kind one way or another. . . . I have no doubt that in that Army there are men whom it might be dangerous to turn loose in passing through an enemy's country; and I suppose the very fact that property has to be guarded is evidence of the fact that there is danger. I know nothing about it personally, although I have heard a great many rumors."[15]

The messenger who supplied the information to the *Louisville Journal* and the *Cincinnati Gazette* happened to be a disciple of conciliation, none other than Colonel Jesse B. Norton of the Twenty-first Ohio. Norton had been captured nearly a year before during a skirmish of volunteer militia along the Scary River in western Virginia. Norton suffered a minor wound, and the rebel commander, former governor Henry Wise, arranged by private agreement to parole Norton in exchange for Colonel George S. Patton, an ancestor of the World War II general. Norton returned home, recovered, reorganized his militiamen as a three-year unit, and went off to serve in Kentucky. Patton stayed home waiting for official word that the exchange had been approved. The matter of the botched exchange first entered official army channels in March, but it did not reach Norton or the Adjutant General's Department until July 4. On that date Norton, armed with a letter from Buell referring to him as "an officer of merit," left his post at Athens for Washington, ostensibly to straighten out the matter of his exchange. Had he limited his visit to the business of his own status, no one would ever have noticed. He had, however, more pressing business on his mind and more papers in his satchel than the letter of recommendation from Buell. He left for Washington to derail the confirmation of a new brigadier.[16]

With his own personal popularity among the civilians of both Huntsville and Athens, where he had commanded either the provost guard or the occupying garrison, conciliation had no greater proponent than this man who had seen its apparent success. Norton stopped at Louisville on July 9 and took the time to fuel Prentice's new anti-Mitchel and -Turchin fire. Passing through Cincinnati and Pittsburgh on his way east, he checked into Willard's Hotel on July 16, having arrived in the capital at least a day or two before. He was said to have brought with him documents, presumably copies of the affidavits assembled in May by Judge Lane, to support the monetary claims of Athens's citizens.[17] "The papers about the sacking of Athens have been received," was the matter-of-fact intelligence from the *Pittsburgh Gazette,* datelined Washington, Tuesday, July 15.

These news items scarcely amounted to a widespread clamor either favoring Turchin's promotion or demanding his punishment. (Publicity more in his favor would not come until later.) The news items were adequate, however, to put those who needed to know on notice that they had another recent immigrant standing as a nominee for brigadier whose conduct had come into serious question. With the presence of Norton, they had a witness at hand anxiously trying to testify before anyone willing to listen.

Evidently misled by the name of the panel, perhaps naïve as to its members' true radical bent, Colonel Norton chose as his forum the Committee on the Conduct of the War. Were Benjamin Wade not otherwise occupied, preparing and delivering a lengthy tirade on July 16 against George McClellan, few things would have warmed that senator's heart so merrily as a description, however exaggerated, of Turchin's brigade rampaging through Alabama. As it happened, his committee did give Norton a hearing, "at a meeting at which several members of the committee were not present," reportedly on that Wednesday, July 16. But it accorded him no importance. The committee kept a transcript of its proceedings but included only the testimony of another witness, Colonel Gilman Marston. It pointedly omitted any mention of affairs in Alabama.[18] One newspaper account of Norton's testimony, published on July 22 in the *Cincinnati Commercial,* indicates that he condemned Mitchel for dealing illicitly in cotton and Turchin for allowing depredations. The story specifically mentioned rapes and plundering. An account in the *New York Herald* of the same date, moreover, reprints the statement Colonel Norton provided to the senators before the vote on Turchin's confirmation. While written in a tone charitably to be described as hysterical, it fully apprised the legislators of the charges at the court-martial. It both paraphrased them and provided new elaboration, charging that Turchin's men

have stolen horses, mules, bacon, corn and fodder from the inhabitants. . . . I charge that they have plundered houses, taken from them ladies wearing apparel, gentlemen's clothing, and have broken furniture and windows, broken locks of drawers and have destroyed everything in and about various premises. I charge them with committing rape upon servant girls in the presence of their mistresses, while stripping rings from ladies' fingers, cutting bacon upon parlor carpets, piling meat upon pianos, and being quartered in houses when they should have been quartered in their tents, robbing citizens upon the highway, breaking open safes and stores, breaking jars and everything generally in drug stores, in two or three instances. They have also taken away horses, mules, buggies and harness.

Had there been any life left in the policy of conciliation, the news carried by Norton might have had dramatic effect. Instead, despite his shrill tenor and urgent delivery, he was wildly out of step with the times—his attempt completely backfired, and backfired badly. By one account Secretary of War Stanton issued orders for Norton's arrest, thereby running the tattling colonel out of town for being absent from his duty station. Colonel Norton's military career abruptly ended shortly thereafter.[19]

President Lincoln had a keen sensitivity to the political pulse of the country. He had no fear of decisiveness, and during July 1862 the opportunity to lead and to make changes—broad, sweeping changes—stood in plain view. Much of that decision making took place behind closed doors. It was a public fact that there was "a heavy pressure among the Republicans for more earnest and vigorous measures in the conduct of the war, and several Congressmen are waiting now [July 9] only to unite with a declaration, to call on the President tomorrow as soon as he can receive them." On July 12 a caucus of Republican representatives produced a resolution imploring the administration "to punish traitors and treason with fitting severity, and to crush the present wicked and causeless rebellion that no flag of disunion shall ever again be raised."[20] Some had spoken with this harshness before. Now there was the clear prospect of action.

On July 11 Illinois governor Richard Yates issued a public letter arguing that harsh war "will bring the conflict to a speedy close," now that the policy of "[m]ild and conciliatory means . . . has utterly failed to reduce traitors to their allegiance, and to restore the supremacy of the law." Fitted instead with a draconian policy, Yates promised, his state, "resounding with the tread of new recruits, . . . will leap like a flaming sheet into the fight." Within days the *Milwaukee Sentinel,* the *Philadelphia Press,* the *National Republican,* and the *Pittsburgh Press,* among others, reprinted Yates's ringing call for harsh war.[21]

In the background, Washington insiders could hear the relentless drumbeat of Benjamin Wade's Committee on the Conduct of the War, its radical members carefully assembling a record of conciliation's failure during McClellan's recent campaign. On July 10, during friendly cross-examination about another incident, a *Philadelphia Inquirer* correspondent testified: "Whenever we were on the march, General Andrew Porter would send out cavalry and infantry with the advance, and station them at the homes and lanes, with positive orders to prevent any of the soldiers entering under any pretence whatever."

Question: [by Representative John Covode, radical Republican of western Pennsylvania] Would not the taking of that property by our troops hinder the rebels, at least so far as we prevented them from getting it?

Answer: Certainly it would.[22]

The committee's testimonial record and its conclusions—even such obvious points from so minor a source—were ostensibly kept confidential. This went by the boards with Wade's speech on the Senate floor on July 16, which concluded in part, "Had [the Army of the Potomac] been relieved from guarding the property of rebels in arms, many valuable lives would have been saved."[23]

In the midst of this pressure, Lincoln prepared to make explicit declarations of a new harsh-war policy through the orders of his new commander in northern Virginia. Major General John Pope reported for duty in Washington on June 22 and then reluctantly, on June 26, accepted the command of all troops in Virginia, other than those under McClellan on the Peninsula.[24] That Pope would apply a more aggressive brand of strategy and tactics than had McClellan was immediately apparent from his published address to his new charges, delivered on July 14, with language that, if easily criticized as sounding silly, was at least blunt: "Let us look before us and not behind. Success and glory are in the advance. Danger and shame lurk in the rear." Certainly that speech was aimed as much at his superiors as it was toward his men, being his first attempt to impress on the administration that he intended to be the sort of commander it sought.[25]

A stream of orders, all of which cleared the White House before being issued, followed closely on the heels of the speech. First, on July 15, at the beginning of a momentous week, Pope banned the practice of guarding private houses and other rebel civilian property within the area of his command. On July 18 he directed that "the troops of this command will subsist upon the country in which their operations are carried on." Even more, local citizens would not only be held responsible for all damage done to transportation and communication facilities by guerillas and bushwhackers operating in their areas, but they also could be compelled to repair the damage or be assessed to pay to have others do so, as had been done in Missouri with telling effect the year before. Secretary of War Stanton personally drafted the first of these orders. The president and the cabinet approved them all. These startling new directives, which so directly contravened McClellan's views so recently expressed, were not the creation of a new general who had decided to go it on his own.[26] They emanated from the peak of the mount.

Somewhat unfairly—none of Pope's orders overstepped the bounds of legitimate military conduct—this change in the thrust of the operational orders to his troops was promptly construed by officers of the Old Army as leading the soldiers to "believe that they have a perfect right to rob, tyrannize, threaten and mistreat any one they please, under the Orders of Gen.

Pope." Confederate general Richard Ewell perceived this happening in Culpeper County, where he complained of Union troops "systematically destroying all the growing crops," which they were, in order to subsist. Henry Halleck understood the situation, writing to McClellan on August 7: "I think some of General Pope's orders very injudicious, and have so advised him; but as I understand they were shown to the President before they were issued I felt unwilling to ask him to countermand them."[27]

The political drive for a turn explicitly to hard war thus was building to a crescendo during the last week of the congressional session. When it all was over, the *New York Tribune*'s Hill, a ravenous searcher after the words and wisdom of the powerful, recounted for his editor on Friday, July 18, "Arnold, of Ills. tells me tonight that within the last two or three days the President has been subjected to the greatest pressure in favor of vigorous war that was ever brought to bear upon him."[28]

Two circumstances not generally noticed intervened during this crowded time to ease Lincoln's repudiation of conciliation. First, the leading congressional spokesmen for conciliation—the senators and representatives from the border states—came up woefully short in negotiations with the president. Their chance came when they were invited as a group to the White House on Saturday morning, July 12, to hear Lincoln read a written argument for "a decision at once to emancipate gradually," perhaps through colonization in South America. It was time, the president told them, to "fish, cut bait or pull ashore."[29]

Their lengthy, niggling, and negative written response came out on Tuesday, July 15, written by the voluble, peppery, staunchly proslavery Senator Garrett Davis of Kentucky, the negligible Senator "Bob" Wilson of Missouri, and eighteen congressmen. They balked at the figure of $476 million, the price of purchasing emancipation, as it had already been estimated during debate in March. They promised to forward the subject for consideration by their states and districts when the number became more definite. More to the point, they argued for a reaffirmation of the Crittenden Resolution, in effect for adoption of the Harrison's Landing Letter, and for assurance that slavery would be left untouched by a victory of Union arms. The majority of Southerners in rebellion, they wrote, would cease to fight if the federal government were merely to "[r]emove their apprehensions, satisfy them that no harm is intended to them and their institutions; that the government is not making war on their rights of property, but is simply defending its legitimate authority." A minority response to Lincoln's Saturday morning overture emerged at the same time, signed by Senator Whitman Thomas Willey of western Virginia, a captive of the administration, and six members of the House. They proposed lamely to ask "our people to consider the question of emancipation to save the Union . . . calmly, fairly and deliberately."[30]

It is hard to imagine that Lincoln, who had campaigned on a platform where he constantly had tried to reassure Southerners that "no harm was intended to them and their institutions," by this point expected this excursion to end in any more productive a result. By digging when and where they did, Davis and the border staters in effect gave up any moral claim to influence whatever violence the administration might care to work on the remains of a conciliatory policy.

The second circumstance, also unfortunate in itself, that worked to free Lincoln's hand was a striking military event and a sharp blow to the reputation and professional credibility of Don Carlos Buell. Failure on the Peninsula had already destroyed McClellan's standing. Now Buell found himself tarnished by the loss of Murfreesboro and its 1,600 soldiers to a relatively small but patently aggressive Confederate force. The story made headlines across the North on July 14, extending so far as the front page of the *Boston Transcript*. For the benefit of Washington readers, the *National Intelligencer's* story included the extent of the loss by unit. In the view of Prentice at the *Louisville Journal* on July 15, the military disaster "cannot but have created a painful feeling among loyal men everywhere. These events, but mere ripples in the great tide of war, indicate strikingly a want of good management. They should not have been permitted to happen. Nothing like them should be permitted to happen hereafter."

Not for nothing did Buell, as soon as the scope of the disaster became apparent, rail against the unfortunate senior officers who had failed in command at the scene. The general no doubt felt the frustration of soldiers serving as occupiers in an unfriendly land. Buell knew that a want of good management had occurred within his own command. He knew, too, that the loss would draw into question his own abilities. Minds already focused on his lack of action could find in it an easy explanation for this reverse. Buell had refused to seize the initiative. Now his opponents, both in the North and in the South, had snatched it from him.

The Senate had been mixing its own cauldrons of bitter broth for the civilians of the South far longer than had the administration. The second confiscation bill had been simmering in the Senate hopper since December 5, 1861. The bill, introduced by Lyman Trumbull, became, it was almost fair of one of his admirers to say, "the pièce de résistance of senatorial debate for the whole session." After a fierce and protracted debate, McClellan's defeat had as much as anything else brought the matter to a head and allowed its passage. The result, however, was far more intelligibly read as rhetoric than as law.[31]

As the bill finally stood on July 17, 1862, ready for Lincoln's signature,[32] it created a "duty" in the president to seize "all the estate and property, money, stocks, credits and effects" of all Confederate army and navy officers, high government officials and, when the property was to be found in loyal parts of the Union, anyone who "shall hereafter assist and give aid and comfort" to the rebellion. To enforce seizures, the bill provided for proceedings in the federal courts in rem. The government, in a suit, could name as the party defendant the property itself, without need to root out the rebellious owner and serve him with process. Thus, if Union officials learned of a Confederate sutler's account in a St. Louis bank, that account could vanish into the federal treasury with actual notice to no one but the local federal court and the bank.

Further, if a loyal citizen came into possession of the property of a traitor, as defined in the statute, he could raise that owner's treason (often, presumably, just his position in the Confederate armed forces) as an absolute defense to his own title to it, and so walk off with the property. Thus, in theory, a wealthy Georgian commissioned as a major in the Confederate States Army who happened to own a house on Twelfth Street in New York City could lose it in a trice to a squatter. Thus, under this new enactment, privates in the United States Army could claim they committed no crime, but rather enforced the law, when they filched a rebel sympathizer's silver.

The measure was also emancipatory, even though the sections providing for seizure and in rem divestiture of title would seem already to have freed the slaves of most of the active Confederates. It declared "forever free of servitude" all slaves of persons engaged in rebellion "or who shall give aid or comfort thereto," though only if the slaves could make their way to or otherwise fall within federal lines. The bill gave only the vaguest guidance as to its targets, evincing an attitude, perhaps, of "We know who's guilty." It could be read to include virtually every complacent resident of the rebelling states. It clearly fit what Senator Benjamin Wade wanted to achieve; as he stated it during a floor debate on June 25: "I would reduce these aristocratic slave-holders to utter poverty."[33]

To the hard-bitten among the North's editorial writers, and to the readers who read their columns (including tens of thousands of volunteers), the only further logic needed was, as the *Pittsburgh Gazette* put it, again purely *in terrorem*, "inflicting no more than a just punishment upon those who have originated and do now uphold this nefarious rebellion." That blunt thought echoed up the smallest valleys of the North, into the very grassroots of the country. As the *Courier* in little Lebanon, Pennsylvania, put it, "The traitors shall be made [to] pay the cost of their folly and crime."[34]

Not surprisingly, no newspaper appeared more stridently an advocate of confiscation than the *Chicago Tribune*. There Charles Ray caught the ingenious and important point that this bit of lawmaking would emancipate a great many slaves. It depended not at all upon any ideology of abolitionism to do it. "Here is a plain, easily understood issue," the paper editorialized early in the debate, on March 12. "No pettifogging, no demagogical humbug, no howling at 'abolitionists' can befog this issue, or blink it. It looms up like a mountain. It smokes out rebel sympathizers in our midst. Every man opposed to confiscation is an ally of Jeff. Davis & Co. He is in favor of 'subjecting the people of the North to burthens which must continue to oppress them for generations to come' in order that his traitor friends in Secessia, may escape the just penalty of their crimes." Privately, publisher Medill noted in a letter to Senator Trumbull that the confiscation bill once enacted would be exceedingly difficult to repeal. Should Democrats ever regain power in Congress, they would be hard-pressed to put blacks back in chains.[35]

Another congressional assault on the civilians of the South, the militia bill, would strike a double blow as it stood the morning of July 17.[36] First, it authorized the acceptance into federal service of "persons of African descent." Though ostensibly "for the purpose of constructing entrenchments, or performing camp service, or any other labor," it also allowed black men to serve in "any other military or naval service for which they may be found competent." This did not exclude combat service. As secretary of war, Simon Cameron had raised the prospect of enlisting blacks in November 1861.[37] In the Senate on April 14, 1862, while debating a proposed new article of war forbidding the return of fugitive slaves, Iowa's James Grimes, a man personally close to the president, argued "unhesitatingly" that Union forts should be garrisoned "in whole or in part, by soldiers of African descent; that instead of returning slaves to their rebel masters to fight against us, we should employ them in our own military service." At Fessenden's request, the historian George Bancroft produced precedent from the Revolutionary War for armed service by blacks.[38]

Armed slaves would form the honor guard gathered around the grave of conciliation. Its profound effect upon the Southern mind appears as sharply as anywhere in the opinion expressed a year later by Garlick Kean, the normally temperate, highly intelligent young patrician Virginia lawyer who headed an important Confederate administrative bureau in Richmond. "[I]t is quite clear that the enlistment of our slaves is a barbarity which no people, who regarded anything save the gratification of a devilish lust of revenge and hatred, could tolerate on the principle, the use of savages, which Chatham denounced and the Declaration of Independence recorded as infamous."[39] Now the United States government was on the verge of doing that which John Brown had been hanged for only two and one-half years before.

Southerners thus faced two new weapons harnessed by the statutes. Forced emancipation breached forever the doctrine of states' rights and the thought that a state could regulate its own "established institutions." Even more terrifying to those supporting the rebellion, their slaves could, and would, be armed to bring about their own defeat. This all stood in stark contrast to the platform upon which Lincoln had campaigned, to the Crittenden Resolution of only a year before, to the border state Unionists' response to Lincoln just days earlier, and to the conciliatory policies previously espoused by Lincoln and still dear to the hearts and senses of honor of professional soldiers like George B. McClellan and Don Carlos Buell. As rejections of conciliation, no sharper messages could be sent. But how best to let the army know that times had changed? Pope's orders had caught Henry Halleck, now commanding general of the armies, by surprise. Perhaps other events would clarify the administration's new drift.

13
Confirmation

If the President has initiated some decidedly new steps in his intercourse with Congress, so also the Senate has done a like thing by transacting ordinary public business with closed doors. This went on for hours to-day, and what was said and done is of course a sealed book to correspondents. Actions upon the Presidential appointments is the excuse. . . . A shrewd republican suggests that it will be found that a great number of promotions of those who are not recognized as radicals have been passed over.

—*New York Herald*, datelined Washington, July 17, 1862

With more than four dozen nominations for brigadier pending, careful legislative management would be needed to bring any of them to the forefront quickly and successfully so that its message, if one was intended, might be loudly and clearly conveyed. Normally that job would have fallen to the chairman of the Committee on Military Affairs and the Militia, Senator Henry Wilson of Massachusetts, or his vice chairman, Preston King of New York. Senator Wilson had a deep, personal fascination with military matters, even having once accepted a colonel's commission for himself. He "admired the gaudily uniformed men who proposed to crush the rebels" and at first, through the closing months of 1861, coddled McClellan. Now, however, in Washington's suffocating summer heat, Wilson joined the swelling ranks of those fed up with the progress of the war. On July 9 he spoke in the Senate against the "many leaders of our armies [who exhibited] excessive zeal to conciliate rebels and to protect the property of rebels."[1] Preston King, on the other hand, had always been skeptical about the professional military establishment but, like Wilson, was staunchly antislavery. Also on July 9, he assisted James Grimes with the portion of the militia bill that touched on emancipation. Privately he favored creating a combat brigade of black troops. Publicly he was nearly as blunt. "[W]e have got to take off our gloves and our coats and go at these people in earnest," King told his colleagues.[2]

From the nature of their Senate positions Wilson and King could not advance anything so broadly contrary to the ethos of the professional military as the promotion of a colonel who was in the midst of a court-martial. Their committee posts required close work with the senior uniformed men on matters ranging from supply contracts to drafting regulations. As Wilson put it, officers came to their committee to "make their wishes known to me. . . . It would be very unwise in that committee not to hear those officers and not to hear that Department."[3] Similarly unwise it would have been for the two senior members of the committee to seem oblivious to the core disciplinary values of the military service. Thus Wilson and King would both vote against Turchin's confirmation, even though the nature of the confirmation procedure must have obliged Wilson's clerk to affix Turchin's name to the list of those up for the vote. Neither made an attempt to stymie the nomination in committee.

If the administration wanted Colonel Turchin confirmed, it would have to find a floor leader to gather the votes. Almost inescapable is the conclusion that William Pitt Fessenden acted as that manager. Direct proof is entirely absent, but the circumstantial evidence points unequivocally to the senior senator from Maine and to no one else. Fessenden scrutinized military affairs both from official duty and from the psychological burden of having three sons in uniform. Generally an opponent of conciliation but reticent in his public comments about it "in order not to discourage the people," as one son put it, he accepted an invitation to Stanton's office on April 13 to hear Benjamin Wade rail in favor of giving the country "that vigorous war policy which alone could save it." Privately contemptuous of McClellan, no doubt he harbored similar feelings toward the policies the general espoused.[4]

As to Buell, in whose ranks Fessenden's son Frank had served at Shiloh, his public statements and private writings say nothing—except late that summer, on August 31, when Buell's position had grown tenuous, and Fessenden "rejoiced" that Frank would not be sent back to serve in the West before "a competent commander" could be placed in charge there.[5] A dedicated, probably brilliant, trial lawyer as a young man in Bangor and Portland, Fessenden did not hold military justice and courts-martial in high regard. "It is well known that there is a sort of fellow feeling or something of the kind that very often operates on courts-martial," he would later say, "not constrained as civil courts are, that unquestionably needs correction. . . . [They] after all are mere military tribunals."[6]

Often ignored, recognized chiefly for technical competence as chairman of the Committee of Finance, Fessenden has been thought an unpleasantly aloof figure, excused for it because he bore the torments of dyspepsia in his slender, 130-pound frame. He was aloof. He suffered physically. But quietly and competently, he made good use of a position of great legislative power. Comments from his circle of close personal friends, and in his family correspondence, disclose a charming personality. His comrades enjoyed evenings "laughing at Mr. Fessenden's jokes & stories," and he shared confidential chats with another great storyteller, Abraham Lincoln, about high military matters.[7]

Perhaps because of his rapport with the president, during the spring of 1862 Fessenden, not Wilson, interviewed and recommended Edwin Stanton to replace Simon Cameron as secretary of war. Now, in the midst of the growing debate over war policy, during the week of July 14 Fessenden busied himself mediating between the president and the Senate to reach a satisfactory compromise on the terms of the confiscation bill, though no contemporary account tells exactly what this "mousing around" with the White House (Wade's language) involved.[8] Fessenden filled the role of a discreet force behind the scenes when the administration's military affairs touched on senatorial politics. He was the natural, perhaps the only, choice to guide the Turchin nomination to a quick and positive result.

From what we know of Fessenden's background, there was no question about how he would vote, nor about how enthusiastically he would do so. Similar, if scantier, information makes it possible to assess the votes to be expected from the other senators present in the Senate that July 17. Simple information such as their states, their party backgrounds, and their statements on the Senate floor, even if those sometimes had to be taken with a bit of skepticism, are often sufficient to demonstrate the basis of their votes.[9] Conclusions may also be reached by focusing upon specific tallies; though not robust statistical conclusions, given the mere handful of apposite votes cast by a small group of men in the Senate chamber during the spring and early summer of 1862, some votes are enlightening.[10]

Senators who voted to add emancipatory provisions to the militia bill (drafted originally simply as a measure to raise more troops) could reasonably be expected to vote for the no less incendiary confirmation of a colonel accused of being too hard on Southerners. So also those who voted to emancipate the slaves in the District of Columbia, to bar army officers from slave catching, and to allow blacks to testify in court. It is also reasonable to assume that those who voted to send the Senate's confiscation bill forward were of a nonconciliatory bent. Two votes trenching upon the Regular Army—one limiting the size of staffs, the other the number of brigadiers, and so reflecting attitudes toward the army—might shed a modest light on the inclination of specific senators to defy the high command and vote for Turchin. There is also the contested vote of July 16 on the confirmation of James Streshly Jackson as a brigadier. A Kentucky lawyer and a member of Congress until he resigned to take command of the Third Kentucky Cavalry, he had throughout his career evoked sharply contrasting opinions between supporters and opponents. When the vote came, he stood in command of Don Carlos Buell's cavalry and was highly recommended for promotion by Buell. But he also stood accused, not of malicious misconduct, but rather of displaying undue sympathy for Southern civilians. He was John Basil Turchin's direct opposite.[11]

Using these criteria, nine senators emerge who would never have supported the appointment of Turchin as a brigadier. Five were from the border states: Garrett Davis and Lazarus Powell of Kentucky, John Carlisle of Virginia, John Brooks Henderson and Robert Wilson of Missouri. Not one had cast a single vote favoring emancipation or confiscation. Also based on votes cast on those subjects, votes against Turchin could be expected from Benjamin Stark of Oregon, Joseph Albert Wright of Indiana, and Henry Anthony and James Simon of Rhode Island. Jacob Collamer of Vermont cast the tenth vote against Turchin. On April 25 he had bitterly denounced confiscation in a speech.[12] Collamer by nature could not sanction any unnecessary roughness against the people of the South. More than any other senator, he was, at age seventy-one, looking ahead toward the consequences of the war's end.

On the other side Lincoln, and presumably Fessenden as his manager, could garner sixteen votes from obvious radicals and Republican Regulars whom they had every reason to think favored Turchin's confirmation. Zachariah Chandler of Michigan "detested the Southern aristocrats and never missed an opportunity to attack them." New Hampshire's Daniel Clark stood as "an uncompromising foe of slavery." He had made the motion to expel James Mason, James Chestnut, Louis Wigfall, and seven other Southern senators when they failed to appear at the reconvened Congress on July 10, 1861. Clark had long thought reconciliation impossible. John Parker Hale of New Hampshire first spoke of abolishing slavery in 1847. James Wilson Grimes, one of Fessenden's closer friends, and James Harlan, close to Lincoln and a strong defender of the administration, both of Iowa, stood out as trusted allies.[13]

Jacob M. Howard of Michigan, an early skeptic about McClellan, supported a vigorous prosecution of the war, as he amply demonstrated in his speech on the confiscation bill. Timothy Howe of Wisconsin had introduced the bill to repeal the Fugitive Slave Act and in general "steadfastly supported administration measures." Henry Smith Lane of Indiana voted to confirm Colonel Jackson but also was "regarded as the leader of the antislavery movement" of his state and otherwise took positions consistent with a Turchin voter. Lot M. Morrill of Maine was something of a radical. His support of a man like Turchin came naturally.[14]

Charles Sumner of Massachusetts had famously suffered blows from the cane of a Southern firebrand, and his antipathy for anything favoring the residents of the slave states was well understood. The occasionally ornery Lyman Trumbull of Illinois stood, after Fessenden and Sumner, as the least likely to oppose confirmation. Benjamin Franklin Wade of Ohio would have been delighted to have two hundred Turchins up for confirmation. Minnesota's Morton Smith Wilkinson was a "committed radical" of remarkable consistency. Henry Mower Rice of Minnesota had only lately converted to harsh war, but judging by all his recent votes, he had become a true convert. Finally, David Wilmot of Pennsylvania had established his reputation as a champion of free soil in 1846, when he first proposed his proviso that would have outlawed slavery in all territory gained in Mexico. He never strayed from the cause of abolitionism.[15] There would be no regional prejudice against the Illinois colonel. Indeed, he garnered broad geographic acceptance across the loyal states. Yet the solid votes so far counted left him a few shy of the number needed for confirmation.

There were eight senators who might have voted for Turchin but did not. John Conover Ten Eyck, the obscure Republican senator from New Jersey, waffled ambiguously throughout his career, as did, for that matter, the legislature that sent him to Washington, a coalition in which the status of the Republican Party was often shaky. Ten Eyck had voted to ban slave catching by army officers, to emancipate the slaves in the District of Columbia, and to allow the testimony of blacks in court and had concurred in the confiscation bill. Yet he had voted against the more radical emancipatory sections of the militia bill, and he did represent George McClellan's adopted home state. His vote here may have been a matter of taste, a signal of the sort of person he preferred to see in a general's uniform. Ten Eyck voted to confirm Buell's protégé James S. Jackson and against Turchin.[16]

The votes of the Kansas delegation, James Henry Lane and Samuel Clarke Pomeroy, are harder to explain. Both were fervent and conspicuous abolitionists, as one might expect from the state they represented, Lane "the Knight of the Sorrowful Nigger" to one irreverent young newspaperman. Both owed their all to Lincoln's past favor with patronage for their political and financial fortunes, and each knew that he would be indebted in the future.[17]

Jim Lane, labeled rather carelessly as a "Kansas border ruffian" by the writers for the *New York Herald,* had spoken in the Senate against conciliation as forcefully as any senator there. "I laugh to scorn the policy of wooing back the traitors to their allegiance," he had cried. He held, rather more shockingly, the distinction of being the one United States senator who had personally directed the destruction of a town thought to be Confederate. Back in the West on one of his occasional military forays commanding a volunteer brigade, at Osceola, Missouri, on September 23, 1861, he had led his men in the cannonading, plundering, and final torching of the little town. His personal share of the loot was a piano and a clutch of silk dresses. Lane made a practice, though, of retreating to pious words after outrageous conduct. His vote against Turchin may have been an attempt to appear more pious. It may also have been an attempt to placate the citizens of Missouri who had cause to complain about Turchin's sojourn there hardly a year earlier.[18] Pomeroy, consistently seen with a "bland smile and sanctimonious air," chose to follow Lane's lead. Perhaps both were also sensitive to the complaints about the more recent outrages committed by Kansas troops. They both voted against Turchin.[19]

Five other senators who might normally have favored the Russian did not. Wilson and King, with their ties to the army, could not. Ira Harris of New York, an inveterate master of patronage, would have wanted to defeat Turchin's appointment so that another place would be available for a man of his own.[20] Wisconsin's James Rood Doolittle was engaged in a long-standing personal feud with the *Chicago Tribune,* such that the newspaper's publishers were "doing their utmost to defeat your reappointment to the Senate," or so a friend advised him. He may well have taken an opportunity to reciprocate with a swipe at a *Tribune* pet. Doolittle shared with the president well-reasoned doubts about portions of the confiscation bill, and his personal philosophy was at bottom more Democrat than Republican, even though he was generally an advocate of vigorous military policy. Here something of a personal nature probably governed his vote.[21]

Senator John Sherman of Ohio voted against Turchin. The general's younger brother had always, up to this point, talked with some hesitation about harsh war, voting for the Crittenden Resolution in 1861 from a fear, based on reflection, that "Anglo-Saxons have always warred with each other bitterly and with determination." Yet, he wrote, "a man who has assented in this rebellion forfeits life and property and slave and honor and everything. There is hardly anything I would not do to him." The senator advocated the use of blacks in the army.[22]

The senator always remained in close touch with his brother the general. He took into serious consideration his brother's views on military matters. The general's deep sense of discipline may have mattered most when it came to Turchin's confirmation. Throughout 1862 there were lines William Tecumseh Sherman would not let soldiers cross. As a division commander at the time, he issued standard general orders enjoining depredations, but with a personal edge to them. "Let us respect private property, and if the effects of some secessionists should even escape for a time, it will still be liable to confiscation, as the civil courts follow in our train. We have a higher mission than to destroy the petty property of the families of our enemies."[23] This attitude was manifestly contrary to that of Turchin at Athens. In this case, it appears that the attitude of the general infused that of the senator. When it came to the vote that Thursday morning, John Sherman evidently saw Turchin as having been properly indicted for tolerating petty deeds of pillage, and so unworthy of the brigadier's star.

The administration thus very much needed four more votes to carry the nomination. Only with some effort were they to be gotten, even if in the end the price was fairly cheap. The background and records of the four senators who acquiesced—Waitman Thomas Willey of western Virginia, James A. McDougal of California, Edgar Cowan of Pennsylvania, and Orville Hickman Browning of Illinois—were in each case such that the senator would never have been expected to vote for a confirmation that stood for harsh punishment of Southern civilians. But each man was also vulnerable to suggestion and was irrevocably beholden to the administration either for past assistance or in hope of future aid and favor. There is no evidence that any specific quid pro quo was exchanged for any of the four votes. It would be enough that indebtedness existed and may have been mentioned in the course of the negotiations prior to the vote. Thus Lincoln and his manager were able, and apparently willing, to tolerate the closeness of the vote if it resulted in favorable and quick action.

Waitman Willey, the Virginian, normally felt obliged by local politics to take the position of a border state Unionist—that the nation must be bound back together but without interfering with the South's supposed rights in slavery. When matters came to a vote, Willey consistently rejected emancipation in the District of Columbia and opposed the emancipatory provisions of the militia bill. He came only reluctantly to a position tolerating gradual emancipation. He and his patron, Governor Francis Pierpont, knew that depredations by Union troops had been horrific experiences for their friends and neighbors. They received and read petitions from households seeking aid after Union troops occupying the counties of the proposed new state disrupted their lives. On the other hand, they knew that the rebels in their midst often did far worse. The Union soldiers stole things. Rebels carried off the men and boys, sometimes to army training camps, sometimes into the woods to be murdered. It was abundantly clear, too, that Pierpont's state administration, and thus Willey, served entirely at the pleasure of the Lincoln administration and were beholden to the president. As one analyst of the state's situation has pointed out, "It is inconceivable that the Pierpont Government could have functioned effectively without the support of Federal troops."[24] Willey thus became the one border state senator who signed the reply not dismissive of Lincoln's compromise overture of a few days before the Turchin vote. He was now the one border state senator who voted for Turchin.

Edgar Cowan's dependence on the administration ran deep. He had no other basis of support, having foolishly managed to alienate the backing of his fellow Republicans in a state where the party, dominated by Simon Cameron, was distinctly averse to any softness about the South. A small-town lawyer from the mountains of western Pennsylvania, slipping through the General Assembly in one of Cameron's inattentive moments, he found himself in the national Senate almost by accident. The clumsy extravagance of some of his oratory there suggested his awareness that he was out of his depth. Those speeches trended far to the side favoring conciliation. A victorious Union general could not, he argued in April 1862, "follow the rebel after his surrender, and take from him his house the private property he had left . . . and all this because a Christian civilization has taught the nations that such modes of making war are not only not necessary, but that they are in all cases mischievous and injurious even to the conqueror himself."[25]

By July 1862 Cowan could not but have noticed that such rhetoric, however morally admirable, left him with no support whatever among Pennsylvania Republicans. "Viciously attacked for the position he had taken on party measures," he became the whipping boy of the radical *Pittsburgh Gazette* and won unfortunate praise as a "courageous statesman" in the wrong journal, the near-copperhead *Harrisburg Patriot-Union*. Simply to stay in public life, he needed any succor the White House might then or later care to provide.[26] Cowan's vote could be obtained with a very gentle nudge. Someone jiggled the prod.

The California Democrat James McDougal had a different and darker dependence: alcoholism. A brilliant lawyer, McDougal had been transported from brilliance to flamboyance by alcohol. He appeared in the Senate chamber at times drunk, wearing a vaquero's large black sombrero, brandishing a whip—some sort of advertisement, perhaps, for the color and excitement of his state. Very Unionist, officially a Douglas Democrat, he spoke articulately and voted consistently against both emancipation and confiscation. When confirming generals, his taste would normally have been with the orthodox Regular Army. Thus he voted for James S. Jackson. He bravely made the particular point of standing up for the Regulars' rights and privileges in the case of Brigadier General Charles P. Stone. In July 1862 Stone sat imprisoned in a federal fort, no charges having been filed, a scapegoat for the Union defeat at Ball's Bluff and a victim of rumors spread by Ben Wade and others that he was "unsound on slavery."[27]

McDougal's savior from his debilitating and increasingly obvious drinking problem appears to have been Fessenden, who kept him occupied with the challenging work of the Finance Committee. For that Fessenden would have been owed no small favor. If Fessenden did not ask, Lincoln could have. Back in downstate Illinois in 1843, he and McDougal had been among the candidates for a seat in Congress, and there is evidence that these many years later the president was granting McDougal small favors, treating him with perhaps unexpected respect.[28] For McDougal the prospect of continued decent influence at the White House amidst a collapsing life may well have led him to go along with Lincoln and Fessenden in support of the nominee.

Orville Hickman Browning wanted in the worst way to be a justice of the United States Supreme Court and had been lobbying for the position since taking the senatorial oath in the spring of 1861, supposing himself to be a closer friend and ally of Lincoln than was actually the case. A downstate Illinois Republican, not implausibly accused of being a closet Democrat, by 1862 Browning had taken positions so far in favor of conciliation that the *Tribune*'s Medill, who hated him, would "[r]ather have a pro-slavery democrat & [be] done with it." In fact Browning was not in favor of slavery. He was merely an extreme conservative in general outlook, an "old-time Whig," another voter for the bellwether James S. Jackson and the active supporter of a competitor, a thoroughly conventional brigadier nominee from Illinois, James D. Morgan.[29]

Browning spent some time buzzing about the White House and conferring with Fessenden the week of July 14. As it happened, one Supreme Court vacancy was filled by the nomination Wednesday and the confirmation Thursday of Iowa judge Samuel F. Miller, but another seat remained vacant. Nothing kept Browning from aspiring to it. Nothing would have kept Lincoln and Fessenden from leading him to believe himself under serious consideration. The game went on until the following October when the position went to Lincoln's closer friend, David Davis.[30]

No record informs us of the substance of any of the private conversations Lincoln and Fessenden had on July 16 and 17 with Willey, Cowan, McDougal, and Browning, but it would have been normal for a floor leader like Fessenden, or even for Lincoln himself, to make the contacts needed to line up the votes required. With the tide rising so quickly and decidedly against all things associated with the leadership of generals like McClellan and Buell and for pushing the war onto a harsher course, a vote with the administration on this question would have been made all the easier. The fact that the president was sitting in the next room, ready to sign bills or provide advice, was certainly not lost on those whose votes might waver.[31]

The thirty-eight U.S. senators who came to work on July 17 found a full slate to be dealt with. They formally received scores of nominations from the president, referring them to the appropriate committees for review—those for the navy to the Committee of Naval Affairs, those for local officials to the Committee on the District of Columbia, those for the army to Henry Wilson's Committee on Military Affairs and Militia. Then they moved on to those earlier nominations that had been reported out of committee and that now required action.[32]

Those with no attached controversy came first. After his colleagues gave unanimous approval for the appointment of scores of men to low-ranking positions, Senator John Sherman stood and moved for the consideration of Colonel John Steedman's appointment as a brigadier general. The senators unanimously consented. Motions for action on the appointments of August Willich, hero of the Revolution of 1848 and of Shiloh; Conrad Jackson, a veteran of the peninsular campaign; and John Cochrane, a veteran of Fair Oaks and future sachem of Tammany Hall; as brigadiers also gained universal support. Next, the senators considered the elevation of three of Buell's division commanders—Alexander McCook, William Nelson, and Thomas

Crittenden—to the rank of major general. Not a single voice sounded in opposition.[33]

Then Senator Lyman Trumbull of Illinois rose from his chair in support of one of his constituents. He moved for the consideration of the nomination of Colonel John B. Turchin as a brigadier general of volunteers. New York's senator Ira Harris immediately countered with a motion to table the nomination. (With Congress about to adjourn, tabling action on Turchin's appointment would in effect kill it.) On the vote, seventeen senators sided with Harris. Nineteen joined Trumbull in voting nay. By a vote of eighteen to twenty, the motion to table the nomination failed. The Senate would have to vote up or down on the question. For the first time that day, the senators debated the relative merits of a nominee. We do not know what any of them said. We do not know how long or how heatedly they argued. All we know is the result. Presumably by the same slender margin, the United States Senate, after debate, advised and consented "to the appointment of John B. Turchin agreeably to the nomination."[34] Colonel John Basil Turchin, the scourge of Missouri, Bowling Green, and Athens, Alabama, had his brigadier's star. He had not obtained it by accident.

Immediately, now that the forces favoring harsh war had prevailed across the board in Congress, Lincoln took steps to temper the victory. The greatest problem lay in the confiscation bill, which lacked only his signature to become law. As passed by both houses, in the form preferred by the Senate and sitting on the president's desk from the morning of Tuesday, July 15, its provisions would punish offenders for acts committed before it went into effect and included as one potential punishment a forfeiture of an offender's real estate in perpetuity. The former provision was patently unconstitutional as a penalty ex post facto. The latter smelled like a bill of attainder, a legislative taking without judicial oversight. Both thus fell into question under the proscription of article 1, section 9, clause 3 of the Constitution.[35]

In addition to these constitutional objections, issues that Lincoln could safely have left to the courts, the attainder provisions in the bill almost certainly went farther than he cared to go as a matter of practical political governance. They instead represented Senator Jacob Collamer's scorn, as expressed in his April speech, precisely applied. According to a news dispatch datelined July 15, "The President's [sic] has been closeted all day in his library, refusing to see anyone, engaged in writing a message on the Confiscation bill. It is known that it will be either a veto or a request for supplemental legislation. All hope for the latter. Mr. [Schuyler] Colfax [radical Republican congressman from Indiana] . . . was so in earnest on confiscation as to leave a sick bed and go to a cot, on a cloak, in a room of the House, so that he could be called on to vote for it."[36]

The clash between Congress's vengefulness and Lincoln's constitutional conservatism came to be marked out in a message he sent to the House Thursday, when legislative attention on all fronts must have seemed frenetic. Lincoln said he could not agree to the confiscation bill's forfeiture provisions, specifically those making permanent the attainder of offenders' real property.

> For the causes of treason—the ingredients of treason, but amounting to the full crime—it declares forfeiture extending beyond the lives of the guilty parties, whereas the Constitution of the United States declares that no attainder of treason shall work corruption of blood or forfeiture, except during the life of the person attained [sic]. True, there is to be no formal attainder in this case, still I think the greater punishment cannot be constitutionally inflicted in a different form for the same offense. With great respect, I am constrained to say that I think this feature of the act is unconstitutional.[37]

Fessenden is generally credited—and was at the time sharply criticized—for avoiding a presidential veto by acting as an intermediary between the president and the congressional radicals. His intervention led to the last-minute passage of a joint resolution explicitly providing that the act "shall be so construed as not to apply to any act or acts done prior" to its passage, solving the ex post facto problem, and as to attainder and corruption of blood, that no action taken under it could "be so construed as to work a forfeiture of the real property of the offender beyond his natural life."[38]

Not strangely to Lincoln's purpose of moderating the effect of this measure, he made his message to the House public for reading and printing. Also not strangely, considering the radical senators' purpose of grinding into the South the heel of their harsh resolve, they would have preferred he had not. The *New York Tribune* went to print with the view that the compromise measure "fell like a wet blanket upon [the president's] friends in both Houses of Congress." The private view of the paper's Adams Sherman Hill: "Everybody hoped when a message was received that it was something that would stir up the people and quicken instead of hampering enlistments. Everybody was disappointed." A later and more dispassionate Republican analysis: "The feeling in Congress . . . was far more intense than throughout the country."[39]

Although Lincoln sought to appear measured and responsible, he left little doubt that times had changed. Trimming only slightly the arguments of Joseph Medill and Ben Wade, the message to the House noted about the first point, "That those who make a causeless war should be compelled to pay the cost of it, is too obviously just to be called in question. To give government protection to the property of persons who have abandoned it, and gone on a crusade to overthrow the same Government, is absurd." This statement charted an entirely new course from that mapped out in the president's first inaugural address. When it came to the employment of blacks, Lincoln also expressed agreement in principle, writing, "I am ready to say now that I think it is proper for our military commanders to employ as laborers as many persons of African descent as can be used to advantage."[40] Not quite the call for black troops radical abolitionists had made provision for; still, it was a sweeping change in policy.

The very next day, Major General John Pope began issuing the harsh-war orders that would quickly seize the attention of the Confederate administration, in part directing his troops to subsist on the hostile countryside when it was feasible to do so. On Tuesday, July 22, the president issued an executive order directing that in states where active hostilities were taking place, military commanders were to have the power "to seize and use property, real or personal, which may be necessary or convenient for their several commands as supplies, or for other military purposes." A power he already had, in his view, since at least as early as September 1861, it was nonetheless new official policy. The order went on, allowing the army to employ as laborers "so many persons of African descent as can be advantageously used."[41] This was not a sweeping engine of confiscation, but it was a very prompt application of new policy. From what a frenzied Congress had given him, the president quickly, but carefully, took advantage of all that he thought might be politically palatable.

A similar measured degree of action attached to the Turchin promotion. Lincoln sent a limited message. Numerous other men were confirmed along with Turchin, and only one of them might have been elevated for his harsh-war activities. The "hot-headed Iowa abolitionist" Fitz Henry Warren, at this point commanding the First Iowa Cavalry, had carried on Turchin's campaign against the rebel sympathizers in central Missouri. People in Washington remembered Warren from his incarnation as a *New York Tribune* editor and writer in June and July 1861, when he notoriously authored the editorials daily exhorting, "The Nation's War Cry: Forward to Richmond! Forward to

Richmond!" His nomination drew no objection based on his vigorous views of war, only a cavil from the Boston press that he was insufficiently a professional soldier. In a slightly different fashion, and in not quite so profound a way, Warren could also be seen as a symbol of the new hard-war policy.[42]

Colonel and acting brigadier Randolph Barnes Marcy, a career soldier and George McClellan's chief of staff (and, as it happened, his father-in-law) had been mysteriously deleted from the promotion list, "considered a pretty strong hit at George." Some of the sting of it had been softened on June 22 when Lincoln let it be known that Marcy remained chief of staff to the Army of the Potomac. However, nepotism may well have played its part in garnering stars for Cadwallader Washburn, brother of Lincoln confidant Elihu Washburn, and Frederick Salomon, brother of the governor of Wisconsin.[43]

Good old-fashioned bravery would still win promotion, as demonstrated by the confirmation of twenty-five-year-old Thomas Herron for his heroics at Pea Ridge and of Charles Cruft, who had been wounded at Shiloh. The same slate of officers, moreover, that was confirmed July 16 and 17 ought to have mollified Don Carlos Buell. Most of the officers he had recommended for brigadier's stars back on April 11 got them, including Joshua W. Sill, West Point class of 1853, Regular to the core, and, of course, James S. Jackson. Not least, also elevated was an officer then sitting in judgment of Turchin, Colonel Jacob Ammen. Obviously, military competence counted for much. Equally obviously, allowing men under one's command to treat Southern civilians with a bit of incivility was not any indication of a lack of such competence—not in the minds of the administration, not in the eyes of a majority in the Senate.[44]

None of this had the effect, however, of bringing the proceedings in Huntsville to a halt. The court-martial of the newly elevated brigadier went on apace. Public reaction to all of this remained to be seen.

14
The Verdict

Colonel Turchin is in his third week of trial for not dealing quietly
enough with rebels and their property.
—Brigadier General James A. Garfield, July 24, 1862

The promotion of the new class of brigadiers of which John Basil Turchin
was a member represented the close of business for the United States Senate.
On Thursday, July 17, it confirmed the last of those appointments, wrapped
up all of its other business, and adjourned until December, many of the members, their staffs, and hangers-on catching trains for distant cities and other
objectives. Frank P. Blair, for example, headed to St. Louis to raise yet another regiment.

Taking for granted the validity of Turchin's promotion, the *Chicago Tribune* put it to one of its intended purposes—the encouragement of recruiting
through praise of the new general as an example of a warrior rewarded for
fighting a war the way volunteers ought to fight it. For example, a July 26
editorial said, "Out of the long list of generals whose nominations were not
acted upon by the Senate, exceptions were made of two names, which were
pushed through. The first of these, J. B. Turchin, 19th Illinois, belongs to as
skillful and brave a soldier as our army contains. He was believed to make
war as war should be made, and to hit a head wherever he saw it. To these
peculiarities and to the persecution that he is enduring from others who lack
his faith, his promotion was due." Likely in response to the congressional
fervor exemplified in the action on Turchin, the *Tribune* also reported that
the Chicago Board of Trade Battery had by that date "raised a bounty fund
of $30,000 and have recruited a full battery of artillery and are rapidly filling
up a regiment."[1]

Though word of the promotion reached members of the court-martial
board as early as Saturday, July 19, the news did not slow its progress. On
July 20 orders transferred the proceedings from Athens to Huntsville, where

they went forward at a pace Garfield and Beatty found unbearably slow. Nine days later General Buell took formal note of the question of the court's continued validity and issued his General Order 36 in response. There he affirmed the court without specifying it by its caption and admonished the members: "Courts-martial in the army shall proceed industriously and continuously with the business before them until it is completed." Then he made his real point clear. "Discipline, and consequently the honor, and efficiency of the army is in no [in]considerable degree dependent on courts-martial. Nominal penalties for grave offenses avail nothing, and are neither wise nor merciful." To General Buell, the undisciplined behavior of Turchin's men in Athens would never be a passing matter. Turchin's style of command had no place in his army. Buell's orders, plain and direct, had been disregarded. His brigade commander had countenanced the precise behavior from his volunteers that the general most wanted to avoid. This court had been formed to roll heads.[2] Insofar as Major General Don Carlos Buell was concerned, the action of the Senate had no effect. His warning to Stanton may have gone unheeded. His messenger to the Senate may have been ignored and repudiated. Nonetheless, General Garfield's court-martial panel still could do justice where it most needed to be done.

A story is told, from much later than these events, about the credibility of the witness Turchin and Gazlay picked to begin their defense. In 1862 William B. Curtis, then a twenty-five-year-old lieutenant, served as Turchin's adjutant. In 1874 he refereed a major championship rowing race in New York City. He could have entered a ruling for the Halifax team, representing America, giving it the world championship in four-oar shells. (Rowing competitions were wildly popular sporting events at that time, and competitors could go to great lengths to fix a race, even so far as to saw opponents' shells in half.) Curtis ruled for the opposition, the Thames, representing Britain and, reported *The New York Times*, "it is enough to say that his effigy was burned in Halifax." As for the basis for his decision, Curtis said, "I couldn't help it. It was the only thing I could do. If they don't want me to referee fairly, they need not ask me at all." The *Times*'s comment in Curtis's obituary, after his death on Mount Washington during an unexpected snowstorm in July 1900, was to the point: "And this was the keynote of his character. He couldn't help being honest."[3]

Turchin and Gazlay not only had the savvy to call this man of unshakable integrity as their first witness, where he would do the most good, but they organized his testimony intelligently. It began with a point that would capture the members' attention and which had to be made. At the station in Huntsville the afternoon on May 1, on hearing that two Union soldiers had been killed, General Mitchel had instructed the troops leaving for Athens: "I will build a monument to those two men at Athens. I have dealt gently long enough with those people. I will try another course now."

Curtis's testimony then continued with the customary narrative introduction, this one covering the movement against Athens, happily somewhat foreshortened.

On the evening of the 1st May I was sent forward by Col. Turchin to Col Kennett [commanding] the 4th Ohio Cavalry to give him instructions to proceed to Athens with his command and find out what was there: I accompanied the command when we entered the town driving out five of the rebel cavalry. Col. Kennett went in pursuit of the enemy, leaving some dozen or so of his own men in town. I returned to Col. Turchin to give him the intelligence. We then advanced to the town with artillery and infantry. I was ordered by Col. Turchin to stop the 24th Ill., 37th Ind. and Edgarton's Battery, outside the town—near the residence of Mr. Donnell—and he himself brought in the other troops. When I came back to town I saw the section of Loomis' Battery posted on the corner of the Court House Square. . . . The 18th Ohio was stationed on the Court House yard, and the 19th Ill just behind the artillery. I went around with Col Turchin to the former camp of the 18th Ohio, at the fair grounds, and came back by another road, occupying some three quarters of an hour. About the time of our return Col Turchin received a message from Col. Kennett's command, that the woods were full of the enemy's cavalry, and that they were fighting them; and soon after another messenger came in with the information that the cavalry and artillery of the enemy had taken a position on the other side of a slough, and that Kennett's Cavalry had made an unsuccessful effort to dislodge them, and they wanted artillery and infantry to help them. Col Turchin rode up to the Court House Yard and getting down from his horse gave orders to Col. Given and Lt. Chandler to proceed at once to assist Col Kennett, the men to go in wagons to facilitate the expedition. Some soldiers coming into the Court House Yard about that time with straw hats and summer clothing on, Col. Turchin appointed Col. Stanley Provost Marshal of the town, and ordered him to establish patrol guards, at once, and to keep all soldiers and citizens out of the streets, and to see that all soldiers kept their proper places. I think those were the words. Col. Turchin then went to the Hotel near the Depot, staid [*sic*] there to dinner and right after dinner went round to examine the different roads leading from Athens; and when he returned about 7 o'clock in the evening, word came from the expedition that the enemy had crossed Elk River and escaped before the expedition reached there. These were the leading facts of the day as I remember them.[4]

Curtis had delivered a model performance, providing a straightforward account of events. The only admission was of an apparently trivial wearing by a few troops of summer hats and clothing, a matter Turchin promptly set right by the appointment, at the first chance he got, of Stanley as provost marshal and the appointment of street patrols. All else had been by the book.

Having thus set the slate with their own military language, not that of the craven Southern civilians who had hidden behind the Fifth Amendment on questions of loyalty, Gazlay made good use of Curtis to score points strongly in his client's favor.[5] First, on the march to Athens the night of May 1, the troops were beset with stories of atrocities (later, he testified, ameliorated) told by stragglers of the Eighteenth Ohio to that regiment's men. Second, he had personally made the boarding arrangements at the hotel, and they were made for Turchin and himself only, not for any other officers, countering claims of failure to pay the innkeeper. Third, Turchin had full authority to impress horses for military service, and Curtis confirmed that he personally had seized some of the animals, thus countering claims of horse thievery. Fourth, the troops lacked their own tents during their first few days at Athens but did not quarter in white citizens' homes, only in some slave shanties.

Finally, Gazlay and Curtis put into evidence a brief, but telling, order issued by Turchin on May 3, 1862: "The regimental commanders and the commanders of batteries will see that the men are in the places assigned to them. Strict guard must be put over the camps. No straggling allowed. No depredations permitted. The commanding officers will be responsible for each disorder."[6] (No one noted if any of the court members caught the irony in this last sentence.)

General Mitchel had in fact forcefully reversed himself just as soon as he learned of the outrages committed at Athens. Turchin's order had been issued directly on the heels of a nearly identical one written by Mitchel. The division commander repeated the message four days later on May 7, telling Turchin to "be vigilant and repress pillaging. Shave the heads of offenders, brand them thieves, and drive them out of camp."[7]

Judge Advocate Swaine responded in cross-examination with a rocky start.

> *Question by Judge Advocate:* Did you hear orders from Col. Turchin to any portion of his command directing them to quarter in private homes?
>
> *Answer:* No.
>
> *Question by Judge Advocate:* What orders did you hear from Col Turchin in regard to quartering troops?
>
> *Answer:* Not any.

Swaine later stumbled into eliciting testimony as to Turchin's headquarters after he left the hotel. They were "in his tent."[8]

Better was not to be expected. Curtis was physically, mentally, and psychologically a strong individual, later a major national figure in the growth of American amateur sport, not only in rowing, but also in bicycling, weight lifting, and as a founder of the Amateur Athletic Union. While an abler lawyer than Swaine might have squeezed out admissions about sights on the streets of Athens and in its stores, Swaine stumbled around, only slowly moving beyond the pointless quartering matter.[9]

Swaine turned to questions about looting, but Curtis picked the questions he wished to answer and the answers he wished to give.

> *Question by Judge Advocate:* Were you with Col Turchin at the Court House [yard] when Lieut Chandler and others were reporting to him for orders with reference to the defeat of the enemy, did you hear any conversation between Col Turchin and anyone relative to the articles of clothing that troops were wearing or anything else going on, if so, what was said? Did Col Turchin say to anyone there, or at any other time in your presence, that he did not care, so that soldiers took only what they needed, or words to that effect.
>
> *Answer:* Yes. I heard conversation in reference to the pursuit of the enemy, but none in reference to the wearing of clothes by the troops. There was nothing said that I heard. He did not in my hearing say that he did not care so the soldiers took what "they needed at any time."[10]

It was a clumsy, hurried cross-examination, made of a highly credible witness, and it failed to elicit anything connecting Colonel Turchin with any merrymaking in the streets. Left altogether forgotten, moreover, were Curtis's own observations about the troops, except the implication that they came near enough in costume to Turchin and Curtis to cause the proper response, the appointment of the provost marshal.

After Curtis did this splendid job of setting out the defense case and rebutting what the prosecution had to support a conviction, down to such detailed points as the pressing of horses, Gazlay moved immediately to respond to the charge that a rape had been perpetrated with the defendant's acquiescence. This was a critical matter. Rape, as it should have been, was an odious offense to senior officers in Civil War armies, and so far as records indicate, it seems to have been rare in the army's experience. The idea that Turchin did not take immediate corrective steps when it happened could darkly color the attitude of the board sitting in judgment of him.

There is no question that a rape was in fact committed on May 3 a few miles from Athens upon Mrs. Haines's young servant girl, Mammy. No one challenged that fact. Mrs. Haines herself, the necessary "white witness," had personally identified the perpetrator a few days later, when she and her slave came to Athens in search of him. Gazlay had been reluctant to confine the man except within the regimental lockup, whatever that may have been. Turchin, on the other hand, took one whiff and sent the culprit to the military prison in Huntsville. The record quickly and clearly reflected that Turchin had not acquiesced in any manner in this foul conduct but had instead taken the firm, correct action required of a commander once the charge had come to light.[11]

For other testimony on a wide variety of subjects, the defense had the renewed direct testimony, rather more than perhaps was wanted, of Athens's one Unionist citizen, D. H. Bingham. Blessed more with a strained sense of humor than with useful information, Bingham had advised his neighbor Donnell, early on the morning of May 2, he told the court, that Union troops

would be here before 10 o'clock today with a reinforcement, and I should not be surprised if they destroyed our town. His reply was, Never. Just at the moment I heard the report of a pistol, and saw a Confederate opposite my house on the Florence road, laying flat upon his horse's neck, making all the speed he could in the direction of

Florence with a Federal soldier pursuing & firing at him from about 30 yards behind. In a moment some three or four more men were in sight in full sport. I said to Major Donnell, "Here they are now," meaning the Federals. He replied, "It can't be possible. They must be Confederates." Just at that time my wife called to me, saying "Mr. Bingham, there are more Federals in the Fair Ground than were ever there before." I looked over to Mr. Donnell's residence and said, "Major, look over at your own house. The ground is perfectly black with them."[12]

As for the balance of the defense testimony, Turchin and Gazlay suffered no gaffes, scored no particular triumphs. Argument would prove a different matter, but for a wartime court-martial the defense side of the trial could be regarded as clean and on point, even by strict modern standards.

The court reconvened at 9:00 on Tuesday morning, July 29. After some uneventful testimony given by Colonel Mihalotzy for the defense, the court spent the rest of the day listening to just two people: the defendant, Colonel John B. Turchin, and his counsel, Carter Gazlay. In keeping with military custom, both had prepared detailed written statements that they first read to the court and then filed with it to be attached as exhibits to the transcript of the proceedings. There would be no questioning by the court, no cross-examination by the prosecution, no interference at all with the arguments they wished to make, with the picture they wished to paint. Turchin went first.

The colonel (insofar as the court was concerned he was still a colonel) described in great detail the events of May 1. He told of his conversations with General Mitchel, of reports that the Eighteenth Ohio had been captured whole, of hearing tell of cannon fire and hostile civilians raining shot and shell on the soldiers fleeing Athens as the rebels approached. Turchin told of his initial troop dispositions and of hearing further reports while en route of bridge burnings and train wrecks. There was much worrisome intelligence, especially of large bodies of rebel cavalry moving through the area, of Beauregard's horsemen venturing out away from Corinth, of John Hunt Morgan's riders passing freely through the Union's rear, raising Cain with their supply lines.[13]

In fact, the threats of rebel activity had been very real. On May 4 General Mitchel had reported that "scattered bands of mounted men, partly citizens" were riding along his line threatening bridges and had succeeded in burning one. What was more, Morgan had raided Pulaski, Tennessee, capturing 250 Union soldiers and 15 of their officers, including Mitchel's son, a lieutenant. Guerillas attacked trains, took pot shots at couriers, cut the telegraph wires.[14]

Such reports were not just old news for the court. Buell's very presence in Tennessee and Alabama was at that moment being severely threatened by the constant attacks on his lines of communication with the North by raiders like Forrest and Morgan. If nothing else, the fall of Murfreesboro demonstrated a commander's need to deal swiftly and decisively with such incursions. The fact that Buell had every good reason to place Turchin's own men, including the Nineteenth Illinois, as guards along the precious rail lines in an attempt to keep them open would do nothing to improve his treatment by the Chicago press in the weeks to come.[15]

Next the colonel spoke of his work to establish his men in a strong position after their arrival in Athens, covering his line of communication with Huntsville and establishing a defensive position that could withstand a renewed rebel assault on the town should one come, sending out pickets along the Florence and Brown's Ferry roads to guard against the rebels' return. "I intended to have the town as they did before. . . . I wanted them to do their duty properly to show to the citizens of Athens that the occupation of the town was discontinued only for a short time for prudential reasons," he explained to the court.[16]

Had the colonel limited his explanation of events to the things he did do, to his attentiveness to the placement of his men, to the scouting of the ground that took much of the afternoon in question, and to his quick response to problems when they were brought to his attention, much of which had been supported by the testimony of the witnesses who had come before, Turchin might have done himself considerable good.

May 2 had been a very exciting day. Turchin had initially established a good, logical defensive position in the town, setting up the batteries where they had clear fields of fire and could support his troops nearby. He had ridden for hours through the neighboring countryside, seeing to the disposition of his other men. Learning that the knapsacks of the Eighteenth Ohio had come up missing, he had detailed men from the Nineteenth Illinois to search for them, as the equipment and material they contained were important for troop effectiveness and comfort. Shortly after touring Athens's outlying areas, he had appointed Colonel Stanley as provost marshal. Early the next day he had issued strict orders requiring unit commanders to keep their men at their posts, "no stragglers allowed, no depredations permitted." But

Turchin could not limit himself to reminding the court of all the things he had done. He had to say more.

"The organization of the U.S. Army and particularly that of the Volunteer Army is in many respects defective," he told the court. He had been a colonel of the Imperial Guards. He knew the systems used in all the European armies, and they were better. There, in the Old Country, they had specialized officers, the état major, assigned to all of the larger operating levels of the army. They were its professional staff. They placed the troops, found good locations for camps. Not only did they determine the proper placement for the troops on the field, but they then led the soldiers to it. They posted the guards, made the surveys, scouted the countryside, interrogated civilians, dealt with spies, collected maps. Militarily, it was the état major who managed a well-organized army. Here in America, we had the corps of engineers to handle a small part of this load but, said the colonel, their numbers were "so small that the Army of Volunteers may be considered as not having them."[17] True enough, but such observations could not have helped but grate upon the members of the court. In addition, they gave no small indication of what else may have made the Russian an object of his superior's scorn.

Thence he went on to explain that a brigade commander who has only untrained aides from the volunteers regiments will, "if he understands his business[,] . . . do all of the work belonging to the État Major" and have little or no time for anything else. He thus would not be "able to attend to the small details and irregularities of his brigade."[18] What he seemed to be saying was that because he knew how to do the job of commanding a brigade better than many others did, he did not have time to attend to many of the duties that other, less skilled commanders might think important and pay attention to. He could not have talked more steeply down his nose to the members of the court if he had been twelve feet tall, but this was his first argument: he was not responsible for the misbehavior of his men because he had been too busy attending to more important business.

His second argument was also based on European custom. He told the court that his men, and in fact all men in the Union army, unlike their European counterparts, were predisposed to commit depredations because there was no bounty system for captured goods. Lacking it, he explained, "soldiers disband themselves in search of pillage and cupidity leads to the greatest horrors. These great evils are avoided by a legal division of booty." As for himself, Turchin pointed out that he had overseen the capture of vast rebel stores at Bowling Green and Huntsville and had not benefited one penny.

Why, even officers who captured horses were required by army regulations to surrender them to the quartermaster![19] This time he seemed to be saying that his men weren't wrong to steal; rather, the army was wrong for refusing to let them benefit from it.

"I am charged with taking and keeping at my quarters a mulatto boy named Joe belonging to Mr. Vasser, a resident of Athens." This Turchin admitted but then reminded the court that other witnesses had proven that he had used Joe as a scout, one who delivered important information and who had been rewarded with protection inside the brigade lines, a policy followed by others, including General Mitchel.

> [W]e know that our only friends here are Negroes; but imbued with prejudices we are afraid to acknowledge it manfully. . . . When I retreated from Tuscumbia I heard, I believe it to be true, that there were four or five Negroes hung on the following day by the people, because they were sure those Negroes had given us valuable information. These horrible acts cry against humanity. . . . The rules of war are, "Use all possible means against your enemy." Now we have in slaves the most powerful means of crushing down the rebellion, and until now we have not used them. Take away the slaves from their quarters and the rebellious slave holders will have no means to support their southern confederacy.[20]

His ardent and practical support of abolition was not, as time would tell, the argument that would resound most strongly throughout the North. It was instead this: "The more lenient we are to secessionists the bolder they become, and if we do not change our policy and prosecute the war with vigor, using all means that we possess against the enemy, including the emancipation of slaves, the ruin of the country is inevitable."[21] With that resounding damnation of army policy and claim of right for the behavior of his men as it had occurred, John Basil Turchin sat down and turned the stage over to his attorney, Colonel Carter Gazlay.

Initially Colonel Gazlay did what a lawyer should do. He turned the court's attention to matters of law that favored his client. He noted that in the first specification of the charges, accusing Turchin of neglect of duty, it was alleged that certain things had occurred with the knowledge of Turchin's subalterns. So what? The prosecution had never offered proof that Turchin ever knew in advance of, or consented to, any outrageous conduct of his troops. Instead, Gazlay argued, it had been clearly shown that Colonel Turchin had been attentively tending to his duties as brigade commander and had in fact taken all necessary measures to deal with problems just as soon as he had become aware of them. The colonel promptly appointed a provost marshal and gave clear orders to his unit commanders "to stop all irregularities and keep order." There had been no recalcitrance, no dereliction there.[22]

In fact, he continued, this was exactly the type of conduct anticipated by General Mitchel's order of March 15, 1862, prohibiting pillaging and depredations. That order specified that brigade commanders were to "order their regimental commanders to hold their company commanders and officers responsible for the conduct of their men at all times." Mitchel's order thus placed the responsibility for police matters in the hands of the regimental commanders, freeing brigade commanders like Turchin for more important duties, like planning against counterattacks, just as he had done.[23]

As to the charge of conduct unbecoming an officer and a gentleman, Gazlay addressed the accusation that Turchin had failed to pay his hotel bill. He pointed out to the court that this was a bald attempt to use a court-martial proceeding to collect an outstanding debt. Even if it was owed (and Gazlay here reminded the court of the ample testimony showing that it was not due or at best was severely inflated), he pointed out that accepting the claim might set a dangerous precedent. Criminal proceedings in courts-martial might turn into courts of claims for the benefit of sutlers, tailors, sulking rebels, and all others who might or might not have legitimate civil claims against an officer. This, he pointed out to them, was probably a business they did not want to get into.[24]

The charge that Turchin had acted in disobedience to his orders was more complex, and so was the counterargument. Gazlay claimed that the charge was redundant, covered by the first charge of neglect, and that it was answered by the arguments offered in response to it. He then turned to the specific language of Buell's Order 13a issued on February 26, 1862. "We are in arms not for the purpose of invading the rights of our fellow countrymen anywhere, but to maintain the integrity of the Union and protect the Constitution, under which its people have been prosperous and happy. . . . Peaceable citizens are not to be molested in their persons and property. Any wrongs to either are to be promptly corrected and the offenders brought to punishment."

Gazlay focused on the words "peaceable citizens." He argued that the phrase was legal, technical, and should be interpreted to mean something other than simple inhabitants or residents. It meant, he claimed, "citizen of the United States," and did not "include persons in rebellion against the United States, or those who in any way aid or countenance the Rebellion." This position was, in fact, in keeping with army policy. As early as February 1862 Henry Halleck in his General Order 46 had stated that "persons not in arms are considered non-combatants, and are not to be molested in their persons or property. If, however, they aid and assist the enemy they become belligerents, and will be treated as such. If they violate the laws of war, they will be made to suffer the penalties."[25]

And what, asked Gazlay, constituted giving aid to the rebellion? When residents of a community held town meetings to levy taxes in support of the rebellion or the families of those engaged in revolt, wasn't that the plainest form of aid? Athens had held such meetings, levied, received, and delivered such tribute. He pointed to the witnesses who had come before the court, ready to testify about their claims but unwilling to take the oath of allegiance to the country whose legal system they were trying to make use of. How much weight should such testimony have against the sworn words of "a loyal officer of the Union Army, who is not only willing to take the oath of allegiance, but is willing to risk his life in defence [*sic*] of the banner of the free for the maintenance of the Union?"[26] In Gazlay's opinion, such testimony didn't have the weight of a single straw.

As the day drew on Gazlay tired, and as his guard slowly dropped he finally grew sarcastic. "It may be considered as fortunate that our officers have time to hear the magnified grievances of traitors . . . and see to their redress. It indicates that the rebellion is about suppressed, that there is not much more work to be done, and none on hand at the time." He and everyone in the courtroom knew how preposterous and pointed those remarks were. Just in the past ten days, John Hunt Morgan had led raids into Kentucky, while other rebels had captured Union pickets within five miles of Nashville and burned essential bridges along the rail line leading from there into Alabama and on to Chattanooga. Confederate operatives had tapped into the federal telegraph system and had been reading dispatches for more than a week. Braxton Bragg's Confederate army was engaged in a rapid rail transfer from Tupelo to Chattanooga en route to thwart Buell's molasseslike move to southeastern Tennessee. In Virginia the rebels had tied up McClellan's army at Harrison's Landing, its march toward Richmond long since over. The war was being lost, and here they all were sitting at a trial of a soldier who was being accused of being too harsh on his opponents.

The sad state of affairs was being felt all too painfully right there in Huntsville, right then that day. It was on this day that General Buell had issued his order requiring the officers detailed for court-martial duty to "proceed industriously and continuously with the business before them until it is completed," forbidding members "to absent themselves from the court for the performance of other duty, or on any account whatever," including troop movements. Completing the Turchin case would be just the beginning of their work. Captain Edgarton, whose battery had positioned itself in the Athens village square on that fateful day in May, was scheduled to be tried next, and there was a long line to follow him.[27]

Gazlay's dialogue served to remind the colonels on the board about the competing calls to duty they all felt. "Our troops are on half rations and have been for over two weeks," the attorney for the defense reminded the court. "Men cannot exist on that fare and do the duties of a soldier. They will take provisions and no doubt but that ere long every brigade commander will be required to answer criminally for the bacon, hogs and sheep taken by the soldiers from the Jones' and the Donnell's of the country." Finally offering a disclaimer of any intent on his part to show disrespect for any officer who had preferred charges, meaning Buell, Gazlay closed and filed his written statement with the court. It was 7:00 in the evening, time for supper, time to contemplate, time to rest and, for the defense, time to pray and make copies of their statements for distribution to waiting reporters. The court agreed to reconvene the next morning to deliver its verdict. Apparently none of them saw the need for a long debate about what the decision should be.[28]

Did Turchin order his men to pillage Athens? Despite the prosecution's best efforts to elicit testimony to that effect, Swaine had never gotten anyone to say that they had heard any such order. It had been difficult for him to find any men at all from the brigade willing to testify about anything. Lieutenant Chandler had come the closest to providing such evidence, saying that he had heard Turchin remark "about the affairs [the pillaging] then going on, that he did not care so long as they did not take what they did not need, or words to that effect," words that sounded suspiciously similar to those that had been widely reported, that Turchin "would shut mine eyes for two hours."[29]

Swaine had called three Union enlisted men to provide details about the morning of May 2. Two were privates who had deserted from the Eighteenth Ohio on May 30 while marching through Tennessee and who had been subsequently arrested, circumstances never raised by the defense to impeach their testimony. Even those miscreants would not say that they had heard an order to pillage. They did confirm the testimony of others that Turchin had watched the pillaging begin and that he had done nothing to stop it. Private Joseph Arnold said that Turchin watched from the steps of the courthouse, where he could plainly see "[a]ll the stores and shops there were open [and] as many soldiers as could were going in and out. Those coming out were bringing out goods, and the noise was so great that if a person had . . . ordinary hearing [he] would have had his attention drawn to it."[30]

In fact, many witnesses recalled the great level of noise that drowned out all else when the pillaging began. Carriage maker William McEnary heard it, followed immediately by the appearance of volunteers, their arms filled with "all manner of articles . . . such as coats, caps, kettles, vests, bottles of different kinds of medicines." Thomas Cox heard the same cacophony, although his attention focused on the troops trying to break into Hine's store. Both of the Union privates and Lieutenant Chandler alluded to it, although Chandler thought that the parade of men carrying goods brought his attention to the noise of the pillaging rather than the other way around. Turchin knew what was going on.[31]

Did Turchin do anything to stop it? The same witnesses uniformly said no. Had he taken any steps to locate and punish the thieves? Other than the arrest of Private Bowers for the rape of the young girl, again the witnesses could not recall anyone being punished or even being brought up on charges. The only charges filed came as a result of the investigation conducted by Buell's staff.[32]

Even though there was no testimony that Turchin had ordered the pillaging, was there other evidence that indicated an underlying plan to sack the town? It was entirely circumstantial, but it lay there before the court just as plain as day, if they chose to look for it. Lieutenant Curtis had testified that he had galloped back from Athens to let Turchin know that the rebel cavalry had ridden off. Turchin thus knew there were no rebel troops in Athens. When Turchin arrived at the courthouse with his two regiments, the Nineteenth Illinois and the Eighteenth Ohio, both of those units stopped and stacked their arms, something they never would have done had there been any chance that Scott's cavalry was still nearby. Most telling of all, just as soon as their arms were stacked, both units dispersed and started breaking into the nearby stores and homes, making such a noise that it could be heard all around the town. The fact that two units had acted with such uniformity and coordination indicated very clearly that orders to do so had come from above; and on the morning of May 2 the only higher authority present was John Basil Turchin. In all probability he had not directed anyone to pillage anywhere or steal anything. What he did do was let his men know that if they wanted to do something like that, it would be all right with him. He would file no charges. He would allow his volunteers to do exactly what he knew they wanted to do.[33]

Of course, to an army commander—in fact, to any officer who knew his trade—whether or not Turchin issued the order simply didn't matter. No positive orders to act were needed to disobey Buell's Order 13a. Buell did not direct the officers of his command not to order pillaging. He told them that it would not be allowed. Buell's chief of staff, James Barnet Fry, would later set out very concisely the importance of obedience in the military. "Obedience to command is the chief military virtue, in relation to which all others are secondary and subordinate; and disobedience is reckoned among the principle military crimes, and is justly liable to the most exemplary punishment."[34]

All that mattered was that Turchin had allowed conditions to exist in his command in which his men could feel themselves free to behave in this manner, which was, of course, nothing new to them. They had pillaged and raised havoc with Southern civilians virtually since they first enlisted. And out of the petty crimes festered the conditions that led to the most serious ones, to the intimidation of people who were in fact sometimes on their side, or who were at the worst neutral, just wanting to go about their lives in peace— conditions that led to the rape of slave girls and to the beginnings of rule by terror rather than rule by law. Orders had to be obeyed. Justice had to be done.

All seven members of the court filed into the hearing room, facing Turchin and Gazlay for the final time on the morning of July 30. Future president Garfield continued to preside, although he was ailing and was about to depart for Ohio on convalescent leave. Presumably, he read aloud the findings of the court.[35]

As to the first charge, neglect of duty to the prejudice of good order and military discipline: guilty. The court found that Turchin did allow his men, in his presence, to disperse, plunder, and pillage "without taking adequate steps to restrain them." The court recited nineteen specific instances of conduct they found outrageous. They ranged from the rape of the servant girl (which had happened a day later and far away from Turchin and his staff) all the way to the destruction of the box of Bibles and insulting remarks made by many of the soldiers to the ladies of the town, not to mention the money and clothing stolen from numerous households.[36]

As to the second charge, conduct unbecoming an officer and a gentleman, here the court split hairs. They found that Turchin's conduct was indeed unbecoming for an officer, but they could not conclude that it was necessarily unbecoming of a gentleman to do as he had done. They thus found him not guilty of the charge as laid and cleared him entirely of the accusation that he had knowingly failed to pay his hotel bill. However, they instead found him guilty of engaging in "conduct prejudicial to good order and discipline," in that he failed to "make any responsible and proper effort to prevent the disgraceful behavior of the troops under his command."[37]

As to the third charge, disobedience of orders, the job was much easier, even if the specifications were more detailed. On the charge of violating General Buell's Order 13a, protecting the property of "peaceable citizens": guilty. The court dismissed the legal issue raised by Gazlay regarding the definition of the term "peaceable citizen" by ruling that the order stated "peaceable persons" were not to be molested "in their persons or property." As to the accusation that Turchin had failed to provide fair compensation for materiel properly seized for the use of the army, as also required under the order, again the court found him guilty. However, as to the charge that he had violated the spirit of Order 13a by allowing the taking of provisions, forage, and draft animals without adequate necessity, here the court found him not guilty. It wasn't that the army didn't need the items. As present conditions demonstrated, they did. It was just that the colonel had never paid for them.[38]

Finally there was the fourth accusation of violating orders, of Buell's General Order 4, which forbade women to accompany troops into the field. To this Turchin had pled guilty at the outset, and the court simply confirmed the defendant's guilty plea. No one had ever denied Mrs. Turchin's presence in Alabama. All that was left was to pronounce sentence, a matter that required no additional deliberation, for the law was clear. General Garfield kept it short. Colonel John B. Turchin of the Nineteenth Illinois Infantry was "to be dismissed from the service of the United States."[39]

That wasn't quite all. Despite the lecturing by the defendant, despite the sarcasm of defense counsel, with the course of the conduct of the war hardening all around them, the irony of the defendant's situation had not been lost on the members of the court. There was a sympathy for this man who had been so calm, so polite, during the proceedings, and who had been so obviously attentive to so many things that needed doing on May 2. Before forwarding the transcript and findings to Buell himself, six of the seven members of the court, all save old-line Colonel Curran Pope, signed their names to an addendum: "[I]n view of the fact that the finding of the court acquits Colonel Turchin of any personal dishonesty and believing that the offense was committed under exciting circumstances and was one of omission rather than commission, [we] most favorably recommend him to the consideration of the reviewing officer."[40] They all waited one more week to hear if Major General Don Carlos Buell would listen to their plea to his common sense for leniency for John Basil Turchin.

His answer might have been guessed when the officers of the court read the conclusion of his General Order 36 of July 29 requiring the officers to remain on court-martial duty. "Discipline, and consequently the honor, and efficiency of the army is in no inconsiderable degree dependent on courts-martial. Nominal penalties for grave offenses avail nothing, and are neither wise nor merciful." Buell sent that message directly to the colonels sitting in judgment of the Russian before they passed their sentence. Surely the general would heed his own advice, whatever the nature of the crime.

The answer came on August 6, 1862, in the form of General Order 39 of the Department of the Ohio. Buell had heard the plea for leniency but felt "constrained nevertheless, to carry the sentence into effect." On the question of leniency, the general found it entirely appropriate to look beyond the court record. There he found similar, if less spectacular, displays of undisciplined behavior that had "marred the course of Colonel Turchin's command wherever it has gone."[41] The events and actions in Missouri and Bowling Green had been counted after all.

As to the necessity of prosecuting a harsh war, Buell made it clear that in his view pillage and plunder led to demoralization, disgrace, and disaster "and is punished with the greatest severity in all armies." Moreover, "the circumstances under which the disorders were committed were precisely those that demanded the strictest observation of discipline." The command was supposed to be "in the presence of the enemy," the general reminded everyone. "Every man should have been at his post instead of roaming over the town and country to load himself with useless plunder."[42]

Then Don Carlos Buell made what he must have thought was his most telling point. Had Colonel Turchin instilled a proper sense of discipline in his brigade during the five months he had led them prior to their arrival in

Athens, the outrages never would have happened. The crime lay not in the fact that orders had been breached on this single occasion. Rather, it lay in the fact that to these volunteers "the orders of the commander were unavailing at a time when the observance of it might be of vital importance." He had failed to convert his eager volunteers into soldiers. Therefore, John Basil Turchin's dismissal from the army would stand.

The only problem, as yet unbeknownst to Buell, was that four days earlier, on August 2, 1862, the War Department in Washington had issued its General Order No. 93. Three days after his conviction, the War Department had formally announced to the world the appointment of Colonel Turchin to the rank of brigadier general. The nation had charted a new course for its war to reunify the country. Don Carlos Buell's helm instead held steady on the same rhumb line it had followed for the past nine months. Those paths, once parallel, were now widely divergent. A price would be quickly exacted.[43]

15
The Conquering Hero

What I have done is not much, but what I could do, were I allowed,
might amount to something. . . . We have been talking about the Union
and hurrahing for the Union a great while. Let us now talk and hurrah
for conquest.

—John B. Turchin, August 19, 1862

The former colonel, perhaps brigadier, John B. Turchin kicked around Huntsville for six days before he accepted the fact that he had been cashiered. He
took off his uniform, donned civilian garb, and on August 12 telegraphed his
friends and family in Chicago, telling them that such was the state of affairs.
He would catch a train home the next day, Wednesday, the thirteenth. Four
days later, newspapers from Louisville to New York published the text of his
closing statement, being the best evidence yet that the Russian colonel had in
fact been convicted, dismissed, and sent home. A pledge he had made to
Garfield, to appeal directly to the American people if cashiered, remained
known only to the two men. There had been, and remained, some confusion
in the papers about whether he had been acquitted or convicted. Turchin's
own words settled that matter, but a debate continued in the dailies about
what effect conviction would have in light of the colonel's recent promotion.[1]

More than 550 miles separated Huntsville from Chicago. The very day
Turchin announced his travel plans, John Hunt Morgan and his mounted
rebels captured the Union garrison at Gallatin, Tennessee, breaking yet again
the rail link between Louisville and Nashville. That raid and others, now
happening on almost a daily basis, slowed Turchin's homeward journey to a
crawl. They also served Don Carlos Buell with a clear message about the
price of stagnancy. Rather than pressing into the rebel heartland, Buell began
pulling back toward Nashville and central Tennessee. While the rebels signaled that change was in the air, Don Carlos Buell unwittingly played into
their hands. The Confederates had a new commander, Braxton Bragg. His
eyes faced north.

For six days, Turchin bounced intermittently along on the band of rails that connected his seat of war to his hometown. In the midsummer's heat, the engine's plume of smoke, ash, and cinders moved effortlessly through the open windows of the cars. It permeated hair, skin, and clothing alike with the ashen look, smooth feel, and oily smell of soot. For nearly a week, the colonel sat and listened to the steady clack of the wheels, the chug of the pistons, the hissing of the relief valves, the squeal of the brakes. Then, late in the afternoon of August 19, the train stopped in Valparaiso, Indiana. Dressed in high-topped boots and a plain linen coat, his shirt's collar open and necktie very loosely draped around his neck, without a vest but sporting a light gray fatigue cap, the colonel stepped down onto the station platform to catch a connecting train into Chicago. There he discovered something was up.[2]

Waiting on the platform to greet him stood some of the most prominent men in Chicago. Murray Nelson, George Steele, J. L. Hancock, C. H. Walker, Stephen Clary, and William Bross of the *Tribune*, among others, stood at the head of "a vast crowd of citizens" of Valparaiso who had turned out to greet the former colonel. The committee had come as emissaries of the Chicago Board of Trade to welcome General Turchin back to their city. The crowd in Valparaiso had time to give him "three times three cheers" before he and the committee boarded their own special train for the rest of the trip. At every station along the forty-five mile route, at Wheeler and Hobart and the other hamlets and whistle-stops of northwestern Indiana, and finally across the state line and into the outskirts of Chicago, "the same enthusiasm prevailed." Rather than face the quiet disgrace and sideward glances given a cashiered officer, Turchin was being wildly cheered at every wayside.[3]

Turchin's telegram from Huntsville, and its publication, had given rise to two unexpected results. It triggered a huge public outcry to his dismissal, and it gave his powerful allies in Chicago nearly a week to organize his homecoming. It did not hurt that at almost the same moment she received word of her husband's imminent return, Nadine Turchin had picked up his commission as a brigadier at the War Department in Washington, thereby touching off a widely reported rumor that her personal influence with President Lincoln had resulted in her husband's appointment. The *Tribune* was already in the midst of a vigorous campaign to use "every agency . . . to stir the war spirit and fill the ranks of the soldiers for Uncle Abe." Turchin's predicament provided well-cured fuel for the fire they were igniting.[4]

Having previously and prominently published a resolution of congratulation to Turchin on his supposed acquittal, the *Tribune* didn't miss a beat when it discovered the report had been false. To accept the testimony of avowed secessionists and traitors, of people who openly refused to take the oath of allegiance to "the best government on earth . . . is enough to sink every member of the court-martial to the lowest depth of infamy and shame," the *Tribune* howled on August 15. Admit every charge, and still such testimony from "villainous traitors" tainted the result. Admit the outcome as precedent for cases to come, and the testimony of Jefferson Davis "and his vile gang" would result in President Lincoln and General Winfield Scott "stretching the hemp."

The columnists filled the paper again the next day with vituperation against the decision of the court in general and against Don Carlos Buell in particular. "The injustice to which General Turchin has been made a victim, and the indignities which have been heaped upon him by rebel witnesses before a federal court-martial—a curious spectacle—have naturally created in this community an almost unanimous and freely outspoken sentiment, that the late investigation to which he was the party defendant, was—to use a mild term—an outrage." On the editorial fumed, complaining that their hometown boys, the gallant Nineteenth Illinois, were now scattered by company and squad guarding railroad bridges. Why? "For the reason that Don Carlos Buell is determined *to kill this regiment.*" Neither the editors nor, they assumed, their readers could "appreciate the fact that a general should suffer because he believes in carrying on a war vigorously and energetically; in employing every means Providence places in his power, and waging the strife against rebels with all his zeal and strength, instead of sympathizing with them." For three more days, the paper carried letters from parents of the boys in the Nineteenth and notices of the welcoming rally being organized to greet Turchin on his return. When his train finally pulled into the station, the people of Chicago could not have been more fully primed.

The parade began almost immediately, as the party of dignitaries descended from their cars and straightaway climbed into a waiting row of carriages. Vaas & Dow's Light Guard Band put wind to its instruments and sticks to its drums, a detachment of the Twenty-fourth Illinois formed an honor guard, and they and "an immense crowd of citizens" escorted the cortege all through the south side of the city to the Sherman House Hotel, where Turchin was able to spend a few minutes with his wife. While they took their few private moments, crowds began to gather along the expected route of the procession, which now ran from the hotel all the way to Bryan Hall, the great auditorium where the formal ceremonies would be held, and which was already nearly full to the rafters with another huge crowd of supporters.[5]

For nearly an hour, Robert M. Blackwell had tried to warm up and keep the attention of the packed house, when finally "the swaying of the crowd about the door and the flourish of music in the hallway announced the arrival of General Turchin." He and his entourage elbowed and pushed, making a path through the crushing multitude, slowly working their way toward the stage, "amid a perfect whirlwind of applause." Turchin looked jaded and worn from his travels, but with his "massive chest and neck" he still "looked the general." When he finally came to the front of the stage the crowd went wild, and the frenzy only grew when the band struck up "Lo! The Conquering Hero Comes." Long minutes passed before the applause finally died away and William Bross, on behalf of the board of trade, rose to welcome the general home.[6]

Bross was direct in telling Turchin why it was that he was being welcomed so heartily by so many.

> We welcome you as an officer who understands the malignant character of the rebellion, and who is both ready and able to use all the means at his command to put it down. We honor you as the commander of the 19th Illinois—acknowledged on all hands to be one of the best, if not the best, drilled regiment in the service. . . . The name "Bloody 19th" bestowed on you by the traitors of Missouri . . . is really an honor that your fellow citizens know how to appreciate. Finally, we welcome and honor you, sir, for the patriotic, earnest devotion with which you have sustained the flag of your adopted country.[7]

After touching on the recent decision of the tsar to abolish slavery in Russia and drawing a parallel with Turchin's fight here, Bross turned the stage over to the cast-out colonel. Turchin's strong accent and occasional broken English (mostly smoothed out of the printed version of his remarks) did not weaken the strength of his response. "Fellow citizens of Chicago! When I left this city with my regiment I never expected to receive such a reception as this. *I have simply done my duty; that's all I have done.*" Then began the first of many long bursts of enthusiastic applause that would interrupt the general's otherwise short speech. "I did my duty as a soldier, and I trust as an American citizen also." More applause. "Although I am not versed in politics, I made up my mind that the cause of this rebellion was slavery, and I acted upon the principle that the cause should be removed." Long, continued applause. "At the same time, I knew also that those men who were relying upon the power of slavery must not be handled with soft gloves, but a little roughly, and so I handled them a little roughly." Applause again. "I don't know whether to call it a happy or unhappy result that my superior officer did not approve of it, and thought differently. He thought that I must be court-martialed and dismissed from the service." Groans and hisses came from the crowd, accompanied by cries for Turchin's return to the war.[8]

He referred to hearing that his wife held his brigadier's commission and was again interrupted, this time by a call for three cheers for Madam Turchin. He told the crowd that he rejoiced at receiving the reception he was being given, but that his men of the Nineteenth Illinois should be with him to hear it, rather than spread out doing tedious guard duty along the railroad. Then Turchin took straight aim at his former commander. Such treatment of good soldiers was "low minded; it is contemptible. I cannot but feel the greatest contempt for a man, who at the head of a powerful army will behave thus towards soldiers. I do not care for myself, but it is a shame to punish my men." The crowd broke into a chant of "Shame! Shame!"[9]

Then Turchin made it plain to his audience just what it was that he and his men and, in his mind at least, all Union soldiers were up against when they crossed into Dixie.

I have studied secession and secessionists in Missouri, Kentucky, Tennessee, and Alabama and I tell you it is no use to fight against them unless we use every means in our power. They are too powerful to be fought otherwise. Who are these guerillas? They are citizens who pretend to be peaceful, but who are plotting treason all the time. They are all the time looking out for straggling Yankees. As soon as he finds one, he gets two of his neighbors, they take their shotguns, go out and catch him. They look out for pickets and shoot them. You know how they murdered General McCook. This is what I call a war of extermination. We must do the same, and until we use all men, slaves included, we cannot put them down.[10]

Another huge burst of applause. Obviously energized by the enthusiastic support he was being shown, the general hit his crescendo. "What I have done is not much," he told his supporters, "but what I could do, were I allowed, might amount to something. . . . We have been talking about the

Union and hurrahing for the Union a great while. Let us now talk and hurrah for conquest." With that, he nearly brought the house down. When the cheering finally showed signs of waning, Mrs. Turchin produced the brigadier's commission, the applause swelled anew, and she was forced to take center stage, where the crowd greeted her with a wild ovation and numerous bouquets. There were a few more short speeches by some of the other dignitaries, including a furloughed sergeant of the Nineteenth Illinois who said the men would follow Turchin anywhere. As the *Tribune* noted two days later, whenever Turchin himself or any other speaker "alluded to a more vigorous war policy, to confiscate the slaves and the property of rebels, and generally to crushing out the rebellion in the shortest time possible . . . the people made the welkin ring with their plaudits." When the speakers had finished and the applause died away, the band struck up the Star-Spangled Banner. At the end came singing. The last song, performed by Frank Lombard, was "The Red, White and Blue," and the entire hall joined in the chorus. John Basil Turchin was quite clearly home.[11]

Word of Turchin's triumphant return spread quickly. The *Pittsburgh Gazette* reprinted the *Tribune*'s account two days later. Perhaps more important to those attuned to such things, the war fever mentality spurred enlistments, and within a week two regiments of Illinois troops, the Seventy-second and Eighty-eighth, both sponsored by Chicago's Board of Trade, completed enlistments and left for the war. Turchin himself remained in Chicago, although his friends in high places instantly went to work to see him reassigned. On August 21, just a day and a half after he arrived, the board of trade committee made contact with Governor Yates, asking about Turchin's status, "as his friends are anxious to place him again in the field, if he is all right." Yates in turn went straight to the top, writing to Lincoln on August 29 supporting Turchin's return to active duty. Thanks to the government's escalating frustration with Don Carlos Buell, the governor's inquiry could not have arrived at a more opportune time.[12]

On the day of Turchin's arrival in Chicago, the War Department had created a new command, the Department of the Ohio, which encompassed all of the states of Ohio, Indiana, Michigan, Illinois, and Wisconsin as well as all of Kentucky east of the Tennessee River—nearly all of Kentucky—and named Major General Horatio Wright to command. In describing their expectations of him, General Halleck made it very plain to Wright that there was widespread displeasure with Buell. If he failed to take action soon, Buell's days were at an end. In fact, Halleck admitted, Buell would already have been sacked had he, Halleck, not personally asked that the man be given a little more time. Now even that sand had about run out of the glass.[13]

More important, perhaps, the rebels had seized the initiative. E. Kirby Smith had gathered 10,000 men at Knoxville, and General Bragg had suddenly repositioned his Army of the Mississippi at Chattanooga, where he had no intention of remaining. In a move that in timing matched General Lee's lightning offensive in central Virginia, which was then in the process of whipping John Pope's Union army into the Washington defenses, both Smith and Bragg started north during the week of August 25. Smith rode straight north, battering down the gates of Richmond, Kentucky, on August 30, capturing over 4,000 members of the garrison and sending the rest running pell-mell for Louisville. Bragg marched into middle Tennessee and aimed for the rail connections that made it possible for Buell's army to live, albeit meagerly, without living off the land. Stealthily avoiding Union strong points, such as the reinforced garrisons at Murfreesboro and Nashville, by the first week of September he, too, was well on his way into Kentucky.

The North was in a panic. The male citizens of southern Ohio and Cincinnati dropped everything and started drilling as militia. None too soon, for rebel brigadier Albert Jenkins led his cavalrymen across the river and into the Buckeye State on September 4. Governor Morton of Indiana called out his militia at the same time, sending them to guard the numerous river crossings that led into Kentucky. The flood tide of war came rolling north in a hurry. On September 5, with Buell in full retreat, with Lee in Maryland, Jenkins in Ohio, and Bragg and Smith in Kentucky, Lincoln received the plea from Governor Yates on behalf of Brigadier General John Basil Turchin. It was time to finish the message begun when Turchin's nomination had been pushed through the Senate. It was time to put the lash to the rebellious, to spur on those who would be the sort of fighting generals for which Lincoln so earnestly yearned. It was time to make sure the army got the point. That evening the president took up the governor's letter and endorsed it: "With the concurrence of the Secretary of War and Gen'l Halleck, I should be very glad for General Turchin to be given a brigade, composed as desired, if convenient, and where active duty is now required in Kentucky."[14] Buell's face couldn't have been slapped harder had he been standing in the room.

September 1862 was hectic to say the least. Bragg captured another federal garrison of 4,000 men at Munfordville on the sixteenth. Lee's invasion of Maryland ended two days afterward as a result of the bloodbath outside Sharpsburg, Maryland, along the banks of Antietam Creek. Buell managed to bring his army back into Kentucky on the fourteenth, and on September 25 he camped on the banks of the Ohio River at Louisville. On September 22 President Lincoln issued the preliminary Emancipation Proclamation, and two days later he suspended the writ of habeas corpus. The president seemed to say that the lash would be applied to all traitors alike, whether north or south of the Mason-Dixon Line.

Buell finally moved out to engage the rebel invaders, and a battle eventually took place on October 8, when the Confederates attacked near Perryville, fought to a draw, and then started their withdrawal back into eastern Tennessee. Buell refused to pursue, even when specifically ordered to do so, and the jig was up. On October 30 the War Department appointed Major General William S. Rosecrans to serve as the new commander of the Department of the Cumberland, and five days later Halleck himself ordered a court of inquiry to sit in Cincinnati. The court had the charge of investigating how it was that Buell had allowed the invasion of Kentucky to occur, his conduct at the Battle of Perryville (where he had been close to the battlefield but remained unaware that it was happening for most of the day), his failure to pursue the enemy after that battle, and "such other matters as might be beneficial to the service." In the end, the court did not bring or recommend any charges against General Buell, and it found no basis upon which to question his loyalty.[15]

However, it did conclude that his inactivity and poor strategic decisions had led to the invasion of Kentucky, and that he and his army had been perfectly able to pursue Bragg back into Tennessee and should have done so. The court also found that Buell had quite clearly pursued "the conciliatory policy." But in his doing so they found no blame. "Whether good or bad in its effects, General Buell deserves neither blame nor applause for it," the generals sitting on the board concluded, "because it was at that time understood to be the policy of the Government. At least he could violate no orders on the subject, for there were none." For a year Buell waited for other orders. He was instead mustered out of the volunteer service.[16]

The bureaucracy of the army, more sensitive perhaps to the reaction of Buell and to many other Regular Army officers like him, succeeded in postponing the Russian's reassignment until matters had cooled and Buell had been properly admonished. Then, on March 28, 1863, Brigadier General John B. Turchin was dispatched to Major General Rosecrans, again in the Department of the Cumberland, again in Tennessee. Old Rosey took an immediate liking to Turchin and gave him command of a division of cavalry.

The Cavalry Corps commander, Major General David Stanley, had only contempt for the "dumpy, fat, short-legged Russian, who could not ride a horse." That summer Stanley finally found cause to ask for Turchin's reassignment. Rosecrans moved him to the Third Brigade, Fourth (Reynolds's) Division, Fourteenth Army Corps. Under George H. Thomas, Turchin would have the chance to prove whether Rosecrans or Stanley and Buell had been right about him.[17]

With their disparate reactions, Rosecrans and Stanley demonstrated the most memorable quality about Turchin. Among his peers, he very clearly was a man you loved or you hated. But the volunteers who served under him universally sang his praises, not just the men of the Nineteenth Illinois with whom he had started. His new infantry brigade was composed of six units: the Eighteenth Kentucky; the Eleventh, Thirty-sixth, Eighty-ninth, and the untested Ninety-second Ohio regiments; and the Twenty-first Indiana Battery. Bouncing around on a small white Arabian mare, using her to move relentlessly from camp to camp, Turchin quickly won these men over with good humor and constant attention to detail. His wife, Nadine, came south again. Often riding at the head of the column, she charmed and cheered the men while they marched along the roads of Tennessee, Alabama, and finally Georgia, as Rosecrans closed on Chattanooga.[18]

The nature of the war he was being asked to fight had completely changed. No longer was Turchin leading a brigade of an army of occupation. No longer was he fighting mainly partisans and guerillas. Instead, the Confederate government had formally organized its Army of Tennessee in November 1862 with General Braxton Bragg at its head. The Union's Army of the Cumberland at last faced an organized, uniformed foe. Brigadier General Turchin became part of an army that would fight conventional military opponents in conventional ways. He now had the chance to put his formal training and experience, rather than his volunteer's prejudice and enthusiasm, to work.

His first great test came along the banks of Chickamauga Creek six months after his return to the army. The Union army's situation during its first day at Chickamauga, September 19, 1863, may best be described as fluid. Brigades and units were placed here and there as needed, the Union line often being a series of patches as the Confederates poked and penetrated. Turchin was leading his brigade to reinforce the Union left when a courier rode up to tell him that his trailing regiments had already been pulled away to fill a hole in the center and that he should follow with the rest. A quick about-face and a short march brought him up behind the first of his regiments to be pulled away. An hour passed, Hazen's brigade withdrew from Turchin's right flank to get more ammunition, and Turchin decided to face right, move over to support the left flank of Cruft's brigade, filling the gap but aligning at an acute angle with Cruft's front.[19]

Luck marched with the Russian. Just after his men had formed into two lines, Law's brigade of Hood's rebel division stumbled upon Cruft. Characteristically of hounds on a fresh scent, the Alabamians immediately charged. Cruft's men fired first volley too high, and Law's men just picked up their pace. Two of Cruft's three regiments then broke for the rear, leaving Cruft exhorting only the Nineteenth Ohio and Battery B of the First Ohio Light Artillery to hold their ground. In the midst of what he called wavering and indecision, into that breach stepped Brigadier General Turchin, his line already aimed fortuitously at the rebel's right flank. He gave simple orders: Fix bayonets and charge! Taking hold of his plumed hat and waving it to his men, the little brigadier shouted out, "Bully for mine brigade!" An old soldier recalled years later that Turchin's spirit was infectious that afternoon. As one, the brigade line gave a cheer that echoed over the sound of the battle and leapt forward. "We charged bayonets on them with a rush and a yell. The Alabamians were stunned, and in a moment faced about and ran," Turchin himself later wrote. For Major General John Palmer, the events appeared even more dramatic. "As if by magic the line straightened up," he wrote in his official report. "[T]he men [those of the Second Kentucky and Cruft's own Thirty-first Indiana, who had broken in the face of the charge] turned upon their pursuers with the bayonet, and as quickly they [the rebels] turned and fled, and were in turn pursued." The "Russian Thunderbolt" had struck for the first time.[20]

The work of the next day was perhaps the hardest ever for the Army of the Cumberland, as disaster struck when a division mistakenly pulled out of the center of the line just before Longstreet launched an attack on that very point. The Union right crumbled and fled. The line of the left, mainly composed of Thomas's Fourteenth Corps, slowly bent back at both ends. Turchin's men had little trouble holding their section of line near the right end of the shoe, reinforced as it was by breastworks, but as the afternoon passed they were forced to change front to the right. It was increasingly obvious that the rebels threatened to cut off all lines of retreat.

At one bleak point during the afternoon, Turchin found himself standing near Lieutenant Colonel Douglas Putnam of the Ninety-second Ohio. Putnam, in his first battle, expressed a hope that night might fall so that they could escape the predicament and then asked Turchin what he intended to do until they could. "Do?" cried the frustrated Russian. "This brigade stays right here until we are all cut to pieces, that's what we'll do!" Finally, orders arrived for the division to pull out of the line to begin their retreat. Turchin's brigade would lead the way north along the La Fayette Road toward Rossville. The general rode down the line, personally spreading the word to speak only at a whisper, to drop everything that might rattle, and to move in silence.[21]

Approaching the northern end of the Union mule shoe, Turchin encountered Major General George H. Thomas himself. The corps commander had just been alerted that the rebels were advancing westerly across the road and were about to cut it off. The road had to be cleared, and now. Despite having marched by the right flank (to be ready to repel an attack from the rear), Turchin's four regiments rapidly deployed into a double line in a patch of woods, out of which they could see Liddell's division of rebels moving across a field to their front. The general trotted his mare to the center of the brigade, drew his saber, and yelled at the top of his lungs, "Charge bayonets! Give dem hell, Got damn 'em."[22]

As the Union line moved forward, the rebels, who had only a few moments' notice of the impending attack, had the chance to get off but a single volley. It brought down a few unlucky soldiers and the general's little white mare, but it did nothing to slow the pace of the attack. Instead, the boys in blue broke into a full-fledged charge, and the rebels, two brigades formed into eight lines, were swept away. Turchin, only scratched when his mount collapsed, ran ahead with his troops, brandishing his blade, shouting encouragement. He and they overran and captured more than five hundred Johnnies and two cannons, only stopping because they were winded from the long five-hundred-yard sprint. The route to Rossville lay open. The corps' line of retreat had been secured.[23]

Accolades followed as never before. Reynolds and Palmer were glowing in their after-action reports. General Thomas recommended Turchin for promotion to major general "for gallantry and skillful conduct" shown on the battlefield at Chickamauga. Assistant Secretary of War Charles A. Dana sent daily battlefield reports to Secretary Stanton in Washington and singled out only three brigade commanders for special mention: Brigadier General John B. Turchin was the first. "He charged through rebel lines with the bayonet, and becoming surrounded, forced his way back again," the beaming Dana wired his chief. But the praise that may have meant the most to Turchin came in a message sent to Rosecrans at Rossville as the battle closed. Only one brigadier was spoken of: "Turchin charged the rebel lines and took 500 prisoners, became enveloped, swept around behind their lines and cut his way to another place," the report glowed.[24] The army's chief of staff, James A. Garfield, signed it. What more could there be? Where else could bayonets spear fruit? The answer to that question lay at the base of a long, high ridge overlooking the city of Chattanooga, Tennessee.

After the Army of the Cumberland solidified its position in Chattanooga, it went through a reorganization that resulted in the merging of various units. On October 9 Turchin asked for at least two more regiments to build up his depleted brigade. In the letter of request, he asked for one thing more. "My military relations with this brigade having been fairly consolidated on the late battlefield," he wrote with a clear degree of uncharacteristic understatement and humility, "I respectfully request the general commanding the department to leave it under my command." That same day orders issued merging Turchin's brigade with the old First Brigade, Third Division. The Russian, as he wished, now commanded the newly designated First Brigade of Absalom Baird's Third Division, Fourteenth Corps. He had earned, and was entrusted with, the command of seven regiments: the Eleventh, Seventeenth, Thirty-first, Thirty-sixth, Eighty-ninth, and Ninety-second Ohio and the Eighty-second Indiana. Within three weeks General Thomas again sang Turchin's praises after his and General Hazen's brigades completed the job of reopening the Tennessee River supply line.[25]

Wednesday, November 25, 1863, was a gray day in Chattanooga. Baird's division kept busy through the morning and early afternoon hours marching and countermarching. William Tecumseh Sherman, in charge of the forces on the northern end of the Union line, had been ordered to attack the rebels holding the high ground. General Thomas, now in charge of the center of the army, was to attack in support after Sherman had punched his way to the top; but the rebels held. Sherman's men were thrown back time and again. Finally, in the midafternoon, Thomas received orders to move his men forward and seize the rebel rifle pits at the base of Missionary Ridge as a staging area for a push to the top.

Brigadier General Baird was sitting his horse at the northern end of his division's line when a courier found him and delivered a verbal order from Thomas to move ahead to a position from which the rifle pits could be seized, the advance to be signaled by the firing of six guns from Orchard Knob. Baird, a high-ranking graduate of West Point's class of 1849, rode back along the line and was just delivering the order to Colonel Ferdinand VanDerveer, commanding the Second Brigade in the center of his line, when what appeared to be the signal to attack went off. By the time he arrived at Turchin's position at the right end of his line, his other two brigades had already stepped out, as had Wood's division next on the right. To make up for lost time, Baird ordered Turchin "to push to the front, and without halting to take the rifle pits; then conforming his movements to those of the troops on his right, to endeavor to gain the summit of the mountain along with them."[26]

Such orders were by now familiar ground for Turchin, and they called for equally familiar techniques. Just as soon as the advance began, the brush growing along Citigo Creek swallowed up and distorted the brigade line. After his men emerged from the underbrush into a patch of more open woods from which they could see the rebel line a half mile off, Turchin took time to halt, dress the line, and give the order to fix bayonets. Both Van-Derveer's brigade to the left and Brigadier General Samuel Beatty's brigade to the right were already stalled, battling along the line of rifle pits at the opposite side of the clearing. The rebels were pouring in converging artillery fire from the heights above. Without a moment to lose, with every reason to be in the clearing as little time as possible, Turchin ordered the men to advance at the double-quick. "Both lines moved with a run and a cheer," he noted in his report.[27]

When his front line, made up of the Eleventh, Thirty-sixth, and Ninety-second Ohio regiments, hit the line of Confederate rifle pits, they staggered for a moment. Men began to drop, some hit by the incoming fire but most trying hard to avoid its effects. Turchin wouldn't have it. "Knowing that men dropping down under fire are very slow to get up and start again, I urged my regiments on, and they again rushed forward" over the rebels' line, in some cases over and through the lines of the adjoining Union brigades that had stopped at the trench line, and on up the steep slope of the ridge itself. The long, straight battle lines quickly evolved into pointed waves, with flag bearers and enthusiastic officers pulling the peaks of the waves up the slope, while a broad trail of blue blouses streamed steadily upward from down below. From his vantage point far to the rear, General Baird watched in amazement as Turchin's charge moved rapidly up the face of the ridge until three of the brigade's regimental flags were waving in close proximity to one another, sheltered just below the crest. One had been carried by Color Sergeant James B. Bell of the Thirty-sixth Ohio, who held on to his staff until wounded five times. As General Grant noted in his report, the rebels had been driven out of their rifle pits "like bees from a hive."[28]

The flags stayed put for nearly fifteen minutes, during which Baird debated whether to send support or try to pull Turchin back. He did not know that the rebels had not stalled the advance. Rather, all but the most stalwart had become completely winded by the 1,200-yard uphill sprint. Gathered around the flags near the top stood a collection of Turchin's officers. They included Lieutenant Colonel Ogden Street of the Eleventh Ohio, Lieutenant Colonel Frederick Lister of the Thirty-first Ohio, Captain Americus Whedon of the Eighty-second Indiana, and so many others they became impossible to name or remember. Just as a general advance was ordered from down below, these officers hailed the mixed collection of men from the brigade who had gathered around them and burst over the crest of the ridge, broke through the line of breastworks, chased the rebels for a couple of hundred more yards, and then turned their attention to the left and to the batteries that had borne down on them during the early stages of the advance. They mowed down the gun crews and the horses. They seized the cannons and then ran on to take still more. Lieutenant Colonel Hiram Devol, commanding the Thirty-sixth Ohio, made note of the conditions that allowed the charge to succeed: "Never as yet have [we] fallen back in the face of the enemy. In this, all seemed eager to fight, and under the leadership of [our] general, [we] felt confident of success." He took little note of the fact that his own regiment, and the Ninety-second Ohio, which had lined up to his right, had suffered the highest casualties of all regiments in the corps that afternoon. Colonel Henry Morton of the Eighty-second Indiana was more direct in his praise, taking time to express the admiration he and his men felt for "the gallantry displayed by [General Turchin and his staff] in leading the brilliant charge that won Missionary Ridge."[29]

The man the press referred to as the Russian Thunderbolt had completed his redemption. Back in Chicago fifteen months before, he had told his audience, "[W]hat I could do, were I allowed, might amount to something." It had. He had asked his listeners at his rally to "hurrah for conquest." He had shown his men not only how to cheer but also how to triumph. They, too, would conquer.[30]

16
Afterward

The energy and bitterness which they [the Southern public] have
infused into the contest must be met with energy and determination. . . .
Such is not only the lesson of history, the dictate of policy, but it is the
general popular sentiment.
—Senator John Sherman to William T. Sherman, August 24, 1862

General Turchin stayed with the army until July 15, 1864, when he returned
home on furlough due to illness and soon after resigned. Until then he continued to lead and inspire the men who served under him. During an en-
gagement near Dalton, Georgia, in late February 1864, he "gallantly appeared and exposed his life on horseback through the thickest of the fight."
One old veteran of the Ninety-second Ohio wrote in to the *National Tribune*
nearly sixty years later that it was Turchin who had been the true "Rock of
Chickamauga." Perhaps more important, he left an equally favorable impression on his division commander, Absalom Baird. When noting Turchin's departure, the West Pointer Baird wrote that his brigadier was "one of the most
thoroughly educated and scientific soldiers in the country, and a more devout
patriot than most of those born on our soil." His illness and departure thus
"inflicted a great loss upon the service."[1]

John and Nadine Turchin settled for a time in Chicago, where he served
as a solicitor of patents. In 1873 he took possession of a tract of land 250
miles to the south along the line of the Illinois Central Railroad and started
a colony for Polish immigrants called Radom, where he spent most of the rest
of his life. He wrote two books, *Military Ramblings* and *Chickamauga*, and
made a number of contributions to the pages of the *National Tribune*, re-
fighting Chickamauga and—most important to this work—describing his
early service with the Nineteenth Illinois. He died on June 19, 1901, in the
Illinois State Hospital for the Insane.[2]

The Nineteenth Illinois Volunteer Infantry was folded back into the regular organization of the Army of the Ohio (later redesignated the Army of the

Cumberland) during the Kentucky Emergency in September 1862. By the time General Turchin arrived to report to General Rosecrans, they also were serving with the Fourteenth Corps, in the Second Brigade, Second Division, led by Colonel Timothy Stanley of the Eighteenth Ohio. They fought at Stone's River and Chickamauga and at Missionary Ridge, though with less panache and energy than they might have under Turchin. In fact, their patriotic desire to see the war through to the end had been permanently dampened by the events of the spring of 1862, and the Nineteenth was among the minority of the western regiments that did not reenlist as veteran volunteers in the spring of 1864. They fought at Resaca and around New Hope Church that May, and then they went home. Before they left, at the general's request they were briefly reattached to his brigade, and he rode over to bid them adieu. He told them that he hoped that they would be as good citizens as they had been soldiers.[3] We can only wonder how ironic that comment might have sounded to a resident of Athens.

General Turchin's community at Radom never flourished, at least not enough to allow him to put much money in the bank, and when he died he left his wife, Nadine, strapped for funds. The soldiers of the Nineteenth rallied one more time just for her. While neighbors supplied her with her daily bread and butter, the Nineteenth Illinois Veterans' Association raised a stake sufficient to provide her with a temporary stipend of $25 a month. Then they went off on one last campaign, this time to get a special act of Congress passed to provide the widow, whom they warmly remembered riding at the head of their column along the dusty roads of Tennessee, with a general's pension. It passed in the spring of 1902, and Nadine spent the rest of her days quietly and comfortably in Radom.[4]

In the spring of 1864, Ulysses Grant, shortly after his elevation to lieutenant general, thought about ways to mobilize the entire country to bring an end to the war. He suggested that many of the prominent officers who had been relieved of important commands be restored to duty. His list included the fallen stars of McClellan, Burnside, Frémont, Negley, Crittenden, and Don Carlos Buell. For Buell, Grant, perhaps out of a sense of debt due since Shiloh, personally approached the secretary of war, and Stanton agreed to offer him a command. Buell declined, refusing on a point of pride to serve under either of his former subordinates William T. Sherman or Edward Canby. In his memoirs Grant commented, "[T]he worst excuse a soldier can make for declining service is that he once ranked the commander he is ordered to report to." It was the last time Grant ever tried to do Buell a favor.[5]

Buell promptly resigned from the army. For a time he operated coal and iron businesses in eastern Kentucky. During the administration of President Benjamin Harrison in the late 1880s, he received an appointment as a government pension agent, but that disappeared when Grover Cleveland regained the presidency in 1893. The general who had gotten his troops to Pittsburg Landing just in the nick of time, and who stood so solidly behind a policy of conciliation with the civilians of the South, lived another five years, dying in Kentucky at the age of eighty in 1898. The little town where he spent most of his postwar years completely disappeared.[6]

The Turchin controversy and the rampage of the men of the Eighth Brigade were not the only scandalous burrs to catch in the coattails of Ormsby MacKnight Mitchel during the late spring and early summer months of 1862. Pressed for funds to operate the railroads of middle Tennessee, General Mitchel had dismantled a rebel fort made from cotton bales. He first used them to make a temporary bridge three hundred feet long, over which his men crossed and then captured the city of Bridgeport. Then, with prior notice to General Halleck, he had the bales pulled out of the river and sold them for $20,000. The money was indeed used to pay the expense of keeping the railroad running, but rumors of illicit gain quickly circulated, further straining Mitchel's relationship with Buell. After painfully defending his actions to control his men and accounting for the cotton proceeds, the astronomer, ever popular in the Northern press, waited for a new assignment. In September of that year, he went off to command the Tenth Corps and the Department of the South, with headquarters in Hilton Head, South Carolina. Within six weeks of his arrival, he was dead of yellow fever.[7]

Neither General Turchin nor any of the men who had served under him were ever again accused of committing depredations against anyone. Neither he nor the men of the Nineteenth Illinois went with Sherman on the March to the Sea, so none of them experienced living as a daily experience what they had been so harshly criticized for doing in the spring of 1862. But Turchin's name was just as deeply cut into the Southern psyche as it had been in the North's, perhaps more so.

Before General Sherman cut his swath across Georgia, whenever a Confederate leader wanted to conjure up images of the depraved indifference of the Yankee invaders, he had at his disposal a few choice examples. In September 1862, in an attempt to rally the people of Kentucky to the Southern cause, Simon Bolivar Buckner made this appeal. "Freemen of Kentucky!" he called out,

It needs not that you look abroad upon the burning cities and villages and the devastated fields of Tennessee and the Mississippi Valley and of our mother State, Virginia, to convince yourselves of the true character of our oppressors. Our own State shows sufficient evidences of their tyranny. Nor need you listen to the piercing cries of the women of Northern Alabama. Our oppressors would teach us that the nameless brutalities of Mitchel and Turchin were sanctified by the folds of the immaculate banner under which these deeds were perpetrated; for we learn that their master has rewarded these outlaws for their crimes.[8]

The cheering in the North that followed Turchin's appointment was matched by a hue and cry of outrage that spread like seed in the wind among the people of the South.

Well more than a year later, on December 7, 1863, Jefferson Davis delivered to the reconvened Confederate Congress his required "state of the Confederacy" address. He presented his legislators with more than twenty-five pages of printed material. He described the military situation, the reverses in the West, the struggle and the losses in the East. He went on for page after page about the Confederacy's foreign relations and the increasingly hostile positions being taken by Britain and France. He informed his Congress on the state of the army, the prisoner exchange program, and about the status and condition of the navy, which was having a very hard time finding crewmen. He mentioned the post office. Then he ended by turning to a more somber subject.[9]

"I cannot close this message without again adverting to the savage ferocity which still marks the conduct of the enemy in the prosecution of the war," the beleaguered president wrote. "After their repulse from the defenses before Charleston they first sought revenge by an abortive attempt to destroy the city with an incendiary composition thrown by improved artillery from a distance of four miles. Failing in this they changed their missiles, but fortunately have thus far succeeded only in killing two women in the city. Their commanders, Butler, McNeil, and Turchin, whose terrible barbarities have made their names widely notorious and everywhere execrable, are still honored and cherished by the authorities at Washington."[10]

The actions of the offending generals were one thing. The official position of the opposing government was another, even in the late days of 1863, when the pain of Sherman's marches had yet to be felt. President Davis continued:

The frontier of our country bears witness to the alacrity and efficiency with which the general orders of the enemy have been executed in the devastation of farms, the destruction of the agricultural implements, the burning of the houses, and the plunder of everything movable. Its whole aspect is a comment on the ethics of the general order issued by the United States on the 24th of April, 1863, comprising "Instructions for the government of armies of the United States in the field," and of which the following is an example: Military necessity admits of all direct destruction of life or limb of *armed* enemies, and of other persons whose destruction is incidentally *unavoidable* in the armed contests of the war; it allows of the capturing of every armed enemy, and every enemy of importance to the hostile Government, or of peculiar danger to the captor; it allows of all destruction of property, and obstructions of the ways and channels of traffic, travel, or communication, and of all withholding of sustenance or means of life from the enemy; of the appropriation of whatever an enemy's country affords necessary for the subsistence and safety of the Army.[11]

Davis was clearly shocked and concerned about these increasing evidences of the harsh-war policy his government now faced, and of which John B. Turchin was seen as one of the earliest examples and proponents. But Davis went on to expose his own pride and naïveté. "The striking contrast to these teachings and practices presented by our army when invading Pennsylvania," noted the president, "illustrates the moral character of our people. Though their forbearance may have been unmerited and unappreciated by the enemy, it was imposed by their own self-respect which forbade their degenerating from Christian warriors into plundering ruffians, assailing the property, lives, and honor of helpless non-combatants. If their conduct, when thus contrasted with the inhuman practices of our foe, fail to command the respect and sympathy of civilized nations in our day, it cannot fail to be recognized by their less deceived posterity."[12]

The point that the rebel president missed, however, was that the Union army did not face only a uniformed foe. Lee and the Army of Northern Virginia may not have been welcomed into Pennsylvania, but neither did the Keystone State's farmers bushwhack them. In contrast, in August of 1862 William T. Sherman had written to his brother, Senator John Sherman, describing the conditions around Memphis. "All their people are armed and at war," the general reported. "You hear of vast armies at Richmond, at Chattanooga and threatening New Orleans, whilst the whole country is full of guerilla bands numbering hundreds. All the people are armed," he repeated, "and wherever we go we find them well prepared."[13]

The senator, who had voted with what were then the general's sentiments and against Turchin's promotion, stood in a better position to gauge the state of current opinion. On August 24 he wrote a long letter to his brother. After telling the general about the sudden and abrupt change in opinion on the question of emancipation, he changed the subject to war policy. "By the way," he chided his brother,

> the only criticism I notice in your management of Memphis is your leniency to the rebels. I enclose you an extract. I take it those complaints are groundless, but you perceive from it the point upon which public opinion rests. The energy and bitterness which they have infused into the contest must be met with energy and determination. . . . Such is not only the lesson of history, the dictate of policy, but it is the general popular sentiment. I know you care very little for the latter. . . . It is sometimes passionate, hasty, and intemperate, but after a little fluctuation it seems to settle very near the true line. You notice that Frémont, Butler, Mitchel, Turchin and Cochrane are popular, while Buell, Thomas, McClellan and others are not. It is not for military merit, for most persons concede the inferiority on many respects of the officers first named, but it is because these officers agree with and act upon the popular idea.[14]

Did this start in the general's mind a debate as to whether or not "the popular idea" had validity? That we can never know. We do know that before he launched his campaign through Georgia, his views had completely changed.

On December 6, 1941, Anthony Sallazzo was a sixteen-year-old junior in a little high school in upstate New York. Two days later, he was a United States Marine. He volunteered to avenge Pearl Harbor. He jumped from the high school football team into the service of his country because it had been attacked. He had to do something, and he knew exactly what it was.[15] The Marine Corps wanted all the men like Tony it could get. Men, or boys, who had that motivation would win the war for the United States. Such desire, such motivation, was a fact of life of which the military of 1941 could take full advantage. That was not the case in 1861. The men who filled the ranks of the Nineteenth Illinois and the rest of Turchin's regiments came to serve their country with that same emotion, with that deep, excited desire to avenge an attack on their country, to wreak havoc on a land filled with traitors. They had been expected by their senior commanders to rein in that feeling and to treat the people of the Southern States with equanimity, as if nothing had happened. That state of affairs had frustrated both the volunteers and the people who cheered them on their way to the war, but it did not change the widely held popular notion that Southerners should feel the pain of a war they had brought upon themselves. John Sherman very correctly pointed to the popularity of generals like Ben Butler and John Basil Turchin as proof of that pudding.

But was this motivation that had brought Turchin's volunteers into the army something of which the Civil War army could take advantage? Although the elevation of Turchin did not immediately cause that to occur, was not the long-term effect of the broader decision to wage harsh war, in effect, also a decision to take advantage of that added weapon: the desire of the average Union soldier to take his measure of revenge on the people of the South? It became incorporated into numerous orders and regulations governing the conduct of the war, including those governing martial law, the treatment of partisans, and the rules regarding insurrection, civil war, and rebellion, which were among those issued on April 24, 1863.

Paragraph 156 stated the case simply. "The commander will throw the burden of war, as much as lies within his power, on the disloyal citizens." Those people could be forced to take loyalty oaths, if the commander thought he could rely on such oaths. He could expel them, fine them, or throw them in jail, just as Turchin had done in Missouri at the war's outbreak. Paragraph 157 made it even plainer. "Armed or unarmed resistance by citizens of the United States against the lawful movements of their troops is levying war against the United States, and is therefore treason."[16] The door flung open to wage war on the war-making capacity of the South became part of official army doctrine. Who better to carry on such a conflict than loyal volunteers? When the time came to do exactly that, nary a Union soldier would complain. William Tecumseh Sherman and Phil Sheridan would lead men along the trail that had been blazed by John B. Turchin two years before, and nearly all of them would do it without regret.

For the army, the official change of policy was probably first evidenced by the presidential sanction given the general orders of John Pope when he took command in Virginia in July 1862. But as early as August 2, 1862, while

Turchin awaited the final decision of Don Carlos Buell as to his fate, the word went west to do much as Turchin had done. On that day General Halleck told Grant that he was to clear western Tennessee of "all organized enemies. If necessary, take up all active sympathizers, and either hold them as prisoners or put them beyond our lines. Handle that class without gloves, and take their property for public use." Just as he was urging Buell to do in Tennessee, he told Grant to "get all the supplies you can from the rebels in Mississippi. It is time that they should begin to feel the presence of war on our side."[17]

The observations made by William Tecumseh Sherman at Memphis and the new authority given Grant had far-reaching consequences. Authorized to live off the land and released from his line of supply, Grant could now think ahead and plan the campaign that would take Vicksburg from the south and east. Sherman, too, was free to contemplate the sort of war that would be required to bring the rebellion to an end, free not only to think about how to break the Southern armies but free also to contemplate the destruction of the war-making capacity of the Confederacy itself. No one would take more to heart the statement in the regulations: "The commander will throw the burden of war, as much as lies within his power, on the disloyal citizens."

Had John Basil Turchin been nothing but the ruffian that the rebels portrayed him as, or had George McClellan or Don Carlos Buell been just a bit more daring as warriors, policy might have changed far more slowly, and Grant and Sherman might have felt far more constrained in deciding how to continue the war, had they even risen in such circumstances to positions where they had to make those decisions. But the most important military proponents of the conciliatory policy, McClellan and Buell, failed miserably on the battlefield, and the first brigade commander to be indicted for allowing a harsher policy had become a hero with the public, had been promoted for it, and everyone knew it. Halleck told Grant to make the rebels feel war from "our side." Turchin stood as the living proof that neither Grant, nor Sherman, nor any other Union commander need fear any consequences for doing so. (All but one of Turchin's regimental commanders survived the affair at Athens with their military careers intact.)[18]

The nature of the war would change, too. While he faced the Confederate Army of Tennessee, Sherman and his men fought a conventional war against a conventional foe. Complaints about the conduct of Sherman's men on their way to Atlanta were few and far between. However, after Atlanta's fall and Hood's decision to move his army away from Sherman, there was no conventional foe to face. From this point forward, the people of the South would feel the full weight of the war. On the way to Savannah, every brigade commander in Sherman's army would be watching his men do the very same things Turchin and his men had been castigated for in the spring of 1862. Those volunteers, free to invade, would offer no apologies for doing that which they had come to do. Turchin's men never did, either.

Epilogue
Revenge

Vengeance is mine; I will repay, saith the Lord.
                    —Epistle of Paul to the Romans, 12:19

There is a danger in bringing men together to fight for a cause. The danger lies in the risk that the people will volunteer for a cause that is different than that for which their government seeks their service. If not adequately trained, if left to fend for themselves, untrained, undisciplined, their own dark motives can quickly determine the actions they take, especially where commanders themselves are absent or, even worse, where they have failed to establish or have lost their authority over the men they are supposed to lead.

In the late summer of 1862, for the men of the Nineteenth Illinois, everything had gone wrong. Colonel Turchin was gone, sent home in disgrace for allowing them to carry on the war just as they had expected to. The war itself appeared to be on the verge of being lost. The army in the east had abandoned the assault on Richmond. In the west, the rebels were advancing from Georgia all the way to the banks of the Ohio River. As a result, the men of the Nineteenth Illinois were about to abandon Tennessee, a state they had occupied for nearly six months. These men were worn and disenchanted by the failure of their leaders and by the ignominy of their service. We can assume from the events about to transpire that their own leaders, the field and line officers of the regiment, were just as disenchanted as they were. Consequently, those captains and lieutenants were completely ineffectual as leaders. But no matter how demoralized, these men were still very capable of getting even, of venting the frustration they felt because of the course of the war, because of the year they had lost in the army seemingly accomplishing nothing.

Who would they revile more than a traitor? Perhaps it would be a traitor who was also a snitch, a complainer, someone who whined to the authorities about minor losses and inconveniences that were obviously, in the minds of the snitched upon, well deserved. J. B. Davidson fit the bill. He owned the hotel on the square in Athens first made famous in the town decades before when a former proprietor, who was certain the general had overpaid his bill, chased down Andrew Jackson, Old Hickory himself, to issue a refund. It was also where Colonel Turchin had stayed during his first days in Athens. Davidson admitted he had never even bothered to discuss his daily rates for room or for board, nor had he raised the issue of the manner of being paid with anyone. And yet he had the temerity to personally testify against Turchin at his trial, trying not only to collect monies not due but also smearing the reputation of a commander valued by his men. Davidson, as much as anyone living in Athens, presented the men of the Nineteenth Illinois with a score they could easily settle given the chance.[1]

Turchin's men revered their little colonel. On the other hand, there could be no doubt in a volunteer's mind that J. B. Davidson was a traitor. Undoubtedly, they all knew that after giving his testimony the hotelkeeper had declined the opportunity to take the oath of allegiance. In their eyes he was just another rebel trying to collect from the government, trying to take advantage of a policy that protected his rights and property, rewarded him in court, and left him and his friends free to plot treason. The men of the Twenty-first Ohio had known Davidson's Hotel as "rebel headquarters." Perhaps the nickname dated back to the time Turchin's men garrisoned the place. There, all during the summer, while Turchin stood trial, while the Nineteenth Illinois spent day after boring day guarding railroad bridges and culverts, and while Buell's inactivity allowed the rebel army to seize the initiative, the witnesses who had refused to take the oath and others who thought like them gathered at the hotel to share news and stories—and, no doubt, in the minds of the volunteers who watched them come and go, to hatch plans. During those long, hot weeks of summer, all the volunteers did was watch.[2]

The men of the Nineteenth Illinois festered in their small, isolated camps along the rail line. Their colonel under arrest, then sent home, their assignment to the lowest duty known (at least to them), their company officers no doubt feeling as depressed as the men in the ranks, morale plummeted. Their angry frustration simmered until it began to boil over. They would be quick to take the chance to relieve themselves of it. None of the company officers stepped up to try to rebuild that morale. None of them had a cure for the malaise that permeated the camps. One who finally tried was Fred Harding,

Ellsworth disciple, drill instructor extraordinaire, the regiment's major—but he took up the challenge too late. Rather than respond to his orders to get in line and shape up, the men simply snarled at him. Rather than obey him, they came at him with death threats. The threats were clear and convincing to Harding, but it took two letters of resignation for him to convey that point to his superiors. Finally, at the end of August, he was allowed to go while the going was good.[3]

At about the same time, while the rebels began to mount their drive into Kentucky, orders arrived. The troops that had been left guarding the railroads of northern Alabama were to gather together and head north toward Nashville. The road to ride was the Nashville & Decatur. On August 27 the men of the Twenty-first Ohio made camp for the final time around the Limestone County Court House in the center of Athens. The following afternoon the regiment's wagon train formed on the streets to head north, while the men waited for empty railroad cars. Shortly after, an engine pulling cars stopped on the edge of town. The train had been picking up detachments of the Nineteenth Illinois as it chugged its way north toward Athens. No one made note of seeing anyone get off, but very soon thereafter everyone's attention abruptly turned away from the railroad.[4]

The first smoke anyone noticed came from Davidson's Hotel, the infamous "rebel headquarters." The flames spread rapidly through the tinder contained in the old building. Then another fire broke out, and another and another. Soon the entire north side of the town was in flames. The new buildings at the fairgrounds where the Eighteenth Ohio had made its camp, four blocks away from the hotel, were quickly swallowed up in the conflagration. The blaze surrounded the courthouse on the square, licked at its brick façade, and then ignited the roof. By daybreak, all of them—the hotel, the grandstand and fair buildings, the business blocks in between, and the courthouse—had been reduced to smoldering ash.[5]

By then the Yankees were gone, angry bushwhackers and guerillas harassing them every step of the way back to Nashville. Fred Harding's own company had carried a banner to the war that bore the pledge: "Retaliation—No mercy to traitors." The men of the Nineteenth Illinois had retaliated in spades, and this time none of them would be charged with anything.

Abbreviations

In citing published works in the notes, short titles have been used, and the full name of the author, the work, and the details of publication can be found in the bibliography. Works or repositories frequently cited have been identified by the following abbreviations. Full citations are contained in the bibliography.

CMSR	Compiled Military Service Record (of a named individual soldier), National Archives and Records Administration.
CMT	The Turchin Court-Martial Trial Transcript, found in the CMSR of Col. John B. Turchin, National Archives and Records Administration.
ExPro	U.S. Congress, *Journal of the Executive Proceedings of the Senate of the United States.*
IAGR	Illinois Adjutant General's Department, *Reports.*
JCCW	U.S. Congress, *Report of the Joint Committee on the Conduct of the War.*
LOC	Library of Congress.
NCAB	*National Cyclopedia of American Biography.*
MHI	United States Army Military History Institute.
NA	National Archives and Records Administration.
OR	United States War Department, *War of the Rebellion: A Compilation of Official Records.* Unless otherwise specifically noted, all references are to Series 1.

Stanley Board   The record of the proceedings of a board of inquiry
                 into the performance of Col. Timothy Stanley, 18th
                 Ohio Infantry, which can be found in Stanley's
                 CMSR.

Notes

INTRODUCTION

1. Murray, *Discipline,* 7; United States War Department, *Basic Field Manual, 1941,* 1.

CHAPTER 1

1. Basler, *Collected Works,* 4:249–61.
2. Ibid., 262.
3. Ibid., 263.
4. Ibid.
5. Ibid., 266.
6. Ibid., 271; *Charleston Mercury,* quoted in Long, *Civil War Day by Day,* 46.
7. Grimsley, *Hard Hand,* 8–10; Basler, *Collected Works,* 4:272.
8. Basler, *Collected Works,* 4:316–17. It is believed that the letter from Lincoln to Seward setting out these points was never delivered but that the president did convey his points verbally.
9. Grimsley, *Hard Hand,* 49, citing General Order No. 3, *OR,* 8:370.
10. Engle, *Don Carlos Buell,* 1–17, 75, 119.
11. Ibid., 50–51, 64–65.
12. Ibid., 18, 48–49, citing McClellan to Fredericka English, January 1, 1853, and Mahan to McClellan, August 3, 1861, McClellan Papers, LOC.
13. Ibid., 117.
14. Ibid., 48, 88, 94.
15. Grimsley, *Hard Hand,* 63–64.
16. Diary of Edward L. Witman, Co. F., 25th Pennsylvania Volunteers, Richard Johnston Collection.
17. Grimsley, *Hard Hand,* 14–16.
18. Ibid., 22.

CHAPTER 2

1. Turchin, *Chickamauga*, 5; *Chicago Tribune*, Feb. 6, 1886; Parry, "Turchin," 45; Seaton, *Crimean War*, 25; Alston, *Education*, 33, 35. Novocherkassk, founded in 1805, is today a city of about 188,000 people on the Askai River, about twenty miles northeast of Rostov-on-Don.

2. Quoted in Miller, *Miliutin*, 96.

3. Brooks, *Reform*, 71; Miller, *Miliutin*, 94–95.

4. Parry, "Turchin," 45; Curtiss, *Russian Army*, 114–15.

5. Parry, "Turchin," 45–46; Curtiss, *Russian Army*, 77–78.

6. Deak, *Lawful Revolution*, 301; Lincoln, *Nicholas I*, 314; Curtiss, *Russian Army*, 220.

7. Deak, *Lawful Revolution*, 292, 306; Lincoln, *Nicholas I*, 315.

8. Curtiss, *Russian Army*, 143–44, 311.

9. Lee, *Crowds and Soldiers*, 194.

10. Deak, *Lawful Revolution*, 305.

11. *Chicago Tribune*, Feb. 6, 1886.

12. Van Dyke, *Military Doctrine*, 20–23, 34–35; Miller, *Miliutin*, 4–5.

13. *Chicago Tribune*, Feb. 6, 1886. He learned his lessons imperfectly. The short book he wrote near the end of the American Civil War, *Military Rambles,* is no more than its title suggests and less than the intended analysis of Union strategy, not any sort of coherent "history of the present." See Turchin, *Military Rambles.*

14. Turchin, *Chickamauga*, 132.

15. Turchin, *Military Rambles*, 20.

16. Curtiss, *Russian Army*, 107; Brooks, *Reform*, 65, 73n40; Seaton, *Crimean War*, 24; Van Dyke, *Military Doctrine*, 34; Lincoln, *Nicholas I*, 9.

17. Curtiss, *Crimean War*, 283; Malloy, *Miliutin*, 91; *Chicago Tribune*, Feb. 6, 1886.

18. Curtiss, *Crimean War*, 284, 287–88, 296, 327, 419–20.

19. Delafield, *Report*, 24.

20. Ibid., 36; Mordecai, *Military Commission;* McClellan, *Armies of Europe;* Skelton, *American Profession*, 241.

21. Delafield, *Report*, 36; Curtiss, *Crimean War*, 327; Van Dyke, *Military Doctrine,* 37–38; Riasanovsky, *Nicholas I*, 41.

22. Malloy, *Miliutin*, 94; Brooks, *Reform*, 80–81.

23. Parry, "Turchin," 46; East, "Russian General," 121.

24. McElligott, "Diary of Nadine Turchin," 27, 30, 39, 44, 65–66.

25. Ibid., 89.

26. Ibid., 43.

27. *Chicago Tribune*, June 24, 1861.

28. McElligott, "Diary of Nadine Turchin," 23; Parry, "Turchin," 45; Curtiss, *Russian Army*, 192; McClellan, *Armies of Europe*, 104.

29. *Chicago Tribune*, Feb. 6, 1886; Parry, "Turchin," 47; Slotten, *Patronage*, 168–70.

30. *Chicago Tribune*, Feb. 6, 1886; Slotten, *Patronage*, 128, 141–42.

31. *Chicago Tribune*, Feb. 6, 1886; Slotten, *Patronage*, 99, 169.

32. Parry, "Turchin," 47; Stover, *Illinois Central*, 1, 62; McElligott, "Diary of Nadine Turchin," 28.

33. *Chicago Tribune*, Feb. 6, 1886; Stover, *Illinois Central*, 87; Goodrich to Trumbull, June 23, 1862, Trumbull Papers, LOC.

34. *Chicago Tribune*, June 25, Sept. 25, Oct. 18, 1861; Turchin to Ray, Sept. 8, 1861, Ray Papers, Huntington Library. While governor of Massachusetts, Banks was the titular commander in chief of the state's fine militia, to which he personally apparently paid little or no attention. See Harrington, *Fighting Politician*, 16, 41–53, 54.

35. *Chicago Tribune*, June 10, 1897; Wendt, *Chicago Tribune*, 46, 49–50; Kinsley, *Chicago Tribune*, 1:35–36; *NCAB*, 29:327.

36. Bross, "What I Remember," 1, 29–31; Wendt, *Chicago Tribune*, 25, 86; *Chicago Tribune*, Jan. 28, 1890; Pierce, *Chicago*, 413.

37. Wendt, *Chicago Tribune*, 43, 49–50.

38. Boorstein, *Reader*, 107, 109.

39. *Chicago Tribune*, Jan. 28, 1890; *NCAB*, 29:327; Medill, however, was not immediately impressed. See Wendt, *Chicago Tribune*, 45–46.

40. Miller, *City of the Century*, 89–90; Bross, "What I Remember," 1; Boorstein, *Reader*, 108.

41. Medill to Trumbull, Mar. 4, 1861, Trumbull Papers, LOC.

42. Strevey, *Medill*, 61.

43. *Chicago Tribune*, Jan. 28, 1890.

44. Strevey, "Medill," 20; Kinsley, *Chicago Tribune*, 145.

45. On the "dialogue" theory of press influence, see Schudson, *Power of News*, 23.

46. Medill to Trumbull, July 1, 1862, in Baxter, *Browning*, 115–16.

47. The recollection of Chauncey M. DePew, quoted in Carman and Luthin, *Lincoln and the Patronage*, 125n84; originally published in Rice, *Reminiscences of Lincoln*, 436.

48. Donald, *Lincoln*, 242; Harper, *Lincoln and the Press*, 76; Carman and Luthin, *Lincoln and the Patronage*, 126–27; Lincoln to Blair, Mar. 12, 1862, in Basler, *Collected Works*, 4:282.

49. Salmon, *Appointing Power*, 59.

50. *Harrisburg Patriot and Union*, July 22, 1862—not, of course, an unbiased observer.

51. *Chicago Tribune*, Aug. 20, 1862; Keegan, *Warfare*, 12, quoted in Lee, *Crowds and Soldiers*, 2 (both of whom may be paraphrasing Clausewitz); *Chicago Tribune*, May 28, June 13, 15, 1861.

CHAPTER 3

1. Haynie, *Nineteenth Illinois*, 153.

2. Page, "A University Volunteer," 82–83.

3. Randall, *Ellsworth*, 8; Hay, "Young Hero," 355; Miller, "Ellsworth's Zouaves," 18; Andreas, *History of Chicago*, 2:187–88.

4. Cunliffe, *Soldiers and Civilians*, 230–35.

5. *Chicago Tribune,* May 25, 1861; Randall, *Ellsworth,* 161; Cunliffe, *Soldiers and Civilians,* 242–43; Miller, "Ellsworth's Zouaves," 17.

6. Miller, "Ellsworth's Zouaves," 18–19.

7. *Chicago Tribune,* July 3, 1860; Randall, *Ellsworth,* 173.

8. *Chicago Tribune,* e.g., July 11, 23, 24, 26, 28, 1860.

9. Miller, "Ellsworth's Zouaves," 33.

10. *New York Tribune,* reprinted in *Chicago Tribune,* July 18, 1860; *Frank Leslie's Illustrated,* July 28, 1861, quoted in Miller, "Ellsworth's Zouaves," 29–30.

11. *Philadelphia Inquirer,* May 25, 1861.

12. Hay, "Young Hero," 358; Villard, *Memoirs,* 1:150.

13. Basler, *Collected Works,* 4:333.

14. Ingraham, *Elmer E. Ellsworth,* 127–36; Hay, "Young Hero," 359–61.

15. *OR,* Series 3, 1:68–69, 81; IAGR, 1:5–7; *Appleton's Cyclopedia,* 368; Pierce, *Chicago,* 255.

16. IAGR, 1:8.

17. *Chicago Tribune,* Apr. 22, 1861.

18. Haynie, *Nineteenth Illinois,* 53–54; *Chicago Tribune,* Apr. 20, 1861.

19. Haynie, *Nineteenth Illinois,* 150; *New York Times,* May 16, 1912; *NCAB,* 13:275.

20. IAGR, 1:7–8; Haynie, *Nineteenth Illinois,* 5, 136.

21. IAGR, 1:9–10.

22. Ibid., 8; *Springfield State Journal,* quoted in *Chicago Tribune,* May 27, 1861.

23. IAGR, 1:10.

24. *OR,* Series 3, 1:146, 151–53; Meneely, *War Department,* 146.

25. Letter from Arnold, May 30, 1861, in *Chicago Tribune,* June 3, 1861; Wendt, *Chicago Tribune,* 154; Strevey, "Medill," 79.

26. IAGR, 1:10; Dayton, "Raising of Union Forces," 401–38.

27. Haynie, *Nineteenth Illinois,* 68; IAGR, 2:128–29.

28. *Chicago Tribune,* June 8, 1861.

29. Illinois election returns, Illinois State Archives: Jo Daviess County (Galena), Lincoln 2,782, Douglas 1,841; Rock Island County (Moline), Lincoln 2,088, Douglas 1,478; and nearby Whiteside County, Lincoln 2,713, Douglas 1,110; Stark County (Elmira), Lincoln 1,164, Douglas 659; Cass (the close exception), Lincoln 1,046, Douglas 1,301. The votes for Breckinridge and Bell were negligible in all these counties. Haynie, *Nineteenth Illinois,* 82, 105, 113, 119.

30. *OR,* Series 3, 5:647; IAGR, 1:10–11, 2:124–25, 138–39.

31. *Chicago Tribune,* June 17, 1861.

32. Ibid., June 18, 1861.

33. Ingraham, *Elmer E. Ellsworth,* 150–51.

34. Randall, *Ellsworth,* 272–74; *Philadelphia Inquirer,* May 25, 29, 1861.

35. Watson, *When Soldiers Quit,* 22, citing Just, *Military Men,* 9.

36. McPherson, *For Cause and Comrades,* 151; Lee, *Crowds and Soldiers,* 194–96.

37. *Philadelphia Inquirer,* May 29, 1861; *Pittsburgh Gazette,* May 26, 1861; *Chicago Tribune,* May 28, June 13, 15, 1861.

38. Ingraham, *Elmer E. Ellsworth*, 130, citing *New York Tribune*, Apr. 30, 1861.

39. Ingraham, *Elmer E. Ellsworth*, 135.

40. East, "Russian General," 111–12.

41. Barnet, *Martyrs and Heroes*, 105–8, 167–68; Illinois Commandery, *Memorials*, 691–93; Haynie, *Nineteenth Illinois*, 136.

42. Sanford, *Fourteenth Illinois Cavalry*, 310; Petition, [1861], Yates Papers, Illinois State Historical Society.

43. Barnet, *Martyrs and Heroes*, 29–30; *Chicago Tribune*, July 13, 1861.

44. Coffman, *Old Army*, 156, 157.

45. Turchin, "First Steps"; Haynie, *Nineteenth Illinois*, 132, 153.

46. Haynie, *Nineteenth Illinois*, 139; *Chicago Tribune*, July 13, 1861; Turchin, "First Steps."

47. Lee, *Crowds and Soldiers*, 218. Lee's study is of the militia in the Carolinas during the Revolutionary War. However, his excellent analysis of the sociology of the Continental Army and the militia will be of great interest to military historians of any period.

48. See McPherson, *For Cause and Comrades*, 16, where he distinguishes between the motivation men had to enlist early in the war and the motivation that kept them fighting during the course of the war. Winders, *Mr. Polk's Army*, 81.

49. Stewart, *Military Character*, 61–62.

CHAPTER 4

1. Donald, *Lincoln*, 287; Turchin, "First Steps."

2. Schutz and Trenerry, *Abandoned by Lincoln*, 3, 15, 57, 60, 62 63.

3. *Milwaukee Sentinel*, Aug. 7, 1862; Turchin, "First Steps."

4. Turchin, "First Steps."

5. Ibid.

6. Painter, *Brief Narrative*, 6–7, 10; Castel, *Quantrill*, 53–54; Grant, *Memoirs*, chap. 19; McPherson, *For Cause and Comrades*, 153.

7. Turchin, "First Steps."

8. Ibid.

9. Ibid.

10. Ibid.

11. Ibid.; Vreeland Papers, MHI.

12. Turchin, "First Steps."

13. Ibid.

14. Ibid.

15. *OR*, 3:415–16, 458–59, 488.

16. Turchin, "First Steps"; Yates and Pickering, *Richard Yates*, 158–59.

17. Turchin, "First Steps."

18. Basler, *Collected Works*, 4:420, 457, 465, 506–7.

19. Turchin, "First Steps."

20. Keegan, *Warfare*, 12, quoted in Lee, *Crowds and Soldiers*, 2; Lee, *Crowds and Soldiers*, 2, 176, 194.

21. Lee, *Crowds and Soldiers*, 197.

22. Ibid., 203, 207.

23. Watson, *When Soldiers Quit*, 83, 163. Those interested in the phenomenon of the disintegration of military units will find all of Watson's chapter 9 of interest.

24. Lee, *Crowds and Soldiers*, 218, 222.

25. As quoted in McPherson, *For Cause and Comrades*, 153.

26. Turchin, "First Steps"; McPherson, *For Cause and Comrades*, 155.

27. Simon, *Papers of Grant*, 2:213; *OR*, 3:491; Nevins, *Frémont*, 524–25; Tap, *Over Lincoln's Shoulder*, 95–96.

28. *OR*, 3:497.

29. IAGR, 2:143; Haynie, *Nineteenth Illinois*, 144; McElligott, "Diary of Nadine Turchin," 58; W. W. Wythe to Editor, *National Tribune*, Mar. 24, 1910.

CHAPTER 5

1. Bowman and Irwin, *Sherman*, 40; IAGR, 2:143; *Louisville Journal*, Oct. 9, 1861; *New York Times*, Oct. 17, 1861.

2. *Louisville Journal*, Sept. 27, 1861; Wolseley, "General Sherman," 196–97; Liddell-Hart, *Sherman*, 342–43.

3. Ewing, "New Sherman Letters," 26; Villard to John Sherman, Oct. 2, 1861, Papers, LOC ("the character of his present command is no better than his late brigade" of volunteer regiments). The fear that the volunteers would make enemies of the local population had deep roots, as will be discussed later.

4. Turchin to Ray, Nov. 8, 1861, Ray Papers, Huntington Library; Haynie, *Nineteenth Illinois*, 146–47; IAGR, 2:155.

5. Sears, *Papers of McClellan*, 105–6, 127n2.

6. Engle, "Buell: Military Philosophy," 94n15; McClellan, *McClellan's Own Story*, 139.

7. *OR*, 7:460.

8. Chumney, "Don Carlos Buell," 34.

9. Haynie, *Nineteenth Illinois*, 159.

10. IAGR, 2:153; Haynie, *Nineteenth Illinois*, 159; Diary of Martin Moor, Dec. 28, 1861, Jan. 31, Mar. 21, Mar. 24, 1862, MHI.

11. Kelly, "Holding Kentucky," 1:385; Diary of Martin Moor, Jan. 11, Feb. 1, 1862, MHI.

12. *OR*, 7:468; Mitchel, *Ormsby MacKnight Mitchel*, 18, 23–25, 41–42; Mansfield, *Personal Memories*, 277–78.

13. Bruce, *Modern American Science*, 116; Slotten, *Patronage*, 120; Shoemaker, "Stellar Impact," 101–7, 142–44, 165, 189–96.

14. Bruce, *Modern American Science*, 243.

15. *New York Tribune,* Apr. 22, 1861. The conflict over control of the Dudley Observatory is the subject of a fascinating study. See Mary Ann James, *Elites in Conflict: The Antebellum Clash over the Dudley Observatory* (New Brunswick, Rutgers University Press, 1987).

16. Mitchel, *Ormsby MacKnight Mitchel,* 207–8, 214–15, 227–28, 231. Regarding Mitchel's skill as a drillmaster, see Engle, *Don Carlos Buell,* 111.

17. *OR,* 7:451.

18. Vocke, "Military Achievements," 84.

19. Warner, *Generals in Blue,* 448–49.

20. Andreas, *History of Chicago,* 2:195–196; Wagner, *24th Illinois,* 5–7; Kune, *Hungarian Exile,* 103; Burton, *Melting Pot Soldiers,* 48–50, 70–76.

21. Lonn, *Foreigners,* 230; Vasvary, *Lincoln's Hungarian Heroes,* 67.

22. Haynie, *Nineteenth Illinois,* 46; Burton, *Melting Pot Soldiers,* 49; Vasvary, *Lincoln's Hungarian Heroes,* 67; Kune, *Hungarian Exile,* 105; CMSR of Col. Geza Mihalotzy, 24th Illinois Volunteer Infantry.

23. Warren, *Stanley Families,* 161; Reid, *Ohio in the War,* 2:128.

24. Cullum, *Biographical Register,* 2:308.

25. *OR,* 4:354, 359.

26. Diary of Martin Moor, MHI; Puntenney, *Thirty-seventh Indiana,* 13–15; IAGR, 2:143.

27. Puntenney, *Thirty-seventh Indiana,* 14–18. Hazzard, who had retained his Regular Army commission, returned to duty as an artilleryman and was killed in Virginia at the climax of the Peninsular Campaign.

28. CMSR of Col. Carter Gazlay, 37th Indiana Volunteer Infantry; Puntenney, *Thirty-seventh Indiana,* 21.

29. Engle, *Don Carlos Buell,* 100–1, 107, 137.

30. *OR,* 7:450–51, 932.

31. Gatch, "General O. M. Mitchel," 113, 114; Vreeland to parents, Feb. 16, 1862, Vreeland Papers, MHI; Mitchel to Buell, Feb. 13, 1862, *OR,* 7:610–11; Turchin, "First Steps."

32. Puntenney, *Thirty-seventh Indiana,* 17; Vreeland to parents, Feb. 16, 1862, Vreeland Papers, MHI; Beatty, "Regiment in Search of Battle," 439–40; *OR,* 7:615.

33. *OR,* 7:861, 863; *National Intelligencer,* Apr. 23, 1862.

34. Andreas, *History of Chicago,* 2:196–97; Moore, *Rebellion Record,* IV:135–136; Beatty, "Regiment in Search of Battle," 440; Haynie, *Nineteenth Illinois,* 162.

35. Puntenney, *Thirty-seventh Indiana,* 17; Moore, *Rebellion Record,* 135–37; *OR,* 7:419.

36. *New York Times,* Aug, 22, 1862.

37. *OR,* 7:421; Puntenney, *Thirty-seventh Indiana,* 17. Andreas, *History of Chicago,* 2:337–38, records the celebration at the board of trade. Estimates of Confederate losses at Fort Donelson vary from 5,000 to nearly 16,000.

38. Horn, *Army of Tennessee,* 102.

39. *OR,* 7:627.

40. Ibid., 638; Vocke, "Military Achievements," 86–87; Beatty, "Regiment in Search of Battle," 441.

CHAPTER 6

1. *OR,* 16(1):497–98, 7:675–76.

2. Ibid.

3. Ford, *Adams Letters,* 2:111–12.

4. Shakespeare, *Henry V,* act 2, scene 4, lines 103–5.

5. *OR,* 7:669.

6. *OR,* Series 3, 1:168–69; *OR,* 2:907. Soon after uttering this statement, Beauregard was promoted directly to the full rank of general.

7. Bourne, *Red King's Rebellion,* 36.

8. Higginbotham, *War of American Independence,* 325–27; Perret, *Country Made by War,* 52–53. Perret makes the point that this was the one time during the Revolution that the Continentals acted as avengers, a role usually played by militiamen or local partisans.

9. Sugden, *Tecumseh,* 63–82.

10. Josephy, *Patriot Chiefs,* 154–60; Sugden, *Tecumseh,* 314–23.

11. Josephy, *Patriot Chiefs,* 200–8; Perret, *Counrty Made by War,* 135–37.

12. Perret, *Country Made by War,* 172–73; Catton, *Civil War,* 39.

13. Garrison, *New "Reign of Terror,"* 12–15.

14. Ibid., 29–30.

15. Ibid., 32–34, 48, 85.

16. See Royster, *Destructive War,* 80–81, and the sources cited there.

17. Fredrickson, *William Lloyd Garrison,* 64–65.

18. United States Military Academy, *Regulations,* secs. 115, 135, pp. 31, 34; Janowitz, *Professional Soldier,* 215–16.

19. United States Military Academy, *Regulations,* secs. 130, 135, 149, pp. 32, 34, 36.

20. Sears, *Papers of McClellan,* 71–73.

21. Pappas, *To The Point,* 242; Dupuy, *Where They Have Trod,* 137–38; Griess, "Dennis Hart Mahan"; Skelton, *American Profession,* 138–39.

22. Morrison, *Best School,* 64; W. T. Sherman to P. B. Ewing, Feb. 17, 1839, Ewing Papers, Ohio Historical Society; W. T. Sherman to Mrs. Thomas Ewing, July 20, 1836, Ewing Papers, LOC.

23. Skelton, *American Profession,* 272; Chumney, "Don Carlos Buell," 3, says it was "merely customary army discipline."

24. Winders, *Mr. Polk's Army,* 36–37, 72–73.

25. Meade, *Life and Letters,* 1:109; Robertson, *General A. P. Hill,* 15; Myers, *Mexican War Diary of McClellan,* 91.

26. Winders, *Mr. Polk's Army,* 85–86, citing Reuben Davis, *Recollections of Mississippi*

and Mississippians (Boston, Houghton Mifflin, 1890), 223; Giddings, *Sketches,* 81; Engle, *Don Carlos Buell,* 35.

27. Meade, *Life and Letters,* 1:108, 162.
28. Edwards, *Down the Tennessee,* 6; Doubleday, *Old Army,* 65.
29. Doubleday, *Old Army,* 64.
30. Anderson, *Artillery Officer,* 24.
31. Meade, *Life and Letters,* 1:147, 162.
32. Johnson, *Winfield Scott,* 168, 179, 188, 207; Eisenhower, *Agent of Destiny,* 74, 87.
33. Cullum, *Biographical Register,* 2:95; Chumney, "Don Carlos Buell," 3–6.
34. *Philadelphia Age,* July 1864, quoted in *Chicago Tribune,* Aug. 12, 1864. See also Abrams, "Copperhead Newspapers," 131–32; Wainwright, "Loyal Opposition," 306–7, 311 12.
35. 1852 campaign speech at Cincinnati, quoted in Johnson, *Winfield Scott,* 169.
36. Simpson and Berlin, *Sherman's Civil War,* Aug. 12, 1861, 129.
37. Ibid., letter of July 28, 1861, 124–25.
38. Ibid., 128–29.
39. Ibid., letter of Aug. 17, 1861, 131.
40. McPherson, *Drawn with the Sword,* 71. Readers may find Prof. McPherson's essay in this volume "From Limited to Total War" particularly interesting.
41. Sears, *Papers of McClellan,* 26, 35, 47n1, 49, 131–32.
42. Fry, *Operations under Buell,* 87–88.
43. Simpson and Berlin, *Sherman's Civil War,* 129.
44. *Congressional Globe,* 37th Cong., 1st sess., 257–65; Blaine, *Twenty Years,* 1:341.
45. *Congressional Globe,* 37th Cong., 2nd sess., 15.
46. Ibid., 37th Cong., 1st sess., 412; Randall, "Confiscation," 8; Rooke, *Lyman Trumbull,* 76; Blaine, *Twenty Years,* 1:341–43.
47. White, *Lyman Trumbull,* 176; Randall, "Confiscation," 9–10.
48. *OR,* 8:370, 465; *Congressional Globe,* 37th Cong., 2nd sess., 76, 130–31.
49. In this era generally, Americans made egalitarian "leveling attacks" on all professions: in 1800 three-quarters of the states had educational prerequisites to admission to the bar, but by 1860 three-quarters tolerated lawyers who had no formal education; in the same period, licensing requirements for physicians had been swept away everywhere. See Samuel Haber, *The Quest for Authority and Honor in the American Professions, 1750–1900* (Chicago: University of Chicago Press, 1991).
50. Julian, *Political Recollections,* 201; Tap, *Over Lincoln's Shoulder,* 45, 70–71.
51. *Congressional Globe,* 37th Cong., 2nd sess., 162, 204, 206.

CHAPTER 7

1. Haynie, *Nineteenth Illinois,* 163; Dr. John B. Lindsley diary, Feb. 26, 1862, quoted in Durham, *Nashville,* 51; *OR,* 10(2):71, 85.
2. *OR,* 10(2):28–29, 148; Force, *General Sherman,* 39.

3. *OR,* 10(2):71.

4. Ibid., 7:591.

5. Gatch, "General O. M. Mitchel," 116; Keifer, *Slavery,* 1:265; Beatty, "Regiment in Search of Battle," 444; Vocke, "Military Achievements," 87–88.

6. *OR,* 10:46, 48.

7. Ibid., 632.

8. McDaniel, *Clinging to the Union.*

9. Beatty, "Regiment in Search of Battle," 444; *New York Times,* Apr. 14, 1862.

10. Vocke, "Military Achievements," 88; Vreeland, letter of Apr. 28, 1862, Vreeland Papers, MHI; *New York Times,* Apr. 14, 1862; Graf and Haskins, *Papers of Johnson,* 5:269 and n1; *OR,* 10:47.

11. *New York Times,* Apr. 26, 1862, quoting a correspondent for the *Cincinnati Gazette.*

12. *OR,* 10(2):126.

13. Brewer, *Alabama,* 347–48, 357–59; Briant, *Sixth Regiment,* 142; *Chicago Tribune,* Apr. 23, 1862.

14. *Chicago Tribune,* Apr. 23, 1862; Eddy, *Patriotism of Illinois,* 332; Wagner, *24th Illinois,* 10 ("Turchin's impetuous urging prevailed"); Reid, *Ohio in the War,* 2:129; Puntenney, *Thirty-seventh Indiana,* 20 ("Gen. Mitchel was in a hurry"); Beatty, "Regiment in Search of Battle," 445. The other major rail line leading to Corinth was the Mobile & Ohio Railroad.

15. As reprinted in the *New York Times,* Apr. 26, 1862.

16. Ibid.; Beatty, "Regiment in Search of Battle," 444; Vocke, "Military Achievements," 91; Vreeland to his parents, Apr. 28, 1862, Vreeland Papers, MHI; *OR,* 10(2):104, 442; *Chicago Tribune,* Apr. 23, 1862; Black, *Railroads,* 143.

17. Puntenney, *Thirty-seventh Indiana,* 20; Chadick, "Southern Account," 157.

18. Burton, *Melting Pot Soldiers,* 146; Diary of Daniel Finn, Dec. 31, 1861, Apr. 23, 1862, MHI; Keifer, *Slavery,* 1:266, 271; *OR,* 20(2):228, 30(1):63; Pirtle, "Three Memorable Days," 37; Eddy, *Patriotism of Illinois,* 734.

19. *New York Times,* Apr. 26, 1862; *OR,* 10(1):641–43, 10(2):417, 460.

20. Vocke, "Military Achievements," 92–93; Wagner, *24th Illinois,* 10; *OR,* 10(1):642.

21. *New York Times,* Apr. 26, 1862; Puntenney, *Thirty-seventh Indiana,* 21.

22. Vreeland, letters of Apr. 28, 1862, July 8, 1862, Vreeland Papers, MHI; Ill. IAGR, 2:124; Andreas, *History of Chicago,* 2:182; Ash, *When the Yankees Came,* 149.

23. Mitchel to Stanton, May 5, 1862, *OR,* 10(2):166.

24. *OR,* 10(2):114, 115, 124.

25. Reid, *Ohio in the War,* 2:129; Goodloe, *Confederate Echoes,* 82–85.

26. *OR,* 10(2):115, 117, 118; *Chicago Tribune,* May 7, 1862; Vreeland, letter of Apr. 28, 1862, Vreeland Papers, MHI; Henett, *Supplement to the OR,* 2:9, 374; IAGR, 2:125; *New York Herald,* May 6, 1862; Beatty, "Regiment in Search of Battle," 447–48; Keifer to his wife, May 2, 1862, Keifer Papers, LOC; *Chicago Tribune,* May 7, 1862; Wagner, *24th Illinois,* 10.

27. *OR,* 10(2):137; *Louisville Journal,* May 6, 1862; *New York Herald,* May 11, 1862; *Chicago Tribune,* May 7, 1862; Beatty, "Regiment in Search of Battle," 448–49.

28. Keifer, *Slavery,* 274; *New York Tribune,* July 19, 1862.

29. *OR,* 10(2):124, 162, 619; Vreeland to his mother, July 8, 1862, Vreeland Papers, MHI.

30. Cooling, *Fort Donelson's Legacy,* 52.

31. Brewer, *Alabama,* 318; Villard, *Memoirs,* 1:290–91.

32. CMT, 56; *Ohio State Journal,* July 12, 1862; Axford, *Thomas Hubbard Hobbs,* 348; Reynolds, *Editors Make War,* 173; Walker, *Limestone County,* 99.

33. Brewer, *Alabama,* 364; Axford, *Thomas Hubbard Hobbs,* 100, 234; *Louisville Journal,* Sept. 12, 1862; Graf and Haskins, *Papers of Johnson,* 5:282n1; *New York Times,* May 24, 1862.

34. CMT, 74, 171; Axford, *Limestone County,* 18, 28.

35. Brewer, *Alabama,* 324–25; Axford, *Thomas Hubbard Hobbs,* 231; Shy, *People Numerous and Armed,* 219; CMT, 20.

36. Brewer, *Alabama,* 603–4, 632–33, 643–44, 666, 686, 688.

37. Axford, *Thomas Hubbard Hobbs,* ix–x, 110, 113, 190, 230–31, 234–36; Axford, *"To Lochaber,"* 41–42, 238 n37.

38. CMT, 73, 75, 178–79; Axford, *Thomas Hubbard Hobbs,* 65.

39. CMT, 56, 73, 75, 178–79; Axford, *Thomas Hubbard Hobbs,* 65.

40. CMSR of Col. Timothy R. Stanley. His file includes the interesting record of the board of officers (Stanley Board) convened Sept. 19, 1862, to judge his fitness as an officer. These citations: Stanley Board, 7–8, 25, 28, 37; Warren, *Stanley Families,* 161. He survived the inquiry.

41. CMT, 52, 98, 183; Ohio Roster Commission, *Official Roster,* 628–30.

42. CMT, 59, 93, 99–100.

43. Ibid., 183–84; Stanley Board, 43. The *Cleveland Plain Dealer* of May 17, 1862, contains an exculpatory but surprisingly detailed account.

44. Stanley Board, 43; CMT, 184.

45. Stanley Board, 22, 25, 28, 37.

46. CMT, 56–57, 98, 167, 184, 221; Stanley Board, 20, 33, 44.

47. CMT, 57–58, 93–94, 100, 167, 175, 184.

48. Stanley Board, 30, 44, 52; CMT, 184.

49. CMT, 184–85; *Cleveland Plain Dealer,* May 17, 1862.

50. CMT, 58, 160; Cooling, *Fort Donelson's Legacy,* 14; *New York Herald,* May 6, 1862, quoting the *Mobile Advertiser; OR,* 10(2):543–44.

51. *Charleston Mercury,* May 21, 1862, another vivid account.

52. Ibid.; CMT, 58, 59, 109, 142–46, 169–70; Axford, *"To Lochaber,"* 43.

53. CMT, 126–27; Keifer to Mitchel, May 1, 1862, Keifer Papers, LOC; Keifer, *Slavery,* 277; *Louisville Journal,* May 7, 1862.

54. CMT, 147, 194, 218–19; Seaton, *Crimean War,* 28.

55. Chadick, "Southern Account," 158; CMT, 116, 119–20, 147–48, 155–56, 163–64, 194.

56. Puntenney, *Thirty-seventh Indiana*, 23; CMT, 119, 148–49.

57. CMT, 119, 148–49, 219.

CHAPTER 8

1. CMT, 116, A5.

2. Ibid., 116, A6; Mahan, *Elementary Treatise*, 84, para. 225.

3. CMT, 51, 77, A8.

4. Ibid., 24, 27, 38, 99.

5. Chadick, "Southern Account," 157; CMT, 21–22, 39.

6. CMT, 92–93, 100, 172, 186.

7. Ibid., 102, 104.

8. Puntenney, *Thirty-seventh Indiana*, 24; CMT, 28, 100, 104, 110–11.

9. Stewart, *Summer Soldiers*, 163; Diary of Alfred H. Trego, Nov. 23, 1864, Chicago Historical Society; Oliphant et al., *Letters of William Gilmore Simms*, 4:484–85n48.

10. CMT, 16–17, 29, 40, 108.

11. Osborne, *Fiery Trail*, 110.

12. CMT, 30, 85–86, 94, 130, A11.

13. Ibid., 39, 77.

14. Puntenney, *Thirty-seventh Indiana*, 24.

15. CMT, 190; Vreeland, letter of May 17, 1862, Vreeland Papers, MHI; Meron, *Henry's Wars*, 22–23; Vale, *Minty and the Cavalry*, 28; Horton and Teverbaugh, *Eleventh Regiment*, 262; Fleming, *Reconstruction in Alabama*, 63 ("Turchin retired to his tent and gave over the town to the soldiers to be sacked after the old European custom"). This "custom" was cited elsewhere during the Civil War, one example being to justify the extensive pillaging of Fredericksburg, Virginia, in December 1862. Walker, *Second Army Corps*, 153. The "custom" in fact has Old Testament origins (Deuteronomy 20:10–14) and Shakespearean echoes.

16. CMT, 117, 186, A11–A12.

17. Ibid., A12.

18. Ibid., 40, 181; Puntenney, *Thirty-seventh Indiana*, 25.

19. CMT, 99, 117, 186–87.

20. Ibid., 39, 44, 64, 101–3, 173.

21. Ibid., 159, A12–A13.

22. *Charleston Mercury*, May 21, 1862; *Cleveland Plain Dealer*, May 17, 1862; *New York Times*, May 17, 1862.

23. *OR*, 10(1):874–76, 10(2):162, 640; Ohio Roster Commission, *Official Roster*, 628–30; Cooling, *Fort Donelson's Legacy*, 54, 67.

24. CMT, 120, A13; *Cleveland Plain Dealer*, May 17, 1862.

25. Vreeland to his parents, Apr. 28, 1862, Vreeland Papers, MHI.

26. Beatty, *Memoirs*, 108; *New York Times*, May 29, 1862; Keifer to his wife, May 3, 1862, Kiefer Papers, LOC.

27. CMT, 80, 121–22, 160–62; Curtiss, *Russian Army*, 192.
28. Puntenney, *Thirty-seventh Indiana*, 25; CMT, 125, A16.
29. CMT, 45–46, 150, 152, 206; Edwards and Axford, *Lure and Lore*, 8. General Sir Henry Clinton made the same arrangement at John Hancock's mansion on Beacon Hill in 1775, quaintly gentlemanly on the one side, quaintly trusting on the other. See Hibbert, *Redcoats and Rebels*.
30. CMT, 65, 68; Axford, *Limestone County*, 23.
31. CMT, 18, 53, 68; Beatty, *Memoirs*, 112; *Cincinnati Commercial*, May 29, 1862.
32. CMT, 135, 158, 192; Turchin, "First Steps."
33. CMT, 50, 123, 127, 129, 133.
34. CMT, 17, 24, 42, 59, 124, 128–29, 133–34, 176.
35. Chadick, "Southern Account," 160.
36. Vreeland, letter of May 17, 1862, Vreeland Papers, MHI; *New York Times*, June 1, 1862; Puntenney, *Thirty-seventh Indiana*, 26; Canfield, *21st Ohio*, 49.
37. Kiefer, *Slavery*, 282.
38. CMT, 28–29, 180, 189.
39. Ibid., 95–96, 201, 202.
40. Ibid., 32–36, 157–58, 193–94; Morris, *Southern Slavery*, 230.
41. Kennett, *Marching through Georgia*, 277.
42. Merrill, *Soldier of Indiana*, 1:408; Dargan, *Diary of Martha Abernathy*, 43–54.
43. *New York Times*, May 17, 18, 1862; Keifer to his wife, May 5, 1862, Kiefer Papers, LOC; *Charleston Mercury*, May 29, 1862.
44. CMT, 120–21.
45. *OR*, 10(2):212, 294.
46. Beatty, *Memoirs*, 111.
47. *OR*, 10(2):212–13, 295.
48. Canfield, *21st Ohio*, 49–53; Grimsley, *Hard Hand*, 82; Axford, "To Lochaber," 56.

CHAPTER 9

1. Pease and Randall, *Diary of Browning*, 551; *Washington Evening Star*, June 21, 1862; Pierpont to Lincoln, June 20, 1862, Lincoln Papers, LOC.
2. Yates and Pickering, *Richard Yates*, 196–97; Ambler, *Pierpont*, 154; *ExPro*, 12:364.
3. Ambler, *Pierpont*, 125–26; Cox, *Military Reminiscences*, 1:206; letter of Mar. 6, 1864, Lightburn Papers, West Virginia University Library. Curry reports, for example, that Lightburn's home, Lewis County, had a population of 7,766 whites in 1860, only 230 slaves, and that the county's vote for statehood was 462 in favor, 3 against. See Curry, *A House Divided*.
4. See Bradford, *Union Portraits*, 167, for the extreme view of his weaknesses. For discussions of his strengths, see Thomas and Hyman, *Stanton*, 143–63; Flower, *Edwin McMasters Stanton*, 117.

5. *ExPro*, 13:312, after renomination.

6. Skelton, *American Profession*, 193–95, 287–89; Coffman, *Old Army*, 66–67, 82–83, 88.

7. Riddle, *Recollections of War Times*, 65; Sherman, *Memoirs*, 1:191; Warner, *Generals in Blue*, 423.

8. Abbott, *Cobbler in Congress*, 123–24; *ExPro*, 12:180, 198.

9. *ExPro*, 12:5, 392; *New York Times*, Apr. 26, 1862; *Congressional Globe*, 37th Cong., 2nd sess., 1773.

10. *ExPro*, 12:288; Warner, *Generals in Blue*, 515, 520–21; Peskin, *Garfield*, 90; Beale, *Diary of Edward Bates*, 245; *ExPro*, 12:233.

11. *Congressional Globe*, 37th Cong., 2nd sess., 163; *New York Times*, May 8, 1862.

12. Sparks, *Diary of Marsena Patrick*, 12–16, 50, 52, 54; Rawley, *Edwin D. Morgan*, 154–55.

13. *ExPro*, 12:216, 270; Warner, *Generals in Blue*, 64.

14. Yates and Pickering, *Richard Yates*, 156, 158, 159; Cozzens and Girardi, *Memoirs of Pope*, 5.

15. The vote was held June 17, but the issue remained in doubt at least until June 25 and was not officially confirmed until August. A. S. Hill to Gay, June 19, 1862, Gay Papers, Columbia University; Medill to Trumbull, June 25, 1862, Trumbull Papers, LOC; Medill to Yates, July 3, 1862, Yates Papers, Illinois State Historical Society; Cole, *Era of the Civil War*, 269–72; Hesseltine, *War Governors*, 238–39.

16. Schutz and Trenerry, *Abandoned by Lincoln*, 94–95; *Congressional Globe*, 37th Cong., 2nd sess., 1992.

17. Hicken, *Illinois in the Civil War*, 12.

18. Jones, *"Black Jack,"* 100, 131.

19. Warner, *Generals in Blue*, 54, 356.

20. Ibid., 89, 288, 347, 411–12; Illinois Commandery, *Memorials*, 356.

21. Warner, *Generals in Blue*, 556–57.

22. Turchin to Ray, Nov. 8, 1861, Ray Papers, Huntington Library; East, "Russian General," 108.

23. Trumbull Papers, LOC; Andreas, *History of Chicago*, 1:439.

24. Harper, *Lincoln and the Press*, 97; Thomas and Hyman, *Stanton*, 218; *Washington Evening Star*, June 16, 1862.

25. Howard, *Civil-War Echoes*, 58; *Congressional Globe*, 37th Cong., 2nd sess., 1416–17.

26. *ExPro*, 12:269–70, attracting notice in the *Chicago Tribune* the next day; *Congressional Globe*, 37th Cong., 2nd sess., 1914.

27. *Congressional Globe*, 37th Cong., 2nd sess., 1991–94, 2013; *New York Times*, July 18, 1862; *New York Tribune*, June 19, 1862.

28. *ExPro*, 12:284, 336, 341; Warner, *Generals in Blue*, 190, 239, 259, 363, 493, 494; *New York Times*, Apr. 26, May 10, June 13, July 9, 1862; *New York Tribune*, June 2, 1862.

29. *ExPro*, 12:288, 336; Warner, *Generals in Blue*, 54, 177, 513, 515; *New York Times*, May 15, June 10, 1862.

30. *ExPro*, 12:255; *New York Tribune*, June 3, 1862.

31. Warner, *Generals in Blue,* 280, 457; *ExPro,* 12:336, 340, 342; Bowman and Irwin, *Sherman,* 262–63; Dana, *Recollections,* 75; Fellman, *Inside War,* 5.

32. *ExPro,* 12:337.

33. Ibid., 366, 371, 382, 384, 386.

34. *New York Tribune,* June 26, 1862.

35. Durham, *Nashville,* 57, 77; Graf and Haskins, *Papers of Johnson,* 5:478; *ExPro,* 12:355–56, 382.

36. Graf and Haskins, *Papers of Johnson,* 5:438; Cullum, *Biographical Register,* 1:418–19; Wright to Sherman, July 6, 1862, Sherman Papers, LOC; *Louisville Journal,* June 25, 1862; *National Intelligencer,* July 3, 1862; *New York Times,* July 6, 1862; *Philadelphia Inquirer,* July 7, 1862.

37. Warner, *Generals in Blue,* 271–72; *OR,* 20(1):12; *ExPro,* 12:357.

38. *New York Times,* June 20, 1862; *ExPro,* 12:684.

CHAPTER 10

1. McKinney, *Education in Violence,* 119; *OR,* 16(2):42; Engle, *Don Carlos Buell,* 254–55.

2. Young, "Men Who Reigned," 194; Dyer, *Reminiscences,* 72–74; McDowell, *City of Conflict,* 10–11; Coulter, *Readjustment in Kentucky,* 254.

3. *ExPro,* 12:260. The exception, confirmed Apr. 15, was William Sooy Smith. See *New York Times,* Apr. 16, 1862, *Congressional Globe,* 37th Cong., 2nd sess., 1862.

4. *OR,* 16(2):68, 70.

5. Ibid., 16(2):68, 70, 72; *New York Times,* July 9, 1862; *Cincinnati Commercial,* July 11, 1862.

6. *OR,* 16(2):72, 80, 85–86, 90–91.

7. Engle, *Don Carlos Buell,* 264.

8. *OR,* 16(2):92; *Cincinnati Commercial,* July 11, 1862; Don Carlos Buell, "Operations in North Alabama," 706–7; Keifer to his wife, July 2, 5, 1862, Keifer Papers, LOC; Vocke, "Military Achievements," 101–2.

9. *OR,* 16(2):592; Shanks, *Personal Recollections,* 198–201, 215–18, 231–33; *Washington Evening Star,* June 24, 1864.

10. *OR,* 16(2):98, 99.

11. Ibid., 8:507–8, 17(2):34–35, 53–54; McClernand to Halleck, July 2, 1862, letters received, Secretary of War's Office, NA; Grimsley, *Hard Hand,* 51; Goodrich, *War to the Knife,* 220.

12. Halleck to Quinby and Halleck to McClernand, July 3 and 6, 1862, letters received, Secretary of War's Office, NA; *OR,* 17(2):77. See Starr, *Jennison's Jayhawkers,* 166–90, for more details on Halleck's attitude.

13. Doster, *Lincoln,* 173; Stanley, *Personal Memoirs,* 15; Ambrose, *Halleck,* 8, 206; Wilson, "Halleck—A Memoir," 548.

14. Dispatch from Joseph P. McCullough, late spring, 1862, quoted in Clayton, *Little Mack,* 19; Shanks, *Personal Recollections,* 245, 246.

15. Ash, *When the Yankees Came*, 150. See also McPherson, *Battle Cry of Freedom*, 501–2; Teitler, *Genesis*, 4, 19–20.

16. Blegen, *Hans Christian Heg*, 67, 98–99; Graf and Haskins, *Papers of Johnson*, 5:371–72.

17. *OR*, 16(2):40; *Milwaukee Sentinel*, June 19, 1862; *New York Herald*, June 20, 1862. Oliver Greene's conciliatory tendencies may have been the cause of his unpopularity with Andrew Johnson, who at this time was demanding his removal. See *OR*, 16(2):47. Greene, reassigned to the Army of the Potomac, received the Congressional Medal of Honor for his services on the 6th Corps staff at Antietam.

18. Grebner, *"We Were the Ninth,"* 104–5.

19. *OR*, 16(2):40, 47, 51.

20. *U.S. Statutes at Large* 12:354, Mar. 13, 1862.

21. *OR*, 10(2):31; *Pittsburgh Gazette*, July 17, 1862.

22. Bogue, *Earnest Men*, 152, 155; Grimsley, *Hard Hand*, 68.

23. Grimsley, *Hard Hand*, 73, citing Force to Kebler, June 16–17, 1862, Manning F. Force papers, University of Washington, Seattle.

24. *OR*, 16(2):69–70.

25. Macomb, *Practice*, 26; CMT, i. The officer who signed the complaint, Charles Champion Gilbert, inspector general of the Department of the Ohio, would himself have his own troubles gaining a general's star, receiving a presidential appointment that the Senate failed to confirm.

26. Chadick, "Southern Account," 161 (with their furniture, by this account); *Chicago Tribune*, July 22, 1862.

CHAPTER 11

1. Julian, *Political Recollections*, 360; Taylor, *Garfield*, 66.

2. Garfield, "My Campaign," 525, 531–32; Taylor, *Garfield of Ohio*, 67–69; Peskin, *Garfield*, 101–18.

3. *OR*, 7:33.

4. Smith, *Life and Letters of Garfield*, 156–57; Taylor, *Garfield*, 73; Peskin, *Garfield*, 128.

5. Peskin, *Garfield*, 136; Smith, *Life and Letters of Garfield*, 210; Garfield, "My Campaign," 527; Hight, *Fifty-eighth Indiana*, 78.

6. Smith, *Life and Letters of Garfield*, 95–96; Williams, *Wild Life*, 89, 114.

7. The most noteworthy example is perhaps a letter to Salmon P. Chase written in July 1863, when Garfield was chief of staff to William S. Rosecrans, taking issue with Rosecrans's command of the Army of the Cumberland—a letter not made public until 1879. Smith, *Life and Letters of Garfield*, 309–11, calls the letter "primarily a cry of distress to a friend and sympathizer whom he wanted to know the truth as to his own feelings." For this trait, Garfield has ample apologists, e.g., Peskin, *Garfield*, 212–18 ("It was too late for Garfield, or anyone else, to set matters right for Rosecrans").

8. Smith, *Life and Letters of Garfield*, 178–79; Williams, *Wild Life*, 116–18.

9. Williams, *Wild Life*, 121.

10. Cullum, *Biographical Register*, 1:475–76, 571–72.

11. *OR*, 7:659–60; Reid, *Ohio in the War*, 1:901–3; *ExPro*, 12:260; *National Tribune*, May 3, 1894. When Ammen received notice of his own promotion to brigadier, fellow members of the court-martial got up an "order" forbidding "anyone hereafter to call him Uncle Jacob, that title being entirely too familiar and undignified for one of his rank." Beatty, *Memoirs*, 122–23.

12. Graf and Haskins, *Papers of Johnson*, 5:311, 312n1.

13. *Kentucky Revised Statutes* (1960), 533–38.

14. Graf and Haskins, *Papers of Johnson*, 5:322–25; *Louisville Journal*, June 21, 1862; *OR*, 16(2):79.

15. Speed, Kelly, and Pirtle, *Union Regiments of Kentucky*, 282–85, *OR*, 10(1).351–52, 648, 682, 1(2):692.

16. Horrall, *Forty-second Indiana*.

17. Thornbrough, *Indiana in the Civil War Era*, 87n4; Stampp, *Indiana Politics*, 21–26; Merrill, *Soldier of Indiana*, 1:404.

18. Quoted in Grimsley, *Hard Hand*, 80, citing Beatty, *Memoirs*, 108–9.

19. Beatty, *Memoirs*, 138–39.

20. Ibid., 9–13, 118; Reid, *Ohio in the War*, 1:924.

21. Beatty, *Memoirs*, 68n2, 111, 113.

22. Cullum, *Biographical Register*, 2:494; *Los Angeles Times*, May 11, 1904; Swaine Papers, MHI, clipping, "Journal," Feb. 27, 1927; Skelton, *American Profession*, 170; Scott, *Military Dictionary*.

23. *Martin v. Mott*, 12 Wheat. (25 U.S.) 19, 34–37, 6 L. Ed. 537 (1827); Newmyer, *Justice Joseph Story*, 74–114.

24. Williams, *Wild Life*, 121.

25. Diary of Almon Rockwell, July 7, 1862, Rockwell Papers, LOC.

26. *CMT*, 2.

27. Ibid., 16; Macomb, *Practice*, 55.

28. *Bickel's Executors v. Fasig's Administrator*, 33 Pa. (9 Casey) 463, 465 (1859); *Taylor v. State*, 62 Ala. 164, 166 (1878); Ky. Rev. St., c. 104, 5 (1960); *Commonwealth v. McGuire*, 84 Ky. 57, 58 (1886).

29. *CMT*, 16.

30. Ibid., 16–20.

31. Ibid., 16.

32. Ibid., 20.

33. Ibid., 18.

34. Ibid., 22–23.

35. Ibid., 32.

36. Ibid., 33.

37. Ibid., 33–34.

38. Ibid.

39. Ibid., 38–44.

40. Ibid., 52–54, 61.

41. Beatty, *Memoirs,* 117; CMT, 45, 46, 68.

42. Beatty, *Memoirs,* 117.

43. CMT, 70.

44. Beatty, *McLean,* 59.

45. CMT, 76–77.

46. Swaine also adduced testimony from Mayor Press Tanner that "I heard a great many soldiers say he had given such orders," i.e., to "act this way" (ibid., 54), but the judge advocate knew this statement was not admissible (Macomb, *Practice,* 52), and any experienced officer would have known it was worthless.

47. CMT, 77, 84–92.

48. Ibid., 92–113.

49. Williams, *Wild Life,* 122–24.

50. Ibid., 123.

51. Smith, *Life and Letters of Garfield,* 225; Beatty, *Memoirs,* 114, 127.

52. Villard, *Memoirs,* 1:290–92; *Louisville Journal,* July 14, 29, Aug. 11, 1862.

53. Ropes, *Story of the Civil War,* 2:390–91; Engle, *Don Carlos Buell,* 273–74.

54. Gay Papers, Columbia University.

55. Drell, *Letters by Richard Smith,* 542–46 (Smith's manifesto); Andrews, *The North Reports,* 287; Beatty, *Memoirs,* 82; Kiefer to his wife, May 2, 1862, Kiefer Papers, LOC.

56. *Cincinnati Commercial,* July 17, 1862.

57. *OR,* 16(2):154, 164.

CHAPTER 12

1. Grimsley, *Hard Hand,* 67.

2. Geary, *We Need Men,* 8; Rawley, *Edwin D. Morgan,* 175; A. S. Hill to S. H. Gay, June 22, July 14, 1862, Gay Papers, Columbia University; Pease and Randall, *Diary of Browning,* 562; Dayton, *Raising of Union Forces,* 411; Nevins and Halsey, *Diary of George Templeton Strong,* 3:241.

3. Grant, *Memoirs,* 1:368–69.

4. For a detailed discussion of the impact of McClellan's defeat on the conduct of the war, see Grimsley, *Hard Hand,* 68–78, 92–95.

5. Letter of July 4, 1862, Trumbull Papers, LOC; Hamlin, *Hannibal Hamlin,* 438.

6. Donald, *Lincoln,* 359–60; Sears, *Papers of McClellan,* 344–45.

7. Sears, *Young Napoleon,* 229; Randall, *Lincoln,* vol. 1, part 2, 103.

8. Grimsley, *Hard Hand,* 75. As to the propriety of the letter and the spectrum of opinion, see Ropes, *Army under Pope,* 13; Hassler, *Shield of the Union,* 178; Williams, *Lincoln and His Generals* 133; Sears, *Young Napoleon,* 228.

9. W. P. Fessenden to his cousin Lizzie, July 6, 1862, Fessenden Papers, Bowdoin College Library.

10. Lincoln to James Conkling, Aug. 26, 1863, Basler, *Collected Works,* 6:408.

11. Sumner, quoted in A. S. Hill to S. H. Gay, Wednesday a.m. [July 9, 1862], Gay Papers, Columbia University.

12. For a full discussion, see Engle, *Don Carlos Buell,* 104–8.

13. *OR,* 16(2):104.

14. *ExPro,* 12:44.

15. *Congressional Globe,* 37th Cong., 2nd sess., 3253.

16. *OR,* Series 2, 3:414–16; 4:124–26.

17. *Louisville Journal,* July 10, 1862; *Washington Evening Star,* July 16, 1862.

18. JCCW, 102.

19. *Louisville Journal,* Aug. 5, 1862; Grimsley, *Hard Hand,* 82.

20. *Pittsburgh Gazette,* July 10, 1862; *Washington Evening Star,* July 14, 1862.

21. Yates's camp claimed the letter a spontaneous effort. See Yates and Pickering, *Richard Yates,* 173–77.

22. JCCW, 101, 286, 290.

23. *Congressional Globe,* 37th Cong., 2nd sess., 3391.

24. Schutz and Trenerry, *Abandoned by Lincoln,* 91, 94.

25. Ropes, *Army under Pope,* 174.

26. Ibid.; *OR,* 12(2):50; *National Intelligencer,* Aug. 16, 1862; Grimsley, *Hard Hand,* 87.

27. Sparks, *Diary of Marsena Patrick,* 109; Sutherland, "Introduction to War," 124. On Stanton's role in Pope's orders, see Thomas and Hyman, *Stanton,* 217–18n9; Sutherland, "Origins of Total War," 577; *OR,* 11(3):359.

28. A. S. Hill to S. H. Gay, Gay Papers, Columbia University.

29. *New York Herald,* July 19, 1862.

30. *Washington Evening Star,* July 18, 1862; *New York Herald,* July 16, 18, 1862. In Congressman George Julian's view, Davis's "volubility of talk bordered on the miraculous; and whenever he began to swathe the Senate in his interminable rhetoric it awakened the laughter or the despair of everybody on the floor or in the galleries." Julian, *Political Recollections,* 358.

31. White, *Lyman Trumbull,* 173. James G. Randall, in making it the subject of his University of Chicago doctoral dissertation, concluded that the months of debates and amendments disclose "a deplorable confusion of logic, and a jarring of opinions even among those who voted together." Randall, "Confiscation," 10.

32. As it stood and as approved after passage of a resolution "clarifying" it, the statute is printed in *U.S. Statutes at Large* 12:589–92; the resolution is on p. 627.

33. *Congressional Globe,* 37th Cong., 2nd sess., 2930.

34. *Pittsburgh Gazette,* Jan. 24, 1862; *Lebanon Courier,* Mar. 22, 1862.

35. Medill to Trumbull, June 25, 1862, Trumbull Papers, LOC.

36. The statute appears in *U.S. Statutes at Large* 12:597–600.

37. Beale, *Diary of Edward Bates,* 203; Bradley, *Simon Cameron,* 201. Cameron argued for it again in his Dec. 1 annual report, saying it "may become the duty . . . of the government to employ [former slaves'] services against the rebels under proper military regulation, discipline and command."

38. *Congressional Globe*, 37th Cong., 2nd sess., 1615; Bancroft to Fessenden, July 11, 1862, Fessenden Papers, Bowdoin College Library; *Congressional Globe*, 37th Cong., 2nd sess., 3200–1.

39. Younger, *Diary of Robert Kean*, 92.

CHAPTER 13

1. Abbott, *Cobbler in Congress*, 30, 118, 126; *Congressional Globe*, 37th Cong., 2nd sess., 3602.

2. Muller, "Preston King," 614, 673–74, 692; Bogue, *Earnest Men*, 161–62; *Congressional Globe*, 37th Cong., 2nd sess., 3251.

3. Muller, "Preston King," 696; *Congressional Globe*, 37th Cong., 2nd sess., 1283.

4. W. P. Fessenden, Feb. 15, 1862, Fessenden Papers, Bowdoin College Library; Fessenden, *Life of Fessenden*, 2:259, 261.

5. Jellison, *Fessenden of Maine*, 151; W. P. Fessenden to Frank Fessenden, Aug. 31, 1862, Fessenden Papers, Bowdoin College Library.

6. *Congressional Globe*, 38th Cong., 1st sess., 557, 559.

7. Blaine, *Twenty Years*, 2:316; Cole and McDonough, *Benjamin Brown French*, 327; W. P. Fessenden to Frank Fessenden, May 17, 1862, Fessenden Papers, Bowdoin College Library.

8. Bogue, *Earnest Men*, 81;.

9. Prof. Allan Bogue greatly enhanced our understanding of the Thirty-seventh Congress with the statistical analysis in his book *The Earnest Men*, drawing precise lines between radicals and moderates in the Senate. Our analysis owes much to his work, though his account is not the whole story.

10. The measures and their legislative roll calls used in this analysis are as they appear in *Congressional Globe*, 37th Cong., 2nd sess.: prohibiting returning fugitive slaves, Mar. 10, 1862, 1142–43; increasing staffs, Mar. 19, 1281–84; emancipating slaves in DC, Apr. 3, 1526; limiting the number of brigadiers to 180, May 8, 2013; allowing blacks to testify, July 7, 3138; continuing the Senate's confiscation bill, July 8, 3166; limiting blacks in the army, July 10, 3333–34; compensating loyalists for slaves in military service, July 10, 3234–37; limiting the emancipatory clause of the militia bill by deleting families, July 11, 3249; rejecting the conference report on the confiscation bill, July 12, 3276; limiting the emancipatory provision of the militia bill, July 13, 3339. The analysis also takes into account the vote to confirm James S. Jackson as brigadier general of volunteers, July 16, *ExPro*, 12:419.

11. *New York Times*, July 6, 1862; *Philadelphia Inquirer*, July 7, 1862; *National Intelligencer*, July 18, 1862; McDonough, *War in Kentucky*, 236–37.

12. *Congressional Globe*, 37th Cong., 2nd sess., 1808–11.

13. Mayer, *Republican Party*, 59; Johnson, *Dictionary of American Biography*, 4:126, 8:268; Bogue, *Earnest Men*, 35; Jellison, *Fessenden of Maine*, 113; Howard, *Civil-War Echoes*, 59. The original copy of Clark's resolution to expel the ten senators is on display in the exhibit hall of the National Archives in Washington.

14. Howard, *Civil-War Echoes*, 274–75; Russell, *Timothy O. Howe*, 94; Sharp, "Henry S. Lane," 96.

15. Bogue, *Earnest Men*, 103, 106; Folwell, *History of Minnesota*, 2:73–74; *Congressional Globe*, 37th Cong., 2nd sess., 3602.

16. Gillette, *Jersey Blue*, 184.

17. Castel, *Civil War Kansas*, 35, 41, 168; *Chicago Tribune*, Mar. 4, 1864; Bogue, *Earnest Men*, 42–43.

18. *New York Herald*, June 7, 1862; *Congressional Globe*, 37th Cong., 2nd sess., 111; Castel, *Civil War Kansas*, 54–55; *OR*, 3:516–17; Stephenson, *James H. Lane*, 116.

19. Castel, *Civil War Kansas*, 24.

20. *New York Tribune*, July 19, 1862; A. S. Hill to S. H. Gay, July 18, 1862, Gay Papers, Columbia University.

21. Norman Eastman to John Locke Scripps, Aug. 6, 1862, Andrew Sherman to J. R. Doolittle, Aug. 13, 1862, James R. Doolittle Papers, LOC; *Congressional Globe*, 37th Cong., 2nd sess., 94–95; Sellers, "James R. Doolittle," 293.

22. *Congressional Globe*, 37th Cong., 1st sess., 262; Simpson and Berlin, *Sherman's Civil War*, 272–73; *Chicago Tribune*, Aug. 2, 1862.

23. Special Order No. 18, Mar. 23, 1862, Special Order Book (Sherman's) Fifth Division, RG 94.2.2, NA.

24. Affidavit of S. P. Bayly, May 12, 1862, Waitman T. Willey Papers, West Virginia University Library; Curry, *A House Divided*, 53–54; Ambler, *Pierpont*, 104–6. Willey, who had been elected by the Pierpont government to fill the vacancy caused by the resignation of James Mason, was at the time Virginia's only serving senator.

25. Dickson, "Edgar Cowan," 20–21; Boucher, *Old and New Westmoreland*, 2:59–60; Persis, "Senator Edgar A. Cowan," 228; *National Intelligencer*, Apr. 7, 1862.

26. Dickson, "Edgar Cowan," 40; *Pittsburgh Gazette*, June 26, 1862; *Harrisburg Patriot and Union*, July 23, 1862; Persis, "Senator Edgar A. Cowan," 232. Cowan's government career ended in 1866, his reelection "plainly impossible" and his nomination to be minister to Austria tabled.

27. Howard, *Civil-War Echoes*, 56–57; Buchanan, "James F. McDougal," 207; Shaw, "McDougal of California," 120–23.

28. Buchanan, "James F. McDougal," 200–1; Fehrenbacher, *Lincoln: Speeches*, 310–11.

29. Baxter, *Browning*, 111; Horner, "Lincoln Rebukes a Senator," 109–10; Joseph Medill to Lyman Trumbull, June 25, 1862, Trumbull Papers, LOC; Bogue, *Earnest Men*, 154. Morgan's commission as a brigadier dated from the same date as Turchin's.

30. Pease and Randall, *Diary of Browning*, 501, 560; Carman and Luthin, *Lincoln and the Patronage*, 178–83; Silver, *Lincoln's Supreme Court*, 67, 74, 79.

31. *Washington Evening Star*, July 18, 1862.

32. *ExPro*, 12:420–34.

33. Ibid., 12:434–35.

34. Ibid., 12:435.

35. Chafee, *Three Human Rights*, 93.

36. *Pittsburgh Gazette*, July 16, 1862.

37. *Congressional Globe,* 37th Cong., 2nd sess., 3406.

38. *U.S. Statutes at Large* 12:627.

39. *New York Tribune,* July 18, 1862; A. S. Hill to S. H. Gay, July 17, 1862, Gay Papers, Columbia University; Julian, *Political Recollections,* 220.

40. *Congressional Globe,* 37th Cong., 2nd sess., 3406.

41. *OR,* 11(3):362–63, 12(2):50.

42. Ritchie, *Press Gallery,* 54–55; Harper, *Lincoln and the Press,* 103; Storr, *Bohemian Brigade,* 34–37; *New York Tribune,* June 14, 1862.

43. *National Intelligencer,* July 18, 1862.

44. It did not promote Col. W. W. Duffield, caught up in the Murfreesboro disaster, nor Col. Stanley Matthews, whose aspirations were scuttled, to Buell's consternation, by Benjamin Wade and John Sherman on grounds of "disloyalty" without participation by the White House. See *OR,* 16(2):48. Marcy did eventually receive an appointment as a brigadier general of the Regular Army, but not until 1878.

CHAPTER 14

1. *OR,* Series 3, 2:253.

2. Beatty, *Memoirs,* 119; *OR,* 16(2):273; Williams, *Wild Life,* 124–24; *OR,* 16(2):230; *Chicago Tribune,* Aug. 18, 1862.

3. *New York Times,* July 8, 1900.

4. CMT, 116–17.

5. Ibid., 121–26.

6. Ibid., 129.

7. *OR,* 10(2):294.

8. CMT, 134–35.

9. *New York Times,* July 8, 1900.

10. CMT, 136.

11. Pvt. Ayer Bowers of Co. B, 37th Indiana, stayed in the lockup at Huntsville less than a fortnight before being released and returned to duty, a sad commentary on the racial attitudes of the times. He remained with his regiment, reenlisted as a veteran, and mustered out with the regiment in 1865. See CMSR of Ayer Bowers.

12. CMT, 137–38.

13. Ibid., Exhibit A, 1–6.

14. *OR,* 10(2):161–62.

15. CMT, Exhibit A, 1–6; Warner, *Generals in Blue,* 52.

16. CMT, Exhibit A, 7.

17. Ibid., 8–10.

18. Ibid.

19. Ibid., 22–25.

20. Ibid., 26–28.

21. Ibid., 32.

22. CMT, Exhibit B, 1–3.

23. Ibid., 3.
24. Ibid., 4.
25. *OR,* 8:564.
26. CMT, Exhibit B, 5–6.
27. *OR,* 16(2):230.
28. CMT, Exhibit B, 8–9.
29. CMT, 77.
30. Ibid., 94. The two deserters called to the stand by the prosecution had slipped away on May 30, 1862 and had been subsequently arrested. Perhaps in a deal for their cooperation, both were apparently set free after testifying. Neither ever returned to their posts. Joseph Arnold was last thought to be serving with the Confederate army. Joel C. Stevens was shot during an argument at a home in Prospect, Tennessee, on Sept. 9, 1862. See the CMSRs of Arnold and Stevens.
31. CMT, 28, 38–39, 77, 86.
32. Ibid., 86, 95, 100.
33. Ibid., 77, 92, 99, 116.
34. Fry, *Military Miscellanies,* 167, citing Hough's *Precedents on Military Law.*
35. *Cincinnati Commercial,* Aug. 7, 1862.
36. *OR,* 16(2):273–75.
37. Ibid., 275.
38. Ibid., 276.
39. CMT, 217.
40. Ibid.
41. Ibid.
42. Ibid.
43. Ibid.; *Louisville Journal,* Aug. 2, 1862.

CHAPTER 15

1. *Louisville Journal,* Aug. 16, 1862; *New York Times,* Aug. 17, 1862. The *National Intelligencer* did not get the story straight until Aug. 20. Williams, *Wild Life,* 123.
2. *Chicago Tribune,* Aug. 20, 1862.
3. Ibid.
4. *Louisville Journal,* Aug. 16, 1862; Strevey, "Medill."
5. *Chicago Tribune,* Aug. 20, 1862.
6. Ibid.
7. Ibid.
8. Ibid.
9. Ibid.
10. Ibid. Just two weeks before, a mixed group of rebel cavalry and partisans had ambushed Brig. Gen. Robert McCook's ambulance, in which he lay sick while traveling across southeastern Tennessee. McCook was mortally wounded in the melee and chase, surviving for only a day. The press descriptions of the shooting caused a national uproar

and branded the shooter, Frank Gurley, a war criminal. McCook's loud protests against conciliation (mentioned earlier in chapter 10), amplified his martyrdom.

11. *Chicago Tribune,* Aug. 20, 21, 1862.

12. Andreas, *History of Chicago,* 227–28, 235; East, "Russian General," 116. To meet the rising crisis in Kentucky, the 88th Illinois left in a bit of haste, like Turchin's men had, without arms or equipment, a problem solved two days later when they arrived in Jeffersonville, Indiana.

13. Fry, *Operations under Buell,* 98; Chumney, "Don Carlos Buell," 114.

14. Basler, *Collected Works,* 5:406n.

15. *OR,* 16, 1:6–7.

16. Ibid., 8–12. Grant, on taking command of the armies in 1864, raised the idea that Buell be reactivated, but Buell refused to serve under anyone he had previously commanded.

17. Ibid., 23(3):183, 246; 30(1):43, 173; Cozzens, *This Terrible Sound,* 177. See also Sinclair to Stanley, *OR,* 23(2):567.

18. *OR,* 31(1):42; *National Tribune,* Apr. 6, 1902, Mar. 24, 1910.

19. Turchin's report, *OR,* 30(1):474.

20. Ibid.; Turchin, "Bayonet and Saber"; John T. Booth, "Chickamauga," *National Tribune,* Oct. 2, 1890; Palmer's report, *OR,* 30(1):714.

21. Turchin's report, *OR,* 30(1):474; Cozzens, *This Terrible Sound,* 492, citing the manuscript history of the 36th Ohio Infantry contained in the John C. Booth Papers, Ohio Historical Society; Clayton, "Turchin's Great Charge."

22. Clayton, "Turchin's Great Charge"; Camp, "Turchin's Brigade at Chickamauga."

23. Reynolds's report, *OR,* 31(1):442; Turchin, *Chickamauga,* 147–50.

24. Reynolds's report, *OR,* 31(1):442; Palmer's report, ibid., 30(1):714; G. H. Thomas to Lorenzo Thomas, Nov. 20, 1863, ibid., 31(3):201; Dana to Stanton, Sept. 21, 1863, ibid., 31(1):194; Garfield to Rosecrans, ibid., 31(1):145.

25. Ibid., 30(4):212, 215; 31(1):40.

26. Baird's report, ibid., 31(2):508.

27. Turchin's report, ibid., 31(2):512–13.

28. Ibid, 513; Grant's, Baird's, and Street's reports, ibid., 34, 509, 519.

29. Hunter's, Street's, Shower's, Lister's, and Devol's reports, ibid., 518–24.

30. Ibid; *Chicago Tribune,* Aug. 20, 1862; Fox, *Regimental Losses,* 443; A. C. Shafer, "Mission Ridge Cannon," *National Tribune,* Oct. 5, 1922.

CHAPTER 16

1. Stinebeck's report, *OR,* 32(1):466; Baird's report, ibid., 38(1):755; Clayton, "Turchin's Great Charge."

2. *New York Times,* June 20, 1901; Warner, *Generals in Blue, 512.* Today, Radom is a small country crossroads, home to 174 people (as of 1990). The Athens, Alabama, newspaper, on learning of Turchin's confinement at the asylum, carried a banner headline that

read, "Gen. Turchin Insane!" See Holly Holman, "The Sack of Athens," *Decatur Daily News*, Apr. 11, 2005.

3. Dyer, *Compendium*, pt. 3, 1052; OR 30(1), 41; Wythe, "Mrs. Turchin." Stanley received a brigadier's star by brevet in 1865.

4. *National Tribune*, Apr. 6, 24, 1902.

5. Grant, *Memoirs*, 471–73.

6. Warner, *Generals in Blue*, 52.

7. *OR*, 10(2):291–92; Warner, *Generals in Blue*, 327.

8. *OR*, 52(2):359–60.

9. Ibid., Series 4, 2:1024–47.

10. Ibid., 1047.

11. Ibid., 1047–48.

12. Ibid., 1048.

13. Simpson and Berlin, *Sherman's Civil War*, 160.

14. Ewing, "New Sherman Letters," 157–58.

15. Interview, July 28, 2004, with Anthony Sallazzo, a veteran of the 1st and 4th Marine divisions, who landed at both Guadalcanal and Iwo Jima.

16. *OR*, Series 3, 3:163–64.

17. *OR*, 17(2):150.

18. The only exception was Turchin's defense attorney, Col. Carter Gazlay of the 37th Indiana. He was dismissed from the service in early August 1862, the victim of accusations that he had been profiting from the sale of contraband, charges that dated back to the days when he had clashed with the first colonel of the 37th, George W. Hazzard. See CMSR of Carter Gazlay.

EPILOGUE

1. CMT, 80–81; Dunnavant, "Arsonists."

2. Canfield, *21st Ohio*, 56.

3. Letter of resignation dated Aug. 31, 1862, CMSR of Maj. Fred Harding, 19th Illinois.

4. Canfield, *21st Ohio*, 56; IAGR, *Regimental History, 19th Illinois*.

5. Ibid.

Bibliography

UNPUBLISHED DOCUMENTS AND PRIMARY SOURCES

Bowdoin College Library, Brunswick, Maine
William Pitt Fessenden Papers

Chicago Historical Society
Diary of Alfred H. Trego

Columbia University, New York
Sidney Howard Gay Papers

Huntington Library, Stanford University
Charles H. Ray Papers

Illinois State Archives, Springfield
Election returns, 1861

Illinois State Historical Society, Springfield
Richard Yates Papers

Richard Johnston Private Collection, Harrisburg, Pennsylvania
Diary of Edward L. Witman

Library of Congress, Washington, DC
James R. Doolittle Papers
Thomas Ewing Papers
Joseph Warren Keifer Papers
Abraham Lincoln Papers

Almon Rockwell Papers
John Sherman Papers
Lyman Trumbull Papers

National Archives and Records Administration, Washington, DC

Carter Gazlay Military Service Record, Record Group 94
Compiled Military Service Records, Record Group 94
John Basil Turchin Military Service Record, including the record of the Court-Martial
    Trial Transcript, Record Group 94
Letters received, Secretary of War's Office (RG Microform 494)

Ohio Historical Society, Columbus

P. B. Ewing Papers

United States Army Military History Institute, Carlisle Barracks, PA

Civil War Miscellaneous Collection: Daniel Finn Diary
Diary of Martin C. Moor, 37th Indiana Volunteer Infantry
Vreeland Papers

United States Military Academy Archives, West Point

Peter T. Swaine Papers

West Virginia University Library, Morgantown

A. J. Lightburn Papers
Waitman T. Willey Papers

PERIODICALS

Charleston Mercury
Chicago Tribune
Cincinnati Commercial
Cleveland Plain Dealer
Frank Leslie's Illustrated Newspaper
Harrisburg Patriot and Union
Harrisburg Telegraph
Lebanon Courier
Los Angeles Times
Louisville Journal
Military Affairs
Milwaukee Sentinel
National Intelligencer
National Tribune
New York Herald

New York Times
New York Tribune
Ohio State Journal
Philadelphia Age
Philadelphia Inquirer
Pittsburgh Gazette
Reading Times
Springfield State Journal
Washington Evening Star

PUBLISHED SOURCES

Abbott, Richard H. *Cobbler in Congress: The Life of Henry Wilson, 1812–1875.* Lexington: University Press of Kentucky, 1972.

Abrams, Ray H. "Copperhead Newspapers and the Negro." *Journal of Negro History* 20 (1935).

Alston, Patrick L. *Education and the State in Tsarist Russia.* Stanford: Stanford University Press, 1969.

Ambler, Charles Henry. *Francis H. Pierpont: Union War Governor of Virginia and Father of West Virginia.* Chapel Hill: University of North Carolina Press, 1937.

Ambrose, Stephen E. *Halleck: Lincoln's Chief of Staff.* Baton Rouge: Louisiana State University Press, 1962.

Anderson, Robert. *An Artillery Officer in the Mexican War, 1846–1847: Letters of Robert Anderson, Captain 3rd Artillery, USA.* New York: Knickerbocker, 1911.

Andreas, Alfred Theodore. *History of Chicago from the Earliest Period to the Present Time.* 3 vols. New York: Arno, 1975. Originally published 1884–86.

Andrews, J. Cutler. *The North Reports the Civil War.* Pittsburgh: University of Pittsburgh Press, 1955.

Appleton's American Annual Cyclopedia and Register of Important Events of the Year 1861. New York: D. Appleton, 1873.

Ash, Steven V. *When the Yankees Came: Conflict and Chaos in the Occupied South, 1861–1865.* Chapel Hill: University of North Carolina Press, 1995.

Axford, Faye Acton, ed. *The Journals of Thomas Hubbard Hobbs.* Tuscaloosa: University of Alabama Press, 1976.

———. *Limestone County after Appomattox, 1865–1870.* Athens, AL: Athens, 1985.

———, ed. *"To Lochaber Na Mair": Southerners View the Civil War.* Athens, AL: Athens, 1986.

Barnet, James, ed. *The Martyrs and Heroes of Illinois in the Great Rebellion.* Chicago: J. Barnet, 1865.

Basler, Roy P., ed. *The Collected Works of Abraham Lincoln.* 9 vols. New Brunswick, NJ: Rutgers University Press, 1953–55.

Baxter, Maurice G. *Orville H. Browning: Lincoln's Friend and Critic.* Bloomington: Indiana University Press, 1957.

Beale, Howard K., ed. *The Diary of Edward Bates, 1859–1866*. Washington, DC: Government Printing Office, 1933.

Beatty, John. *McLean: A Romance of the War*. Columbus, OH: Fred J. Heer, 1904.

———. *Memoirs of a Volunteer, 1861–1863*. Edited by Henry S. Ford, introduction by Lloyd Lewis. New York: W. W. Norton, 1946. Originally published 1878.

———. "A Regiment in Search of Battle." In *Sketches of War History, 1861–1865, Ohio Commandery, Loyal Legion*, vol. 3. Wilmington, NC: Broadfoot, 1991. Originally published 1890.

Black, Robert C., III. *The Railroads of the Confederacy*. Chapel Hill: University of North Carolina Press, 1952.

Blaine, James G. *Twenty Years of Congress, from Lincoln to Garfield*. 2 vols. Norwich, CT: Henry Bill, 1884–86.

Blegen, Theodore C., ed. *The Civil War Letters of Colonel Hans Christian Heg*. Northfield, MN: Norwegian-American Historical Association, 1936.

Bogue, Allan C. *The Earnest Men: Republicans of the Civil War Senate*. Ithaca, NY: Cornell University Press, 1981.

Boorstin, Daniel J. *The Daniel J. Boorstin Reader*. Edited by Ruth F. Boorstin. New York: Modern Library, 1995.

Boucher, John N. *Old and New Westmoreland*. 2 vols. New York: American Historical Society, 1918.

Bourne, Russell. *The Red King's Rebellion: Racial Politics in New England, 1675–1678*. New York: Atheneum, 1990.

Bowman, Col. Samuel Millard, and Lt. Col. Richard Biddle Irwin. *Sherman and His Campaigns: A Military Biography*. New York: Charles B. Richardson, 1865.

Bradford, Gamaliel. *Union Portraits*. Boston: Houghton Mifflin, 1916.

Bradley, Erwin Stanley. *Simon Cameron, Lincoln's Secretary of War: A Political Biography*. Philadelphia: University of Pennsylvania Press, 1966.

Brewer, William. *Alabama: Her History, Resources, War Record, and Public Men, from 1540 to 1872*. Montgomery: Barrett & Brown, 1872.

Briant, Charles C. *History of the Sixth Regiment Indiana Volunteer Infantry*. Indianapolis: Wm. E. Buford, 1891.

Brooks, E. Willis. "Reform in the Russian Army, 1856–1861." *Slavic Review* 43 (1984).

Bross, William. "What I Remember of Early Chicago." In *Reminiscences of Chicago during the Forties and Fifties*, edited by Mabel McIlvaine. Chicago: R. R. Donnelley, 1913.

Bruce, Robert V. *The Launching of Modern American Science, 1846–1876*. New York: Alfred A. Knopf, 1987.

Buchanan, Russell. "James F. McDougal: A Forgotten Senator." *California Historical Society Quarterly* 15 (Sept. 1936).

Buell, Don Carlos. "Operations in North Alabama." In *Battles and Leaders of the Civil War*, vol. 2, edited by Robert Underwood Johnson and Clarence Clough Buell. New York: Century, 1887.

Burton, William L. *Melting Pot Soldiers: The Union's Ethnic Regiments.* Ames: Iowa State University Press, 1988.

Camp, G. L. "Turchin's Brigade at Chickamauga: Cutting Their Way through at the Close of the Fight." *National Tribune*, Oct. 22, 1908.

Canfield, Silas S. *History of the 21st Regiment Ohio Volunteer Infantry in the War of the Rebellion.* Toledo: Vrooman, Anderson, & Bateman, 1893.

Carman, Harry J., and Reinhard H. Luthin. *Lincoln and the Patronage.* Gloucester, MA: Peter Smith, 1964. Originally published 1943.

Castel, Albert. *Civil War Kansas: Reaping the Whirlwind.* Lawrence: University Press of Kansas, 1997. Originally published 1958.

——. *William Clarke Quantrill: His Life and Times.* Marietta, OH: Camp Chase, c. 1992. Originally published 1962.

Catton, Bruce. *The American Heritage Picture History of the Civil War.* New York: American Heritage, 1960.

Chadick, Mary. "A Southern Account of the War in the Valley." In *The Alabama Confederate Reader,* edited by Malcolm C. McMillan. Tuscaloosa: University of Alabama Press, 1963.

Chafee, Zachariah, Jr. *Three Human Rights in the Constitution of 1787.* Lawrence: University of Kansas Press, 1956.

Chumney, James Robert, Jr. "Don Carlos Buell, Gentleman General." Ph.D. diss., Rice University, 1964.

Clayton, B. M. "Turchin's Great Charge: He Cut His Way out and Saved the Army." *National Tribune*, Aug. 18, 1921.

Clayton, Charles C. *Little Mack: Joseph B. McCullagh of the St. Louis Globe Democrat.* Carbondale: Southern Illinois University Press, 1969.

Coffman, Edward M. *The Old Army: A Portrait of the American Army in Peacetime, 1784–1898.* New York: Oxford University Press, 1986.

Cole, Arthur Charles. *The Era of the Civil War, 1848–1870,* vol. 3 of *Centennial History of Illinois.* Freeport, NY: Books for Libraries, 1971. Originally published 1919.

Cole, Donald B., and John J. McDonough, eds. *Benjamin Brown French, Witness to the Young Republic: A Yankee's Journal, 1828–1870.* Hanover, NH: University Press of New England, 1989.

Cooling, Benjamin Franklin. *Fort Donelson's Legacy: War and Society in Kentucky and Tennessee, 1862–1863.* Knoxville: University of Tennessee Press, 1997.

Coulter, E. Merton. *The Civil War and Readjustment in Kentucky.* Gloucester, MA: Peter Smith, 1966. Originally published 1926.

Cox, Jacob Dolson. *Military Reminiscences of the Civil War.* 2 vols. New York: Charles Scribner's Sons, 1910.

Cozzens, Peter. *This Terrible Sound: The Battle of Chickamauga.* Urbana and Chicago: University of Illinois Press, 1992.

Cozzens, Peter, and Robert I. Girardi, eds. *The Military Memoirs of General John Pope.* Chapel Hill: University of North Carolina Press, 1998.

Cullum, George Washington. *Biographical Register of the Officers and Graduates of the U.S. Military Academy.* 2 vols. New York: D. Van Nostrand, 1868.

Cunliffe, Marcus. *Soldiers and Civilians: The Martial Spirit in America, 1775–1865.* Boston: Little, Brown, 1865.

Curry, Richard Orr. *A House Divided: A Study of Statehood Politics and the Copperhead Movement in West Virginia.* Pittsburgh: University of Pittsburgh Press, 1964.

Curtiss, John Shelton. *The Russian Army under Nicholas I, 1825–1855.* Durham, NC: Duke University Press, 1965.

———. *Russia's Crimean War.* Durham, NC: Duke University Press, 1979.

Dana, Charles A. *Recollections of the Civil War.* Edited by Paul M. Angle. New York: Collier, 1963.

Dargan, Elizabeth Paisley, ed. *The Civil War Diary of Martha Abernathy, Wife of Dr. Charles C. Abernathy of Pulaski, Tennessee.* Beltsville, MD: Professional Printing, 1994.

Dayton, Aretas A. "The Raising of Union Forces in Illinois during the Civil War." *Journal of the Illinois State Historical Society* 34 (Dec. 1941).

Deak, Istvan. *The Lawful Revolution: Louis Kossuth and the Hungarians, 1848–1849.* New York: Columbia University Press, 1979.

Delafield, Richard. *Report on the Art of War in Europe in 1854, 1855, and 1856.* 36th Cong., 1st sess., Senate, Ex. Doc. 59 (1860).

Dickson, Clifford Garrett. "Edgar Cowan." Master's thesis, University of Pittsburgh, 1936.

Donald, David Herbert. *Lincoln.* London: Jonathan Cape, 1995.

Doster, William E. *Lincoln and Episodes of the Civil War.* New York: G. P. Putnam's Sons, 1915.

Doubleday, Abner. *My Life in the Old Army: The Reminiscences of Abner Doubleday from the Collections of the New York Historical Society.* Edited by Joseph E. Chance. Fort Worth: Texas Christian University Press, 1998.

Drell, Muriel Bernitt, ed. "Letters by Richard Smith of the Cincinnati Gazette." *Mississippi Valley Historical Review* 26 (Mar. 1940).

Dunnavant, Bob. "Arsonists Set Town Aflame." *Athens News Courier,* Dec. 18, 1976.

Dupuy, R. Ernest. *Where They Have Trod: The West Point Tradition in American Life.* New York: Frederick A. Stokes, 1940.

Durham, Walter T. *Nashville: The Occupied City.* Nashville: Tennessee Historical Society, 1985.

Dyer, Frederick H. *A Compendium of the War of the Rebellion.* 3 vols. New York: T. Yoseloff, 1959.

Dyer, John Will. *Reminiscences; or Four Years in the Confederate Army.* Evansville, IN: Keller, 1898.

East, Ernest E. "Lincoln's Russian General." *Journal of the Illinois State Historical Society* 52 (1959).

Eddy, T. M. *The Patriotism of Illinois.* Chicago: Clarke, 1865.

Edwards, Chris, and Faye Acton Axford. *The Lure and Lore of Limestone County.* Tuscaloosa, AL: Portals, 1978.

Edwards, R. M. *Down the Tennessee: The Mexican War Reminiscences of an East Tennessee Volunteer.* Edited by Stewart Lillard. Charlotte, Loftin, 1997.

Eisenhower, John S. D. *Agent of Destiny: The Life and Times of General Winfield Scott.* New York: Free Press, 1998.

Engle, Steven D. "Don Carlos Buell: Military Philosophy and Command Problems in the West." *Civil War History* 41 (June 1995).

———. *Don Carlos Buell: Most Promising of All.* Chapel Hill: University of North Carolina Press, 1999.

Ewing, Joseph H., ed. "The New Sherman Letters." *American Heritage* 38 (July–Aug. 1987).

Fehrenbacher, Don E., ed. *Abraham Lincoln: Speeches and Writings, 1859–1865.* New York: Library of America, 1989.

Fellman, Michael. *Inside War: The Guerrilla Conflict in Missouri during the American Civil War.* New York: Oxford University Press, 1989.

Fessenden, Francis. *Life and Public Services of William Pitt Fessenden.* 2 vols. New York: Da Capo, 1970.

Fleming, Walter L. *Civil War and Reconstruction in Alabama.* New York: Columbia University Press, 1905.

Flower, Frank Abial. *Edwin McMasters Stanton, the Autocrat of Rebellion, Emancipation, and Reconstruction.* New York: Western W. Wilson, 1905.

Folwell, William Watts. *A History of Minnesota.* 4 vols. St. Paul: Minnesota Historical Society, 1956–69.

Force, Manning F. *General Sherman.* New York: Appleton, 1899.

Ford, Worthington Chauncey, ed. *A Cycle of Adams Letters, 1861–1865.* Boston: Houghton Mifflin, 1920.

Fox, William Freeman. *Regimental Losses in the American Civil War, 1861–1865.* Albany: Albany Publishing, 1889.

Fredrickson, George M. *William Lloyd Garrison.* Englewood Cliffs, NJ: Prentice-Hall, 1968.

Fry, James Barnet. *Military Miscellanies.* New York: Brentano's, 1889.

———. *Operations of the Army under Buell.* New York: D. Van Nostrand, 1884.

Garfield, James A. "My Campaign in Eastern Kentucky." *North American Review* 143 (Dec. 1886).

Garrison, William Lloyd. *A New "Reign of Terror" in the Slaveholding States.* New York: American Anti-slavery Society, 1860.

Gatch, C. H. "General O. M. Mitchel and His Brilliant March into the Heart of the Southern Confederacy." In *War Sketches and Incidents, Iowa Commandery, Loyal Legion,* vol. 2. Wilmington, NC: Broadfoot, 1994. Originally published 1898.

Geary, James W. *We Need Men: The Union Draft in the Civil War.* Dekalb: Northern Illinois University Press, 1991.

Giddings, Luther. *Sketches of the Campaign in Mexico, in Eighteen Hundred Forty-six and Seven.* New York: George P. Putnam, 1853.

Gillette, William. *Jersey Blue: Civil War Politics in New Jersey, 1854–1865.* New Brunswick, NJ: Rutgers University Press, 1995.

Goodloe, Albert Theodore. *Confederate Echoes: A Voice from the South in the Days of Secession and the Southern Confederacy.* Nashville: Smith & Lamar, 1907.

Goodrich, Thomas. *War to the Knife: Bleeding Kansas, 1854–1861.* Mechanicsburg, PA: Stackpole, 1998.

Graf, LeRoy P., and Ralph W. Haskins, eds. *The Papers of Andrew Johnson.* 15 vols. Knoxville: University of Tennessee Press, 1967–.

Grant, Ulysses S. *Personal Memoirs of U.S. Grant.* 2 vols. New York: Library Classics of the United States, 1990.

Grebner, Constantin. *"We Were the Ninth": A History of the Ninth Regiment, Ohio Volunteer Infantry, April 17, 1861, to June 7, 1864.* Translated and edited by Frederic Trautman. Kent, OH: Kent State University Press, 1987.

Griess, Thomas Everett. "Dennis Hart Mahan: West Point Professor and Advocate of Military Professionalism, 1830–1871." Ph.D. diss., Duke University, 1968.

Grimsley, Mark. *The Hard Hand of War: Union Military Policy toward Southern Civilians, 1861–1865.* Cambridge: Cambridge University Press, 1995.

Hamlin, Charles Eugene. *The Life and Times of Hannibal Hamlin.* Cambridge, MA: Riverside, 1899.

Harper, Robert S. *Lincoln and the Press.* New York: McGraw-Hill, 1951.

Harrington, Fred H. *Fighting Politician.* Philadelphia: University of Pennsylvania Press, 1948.

Hassler, Warren W., Jr. *General George B. McClellan: Shield of the Union.* Baton Rouge: Louisiana State University Press, 1957.

Hay, John. "A Young Hero: Personal Reminiscences of Colonel E. E. Ellsworth." *McClure's Magazine* 6 (Mar. 1896).

Haynie, J. Henry. *The Nineteenth Illinois.* Chicago: M. A. Donohue, 1912.

Henett, Janet B., ed. *Supplement to the Official Records of the Union and Confederate Armies.* Multivolume to date. Wilmington, NC: Broadfoot, 1994–.

Hesseltine, William B. *Lincoln and the War Governors.* New York: Alfred A. Knopf, 1948.

Hibbert, Christopher. *Redcoats and Rebels: The American Revolution through British Eyes.* New York: Avon, 1991.

Hicken, Victor. *Illinois in the Civil War.* 2nd ed. Urbana: University of Illinois Press, 1991.

Higginbotham, Don. *The War of American Independence: Military Attitudes, Policies, and Practice, 1763–1789.* New York: Macmillan, 1971.

Hight, John J. *History of the Fifty-eighth Regiment of Indiana Volunteer Infantry.* Edited by Gilbert R. Stormont. Princeton, IN: Clarion, 1895.

Horn, Stanley F. *The Army of Tennessee.* Norman: University of Oklahoma Press, 1993. Originally published 1941.

Horner, Harlan Hoyt. "Lincoln Rebukes a Senator." *Journal of the Illinois State Historical Society* 44 (1951).

Horrall, Spillard F. *History of the Forty-second Indiana Volunteer Infantry.* N.p., 1892.

Horton, Joshua H., and Solomon Teverbaugh. *A History of the Eleventh Regiment (Ohio Volunteer Infantry)*. Dayton: W. J. Shuey, 1866.

Howard, Hamilton Gay. *Civil-War Echoes: Character Sketches and State Secrets*. Washington, DC: Howard, 1907.

Illinois Adjutant General's Department. *Reports, 1861–1865 (Revised)*. Springfield, IL: Phillips Brothers, 1900–1.

Illinois Commandery, Military Order of the Loyal Legion of the United States (MOLLUS). *Memorials of Deceased Companions, from January 1, 1912, to December 31, 1922*. Wilmington, NC: Broadfoot, 1993. Originally published 1923.

———. *Memorials of Deceased Companions, July 1, 1901, to December 31, 1911*. Wilmington, NC: Broadfoot, 1993. Originally published 1912.

Ingraham, Charles Anson. *Elmer E. Ellsworth and the Zouaves of '61*. Chicago: University of Chicago Press, 1925.

Janowitz, Morris. *The Professional Soldier: A Social and Political Portrait*. Glencoe, IL: Free Press, 1960.

Jellison, Charles A. *Fessenden of Maine, Civil War Senator*. Syracuse, NY: Syracuse University Press, 1962.

Johnson, Allen, ed. *Dictionary of American Biography, under the Auspices of the American Council of Learned Societies*. 14 vols. New York: Charles Scribner's Sons, 1946–74.

Johnson, Robert Underwood, and Clarence Clough Buel, eds. *Battles and Leaders of the Civil War*. 4 vols. New York: Century, 1887.

Johnson, Timothy D. *Winfield Scott: The Quest for Military Glory*. Lawrence: University Press of Kansas, 1998.

Jones, John Pickett. *"Black Jack": John A. Logan and Southern Illinois in the Civil War*. Carbondale: Southern Illinois University Press, 1995. Originally published 1967.

Josephy, Alvin M., Jr. *The Patriot Chiefs: A Chronicle of American Indian Leadership*. New York: Viking, 1961.

Julian, George W. *Political Recollections, 1840 to 1872*. Chicago: Jansen, McClurg, 1881.

Just, Ward. *Military Men*. New York: Knopf, 1970.

Keegan, John. *A History of Warfare*. Toronto: Vintage, 1994.

Keifer, Joseph Warren. *Slavery and Four Years of War: A Political History of Slavery in the United States, Together with a Narrative of the Campaigns and Battles of the Civil War in Which the Author Took Part, 1861–1865*. 2 vols. New York: G. P. Putnam's Sons, 1900.

Kelly, Col. R. M. "Holding Kentucky for the Union." In *Battles and Leaders of the Civil War*, edited by Robert Underwood Johnson and Clarence Clough Buel. New York: Castle, 1956. Originally published 1887.

Kennett, Lee. *Marching through Georgia: The Story of Soldiers and Civilians during Sherman's Campaign*. New York: HarperCollins, 1995.

Kentucky Revised Statutes.

Kinsley, Philip. *The Chicago Tribune: Its First Hundred Years*. 2 vols. New York: Alfred A. Knopf, 1943.

Kune, Julian. *Reminiscences of an Octogenarian Hungarian Exile*. Chicago: Julian Kune, 1911.

Lee, Wayne E. *Crowds and Soldiers in Revolutionary North Carolina: The Culture of Violence in Riot and War.* Gainesville: University of Florida Press, 2001.

Liddell-Hart, Basil H. *Sherman: Soldier, Realist, American.* Westport, CT: Greenwood, 1978. Originally published 1929.

Lincoln, D. Bruce. *Nicholas I: Emperor and Autocrat of All the Russias.* Bloomington: Indiana University Press, 1978.

Long, Everette B. *The Civil War Day by Day: An Almanac, 1861–1865.* New York: Da Capo, n.d. Originally published 1971.

Lonn, Ella. *Foreigners in the Union Army and Navy.* Baton Rouge: Louisiana State University Press, 1951.

Macomb, Alexander. *The Practice of Courts Martial.* New York: Harper & Brothers, 1841.

Mahan, Denis Hart. *An Elementary Treatise on Advanced-Guard, Out-Post, and Detachment Service of Troops, and the Manner of Posting and Handling Them in Presence of an Enemy.* New York: John Wiley, 1853.

Malloy, James A., Jr. "Miliutin." In *The Modern Encyclopedia of Russian and Soviet History,* vol. 50, edited by Joseph L. Wieczinski. Gulf Breeze, FL: Academic International, 1989.

Mansfield, Edward Deering. *Personal Memories: Social, Political, and Literary.* New York: Arno, 1970. Originally published 1879.

Mayer, George H. *The Republican Party, 1854–1964.* New York: Oxford University Press, 1964.

McClellan, George B. *The Armies of Europe.* Philadelphia: J. B. Lippincott, 1862. Originally published 1857.

———. *McClellan's Own Story: The War for the Union, the Soldiers Who Fought It, the Civilians Who Directed It, and His Relations to It and to Them.* New York: Charles L. Webster, 1887.

McDaniel, Deangelo. "Clinging to the Union." *Decatur Daily News,* Apr. 10, 2005.

McDonough, James Lee. *War in Kentucky from Shiloh to Perryville.* Knoxville: University of Tennessee Press, 1994.

McDowell, Robert Emmett. *City of Conflict: Louisville in the Civil War, 1861–1865.* Louisville: Louisville Civil War Round Table, 1962.

McElligott, Mary Ellen, ed. "'A Monotony Full of Sadness': The Diary of Nadine Turchin, May 1863–April 1864." *Journal of the Illinois State Historical Society* (February 1977).

McIlvaine, Mabel, ed. *Reminiscences of Chicago during the Civil War.* Chicago: R. R. Donnelly, 1914.

McKinney, Francis F. *Education in Violence: The Life of George H. Thomas and the History of the Army of the Cumberland.* Detroit: Wayne State University Press, 1964.

McPherson, James M. *Battle Cry of Freedom: The Civil War Era.* New York: Oxford University Press, 1988.

———. *Drawn with the Sword: Reflections on the Civil War.* New York: Oxford University Press, 1996.

———. *For Cause and Comrades: Why Men Fought in the Civil War.* New York: Oxford University Press, 1997.

Meade, George G., ed. *The Life and Letters of George Gordon Meade.* 2 vols. New York: Charles Scribner's Sons, 1913.

Meneely, A. Howard. *The War Department, 1861.* New York: Columbia University Press, 1928.

Meron, Theodor. *Henry's Wars and Shakespeare's Laws: Perspectives on the Law of War in the Later Middle Ages.* Oxford: Clarendon, 1993.

Merrill, Catherine. *The Soldier of Indiana in the War for the Union.* 2 vols. Indianapolis: Merrill, 1866, 1869.

Miller, Donald I. *City of the Century: The Epic of Chicago and the Making of America.* New York: Simon & Schuster, 1996.

Miller, Forrest A. *Dmitrii Miliutin and the Reform Era in Russia.* Nashville: Vanderbilt University Press, 1968.

Miller, Henry H. "Ellsworth's Zouaves." In *Reminiscences of Chicago during the Civil War,* edited by Mabel McIlvaine. Chicago: R. R. Donnelly, 1914.

Mitchel, Frederick A. *Ormsby MacKnight Mitchel, Astronomer and General: A Biographical Narrative.* Boston: Houghton Mifflin, 1887.

Monaghan, Jay. *The Man Who Elected Lincoln.* Westport, CT: Greenwood, 1973. Originally published 1956.

Moore, Frank, ed. *The Rebellion Record: A Diary of American Events.* Vol. 4. New York: G. P. Putnam, 1862.

Mordecai, Alfred. *Military Commission to Europe, in 1855 and 1856.* 36th Cong., 1st sess., Senate, Ex. Doc. 60 (1860).

Morris, Thomas D. *Southern Slavery and the Law, 1619–1860.* Chapel Hill: University of North Carolina Press, 1996.

Morrison, James L., Jr. *"The Best School in the World": West Point, the Pre-Civil War Years, 1833–1866.* Kent, OH: Kent State University Press, 1986.

Muller, Ernest Paul. "Preston King: A Political Biography." Ph.D. diss., Columbia University, 1957.

Murray, Lt. Stewart. *Discipline: Its Reason and Battle Value.* London: Gale & Polden, 1894.

Myers, William Starr, ed. *The Mexican War Diary of George B. McClellan.* Princeton, NJ: Princeton University Press, 1917.

National Cyclopedia of American Biography. Vols. 1–65B. New York: James T. White, 1892–1984.

Nevins, Allan. *Frémont: Pathmaker of the West.* New York: Longmans, 1955.

Nevins, Allan, and Thomas Milton Halsey, eds. *The Diary of George Templeton Strong.* 4 vols. New York: Macmillan, 1952.

Newmyer, R. Kent. "Charles Stedman's History of the American War." *American Historical Review* 63 (1958).

———. *Supreme Court Justice Joseph Story: Statesman of the Old Republic.* Chapel Hill: University of North Carolina Press, 1985.

Ohio Roster Commission. *Official Roster of the Soldiers of the State of Ohio in the War of the Rebellion, 1861–1866.* Vol. 2. Cincinnati: Wilstach, Baldwin, 1886.

Oliphant, Mary C. Simms, Alfred Taylor Odell, and T. C. Duncan Eanes, eds. *The Letters of William Gilmore Simms.* 6 vols. Columbia: University of South Carolina Press, 1952–82.

Osborne, Thomas Ward. *The Fiery Trail: A Union Officer's Account of Sherman's Last Campaigns.* Edited by Richard Harwell and Philip N. Racine. Knoxville: University of Tennessee Press, 1986.

Page, John A. "A University Volunteer." In *Reminiscences of Chicago during the Civil War,* edited by Mabel McIlvaine. Chicago: R. R. Donnelly, 1914.

Painter, Henry M. *Brief Narrative of Incidents in the War in Missouri, and of the Personal Experience of One Who Has Suffered.* Boston: Daily Courier, 1863.

Pappas, George S. *To The Point: The United States Military Academy, 1802–1902.* Westport,CT: Praeger, 1993.

Parry, Albert. "John B. Turchin: Russian General in the American Civil War." *Russian Review* 1 (Apr. 1942).

Pease, Theodore Calvin, and James G. Randall. *The Diary of Orville Hickman Browning.* Vol. 1, *1850–1864.* Springfield: Illinois State Historical Library, 1925.

Perret, Geoffrey. *A Country Made by War: From the Revolution to Vietnam—The Story of America's Rise to Power.* New York: Random House, 1989.

Persis, B. F. "Senator Edgar A. Cowan." *Western Pennsylvania Historical Magazine* 4 (Oct. 1921).

Peskin, Allan. *Garfield.* Kent, OH: Kent State University Press, 1978.

Pierce, Bessie Louise. *A History of Chicago.* Vol. 2., *From Town to City, 1848–1871.* New York: Alfred A. Knopf, 1940.

Pirtle, Alfred. "Three Memorable Days—A Letter from Chattanooga, November, 1863." In *Sketches of War History, 1861–1865, Ohio Commandery, Loyal Legion,* vol. 6. Wilmington, NC: Broadfoot, 1992. Originally published 1908.

Puntenney, George H. *History of the Thirty-seventh Regiment of Indiana Infantry Volunteers.* Rushville, IN: Jackson Book and Job Department, 1896.

Randall, James Garfield. "The Confiscation of Property during the Civil War." Ph.D. diss., University of Chicago, 1913.

———. *Lincoln, the President.* 2 vols. New York: Da Capo, 1997. Originally published 1945–55.

Randall, Ruth Painter. *Colonel Elmer Ellsworth: A Biography of Lincoln's Friend and the First Hero of the Civil War.* Boston: Little, Brown, 1960.

Rawley, James A. *Edwin D. Morgan, 1811–1883: Merchant in Politics.* New York: Columbia University Press, 1955.

Reid, Whitelaw. *Ohio in the War: Her Statesman, Her Generals, and Soldiers.* 2 vols. Cincinnati: Moore, Wilstach, & Baldwin, 1868.

Reynolds, Donald E. *Editors Make War: Southern Newspapers in the Secession Crisis.* Nashville: Vanderbilt University Press, 1970.

Riasanovsky, Nicholas V. *Nicholas I and Official Nationality in Russia.* Berkeley: University of California Press, 1961.

Rice, Allen Thorndike. *Reminiscences of Abraham Lincoln, by Distinguished Men of His Time.* New York: North American Review, 1888.

Riddle, Albert Gallatin. *Recollections of War Times: Reminiscences of Men and Events in Washington, 1860–1865.* New York: G. P. Putnam's Sons, 1895.

Ritchie, Donald A. *Press Gallery: Congress and the Washington Correspondents.* Cambridge, MA: Harvard University Press, 1991.

Robertson, James I. *General A. P. Hill: The Story of a Confederate Warrior.* New York: Random House, 1987.

Ropes, John Codman. *The Army under Pope.* New York: Charles Scribner's Sons, 1885.

———. *The Story of the Civil War.* 3 vols. New York: G. P. Putnam's Sons, 1933. Originally published 1898.

Roske, Ralph J. *His Own Counsel: The Life and Times of Lyman Trumbull.* Reno: University of Nevada Press, 1979.

Royster, Charles. *The Destructive War: William Tecumseh Sherman, Stonewall Jackson, and the Americans.* New York: Knopf/Random House, 1991.

Russell, William H. "Timothy O. Howe, Stalwart Republican." *Wisconsin Magazine of History* 35 (Winter 1951).

Salmon, Lucy M. *History of the Appointing Power of the President.* New York: G. P. Putnam's Sons, 1886.

Sanford, Washington L. *History of the Fourteenth Illinois Cavalry.* Chicago: R. R. Donnelley & Sons, 1912.

Schudson, Michael. *The Power of News.* Cambridge, MA: Harvard University Press, 1995.

Schutz, Wallace J., and Walter N. Trenerry. *Abandoned by Lincoln: A Military Biography of General John Pope.* Urbana: University of Illinois Press, 1990.

Scott, H. L. *Military Dictionary: Comprising Technical Definitions; Information on Raising and Keeping Troops; Actual Service, Including Makeshifts and Improved Matériel; and Law, Government, Regulation, and Administration relating to Land Forces.* New York: D. Van Nostrand, 1861.

Sears, Stephen W., ed. *The Civil War Papers of George B. McClellan: Selected Correspondence, 1860–1865.* New York: Ticknor & Fields, 1989.

———. *George B. McClellan: The Young Napoleon.* New York: Ticknor & Fields, 1988.

Seaton, Albert. *The Crimean War: A Russian Chronicle.* New York: St. Martin's, 1977.

Sellers, James L. "James R. Doolittle." *Wisconsin Magazine of History* 17 (1933–34).

Shanks, William F. G. *Personal Recollections of Distinguished Generals.* New York: Harper & Brothers, 1866.

Sharp, Walter Rice. "Henry S. Lane and the Formation of the Republican Party in Indiana." *Mississippi Valley Historical Review* 7 (Sept. 1920).

Shaw, William Lawrence. "McDougal of California." *California Historical Quarterly* 43 (June 1964).

Sherman, William T. *Memoirs.* 2 vols. Bloomington: Indiana University Press, 1957. Originally published 1875.

Shoemaker, Philip S. "Stellar Impact: Ormsby MacKnight Mitchel and Astronomy in Antebellum America." Ph.D. diss., University of Wisconsin, 1991.

Shy, John. *A People Numerous and Armed: Reflections on the Military Struggle for American Independence.* New York: Oxford University Press, 1976.

Silver, David M. *Lincoln's Supreme Court.* Urbana: University of Illinois Press, 1957.

Simon, John Y., ed. *The Papers of Ulysses S. Grant.* 22 vols. Carbondale: Southern Illinois University Press, 1967–.

Simpson, Brooks D., and Jean V. Berlin. *Sherman's Civil War: Selected Correspondence of William T. Sherman, 1860–1865.* Chapel Hill: University of North Carolina Press, 1999.

Skelton, William B. *An American Profession of Arms: The Army Officer Corps, 1784–1861.* Lawrence: University Press of Kansas, 1992.

Slotten, Richard. *Patronage, Practice, and the Culture of American Science: Alexander Dallas Bache and the U.S. Coast Survey.* Cambridge: Cambridge University Press, 1994.

Smith, Theodore Clarke. *The Life and Letters of James Abram Garfield.* Vol. 1. New Haven, CT: Yale University Press, 1948. Originally published 1925.

Sparks, David S., ed. *Inside Lincoln's Army: The Diary of Marsena Patrick, Provost Marshal General, Army of the Potomac.* New York: Thomas Yoseloff, 1964.

Speed, Thomas, R. M. Kelly, and Alfred Pirtle. *The Union Regiments of Kentucky.* Louisville: Courier-Journal Job Printing, 1897.

Stampp, Kenneth M. *Indiana Politics during the Civil War.* Indianapolis: Indiana Historical Bureau, 1949.

Stanley, David Sloane. *Personal Memoirs.* Cambridge, MA: Harvard University Press, 1917.

Starr, Steven Z. *Jennison's Jayhawkers: A Civil War Cavalry Regiment and Its Commander.* Baton Rouge: Louisiana State University Press, 1973.

Stephenson, Wendell Holmes. *The Political Career of General James H. Lane.* Publications of the Kansas State Historical Society, vol. 3. Topeka: B. P. Walker, 1930.

Stewart, A. T. Q. *The Summer Soldiers: The 1798 Rebellion in Antrim and Down.* Belfast: Blackstaff, 1995.

Stewart, Capt. Merch Bradt. *Military Character, Habit, Deportment, Courtesy, and Discipline.* Menasha, WI: George Banta, 1913.

Storr, Louis M. *Bohemian Brigade: Civil War Newsmen in Action.* Madison: University of Wisconsin Press, 1987.

Stover, John F. *History of the Illinois Central Railroad.* New York: Macmillan, 1975.

Strevey, Tracy Elmer. "Joseph Medill and the *Chicago Tribune* during the Civil War Period." Ph.D. diss., University of Chicago, 1930.

Sugden, John. *Tecumseh: A Life.* New York: Henry Holt, 1997.

Sutherland, Daniel E. "Abraham Lincoln, John Pope, and the Origins of Total War." *Journal of Military History* 56 (Oct. 1992).

———. "Introduction to War: The Civilians of Culpepper County, Virginia." *Civil War History* 37 (June 1991).

Tap, Bruce. *Over Lincoln's Shoulder: The Committee on the Conduct of the War.* Lawrence: University Press of Kansas, 1998.

Taylor, John M. *Garfield of Ohio: The Available Man.* New York: W. W. Norton, 1970.

Teitler, Gerke. *The Genesis of the Professional Officers' Corps.* Translated by C. N. Ter Heide-Lopy. Beverly Hills, CA: Sage, 1977.

Thomas, Benjamin B., and Harold M. Hyman. *Stanton: The Life and Times of Lincoln's Secretary of War.* New York: Alfred A. Knopf, 1962.

Thornbrough, Emma Lou. *Indiana in the Civil War Era, 1850–1880.* Indianapolis: Indiana Historical Bureau & Indiana Historical Society, 1965.

Turchin, John Basil. "Bayonet and Saber: Their Value as Weapons in Modern Warfare." *National Tribune,* Feb. 11, 1886.

———. *Chickamauga.* Chicago: Fergus, 1888.

———. "First Steps in War: Organizing a New Regiment and Taking It to the Field." *National Tribune,* Aug. 2, 1888.

———. *Military Rambles.* Chicago: John R. Walsh, 1865.

U.S. Congress. *Congressional Globe.* 46 vols. Washington, DC, 1834–73.

———. *Report of the Joint Committee on the Conduct of the War.* 9 serials in 3 volumes. Washington, DC: Government Printing Office, 1863–66.

———. Senate. *Journal of the Executive Proceedings of the Senate of the United States.* Numerous vols. Washington, DC: Government Printing Office, 1828–.

U.S. Military Academy. *Regulations of the United States Military Academy at West Point, New York.* New York: John Trow, 1853.

U.S. Statutes at Large.

U.S. War Department. *Basic Field Manual Military Training FM 21–5, July 16, 1941.* Washington, DC: Government Printing Office, 1941.

———. *War of the Rebellion: A Compilation of the Official Records of the Union and Confederate Armies.* 128 vols. Washington, DC: Government Printing Office, 1880–1901.

Vale, Joseph G. *Minty and the Cavalry: A History of the Cavalry Campaigns in the Western Armies.* Harrisburg, PA: Edwin K. Meyers, 1886.

Van Dyke, Carl. *Russian Imperial Military Doctrine and Education, 1832–1914.* New York: Greenwood, 1990.

Van Tassel, David D. *Recording America's Past: An Interpretation of the Development of Historical Studies in America, 1607–1884.* Chicago: University of Chicago Press, 1960.

Vasvary, Edmund. *Lincoln's Hungarian Heroes: The Participation of Hungarians in the Civil War, 1861–1865.* Washington, DC: Hungarian Reformed Federation of America, 1939.

Villard, Henry. *Memoirs.* 2 vols. Boston: Houghton Mifflin, 1904.

Vocke, William. "The Military Achievements of Major-General Ormsby MacKnight Mitchel." In *Military Essays and Recollections, Illinois Commandery, Loyal Legion,* vol. 6. Wilmington, NC: Broadfoot, 1992. Originally published 1907.

Wagner, William. *History of the 24th Illinois Volunteer Infantry Regiment (Old Hecker Regiment).* N.p., 1911. Originally published 1864.

Wainwright, Nicholas B. "The Loyal Opposition in Civil War Philadelphia." *Pennsylvania Magazine of History and Biography* 88 (1964).

Walker, Francis A. *History of the Second Army Corps in the Army of the Potomac.* New York: Charles Scribner's Sons, 1887.

Walker, Robert Henry, Jr. *History of Limestone County, Alabama.* Athens, AL: privately printed, 1973.

Warner, Ezra J. *Generals in Blue: Lives of the Union Commanders.* Baton Rouge: Louisiana State University Press, 1964.

Warren, Israel P. *The Stanley Families of America.* Portland, ME: B. Thurston, 1887.

Watson, Bruce Allen. *When Soldiers Quit: Studies in Military Disintegration.* Westport, CT: Praeger, 1997.

Wendt, Lloyd. *Chicago Tribune: The Rise of a Great American Newspaper.* Chicago: Rand, McNally, 1979.

White, Horace. *The Life of Lyman Trumbull.* Boston: Houghton Mifflin, 1913.

Williams, Frederick D. *The Wild Life of the Army: Civil War Letters of James A. Garfield.* Lansing: Michigan State University Press, 1964.

Williams, T. Harry. *Lincoln and His Generals.* New York: Alfred A. Knopf, 1952.

Wilson, James Grant. "General Halleck—A Memoir." *Journal of the Military Service Institution of the United States* 36 (May–June 1905).

Winders, Richard Bruce. *Mr. Polk's Army: The American Military Experience in the Mexican War.* College Station: Texas A & M University Press, 1997.

Wolseley, Garnet Joseph, Viscount. "General Sherman, II." *United Service Magazine,* n.s., 3 (June 1891).

Wythe, W. W. "Mrs. Turchin: A Woman Idolized by the Whole Regiment." *National Tribune,* Mar. 24, 1910.

Yates, Richard, and Catherine Yates Pickering. *Richard Yates: Civil War Governor.* Edited by John K. Krenkel. Danville, IL: Interstate, 1966.

Young, John Russell. "Men Who Reigned: Bennett, Greeley, Raymond, Prentice, Forney." *Lippincott's Monthly Magazine* 51 (Feb. 1893).

Younger, Edwin, ed. *Inside the Confederate Government: The Diary of Robert Garlick Hill Kean.* New York: Oxford University Press, 1957.

Index